Commemorating 20 years of civil liability legislation in Australia – 100 cases that shaped the law

Disclaimer

Wolters Kluwer

Commemorating 20 years of civil liability legislation in Australia – 100 cases that shaped the law

2022

CCH AUSTRALIA LIMITED
GPO Box 4072, Sydney, NSW 2001
Head Office Macquarie Park
Phone: (02) 9857 1300 Fax: (02) 9857 1600
Customer Support
Phone: 1 300 300 224 Fax: 1 300 306 224
https://shop.wolterskluwer.com.au
Book Code: 10097740-0001

About Wolters Kluwer

Wolters Kluwer is a leading provider of accurate, authoritative and timely information services for professionals across the globe. We create value by combining information, deep expertise, and technology to provide our customers with solutions that contribute to the quality and effectiveness of their services. Professionals turn to us when they need actionable information to better serve their clients.

With the integrity and accuracy of over 45 years' experience in Australia and New Zealand, and over 175 years internationally, Wolters Kluwer is lifting the standard in software, knowledge, tools and education.

Wolters Kluwer – *When you have to be right.*

Enquiries are welcome on **1300 300 224**.

"Cataloguing-in-Publication Data available through the National Library of Australia."

First edition 2022

ISBN 978-1-922509-97-0

CONTENTS

SOUTH AUSTRALIA

Page

TASMANIA

VICTORIA

WESTERN AUSTRALIA

Page

Wolters Kluwer Acknowledgments

Wolters Kluwer wishes to thank the following who contributed to and supported this publication:

Director, General Manager, Research & Learning, Wolters Kluwer Asia Pacific

Lauren Ma

Head of Legal Content, Wolters Kluwer Australia

Carol Louw

Senior Content Specialist, Wolters Kluwer Australia

Jacqueline Waugh

Books Coordinator, Wolters Kluwer Asia Pacific

Alexandra Gonzalez

Introduction

The need for tort reform in Australia

Chaired by the late The Hon David Ipp, the Panel charged with reviewing the law of negligence in Australia tabled its final report ''Review of the Law of Negligence Final report'', in September 2002. Also known as the Ipp Report, the Review noted that the prime task of the Panel, as stated by the Terms of Reference, was ''to examine a method for the reform of the common law with the objective of limiting liability and quantum of damages arising from personal injury and death'' and ''to assist governments in developing consistent national approaches for implementing measures to tackle the problems of rising premiums and reduced availability of public liability insurance.'' [1.8], [1.9]

The Panel's overarching recommendation was that a single statute be enacted in each jurisdiction and that the proposed legislation should be expressed to apply to any claim for damages for personal injury or death resulting from negligence regardless of whether the claim is brought in tort, contract, under a statute or any other cause of action.

Tort reform in each jurisdiction

Legislation governing civil liability is an Australia-wide initiative.

The *Civil Liability Act 2002* (NSW) is the first tort reform legislation to have been enacted, with all other states and territories following shortly after and various other civil liability legislation being enacted (or existing legislation being amended), namely:

Civil Law (Wrongs) Act 2002 (ACT)

Personal Injuries (Liabilities and Damages) Act 2003 (NT)

Civil Liability Act 2003 (Qld)

Civil Liability Act 1936 (SA)

Civil Liability Act 2002 (Tas)

Wrongs Act 1958 (Vic)

Civil Liability Act 2002 (WA).

The civil liability legislation dramatically changed the landscape of the law of negligence in Australia.

The initial target of these tort reforms was the liability for personal injury in the medical, public space and recreational services contexts, where insurance was said to be increasingly unaffordable. Despite this, many of the provisions apply to any negligence claim, whether based on tort, contract or statute.

Other important reforms have also transformed liability for property damage and economic loss by introducing proportionate liability.

A tort claim (including areas such as public liability, medical negligence, motor accidents and workers' compensation, as well as emerging areas such as institutional liability for child sexual abuse) can rarely be considered without some reference to applicable civil liability legislation.

Civil liability legislation not only introduced statutory provisions dealing with liability in negligence (eg duty of care and causation), it also placed restrictions on aspects of the recovery of damages for personal injury, forever altering the common law approach to assessing damages for particular heads of damage such as non-economic loss (pain and suffering), loss of earning capacity and gratuitous assistance.

Tort law is now a complex web of common law principles and civil liability statutory provisions, themselves subject in turn to much judicial interpretation in case law. While the High Court has emphasised that there is one common law of Australia (see *Farah Constructions Pty Ltd* v *Say-Dee Pty Ltd* (2007) 230 CLR 89; [2007] HCA 22), and while states often follow a similar pattern of reform, variations in state civil liability legislation have made the law of torts even more complex.

Recognising the 20th anniversary of tort reform

In recognition of the 20th anniversary of the commencement of the various civil liability legislation around Australia (commencing with New South Wales in 2002), we (the Wolters Kluwer editors) have curated what we consider to be the top 100 cases over the last 20 years in which the courts have discussed, interpreted and applied the civil liability legislation provisions.

This commemorative case book covers all Australian jurisdictions. It also includes a supplementary list of an additional 100 prominent cases that delve deeper into the specific civil liability legislation provisions in each jurisdiction.

The cases in this commemorative case book are not an exhaustive list of all civil liability cases from the last 20 years, but rather an expertly curated collection showcasing what we consider to be some of the most prominent cases.

We trust you will find this commemorative case book an invaluable tool and guide as you navigate the complex area of negligence law in Australia.

Australian Capital Territory

[¶82-801] Austen v Tran

(2022) Aust Torts Reports ¶82-801
Medium neutral citation: [2022] ACTSC 114
Supreme Court of the Australian Capital Territory
24 May 2022

Medical negligence — General practitioner — Delay in diagnosis of non-Hodgkin's lymphoma — Blood tests ordered at initial presentation and practitioner did not follow up — Whether breach of duty of care — Whether practitioner should have ordered an MRI at a subsequent presentation — Whether any breach caused a delay in diagnosis — Damages — Whether "household" includes extended family — Civil Liability Act 2002 (NSW), s 5D — Civil Law (Wrongs Act) 2002 (ACT), ss 42, 43, 44, 45, 46, 99, 100.

The plaintiff, Ms Sandra Austen, first consulted the defendant, Dr Tuan Quoc Tran, a general practitioner, on 17 October 2016. Dr Tran was the principal doctor at the Wattle Street Medical Practice (the Practice). Ms Austen complained of pain in her left leg, although the clinical records of Dr Tran noted a presentation of pain in the right leg. Dr Tran did not prescribe any x-rays of any particular leg. Blood test results were received in the Practice the following day (18 October 2016) and indicated a normal range for iron levels. Ms Austen went to the Practice that day in person and was told that her test results were "all good". At the time Ms Austen received the results of the blood tests, no one at the Practice requested she make a further appointment. Dr Tran did not subsequently call Ms Austen or refer her for any further investigations.

On 19 June 2017, Ms Austen attended the Practice and saw a different doctor. She reported left foot/leg pain for the last 3 nights. The provisional diagnosis was nerve root compression, or a disc prolapse. She was referred for a CT of the lumbar spine and underwent blood tests.

On 15 July 2017, Ms Austen had her second consultation with Dr Tran and reported worsening lower back and left leg pain, as well as unexplained weight loss, lethargy and incontinence. Dr Tran prescribed her with a moderate level painkiller and referred her for x-rays and an ultrasound on her left hip and left knee. Dr Tran did not refer Ms Austen to any specialist for further investigations to exclude possible causes of the pain. The x-ray and ultrasound were reported as unremarkable but did note that consideration could be made performing either CT of MRI of the lumbosacral spine. Dr Tran did not take action to follow up that recommendation or refer Ms Austen for further x-rays.

On 21 August 2017, Ms Austen saw a different doctor at the Practice and was referred to orthopaedic specialist Dr Damian Smith for an MRI of the lumbar spine, which identified "bony lesions – metastasis multiple". On 19 September 2017, Ms Austen was diagnosed with non-Hodgkin's lymphoma and the illness is terminal.

Ms Austen commenced negligence proceedings against Dr Tran and claimed damages. She alleged that Dr Tran was negligent in that he failed to take steps which would have led to an earlier diagnosis of the condition, and that an earlier diagnosis would have improved Ms Austen's prognosis and life expectancy.

Dr Tran denied liability. He claimed that at each consultation, he took reasonable steps that were consistent with his duty of care. Further, in relation to the first consultation, Dr Tran submitted that any further reasonable investigations that may have been taken at that

time would not have revealed the presence of the disease (due to it being at an early stage, if it existed at all).

Held: judgment for the defendant.

1. The risk of harm identified was the risk of a delay in diagnosis and subsequent worsening of Ms Austen's non-Hodgkin's lymphoma. The risk of harm arising from a delay in diagnosis was that the lymphoma (which may have been curable) would be left untreated and develop to a point where it was terminal for Ms Austen. There was no dispute that the risk of lymphoma and its progression if undetected, including an increase in size of Ms Austen's osteoblastic skeletal metastases, was a foreseeable risk within the meaning of s 43(1)(a) of the *Civil Law (Wrongs Act) 2002* (ACT) (the Act). [72], [73]

2. There was no breach of Dr Tran's duty of care in the circumstances of this case. It was made out on the evidence that Dr Tran did not investigate Ms Austen's symptoms and complaints as fully as what ought to have occurred, but the consult as a whole and the circumstances that existed at that time must be viewed together to determine whether an individual failure was also sufficient to establish a breach of duty of care. The other matters of not following up with Ms Austen after the consultation, not referring for any further investigations, and not referring to a specialist were also made out on the evidence. However, establishing that the conduct occurred does not prove that a breach of duty occurred. [92], [93]

3. It was not established that Dr Tran acting with reasonable competence ought to have been more proactive. Following that first consultation, a reasonable general practitioner would not have first relied in some way on seeing whether the pain dissipated over time with pain relief to manage the symptom in the meantime, and Ms Austen then re-presenting — either at the Practice or elsewhere in the system — if her pain had not resolved. [143]

4. On balance, the expert evidence did not establish Ms Austen's symptoms were such that they would have caused the reasonably skilled general practitioner to take different precautions. Requesting x-rays of Ms Austen's hip, left knee and a pelvic x-ray, and an ultrasound of her left gluteus muscles was reasonable insofar as those scans targeted areas where pain was reported. [154]

5. Dr Tran could have sent Ms Austen for an MRI of the lumbar spine, given that the pain in that area was acute, but not that acting reasonably, he should have done so, in circumstances where other areas of pain had also been identified by Ms Austen and the CT scan of the lumber spine had not shown any abnormality. [157]

6. Properly characterised, the second consultation on 21 August 2017 was part of an iterative diagnostic process, which occurred throughout June to August 2017. Having regard to the circumstances of the previous consultation at the Practice, and the fact that the second consultation was a step in the process and not a concluded investigation or diagnosis, Dr Tran's conduct did accord with that of a reasonably skilled general practitioner. [162]

7. On balance then, and for the purpose of dealing with the arguments fully notwithstanding the findings on breach, it was accepted that Ms Austen had low grade lymphoma from at least October 2016, and that it became high grade lymphoma from shortly before 2017. On the basis of the finding that low-grade lymphoma existed in Ms Austen as at October 2016, the counterfactual arises for consideration. It could have been detected, but only by a PET scan at that early stage. Drawing on the expert evidence, if x-rays were carried out of Ms Austen's left leg, hip, and pelvis, including perhaps a CT of the lumbar spine in October 2016, and with the blood tests that were normal, her low-grade lymphoma would not have been detected. A PET scan at a first consultation would have been unjustifiable and it is important to note that a referral would have first been necessary because the evidence was that a general practitioner could not order a PET scan. Accordingly, on the counter-factual,

with Dr Tran ordering bloods and x-rays (of the left leg), even if that extended to include an MRI, it is hard to accept that it would have disclosed the condition. [190]–[193]

8. Realistically a process whereby Ms Austen ended up with a referral to a specialist and a PET scan at a point earlier than when the disease escalated in June/July 2017 was unlikely. Assuming any breach by Dr Tran at the first consultation, the evidence does not establish that the breach caused a delay in diagnosis at that time, because the disease was in such an early stage that reasonable testing would not have been likely to identify it. [195]–[198]

9. As to whether any breach arising out of the second consultation caused any delay in diagnosis, assuming an MRI of the lumbar spine was carried out on 8 August 2017 (24 days after the second consultation), and the report given to the Practice on 9 August 2017, and assuming that the subsequent testing occurred with the same urgency once the results of the MRI were known, at best, the delay in diagnosis was a little over 3 weeks. Had there not been that brief delay, even if diagnosed and consequently treated a number of weeks earlier, Ms Austen would still have relapsed. What Ms Austen thus lost, in respect of an assumed breach arising out of the second consultation, was the chance of a better outcome in terms of a longer period of remission. For the purposes of assessing damages, that better outcome (an extra 12 months' remission) would have materialised. [199]–[205]

[*Headnote by the Wolters Kluwer editors*]

D Richards (Maliganis Edwards Johnson) for the plaintiff.

W Sharwood (4 March 2021) and A Muller (3, 4, 6, 7, 12 May 2021) (Minter Ellison) for the defendant.

Before: McWilliam AJ.

[¶82-770] Buljat v Coles Supermarkets Australia Pty Ltd

(2022) Aust Torts Reports ¶82-770

Medium neutral citation: [2022] ACTSC 47

Supreme Court of the Australian Capital Territory

18 March 2022

Occupiers liability — Slip on a grape in the supermarket — No breach of duty by occupier — Civil Law (Wrongs) Act 2002 (ACT), ss 42, 43, 45, 46, 168.

Coles not liable in negligence for slip and fall at supermarket

A woman who was injured when she slipped on a grape on the floor while shopping at Coles, was unsuccessful in her claim of negligence against the supermarket owner and operator. Whilst the court found that the plaintiff did slip on a grape on the floor, it found that the plaintiff failed to prove breach of duty, that there were available precautions which a reasonable person in the position of Coles would have taken to avoid the risk of harm. The court noted that the High Court decision of *Strong* v *Woolworths Ltd* (2012) Aust Torts Reports ¶82-099; [2012] HCA 5 should not be seen as a directive from the High Court as to how cleaning should be undertaken in commercial premises in Australia, and that many authorities have considered alternative systems, including Clean as you Go systems (such as in this case), without finding them insufficient on the sole ground of a failure to have a periodic and documented system of inspection.

Before: Balla AJ.

[¶82-769] Alrifai v Australian Capital Territory

(2022) Aust Torts Reports ¶82-769
Medium neutral citation: [2022] ACTSC 48
Supreme Court of the Australian Capital Territory
18 March 2022

Medical negligence — Causation — Where plaintiff diagnosed with pancreatic cancer — Whether plaintiff would have undergone surgery earlier but for the alleged negligent acts relating to diagnosis — Whether earlier surgical intervention would have prevented injuries particularised — Civil Law (Wrongs) Act 2002 (ACT), ss 42, 43, 44, 45, 46 — Court Procedures Rules 2006, r 443(5).

The plaintiff, Ms Alrifai presented to Canberra Hospital (the hospital) on the evening of 25 December 2017 complaining of chest pain. She was told that she possibly had gastro-oesophageal reflux disease or early pancreatitis and was discharged home.

During early 2018, the plaintiff again presented to the hospital and underwent 3 separate CT scans between January and April 2018: a CT scan on 1 January 2018, a CT scan on 6 April 2018, a CT scan on 22 April 2018 and an endoscopic ultrasound on 26 April 2018. She was diagnosed with pancreatic cancer in November 2018.

The plaintiff commenced negligence proceedings against the Australian Capital Territory being the entity responsible for the hospital. She claimed that the hospital was negligent in failing to diagnose and treat the condition sooner and that as a consequence of the hospital's negligence, the she lost the opportunity for a prompt diagnosis of pancreatic cancer on or shortly after 3 January 2018 (or alternatively, 6 or 26 April 2018) and was thereby deprived of the opportunity of being properly treated for that disease by the performance of a timely partial pancreatectomy which did not occur until November 2018. She claimed that each scan showed a discrete mass in the pancreas and that the hospital was negligent in failing to obtain a surgical opinion, and that had that been done, the tumour would have been removed earlier than it was on 11 November 2018.

The hospital admitted that the failure to obtain a surgical opinion after 26 April 2018 was a breach of its duty of care to the plaintiff but denied that the breach caused any of the injury, loss or damage claimed by the plaintiff. The hospital otherwise denied that it breached its duty of care to the plaintiff.

Held: judgment for the defendant.

1. Section 42 of the *Civil Law (Wrongs) Act 2002* (ACT) sets the standard of care. That section reflects the common law test which was that "the standard of reasonable care and skill required is that of the ordinary skilled person exercising and professing to have that special skill". [106], [107]

2. In determining the issue of the liability of the hospital, the plaintiff expressly resiled from making any claim against the hospital on the basis that any of the 3 radiologists who performed the CT scans were negligent. Each of the particulars of negligence represented a "precaution" that, on the plaintiff's case, should have been taken. [110], [111]

3. After the plaintiff was diagnosed with acute pancreatitis in January 2018 based on her symptoms, investigations were commenced to ascertain the cause of the condition. There was no evidence that the hospital abandoned the differential diagnosis of pancreatic cancer. The plaintiff failed to show that the hospital failed on or by 3 January, 6 or 26 April 2018 to have made or properly considered a differential diagnosis of pancreatic cancer. [151]–[167]

4. As to whether the hospital should have discussed the plaintiff's presentation with a surgeon, involved a surgeon in her care and sought an opinion from a surgeon who could have explained to her the pros and cons of further imaging or simply removing the mass, the plaintiff failed to show that a surgical opinion should have been obtained in January or April 2018. Further, there was no evidence to conclude that the involvement of a surgeon in

January or April 2018 would have meant a different course would have been pursued in the investigation and management of the plaintiff's condition up to April 2018. [209]–[223]

5. The plaintiff failed to show that, if a surgical opinion had been obtained on 26 April 2018, she would have undergone surgery earlier than November 2018. [228]

6. In the alternative, if there had been a finding that the plaintiff had shown the mass should have been removed earlier than 11 November 2018, the plaintiff failed to show that if the mass had been removed in January or April 2018 it would have affected the prognosis of her condition or her life expectancy. [258]–[266]

[*Headnote by the Wolters Kluwer editors*]

D Richards with L Edwards (United Legal) for the plaintiff.

V Thomas with K Beattie (ACT Government Solicitor) for the defendant.

Before: Balla AJ.

[¶82-742] Rubino v Ziaee

(2021) Aust Torts Reports ¶82-742
Medium neutral citation: [2021] ACTSC 331
Supreme Court of Australian Capital Territory
23 December 2021

Medical negligence — Standard of care — Referrals to specialties — Duty to follow up — Assessment of damages — Quantification — General damages — Economic loss — Whether defendant had been negligent in failing to follow-up surgical referral — Civil Law (Wrongs) Act 2002 (ACT), ss 40, 42, 43, 44, 45, 46.

The plaintiff, Mr Michael Rubino (Mr Rubino), who was 39 years old at the time of the hearing, had worked as both a storeman and as a security guard. On 24 July 2013, he presented to the general practice conducted by Tristar Medical Group (the practice) in the Australian Capital Territory. The defendant, Dr Sourosh Ziaee (Dr Ziaee), was a general practitioner within the practice. Mr Rubino's presenting complaint was a lump on the sole of his right foot which was causing him pain and inhibiting his gait. Dr Ziaee diagnosed the lump as a hyperkeratosis (also known as a corn) and prescribed Mr Rubino Panadeine Forte for pain relief. He also advised him to obtain insoles for his shoes.

The corn persisted and Mr Rubino saw Dr Ziaee several more times during 2013, including 3 times in September 2013. On those visits, Dr Ziaee took swabs of the corn and prescribed antibiotics after noting signs of infection. Mr Rubino completed the courses of antibiotics and made efforts to let the corn heal over the following months. However, in February 2014, he was still having problems and so he returned to Dr Ziaee in that month. There was some dispute at what happened in the consultations at that time, but Mr Rubino (and his partner) attested that Dr Ziaee attempted an excision of the corn or some part of it. More antibiotics were also prescribed together with a referral for an ultrasound.

This treatment did not fix the problem and so Mr Rubino had further consultations with Dr Ziaee during March 2014. During those consultations, Dr Ziaee noted that the ultrasound showed a deep cyst containing debris and so he made a referral to a general surgeon at Canberra Hospital. However, for reasons relating to the administrative system used by Canberra Hospital, Mr Rubino did not receive an appointment to see the surgeon and so he raised the issue with Dr Ziaee again in May 2014. Dr Ziaee then made another referral which went to Canberra Hospital but it was cancelled because there was an existing referral within the system.

Over the course of the next 2 years, Dr Ziaee saw Mr Rubino for other issues and assumed that the referral was still pending. However, Mr Rubino received no appointment to see a surgeon and in August 2016 the hyperkeratosis deteriorated to the point that Mr

Rubino could not stand the pain and presented to an emergency department. He was immediately admitted to the hospital for a rapidly spreading foot infection and underwent 2 emergency procedures. The first was a drainage of the infected abscess and the second was a further washout and debridement of the area. Mr Rubino was in hospital for 2 weeks for these procedures.

Following these procedures, Mr Rubino had difficulties walking and suffered from an antalgic gait that was said to limit his capacity for work. This also gave rise to a somatic symptom disorder and an adjustment disorder with depressive mood as a result of him being unable to undertake his normal range of activities.

Mr Rubino commenced proceedings against Dr Ziaee, in negligence and claimed damages. He alleged that Dr Ziaee was negligent in failing to follow up the referral after March 2014 and that conduct fell short of the reasonable standard of care to be provided by a general practitioner.

Held: judgment for plaintiff.

1. As of 5 February 2014, a reasonable general practitioner would have been aware that Mr Rubino had a large and deep keratosis on his foot that had showed some signs of infection. At that point, a reasonable general practitioner would have formed the view that a surgical referral was required. [100]–[113]

2. A reasonable general practitioner would have also followed-up the referral if no appointment had been received after 3 months. This would have been part of the general practitioner's ongoing care and supervision of the condition while the appointment was pending. [114]–[123]

3. Given that Dr Ziaee was aware that Mr Rubino was having pain and that the condition was causing him psychological distress, Dr Ziaee's duty extended to making enquiries of the hospital in addition to prescribing additional treatments and therapies. [124]–[127]

4. Dr Ziaee failed to meet the applicable standard of care from June 2014, which was 3 months after he made the first referral. His treatment plan from that point should have included some means of follow-up to ensure that Mr Rubino received a surgical review. [137]–[151]

5. As to causation, the evidence established that, if an effective referral had been made, Mr Rubino would have had the abscess drained in the public system within a year. That would have obviated the need for emergency surgery and the resulting injuries (including the psychiatric injuries). [177]–[190]

[*Headnote by the Wolters Kluwer editors*]

A Campbell (Gerard Malouf & Partners) for the plaintiff.

CP O'Neill (Avant Law) for the defendant.

Before: McWilliam AJ.

[¶82-624] Hauraki v Steinhoff Asia Pacific Ltd trading as Freedom Furniture

(2021) Aust Torts Reports ¶82-624
Medium neutral citation: [2021] ACTSC 54
Supreme Court of the Australian Capital Territory
12 April 2021

Torts — Workplace injury — Damages — Workplace accident — Worker plaintiff suffered lower back injury at work — Worker had suffered psychological disturbance from previous assault which were largely resolved at time of workplace accident — Worker suffered chronic pain syndrome and severe psychiatric injury — Catastrophic effect of injury on worker's life — Suicide risk — Assessment of damages — Discount of past and future damages for risk of intervening incapacitating event — Discount of future damages for risk worker taking his own life — Life expectancy — Civil Law (Wrongs) Act 2002 (ACT), s 100.

The plaintiff worker, Mr Hauraki, injured his back in the course of his work in the warehouse of the defendant, Steinhoff Asia Pacific Ltd trading as Freedom Furniture (the employer). The warehouse was cluttered and while he was moving a 120 kg couch on a trolley, a 100 kg table pack fell on him and the sofa causing pain to his shoulder and neck. He momentarily let go of the trolley, then to stop the sofa falling over, he grabbed the trolley bars which caused his lower back injury.

The worker claimed the workplace injury caused him to suffer serious and disabling mental illness which effectively destroyed his earning capacity and left him with a high need for care and future medical treatment. He commenced proceedings before the Supreme Court of the Australian Capital Territory (the court), claiming that the employer:

- **was negligent in that it failed to provide him with a safe system of and access to, the work he was required to perform, and**
- **breached a number of sections of the Work Health and Safety Regulation 2011 (ACT) by failing to take the appropriate steps to assess and manage the risk of injury to the plaintiff arising from his work conditions.**

During the hearing, the employer effectively had abandoned its denial of liability, denial of causation and defence of contributory negligence. The central issue before the court was, therefore, the assessment of tortious damages and what discounts ought to be applied [5], [179]. The parties had agreed on the figure of $493,000 for past out of pocket expenses [161].

The court accepted the medical evidence that the chronic pain syndrome and depressive disorder the worker suffered following the workplace accident had led to extensive pain treatment and aggressive mental health inpatient and outpatient treatment, including 2 courses of Electro Convulsive Treatment and strong pain and psychiatric medication. The worker described that when his pain was bad, he would "shut down" mentally and think of suicide.

The worker had suffered a degree of psychological disturbance following an assault in 2009. The employer contended this resulted in post-traumatic stress disorder which rendered the worker particularly vulnerable, such that the risk of the him taking his own life was extremely high. There was evidence of the worker and his wife of numerous incidents of his suicidal ideation and actual attempts over the years, and the expert opinions explained the risk of suicide. As such, the employer argued that, given the history of unsuccessful treatment, damages should be assessed by reference:

- **to a life expectancy of 5 years, totalling around $1.78 million, or**
- **alternatively, a life expectancy of 30 years, with a reduction for vicissitudes of 50%, totalling around $2.5 million.**

The worker argued against the use of arbitrary discount percentages and warned against an unfair duplication of discounting for vicissitudes based on a pre-existing condition. He argued that at the time of the injury both he and his wife were functioning well in their work, family and social lives. He argued that damages of $9.2 million should be awarded. He submitted, among other things, that:

- a discount for loss of future earnings should not exceed 20% [163]
- a discount of no more than 15% should be applied to damages for future out of pockets, care and support under s 100 of the *Civil Law (Wrongs) Act 2002* (ACT) (CLW Act), since the 3% discount tables already allowed for the ordinary vicissitudes of life. A reduction to this support of 20% was already made for the required 70 day inpatient treatment [166], [168], and
- the high levels of care claimed were to avoid the risk of suicide, so that a high discount for suicide as proposed by the employer did not make sense [167].

Held: judgment for the plaintiff in the sum of $5,624,298.

1. The court accepted the medical evidence that the effect of the workplace accident was catastrophic, leaving the worker with interrelated chronic pain and severe psychiatric conditions. He was likely to require hospitalisations and medications for the rest of his life. The court accepted that given his suicide risk, the level of care the worker claimed was needed (both in respect of commercial care, and the s 100 CLW Act supports indicated in the evidence). [177], [178]

2. The worker's work, family and social life had largely returned to normal by 2016 when the workplace accident occurred. The court accepted the expert opinion of the psychiatrists in this respect, rejecting the employer's assertion that he had a pre-existing personality disorder at the time of the workplace accident. [176]

3. A central issue for determination was what allowance was required for the possibility that the worker might have suffered some other injury or incident in his life which might have caused him to become as psychiatrically compromised as he was now without the lower back injury he had suffered. The court rejected the alternative approaches to damages posited by the employer. It applied the principles in *Malec* v *JC Hutton Pty Ltd* (1990) 169 CLR 638 at 642–643 regarding assessing damages "as to what will be and what would have been". In absence of evidence to the contrary, and accepting he was functioning well at the time of the workplace accident, the risk of suffering such an intervening incapacitating event or trigger without the injury was assessed as "fairly low" (rather than speculative), with 5% possibility of such an intervening event before the present time. [179]–[186]

4. In relation to future capacity, some allowance was similarly required for a future non-tortious intervening incapacitating event, as well as the risk that as a result of his mental condition the worker might succeed in ending his own life due to his depressive illness. It was not unreasonable that a further 34 years of work remained given the worker's age. A total discount of 35% was applied to such future loss of earning capacity. This took into account the combined risk of suicide and an intervening incapacitating event of 25% and the standard discount of 15% reduced so as not to double discount. [187], [188]

5. In relation to the damages claimed for future treatment, and care and assistance, a discount of 30% was applied to take into account the worker's statistical life expectancy (rather than 25%, given for the longer period into the future under consideration). [189]

6. The court set out its calculations with respect to the damages claimed, with a total of $5,624,298, which it acknowledged was large but proportionate and appropriate given the catastrophic effects which the work injury in 2016 had on the worker's life. [230]

7. The total was comprised of general damages and interest, past and future out of pocket expenses, past and future loss of earning capacity and interest, past and future domestic care and assistance and interest, loss of superannuation and *Fox v Wood* damages, with the relevant discounts applied. [190]–[229]

[*Headnote by the Wolters Kluwer editors*]

D Campbell SC and A Muller (Maliganis Edwards Johnson) for the plaintiff.

D Shillington (Hicksons Lawyers) for the defendant.

Before: Crowe AJ.

[¶82-618] Reardon v Seselja

(2021) Aust Torts Reports ¶82-618
Medium neutral citation: [2021] ACTCA 4
Supreme Court of the Australian Capital Territory, Court of Appeal
11 March 2021

Motor vehicle accident — Breach of duty of care — Agony of the moment — Whether primary judge erred in finding breach of duty of care — Whether first appellant's response was affected by violent and threatening attack upon him and a passenger in his car by 2 assailants — Where first appellant's actions accorded with the conduct of a reasonably prudent person — Civil Law (Wrongs) Act 2002 (ACT), ss 42, 43, 44.

At approximately 8:30 pm on 13 July 2015, 17-year-old Linden Reardon was driving home in his mother's Mitsubishi Lancer after seeing a movie with his siblings and a friend. A Commodore, which had been travelling in front of the Lancer, came to an abrupt stop in the middle of the road. Mr Reardon stopped the Lancer. Sophie Seselja, who was driving her Suzuki Swift behind the Lancer, stopped behind the Lancer.

The driver and front seat passenger got out of the Commodore and approached the Lancer. The driver threatened Mr Reardon with a metal object and at the same time the Commodore passenger opened the passenger door of the Lancer and slapped Mr Reardon's friend and attempted to pull him out of the Lancer. In an attempt to escape the Commodore driver and passenger, Mr Reardon put the Lancer into reverse; however, he reversed into Ms Seselja's Suzuki.

Both the Commodore driver and passenger were identified and charged with common assault. The passenger was found guilty; however, a conviction was not recorded.

Ms Seselja commenced proceedings in the Supreme Court of the Australian Capital Territory against Mr Reardon and Insurance Australia Ltd t/a NRMA Insurance, the compulsory third-party insurer, in negligence and claimed damages for injuries she allegedly suffered as a result of the collision. She alleged that Mr Reardon was negligent in failing to keep any, or any proper, lookout, failing to stop in response to traffic conditions and reversing the Lancer when it was unsafe to do so.

Mr Reardon denied negligence. He argued that he reacted reasonably in what was an emergency situation and that, although the collision occurred, it was not caused by any breach of duty of care but rather it was the product of his agony of the moment reaction to the actions of the driver and passenger of the Commodore.

His Honour Crowe AJ found Mr Reardon did not look back to check behind the Lancer immediately before he reversed and that the reason he did not do so was that he was scared and was focused on the actions of the occupants of the Commodore. It may be that Mr Reardon's failure to see and appreciate the presence of the Suzuki was the product of his inexperience as a driver. However, that failure amounted to a breach of the applicable standard of care in the circumstances. Mr Reardon knew that the Commodore had been driving aggressively and erratically. A reasonable driver in those circumstances would have

been carefully checking his/her surrounds and thinking of options for escape even before the Commodore occupants had emerged. A person in that situation should have checked the rear vision mirror and noted the presence of the Suzuki. Crowe AJ found that Mr Reardon negligently failed to keep a proper lookout and that failure caused the collision between the Lancer and the Suzuki. Damages were awarded in the total sum of $260,955: *Seselja* v *Reardon* (2020) Aust Torts Reports ¶82-533; [2020] ACTSC 167.

Mr Reardon appealed the primary judge's findings. He argued that the primary judge should have found that in the particular circumstances facing Mr Reardon, his actions accorded with those of a reasonably prudent driver in the same circumstances.

Held: appeal allowed; set aside the orders made in favour of the plaintiff by Crowe AJ and in lieu thereof order judgment for the defendants.

Per Burns and Perry JJ:

1. The challenge was to inferences drawn by the trial judge from facts found by his Honour. The starting point was Ch 4, Pt 4.2 of the *Civil Law (Wrongs) Act 2002* (the Act). The standard by which reasonable care was measured was objective and the question of whether the duty of care had been breached was a question of fact. With respect to the duty of care owed by those in control of a motor vehicle, it is not subdivided into subcategories such as a duty to keep a proper lookout or to keep a safe distance from the car in front, even though the failure to do such things may constitute a breach of the duty to take reasonable care. In determining whether or not a party had acted in breach of their duty of care, the court must have regard to all the circumstances including an emergency or threat confronting that party. [7]–[15]

2. Both parties accepted that without more, Mr Reardon drove negligently in reversing the Lancer into Ms Seselja's car. Mr Reardon was required to take reasonable steps to know what was happening, or might happen, in the vicinity of his car. He failed to comply with that duty when he looked in the rear-view mirror on stopping behind the Commodore and failed to notice the Suzuki behind him. The reasonableness of Mr Reardon's actions when he put his car into reverse must be assessed by reference to a person in his position armed with the knowledge when he stopped his car that it was probable that at least one car would stop behind him in the coming seconds. That was information of which he ought reasonably to have been aware for the purposes of s 42 of the CL(W) Act. Furthermore, a reasonable driver would be watching cautiously to see why the vehicle ahead had stopped and what was going to happen next, particularly in light of the somewhat erratic driving undertaken by the driver of the Commodore shortly beforehand. [48]

3. However, the court does not agree with the trial judge's further finding that a reasonable person would "have been carefully checking his/her surrounds and thinking of options for escape even before the Commodore occupants had emerged". That finding was made with the benefit of hindsight. At that point in time, there was no reason why a reasonable person might have foreseen that a violent attack or other emergency might ensue necessitating an urgent and immediate escape. [49]

4. Critically, the circumstances of the incident painted a picture of a terrifying and unexpected attack unprovoked by anything done by the occupants of the Lancer, such that any reasonable person would have been really frightened for their safety and that of their young passengers and indeed likely would have been in a state of panic. Specifically, at the moment when Mr Reardon put the Lancer into reverse, the Commodore driver who had been yelling and swearing as he approached the car, was bashing on Mr Reardon's side window and armed with what appeared to be a spanner. At the same time, Mr Reardon's friend, Kyle, was in the process of being dragged out of the car by the Commodore passenger who had also approached the Lancer yelling. Added to this, Mr Reardon's 16-year-old sister was screaming in the back of the car and his 14-year-old brother, also in the back of the car, was crying. [50]

5. The trial judge erred in inferring that, despite being "fearful, and perhaps even panicky", Mr Reardon would not have so lost the capacity for risk assessment as to have reversed in an uncontrolled way if he had been aware that the Suzuki was behind him. Irrespective of whether Mr Reardon had previously known of the approaching car behind him, the immediacy and extent of the crisis were such that it was not unreasonable for him to put the car slowly into reverse without first checking the rear-view mirror as he focused upon the attackers, and then jerked or jumped back at a faster speed only when, it can reasonably be inferred, the Commodore driver unexpectedly grabbed the driver's door on the Lancer. It was reasonable for his attention in all of the circumstances to be focused upon the assailants and making good his escape. The trial judge erred in holding that Mr Reardon's failure to check his rear-view mirror before reversing in all of the circumstances was most likely the product of his inexperience and did not accord with the response that a reasonably prudent person in his position with the imputed knowledge to which we have referred was likely to have had in the happenings of the moment. [51]

6. With the benefit of hindsight, Mr Reardon should have checked the rear-view mirror again before he commenced to reverse and, if he had done so, he would have seen the car behind him and the accident may have been avoided. However, as was plain from s 44(b) of the Act, reasonableness was not assessed with the benefit of hindsight but by looking forward from a time before the accident occurred. So viewed, this was not a case where there was an opportunity for calm reflection. Mr Reardon did not act negligently in making an error of judgment in the so-called "agony of the moment." [53]

Per Elkaim J (dissenting):

1. The stopping of the Commodore, in the eyes of Mr Reardon, would have been at least unusual and ought to have placed him on alert that the situation was not normal. In stopping behind the Commodore, Mr Reardon was aware that he was stopping in an unusual place. That was where the breach of duty occurred. [61]

2. The primary judge found that even though Mr Reardon had said he had looked in his rear-view mirror when he stopped his motor vehicle, he did not see Ms Seselja's vehicle behind him. That was notwithstanding that she was travelling with her headlights illuminated and would have been less than 100 metres behind him. Her presence, and perhaps even that of other motor vehicles travelling behind Mr Reardon, were part of the circumstances relevant to what "might happen in the vicinity of the vehicle." It cannot be said that Mr Reardon should have anticipated the belligerent actions of the Commodore's occupants, or even that he might have to suddenly reverse. Rather, that with the history of the Commodore's behaviour during the recent journey, then coming to a stop in an unusual place on the roadway, Mr Reardon, in stopping himself, should have made himself aware of other traffic, in particular behind him as he came to a halt. [62], [63]

3. Mr Reardon may well have been acting in the agony of the moment in reversing away from the danger created by the 2 occupants of the Commodore. However, his act of reversing was performed in a manner that should have been dictated by knowledge that he ought to have already possessed about the presence of Ms Seselja's vehicle. He would have been armed with this knowledge had he not been in breach of his duty of care as a driver, before the need to reverse arose, by making himself aware of the presence of other vehicles in his vicinity. [66]

[*Headnote by the Wolters Kluwer editors*]

K Rewell SC (HWL Ebsworth Lawyers) for the first and second appellant.

D Campbell SC with A Muller (Maliganis Edwards Johnson) for the respondent.

Before: Burns, Elkaim and Perry JJ.

[¶82-622] Benning v Richardson

(2021) Aust Torts Reports ¶82-622
Medium neutral citation: [2021] ACTSC 34
Supreme Court of the Australian Capital Territory
11 March 2021

Motor Vehicle Accident — Contributory negligence — Whether the plaintiff took hold of steering wheel — Whether the plaintiff was wearing a seatbelt — Entering a vehicle with an intoxicated driver — Damages — Civil Law (Wrongs) Act 2002 (ACT)Pt 7.1.

On 1 February 2014, the plaintiff, 22-year-old Dannielle Benning was an intoxicated passenger in a vehicle driven by the first defendant, Mr Jaime Richardson, who was also intoxicated.

Ms Benning, Mr Richardson and 3 other friends went to a local hotel. The group ordered dinner and drinks and continued to drink. They left the hotel at about 1:30 am. The initial plan to take a taxi was abandoned and Mr Richardson drove his vehicle. Ms Benning was seated in the front passenger seat. Two other passengers, Mr Dunster and Mr Gardner were in the rear seats.

As the vehicle driven by Mr Richardson was travelling along William Slim Drive at about 65 kph it veered to the left, exited the road and hit a tree. Ms Benning suffered fractured ankles that required surgical repair, a right pneumothorax, and an injury to her shoulder. Mr Dunster died in the accident. Mr Richardson had a blood alcohol reading of about 0.190 grams per 100 ml of blood. He was charged with the offences of culpable driving causing death and separately causing grievous bodily harm. He came to trial in March 2016 and was convicted on both counts. A later appeal failed.

Ms Benning commenced proceedings in the Supreme Court of the Australian Capital Territory against Mr Richardson, in negligence and claimed damages. Mr Richardson admitted a breach of duty of care owed to Ms Benning by driving while intoxicated. He claimed, primarily, that the breach did not cause Ms Benning's injuries because the accident was the result of Ms Benning taking hold of the steering wheel and turning it sharply to the left causing the vehicle veered off the road into a tree. In the alternative he claimed that if he was found liable there should be a substantial finding of contributory negligence because Ms Benning voluntarily was a passenger in the vehicle when she knew or ought reasonably to have known that the driver was intoxicated, and in addition, she was not wearing a seatbelt.

Held: judgment for the plaintiff.

1. Mr Richardson's evidence about Ms Benning grabbing the steering wheel was rejected. Mr Richardson was a most unimpressive witness. That was not based on his demeanour but rather on the manner in which he gave a number of answers, especially those in which he seemed to treat offences of drink-driving as more an indication of bad luck at being caught than having any element of the protection of road users. Mr Richardson said that Ms Benning "grabbed the steering wheel and ripped it out of my hands". It could not be accepted that Ms Benning was in a position to so strenuously take hold of the steering wheel and turn it so quickly and so strongly that it would have been "ripped" from the hands of Mr Richardson. While the expert reports did not discount the possibility of interference with the steering wheel, they certainly did not raise the occurrence beyond a possibility. [26]

2. It could not be determined exactly why the vehicle suddenly turned to the left. The important question was whether Mr Richardson's assertion that Ms Benning "ripped" the steering wheel out of his hands and turned the vehicle to the left was to be accepted. It was not. Combined with the expert evidence, the result was that Mr Richardson failed to discharge his onus to establish that Ms Benning interfered with the steering of the vehicle. [27], [28]

3. As to contributory negligence, taken with the seatbelt being in its clasp, Ms Benning's head striking the windscreen was sufficient to conclude that Mr Richardson had established that Ms Benning was not wearing a seatbelt when the collision occurred. The intoxicated state of Ms Benning as demonstrated by her blood alcohol reading and her apparent state depicted in the CCTV footage suggested she was in such a condition that she may not have given consideration to wearing a seatbelt. [40]

4. Ms Benning was not wearing a seatbelt. Her failure to do so contributed to her injuries. A further finding of contributory negligence arose from Ms Benning knowingly travelling in the vehicle with an intoxicated driver. [48]

5. Contributory negligence was assessed at 35%. That took into account that Ms Benning's most enduring injuries were to her ankles and those injuries were not relevant to her not wearing a seatbelt but did play a part in her getting into the vehicle with an intoxicated driver. [55]

6. Damages were assessed in the total sum of $458,429.69, including $160,000 for non-economic loss. A reduction of 35% on account of contributory negligence gave a final award of $297,979.30. [79]–[123]

[*Headnote by the Wolters Kluwer editors*]

A Muller (Maliganis Edwards Johnson) for the plaintiff.

J Pappas (HWL Ebsworth Lawyers) for the defendants.

Before: Elkaim J.

[¶82-568] Hall v Martin

(2020) Aust Torts Reports ¶82-568
Medium neutral citation: [2020] ACTSC 233
Supreme Court of the Australian Capital Territory
26 August 2020

Torts — Negligence — Personal injury — Duty of care — Worker injured by co-worker while working at scrap metal business — Worker has no employment contract with business owner and paid cash in hand for work — Worker alleging negligence by business owner and claiming damages for personal injury — Whether worker in employment relationship with business owner — Whether co-worker negligent — Whether business owner vicariously liable for negligence of co-worker — Civil Law (Wrongs) Act 2002 (ACT), s 43 — Workers Compensation Act 1951 (ACT), s 36B(3)(b), 182D.

Mr Hall worked at a scrap metal business conducted by Mr Martin at Fyshwick in the Australian Capital Territory. Mr Hall was employed on a cash-in-hand basis by Mr Martin. There was no written contract of employment and Mr Hall did not receive payslips or group certificates.

Mr McDonald also worked at the scrap metal business at Fyshwick. On 30 January 2016, Mr Hall and Mr McDonald were tasked with making a delivery of scrap cars to a farm owned by Mr Martin in New South Wales. Mr Hall alleged that when they reached Mr Martin's farm he was standing on the back of a truck when Mr McDonald operated a crane located on the back of the truck in such a way that it knocked him from the vehicle causing him to fall and break his left patella which required surgery. Following the surgery, Mr Hall's knee continued to give him pain. He alleged that he was permanently incapacitated to work as a truck driver or a labourer and the only positions he could work were sedentary, for which he had no training.

Section 182D of the *Workers Compensation Act 1951* (ACT) (the WC Act) provided that the law of the "Territory or State of connection" governed whether or not a damages claim

could be made in relation to a work-related injury to a worker and, if such a claim could be made, the determination of that claim. Although Mr Hall's injury occurred in NSW, by virtue of s 36B(3)(b) of the WC Act, Mr Hall's claim was to be determined in accordance with the law of the ACT, because the "Territory or State of connection" was the Territory or State where the worker was usually based for the purposes of the employment, which in this case was the Fyshwick yard within the ACT.

Section 43(1) of the *Civil Law (Wrongs) Act 2002* (ACT) (the CL Act) provided that a person was not negligent in failing to take precautions against a risk of harm unless the risk was foreseeable (ie, it was a risk of which the person knew or ought to have known), the risk was not insignificant, and in the circumstances, a reasonable person in the person's position would have taken those precautions.

Mr Martin did not hold workers compensation insurance. Mr Hall made a claim upon Default Insurance Fund (DIF), established under the WC Act, and brought proceedings against Mr Martin in the Supreme Court of the Australian Capital Territory in negligence and claimed damages for personal injury. DIF was joined in the proceedings as second defendant.

Mr Martin denied any liability for Mr Hall's injury. He denied that he had an employment relationship with Mr Hall and that he had ever instructed Mr Hall to make the delivery to his farm. He also denied that Mr McDonald had ever been employed at the scrap yard. DIF submitted that the evidence of Mr Hall was unreliable.

Held: judgment for the plaintiff.

1. The outcome of the proceedings depended upon the reliability of the evidence of Mr Hall and Mr Martin. Overall, Mr Hall was a reasonably credible witness and DIF's attacks on the reliability of his evidence were not successful. Mr Martin's approach to the proceedings overall were inconsistent with what one would have expected from an honest businessman who was uninsured at a relevant time. He demonstrated a reluctance to have his business affairs scrutinised and a willingness to tailor his evidence in a way that would advance what he perceived to be his interests in the proceedings. [127], [135], [140], [142]

2. The evidence of Mr Hall was accepted on the balance of probabilities that: (1) Mr Hall had an employment relationship with Mr Martin and that the accident occurred at Mr Martin's farm in NSW; (2) Mr Hall was employed by Mr Martin in Mr Martin's scrap metal business in the period from 11 January to 30 January 2016 and was an employee of Mr Martin on 30 January 2016 when he was injured; (3) Mr Hall was paid $100 per day and was paid in cash once a week. [144], [145]

3. The evidence was also that Mr McDonald was employed by Mr Martin at the time of the accident and that the accident occurred at Mr Martin's farm as a result of Mr Hall being struck by the crane operated by Mr McDonald. Mr McDonald was performing duties that were a necessary part of the task that he was instructed to perform in the course of his employment by Mr Martin. [146], [147], [149]

4. The movement of the arm of the crane caused Mr Hall to fall from the truck and be injured. There was no evidence as to how Mr McDonald had manipulated the controls of the crane. It was likely that the unpredictable movement of the crane was as a result of error on the part of the operator by reason of inexperience or otherwise. [150], [153]

5. The risk of a person on the back of the truck falling as a result of incorrect movement of the boom of the crane was foreseeable and the risk was not insignificant. Furthermore, a reasonable person manipulating the crane would have ensured that: (1) the crane was only moved in a predictable manner, and (2) if he was uncertain as to how the crane was controlled, he gained familiarity with its movements before Mr Hall was put in a position where he was at risk from any unexpected or unintended movements. Mr McDonald was negligent in failing to take those precautions. [154], [155]

6. Accordingly, Mr Martin was negligent because he was vicariously liable for the negligence of his employee, Mr McDonald.

7. Damages were assessed in the total sum of $532,365. [187]

[*Headnote by the Wolters Kluwer editors*]

A Stone SC with D Crowe (AC Lawyers) for the plaintiff.

The first defendant (Mr Martin) was self-represented.

D Richards (Minter Ellison) for the second defendant.

Before: Mossop J.

[¶82-525] Ivers v Mehdi

(2020) Aust Torts Reports ¶82-525
Medium neutral citation: [2020] ACTSC 112
Supreme Court of the Australian Capital Territory
12 May 2020

Torts — Negligence — Personal injury — Plaintiff sustained psychological injury when she saw a motor vehicle strike a pedestrian — Motor vehicle driven by first defendant — Whether the first defendant owed the plaintiff a duty of care — Whether the first defendant breached that duty of care — Whether the pedestrian was guilty of contributory negligence — Consideration of the medical evidence — Consideration of damages — Consideration of Civil Law (Wrongs) Act 2002 (ACT), s 34 — Civil Law (Wrongs) Act 2002 (ACT), s 34.

On 25 November 2016, Ms Wendy Ivers witnessed a motor vehicle accident in which a motor vehicle driven by Mr Shahid Mehdi struck a pedestrian in a shopping centre underground carpark.

Ms Ivers commenced proceedings in the Supreme Court of the Australian Capital Territory against Mr Mehdi, in negligence and claimed damages for psychological injury she claimed was caused by witnessing the accident. The Transport Accident Commission, the compulsory third party insurer of the vehicle driven by Mr Mehdi, was named as a party pursuant to s 151 of the *Road Transport (Third Party Insurance) Act 2008* (ACT).

Ms Ivers claimed that Mr Mehdi was negligent in failing to keep a proper lookout, failing to steer the motor vehicle he was driving so as to avoid the accident, and failing to apply the brakes on the motor vehicle he was driving when necessary to do so.

Mr Mehdi admitted that he struck the pedestrian but denied that he owed a duty of care to Ms Ivers or, in the alternative, that he had breached any such duty. He also did not admit that Ms Ivers suffered any injury or loss as she claimed. In the alternative, he claimed that the pedestrian was contributorily negligent in placing himself in the path of the vehicle.

Held: judgment for the plaintiff.

1. The evidence established that Mr Mehdi reversed his motor vehicle into the pedestrian, knocking him to the ground. There was no reason why the pedestrian should have apprehended that someone would reverse a vehicle from the parking bays near where he was standing and he did not have an opportunity to observe the brake lights or reversing lights illuminate on the vehicle because of the position in which he was standing. It is beyond any argument that the collision between Mr Mehdi's vehicle and the pedestrian was solely attributable to the fault of Mr Mehdi. There is no occasion for reduction of Ms Ivers' damages by reason of the operation of s 104 of the *Civil Law (Wrongs) Act 2002* (ACT). [151]

2. As someone who witnessed at least part of the accident, who was present at the scene and ran to provide assistance to the pedestrian, Ms Ivers falls within the class of persons whom Mr Mehdi should have foreseen may suffer a recognised psychiatric injury if he negligently collided with a pedestrian. [157]

3. Whether a duty of care is negated by s 34 of the Civil Law (Wrongs) Act depends not on the personal characteristics of the plaintiff, but on the nature of the event said to have caused the plaintiff's psychological reaction. If the event was one which a reasonable person in the defendant's position would have foreseen might, in the circumstances of the case, cause a person of reasonable fortitude in the plaintiff's position to suffer a recognised psychiatric illness if reasonable care was not taken, then the defendant's duty of care is not negated by the section irrespective of whether the plaintiff is not a person of normal fortitude. [158]

4. The question then becomes one of whether Mr Mehdi should have foreseen that a person of normal fortitude who observed what Ms Ivers observed from her vantage point when Mr Mehdi hit the pedestrian might suffer a recognised psychiatric illness if he did not take reasonable care? Ms Ivers' evidence is to be accepted that from her vantage point she believed that the pedestrian had been killed or seriously injured. Further, the expert evidence is to be accepted that Ms Ivers perceived and her actions in coming to the assistance of the pedestrian, in combination, might cause a person of normal fortitude to develop a recognisable psychiatric illness. [159]

5. Mr Mehdi owed Ms Ivers a relevant duty of care not to cause her mental harm by reversing the car without reasonable care. He breached that duty when he reversed the car without reasonable care, striking the pedestrian. The duty of care owed to Ms Ivers is not negated by the terms of s 34 of the Civil Law (Wrongs) Act. As a consequence of Mr Mehdi's negligence, Ms Ivers developed a recognised psychiatric illness, being Post Traumatic Stress Disorder. [160]

6. Damages are assessed in the total sum of $176,312.43.

[*Headnote by the Wolters Kluwer editors*]

D Crowe (Maliganis Edwards Johnson) for the plaintiff.

J Turnbull SC with ND Compton (Moray and Agnew Lawyers) for the first and second defendants.

Before: Burns J.

[¶82-522] Cornwall v Jenkins as Trustee for the iSpin Family Trust

(2020) Aust Torts Reports ¶82-522
Medium neutral citation: [2020] ACTCA 2
Supreme Court of the Australian Capital Territory, Court of Appeal
19 February 2020

Torts — Negligence — Breach of duty — Duty to take preventative steps — Expert evidence — Assessment of damages — Contributory negligence — Appeals — Notice of contention — Appellant was injured while participating in an "aerial sling" exercise class — Class was being run in a studio operated by respondent — Primary judge held that respondent had not breached her duty of care to appellant by failing to require her to use a crash mat — Appellant appealed claiming that primary judge had erred in assessing breach of duty — Respondent did breach duty to appellant by not insisting that she use a crash mat — Appellant had been contributorily negligent for her injuries in amount of one-third of total liability — Civil Law (Wrongs) Act 2002 (ACT), s 40–46, 102.

On 11 February 2014, the appellant, Ms Carrie Cornwall (Ms Cornwall), was injured while participating in an "aerial sling" exercise class at a studio run by the respondent, Sophie Jenkins as Trustee for the iSpin Family Trust Trading as iSpin (Ms Jenkins). That class involved participants using a fabric sling attached to the ceiling. While practicing a particular manoeuvre, Ms Cornwall fell from the sling and broke both wrists. At that time, she was using a relatively thin yoga mat as fall protection. The studio had a supply of thicker mats, referred to as "crash mats", but did not require the participants to use them.

Ms Cornwall commenced proceedings in the Supreme Court of the Australian Capital Territory in negligence and claimed damages. She alleged that Ms Jenkins, who ran the fitness class and who was the occupier of the premises, was negligent in that she failed to warn of the risks, failed to supervise, failed to operate a safe system, and failed to direct the use of a spotter. iSpin denied liability and argued that the risk of injury was not foreseeable and in the alternative if negligence was proven, Ms Cornwall was contributorily negligent.

The primary judge found that the evidence did not reveal any breach of duty on the part of Ms Jenkins or anyone else responsible for the studio or the running of the aerial sling class, and dismissed Ms Cornwall's claim. Damages were awarded on a notional basis only: *Cornwall v Jenkins as trustee for the iSpin Family Trust* (2019) Aust Torts Reports ¶82-435; [2019] ACTSC 34.

Ms Cornwall appealed the primary judge's findings. She argued that the primary judge erred in finding that Ms Jenkins had not breached her duty of care to Ms Cornwall by failing to require her to use a crash mat and that any breach of duty had not caused Ms Cornwall's injuries.

Ms Jenkins filed a notice of cross-appeal seeking orders that Ms Cornwall's damages be reduced by reason of contributory negligence in the event that she succeeded on her appeal. She also argued that the primary judge should have made three additional findings. Firstly, it should have been found that the risk of harm was not reasonably foreseeable and not "not insignificant" within the meaning of s 43 of the *Civil Law (Wrongs) Act 2002* (ACT) (the Wrongs Act). Secondly, the primary judge should have found that the risk of harm was the risk of Ms Cornwall falling whilst performing the hip lock move with the assistance of a spotter. And thirdly, the primary judge should have found that the presence of crash mats would not have prevented the injury within the meaning of s 45 of the Wrongs Act.

Held: appeal allowed.

1. Section 43(1)(b) of the Wrongs Act provided that a person was not negligent in failing to take precautions against a risk of harm unless that risk was not insignificant. That required the risk to be assessed prospectively. The double negative "not insignificant" imposed a more demanding standard than that imposed by the common law, but not greatly so. [25]–[29]

2. In that respect, the onus fell on the plaintiff to establish that there was a reasonably practicable precaution that could have been taken to avoid the risk of injury. Ms Cornwall sought to discharge that onus in the present case by relying on expert testimony to the effect that, if crash mats had been obligatory, her injuries would not have occurred. [30]–[35]

3. The evidence that Ms Jenkins relied upon to rebut that proposition showed some internal contradiction. More particularly, Ms Jenkins' expert had said that the risk to Ms Cornwall could not be completely eliminated while at the same time appearing to accept that the crash mats may have prevented her injuries. [36]–[56]

4. When that evidence was considered as a whole, it had to be concluded that the primary judge erred in finding that Ms Jenkins had not breached her duty to Ms Cornwall by failing to insist on the use of the crash mats. The risk of injury was plainly foreseeable and insistence on use of a crash mat would not have been unreasonable. [57]–[62]

5. However, the evidence also demonstrated that Ms Jenkins had failed to follow the instructions given to her as to the correct method of performing the manoeuvre when she fell and failed to use a spotter. In those circumstances, Ms Jenkins was to be held contributorily negligent in the amount of one-third. [63], [64]

6. The parties agreed that the primary judge had made an error in assessing past economic loss. On that basis, the damages assessed by the primary judge, when corrected to

account for that error, amounted to $558,446.00. Reducing this amount by one-third resulted in an amount of $372,297.34. Judgment was to be entered for Ms Cornwall in that amount. [65]–[67]

[*Headnote by the Wolters Kluwer editors*]

C Erskine SC with D Richards (Maliganis Edwards Johnson) for the appellant.

A Cheshire SC with E Esber (Colin Biggers & Paisley Lawyers) for the respondent.

Before: Burns, Loukas-Karlsson JJ and Crowe AJ.

[¶82-518] Nouri v Australian Capital Territory

(2020) Aust Torts Reports ¶82-518
Medium neutral citation: [2020] ACTCA 1
Supreme Court of the Australian Capital Territory, Court of Appeal
13 February 2020

Torts — Negligence — Duty of care — Breach of duty — Causation — Damages — Wrongful birth — Congenital anomalies — Prenatal care — Prenatal testing — Duty of disclosure — Appeals — Daughter of appellants was born with significant congenital anomalies — Respondent was responsible for hospital at which mother had received prenatal care — Parents had not been advised that their daughter might be born with congenital anomalies — Proceedings brought by parents for costs of supporting child with severe disabilities — Primary judge held that hospital had breached duty of care but that causation had not been established — Appeal brought to Court of Appeal — Appeal dismissed — Appellants had not established causation — They had not proved that they would have terminated pregnancy had they been properly advised — Civil Law (Wrongs) Act 2002 (ACT), s 45, 46.

The first appellant, Ms Einas Nouri (Ms Nouri), and the second appellant, Mr Musab Shaor (Mr Shaor) were the parents of Saba Nouri (Saba), who was born on 3 November 2011 with severe congenital anomalies. More particularly, her consequential disabilities were categorised as "VACTERL association", which referred to abnormalities in the following areas: vertebral anomalies, anal atresia, cardiac defects, tracheoesophageal fistula (TOF), renal abnormalities and limb defects. She suffered from developmental delay and required 24-hour care. Saba, who was referred to as "Twin B", was also one of non-identical twins. The other twin did not have the anomalies. Ms Nouri and Mr Shaor had three other children in addition to the twins.

Ms Nouri's prenatal medical care had been conducted in Canberra Hospital to which she had been referred after an ultrasound scan in July 2011. In the period from July 2011 to October 2011, she had multiple appointments at that hospital's foetal medical unit as well as several ultrasounds and an amniocentesis. The doctors that Ms Nouri saw during that time initially expressed some concerns about Twin B and so she was referred to Sydney Children's Hospital. However, the outcome of that appointment was that the observed variation was within normal limits. Subsequently when Ms Nouri had to undergo amnioreduction for polyhydramnios, she was not advised that Twin B had any congenital anomaly.

It followed that, when Saba was born on 3 November 2011, neither Ms Nouri nor Mr Shaor were expecting anything other than a possible cardiac abnormality.

Ms Nouri and Mr Shaor commenced proceedings in the Supreme Court of the Australian Capital Territory against the Australian Capital Territory (the ACT), as the entity responsible for Canberra Hospital, in negligence and claimed damages. They alleged that their lives had been irreparably changed due to the additional obligations that came with raising a severely disabled child. They alleged that Canberra Hospital should have provided them with certain information that would have given them the option of terminating the pregnancy in relation to Twin B. The ACT denied any breach of duty and causation of damage.

Before the primary judge, the central point on breach of duty was whether or not the information about Twin B's condition had been disclosed to Ms Nouri or Mr Shaor. On causation, the central issue was whether they would have, or could have, secured a termination at the late stage in the pregnancy when information about Twin B's condition should have been supplied. The primary judge found that the ACT did breach its duty of care but that causation had not been established. His Honour did, however, conduct a contingent assessment of damages in the sum of $1,813,807. That assessment did not include any award of general damages and was performed on the basis that damages were only recoverable up until Saba reached the age of 18 years: (2018) Aust Torts Reports ¶82-415; [2018] ACTSC 275.

Ms Nouri and Mr Shaor appealed the primary judge's findings as to liability as well as to damages. They argued on appeal that the date upon which they should have been informed of the possibility that Twin B suffered from a TOF was earlier than that identified by the primary judge. They also contested the finding on causation, which turned upon whether or not Ms Nouri and Mr Shaor would have been able to arrange a termination of Twin B. In relation to the assessment of damages, they contended that the primary judge erred in failing to award them general damages and in failing to award them economic loss beyond Saba's 18th birthday.

Held: appeal dismissed.

1. The case run on behalf of Ms Nouri and Mr Shaor on appeal was that, had they been advised of the possibility of a TOF earlier than the primary judge found that they should have been, then there was a greater chance of them deciding to terminate the pregnancy. However, it was not clear that such a finding would have altered the conclusion on causation. [34]–[48]

2. In any event, that was not the case that Ms Nouri and Mr Shaor put at trial. That was for the reason that the expert evidence did not support the proposition that reasonable professional diligence required disclosure of the possibility of a TOF at the time that they were now claiming it should have been disclosed. [49]–[61]

3. Ms Nouri and Mr Shaor had claimed at first instance that, had they been informed of the possibility of a TOF when they argued they should have been, they would have made arrangements to fly to the United States for a termination of the pregnancy. However, the evidence adduced at first instance did not support that claim. [62]–[66]

4. In particular, the evidence given by the doctor who had agreed to see Ms Nouri was that he would consider undertaking the termination for her. His evidence was not to the effect that he would have definitely carried out the procedure. He would have required considerable assurances that Ms Nouri had access to appropriate counselling and support. [67]–[78]

5. There was also evidence that, given her state of polyhydramnios, it would have been difficult for Ms Nouri to fly and that it would have been difficult to find an airline who allowed her to do so. In addition, it was not clear that Ms Nouri and Mr Shaor were in a financial position to travel to the United States. [79]–[91]

6. Another unknown factor was the effect that counselling might have had on the decision of Ms Nouri and Mr Shaor. It was not known whether, following such counselling, they may have decided to continue with the pregnancy in spite of the TOF risk. This related to the issue of hindsight and the risks to the other twin of the termination procedure. [92]–[104]

7. For these reasons, there was no error in the primary judge's finding on causation. His Honour was entitled to conclude that, even if Ms Nouri and Mr Shaor had been advised of the TOF risk, they had not proved that the pregnancy of Twin B would have been terminated. It was, therefore, not appropriate or necessary to determine the other grounds of appeal. [92]–[104]

[*Headnote by the Wolters Kluwer editors*]

B Walker SC with A Campbell and U Okereke-Fisher (Gerard Malouf and Partners) for the appellant.

D Higgs SC with K Sant (ACT Government Solicitor) for the respondent.

Before: Murrell CJ, Mossop and Rangiah JJ.

[¶82-481] Hargrave v Singh

(2019) Aust Torts Reports ¶82-481
Medium neutral citation: [2019] ACTSC 139
Supreme Court of the Australian Capital Territory
4 June 2019

Torts law — Personal injury — Pedestrian struck by taxi — Taxi driven by first defendant — Whether collision was caused by negligence of first defendant — Whether plaintiff is guilty of contributory negligence — Consideration of degree of intoxication of plaintiff — Consideration of s 95 of the Civil Law (Wrongs) Act 2002 (ACT) — Consideration of damages — Consideration of the medical evidence — Civil Law (Wrongs) Act 2002, s 95.

On 23 May 2014, 21-year-old Joshua Hargrave and his girlfriend Tegan Lovelock went to the home of friends, Murray Anderson and Rebecca Burrows, where Mr Hargrave consumed about two beers before his mother drove the four of them into Civic, arriving at Mooseheads Nightclub at about 11 pm. At Mooseheads they danced and consumed further alcoholic drinks. They decided to leave at about 3 am on Saturday 24 May 2014 and the group got into a "van maxi-taxi" driven by Mr Amandeep Singh. After some discussion, Mr Singh agreed to commence the journey without up-front payment. After dropping the other passengers home, Mr Hargrave and his girlfriend alighted from the taxi and proceeded to walk the rest of the way home, after disputing a credit card surcharge. As they were walking, Mr Hargrave saw the taxi come over the crest of the hill in front of him. As the taxi came over the rise, Mr Hargrave heard the engine rev and the taxi continued to accelerate. Mr Hargrave waved his hands above his head to try to get Mr Singh's attention, but the taxi continued to move towards him. The taxi struck him and he ended up in the gutter. The taxi did not stop.

Mr Hargrave received treatment at the hospital. A blood alcohol sample was taken which detected a concentration of not less than 0.109 grams per 100 millilitres of blood.

Mr Hargrave commenced proceedings in the Supreme Court of the Australian Capital Territory against Mr Singh and Insurance Australia Limited Trading as NRMA Insurance, in negligence and claimed damages. The defendants admitted that the taxi driven by Mr Singh struck Mr Hargrave, but deny that this collision was caused by the negligence of Mr Singh. In alternative, the defendants claimed that Mr Hargrave was contributorily negligent.

***Held:* judgment for the plaintiff in the total sum of $275,082.26.**

Burns J:

1. The evidence established that Mr Singh saw Mr Hargrave, accelerated, and veered towards him. [17]

2. Mr Singh simply drove off after the collision, leaving Mr Hargrave laying on the ground. Mr Singh did not know what injuries Mr Hargrave had sustained, and certainly was in no position to form a belief that he had not been injured. [15]

3. Mr Singh's driving involved a gross departure from his duty to exercise reasonable care and skill in driving the taxi. [18]

4. As to contributory negligence, two issues arose. Firstly, what was the degree of Mr Hargrave's intoxication at the time of this incident, and, secondly, to what extent was Mr Hargrave guilty of contributory negligence? [19]

5. Section 95(1) of the *Civil Law (Wrongs) Act 2002* (ACT) provides that contributory negligence must be presumed if an injured person was intoxicated at the time of an accident giving rise to a claim for damages for personal injury and the defendant claims contributory negligence. [20]

6. There is a respectable argument that Mr Hargrave's level of intoxication was not in any way causally connected with the injuries he sustained. This is not a case where Mr Hargrave was not seen by Mr Singh after walking out onto a dimly lit road in the middle of the night. This was a case where it has been established that Mr Singh saw Mr Hargrave on the road and deliberately veered his taxi onto the wrong side of the road with the intention of either hitting or scaring him. The contribution made by Mr Hargrave's intoxication to his injuries was minimal. If Mr Singh had simply continued driving on his correct side of the road, no collision would have occurred. By far and away, responsibility for the accident rests with Mr Singh. He saw Mr Hargrave and deliberately changed the course of the taxi to drive at him. Mr Hargrave's contributory negligence is to be assessed at 10%. [27]

[*Headnote by the Wolters Kluwer editors*]

A Muller (Maliganis Edwards Johnson) for the plaintiff.

W Fitzsimmons (Sparke Helmore) for the defendants.

Before: Burns J.

[¶82-376] KS and XT v Calvary Health Care ACT Trading as Calvary Hospital and Dr Andrew Foote

(2018) Aust Torts Reports ¶82-376
Medium neutral citation: [2018] ACTSC 84
Supreme Court of the Australian Capital Territory
Judgment delivered 5 April 2018

Negligence — Medical practitioner — Hospital — Psychological harm to plaintiffs — Liability — Whether there were breaches of duty — Content of duty of care — Whether the breaches of duty were causative of the injuries sustained — Assessment of damages — Contribution — Civil Law (Wrongs) Act 2002 (ACT), ss 32–35, 42–45 — Civil Liability Act 2002 (NSW), s 5O.

On 13 January 2011, Ms KS was admitted to Calvary Private Hospital as a patient of Dr Andrew Foote, an obstetrician and gynaecologist. Ms KS was pregnant with her first child, which had been conceived by IVF. Dr Foote had been attending to Ms KS since August 2010. By 13 January 2011, the baby was one week overdue and it was agreed that Ms KS would be induced. The induction process was started at about 4.30 pm. By 4.58 pm, abnormalities were apparent in the baby's heart activity, detected via a foetal heart rate monitor. In the period following, there were three separate episodes of bradycardia. The midwife attending to Ms KS did not contact Dr Foote until sometime between 5.50 pm and 6.00 pm. Dr Foote ordered a Caesarean section, with Ms KS arriving at theatre at 6.35 pm. However, the baby was delivered stillborn at 7.00 pm.

Ms KS and her husband Mr XT commenced proceedings in the Supreme Court of the Australian Capital Territory against the hospital and Dr Foote, in negligence and claimed damages for psychological harm caused by the stillbirth of their first baby. Ms KS and Mr XT alleged various particulars of negligence, including but not limited to allegations that the hospital and Dr Foote were negligent in failing to adequately interpret the cardiograph, failing to classify and urgently carry out an emergency Caesarean section, failing to resuscitate the baby properly or adequately, and as against Dr Foote, failing to make himself available to perform the Caesaran section earlier and failing to seek assistance and arrange for another competent surgeon to perform the procedure.

The hospital conceded liability. Dr Foote made limited admissions of breach of duty without conceding liability.

The main issues at trial were determining the scope of the Dr Foote's duty of care and causation.

Held: judgment in favour of Ms KS for $669,518.15; judgment in favour of Mr XT for $220,373.00.

Per Burns J:

1. Ms KS had a troubled medical history. She was older, had difficulties conceiving, endured several IVF cycles and a miscarriage and lost the twin foetus of baby A, the focus of these proceedings. There was little doubt she was a high-risk patient. Dr Foote knew, or ought to have known that, given Ms KS' medical history, she would place significance on any risk which might arise from delaying labour. Instead, Dr Foote advised them that delivery beyond 40 weeks was not a concern and assured them of their baby's health. Dr Foote failed to mention that Ms KS was at increased risk of stillbirth.

2. A decision as to induction was delayed another week, due to Dr Foote's leave. Dr Foote failed to explore options in attempting to find an alternative hospital or practitioner who could perform the induction sooner.

3. Dr Foote failed to confirm to the nursing staff that Ms KS was going to have an emergency caesarean. Hence, there was no sense of urgency in preparing and moving Ms KS to theatre.

4. Following her daughter's death, Ms KS experienced severe psychological harm which impacted her personal relationships and career aspirations. She was diagnosed with post-traumatic stress disorder (PTSD). The event also led to Mr XT being detached, angry and bitter. His faith in the medical profession was eroded. He lacked motivation and turned to alcohol.

5. Expert evidence was submitted by several medical professionals. A competent midwife should have alerted Dr Foote earlier and taken immediate remedial action. Discontinuing foetal heart rate monitoring suggested that the staff did not appreciate the urgency of the situation. Further, there was an unacceptably long interval between the decision to perform a caesarean and the delivery. An emergency caesarean could be performed in 20 to 30 minutes. The hospital had seven theatres; yet only one was in use at the time. The event which occurred went against normal hospital procedure. A theatre supervisor charged with bringing Ms KS to theatre was not told that this was a life-threatening event; nor was the midwife who attended to Ms KS. Hence, there was no sense of urgency.

6. Dr Foote declined to give evidence. However, hospital records show that Dr Foote attended to other non-urgent cases at the time — cases which could have been handed to another medical practitioner.

7. The hospital admitted liability. The midwife failed to recognise the significance of the deceleration of the baby's heartbeat, and failed to notify Dr Foote with sufficient urgency. These constituted breaches of the duty of care owed to Ms KS and Mr XT and were an operative cause of Ms KS' daughter being stillborn.

8. Dr Foote admitted liability in failing to advise hospital staff of the emergency nature of the caesarean. He failed to recognise Ms KS' higher risk of stillbirth to advise her accordingly as to the timing of induction. Dr Foote had a duty to warn Ms KS of a material risk inherent in delaying delivery: *Rogers* v *Whitaker* (1992) 175 CLR 479. The risk was material because Dr Foote was aware, or should have been aware, that a reasonable person in Ms KS' position would likely attach significance to it.

9. Dr Foote breached his duty of care in not affording Ms KS the opportunity and right to make an informed decision about the timing of an induction. He failed to make enquiries as to alternative options for induction in a public hospital by a different practitioner — options which Ms KS would most probably have accepted. Dr Foote's failure to arrange an urgent caesarean and his participation in other non-urgent procedures constituted a very serious departure from the duty owed to Ms KS. If Dr Foote had recognised the significance of the foetal heartbeat reading as constituting an emergency, and responded accordingly, Ms KS' daughter may have been born alive and Ms KS and Mr XT would not have sustained injuries.

10. Each defendant is liable. However, Dr Foote was significantly more culpable than the hospital. Liability is apportioned 70% to Dr Foote and 30% to the hospital.

[Headnote by the Wolters Kluwer editors]

Mr I Roberts SC with Mr Ingram (instructed by Commins Hendriks) for the first and second plaintiffs.

Ms K Burke (instructed by Sneddon Hall and Gallop) for the first defendant.

Ms K Oldfield (instructed by Ken Cush and Associates) for the second defendant.

Before: Burns J.

[¶82-315] Roberts v Westpac Banking Corporation

(2016) Aust Torts Reports ¶82-315
Medium neutral citation: [2016] ACTCA 68
Supreme Court of the Australian Capital Territory, Court of Appeal
Judgment delivered 13 December 2016

Negligence — Duty of care — Whether bank owes a duty to customers to protect them from the actions of criminal third parties — Where primary judge found no duty owed — Appeal dismissed — Civil Law (Wrongs) Act 2002 (ACT), ss 40, 42, 43, 45.

On 1 February 2010, Mr Roberts went to Westpac bank in Fyshwick to bank a cheque. As he approached the counter, he noticed something flick past his right side and heard a male yelling behind him "Put the money in the bag. Put the money in the bag". Mr Roberts was told by the offender to place his hands on the counter. The offender was armed with a gun and was wearing a black balaclava. Mr Roberts perceived that the gun was pointed at himself and he was frightened of being shot. He lay on the ground and while on the ground, he heard the offender say, "I'll shoot him. Put the money in the bag. Don't press the button. I'll kill him". Mr Roberts believed that he was going to die. The security shutters were triggered, being activated by the bank teller using a fly-up screen. The offender fired a shot and ran out of the bank. Mr Roberts got up and chased after the offender to see where he went.

As a result of the incident, Mr Roberts to develop post-traumatic stress disorder.

Mr Roberts commenced proceedings in the Supreme Court of the Australian Capital Territory against Westpac Banking Corporation (WBC) in negligence, and claimed damages. He alleged that the bank teller was negligent in activating the security screen as it was unsafe to do so in the situation, and that the WBC failed to instruct staff how to respond during a bank robbery.

Her Honour Ashford AJ found that WBC had no control over the offender and although WBC had a duty to ensure reasonable care was taken, they had no duty to control the actions

of the offender, as the conduct of the offender was unpredictable. Her Honour relied upon the decision of the High Court in *Modbury Triangle Shopping Centre Pty Ltd* v *Anzil* [2000] HCA 61; 205 CLR 254 (*Modbury*). Ashford AJ found that there was no breach of duty of care owed by WBC to Mr Roberts. Her Honour accepted the evidence of the bank teller, that she did not hear the offender threatening to kill Mr Roberts and that she believed the gun was pointed at another bank teller and activated the fly-up screen in accordance with her training.

Her Honour also rejected the scope of any duty owed to Mr Roberts by WBC to train its staff as to how to respond in the event of an armed robbery and such training would not be able to assist how staff react during a robbery as discretion must be maintained in a tense situation. Ashford AJ found that WBC owed a duty to both its staff and customers but no duty to prevent criminal activities of a third party.

Mr Roberts appealed the primary judge's findings. He argued on appeal that the primary judge erred in not rejecting the evidence of the bank teller, and that the primary judge erred in finding that the bank teller did not hear the offender's threat towards Mr Roberts. He also argued that the primary judge erred in finding that the WBC did not owe a duty to Mr Roberts to take reasonable care to avoid the foreseeable risk of injury associated with unpredictable conduct of a bank robber. On the issue of causation, Mr Roberts argued that if the bank teller had been trained to comply with all directions of a bank robber, she would not have activated the pop-up screens and the gun would not have been fired and he would not have sustained an injury.

Held: the appeal be dismissed.

Per Murrell CJ:

1. The primary judge was entitled to accept the employee's evidence that she did not "hear" the offender's threat to shoot Mr Roberts if the security screens were activated.

2. The primary judge was correct in finding that Mr Roberts established neither breach of duty nor causation. It was not open on the evidence to find that training about harm minimisation should have been to the effect that bank employees must always follow the directions of a bank robber. Further, the evidence did not establish the likelihood that, had the bank teller been "properly" trained, the employee would have reacted differently, causing the robber to behave differently, and thereby avoiding injury to Mr Roberts. [23].

Per Burns and Gilmour JJ:

1. The scope of the duty was said to be one on the part of Westpac to take reasonable care not to invite an adverse response from the offender or not to take any step to endanger customers who were lawfully on the bank's premises, and that this was the formulation whether the duty was described as one to behave so as to minimise the danger arising or a duty not to behave so as to increase the danger arising from the presence of the offender on the premises. [51]

2. Westpac did not have any indirect practical control over the offender by its control of its staff, as to how they must respond when confronted by an armed offender. Westpac had no capacity to fulfil such a duty.

3. The primary judge was correct in finding that Westpac had no control of an offender coming onto its premises, and there was no breach of duty of care. That the risk of harm to a customer during the course of an attempted armed robbery was foreseeable is not sufficient of itself to impose upon Westpac, as the occupier of the bank premises, a duty to take reasonable care not to increase the risk of harm to a customer from the criminal behaviour of a third party. [96]

4. The primary judge was entitled to find that Mr Roberts had failed to establish a breach of any duty to train, and was also correct to reject Mr Roberts' argument of causation. Even if Westpac was in breach of the assumed duty by failing to train the bank teller to always obey an offender's instructions, this does not establish causation of the harm suffered by Mr Roberts. Factual causation was not established.

[*Headnote by the Wolters Kluwer editors*]

Mr D Campbell SC with Mr A Muller (instructed by Slater and Gordon) for the appellant.

Mr V Higgs SC with Ms V Thomas (instructed by Wotton Kearney Insurance Lawyers) for the respondent.

Before: Murrell CJ, Burns and Gilmour JJ.

[¶82-313] Jausnik v Nominal Defendant (No 5)

(2016) Aust Torts Reports ¶82-313
Medium neutral citation: [2016] ACTSC 306
Supreme Court of the Australian Capital Territory
Judgment delivered 18 October 2016

Torts — Negligence — Police involved in pursuit of fleeing vehicle across NSW/ACT border — Failure to comply with police protocols for safe driving and cross-border pursuits — Passenger in police vehicle suffering mental harm arising from attending scene of accident arising from police pursuit — Liability of State of New South Wales for failure to provide training in use of radios and cross-border pursuit protocols — Liability of police driver for injury to passenger.

Choice of law — Statutory contribution between tortfeasors — Accident in the territory following police pursuit from New South Wales — Claim for contribution by ACT Nominal Defendant against New South Wales police office and State of New South Wales — Characterisation of apportionment legislation — Applicable choice of law rule.

Torts — Causation — Police pursuit of driver cross-border — Pursued driver involved in fatal accident — Whether pursued driver would have avoided accident if pursuit terminated earlier — Expert evidence based on aggregate statistics — Whether likely conduct of pursued driver proved on balance of probabilities — Causation not established.

Torts — Statutory contribution — Nominal Defendant liable for conduct of pursued driver who caused an accident — State of New South Wales and police officer also negligent — Contingent assessment of appropriate contribution.

Civil Law (Wrongs) Act 2002 (ACT), ss 21, 32, 34, 42, 43, 44, 45, 46 — Civil Liability Act 2002 (NSW), ss 5D, 5E — Workers Compensation Act 1951 (ACT), s 182D — Workers Compensation Act 1987 (NSW), s 150A

On 20 March 2010, Mr Edward Jausnik and the first third party, Mr Michael Hannaford, were performing their duties as New South Wales police officers. They were conducting random breath testing on Richard Avenue in Queanbeyan, NSW. While conducting the breath testing, they observed a vehicle driving at high speed across a roundabout further down Richard Avenue. The officers got into their police vehicle and pursued the vehicle.

The vehicle being pursued was an unregistered silver Mazda being driven by Mr Justin Williams. The police vehicle pulled up behind the Mazda at a set of traffic lights and Mr Hannaford activated his police vehicle lights which resulted in the Mazda taking off through a set of red traffic lights from Kendall Ave onto Canberra Avenue. The car made the distance of 50 m down Canberra Avenue and crossed the border between New South Wales and the Australian Capital Territory with the police officers in pursuit. After notifying the NSW police the officers attempted to radio contact the Australian Federal Police to advise them of

the pursuit and take instruction upon crossing the border, however, they were unable to effectively use the newly installed radio system.

The Mazda proceeded through a further three sets of traffic lights travelling at high speed which was recorded at one point at 157 km/h. The pursuit continued toward the intersection with Ipswich and the Monaro Highway where there were two sets of traffic lights. Another vehicle was turning right on a green light from the Monaro Highway exit onto Canberra Avenue when the Mazda drove through the two sets of red lights and collided with the turning vehicle, killing the driver, his partner, and their infant son.

Mr Jausnik attended to the victims at the crash scene and attempted first aid to the occupants of all vehicles.

Mr Williams survived the impact but later died in hospital due to his injuries. He was recorded as having a blood alcohol level of 0.154%. Mr Williams also had a passenger, who was conveyed to hospital in a critical condition, but survived.

Mr Jausnik commenced proceedings against the Nominal Defendant, a statutory office existing to allow those injured by unregistered vehicles without CTP insurance to seek compensation. Mr Jausnik sought compensation for a psychiatric illness identified as chronic post-traumatic stress disorder and major depression which resulted from his attempts to render first aid to the occupants of the vehicles following the collision. Mr Jausnik succeeded in his claim against the Nominal Defendant and was awarded damages in the sum of $1,225,000 plus costs.

The Nominal Defendant filed a third party notice on November 2012 seeking contribution against Mr Hannaford and the State of New South Wales claiming contributory negligence. The Nominal Defendant sought contribution. It alleged that the third parties were also liable to Mr Jausnik on the basis that Mr Hannaford continued the pursuit despite the excessive speed of Mr Williams; failed to adequately consider the risks; failed to heed Mr Jausnik's advice to terminate the pursuit and failed to comply with protocols of cross border pursuits. The claim against the State of New South Wales was based on the grounds that they failed to adequately train officers on the use of the new radio system, on cross-jurisdictional pursuits, and failed to instruct Mr Hannaford to terminate the pursuit.

***Held:* judgment in favour of the first third party and second third party against the defendant.**

Per Mossop AsJ:

1. In order to seek contribution it must first be established that the Nominal Defendant was liable. It must be shown that Mr Williams should have foreseen that Mr Jausnik might suffer a recognised psychiatric illness as a result of Mr Jausnik being required to attend to persons suffering injuries caused by Mr Williams' negligent driving.

2. The duty of a driver extends to persons who may suffer mental harm as a consequence of his/her negligent driving. Clearly there was negligent driving on Mr Williams' part in the present case. The evidence established that Mr Jausnik suffered damage in the form of post-traumatic stress disorder and depression as a consequence of what he saw and otherwise experienced at the site of the accident. It was therefore accepted that the Nominal Defendant was liable.

3. The state also owed Mr Jausnik a duty to take reasonable care to avoid exposing him to unnecessary risks of injury: *Grills* v *Leighton Contractors Pty Ltd* [2015] NSWCA 72. The state breached this duty in two ways, firstly by failing to appropriately instruct the officers on the new radio system and secondly by failing to provide sufficient training to either Mr Jausnik or Mr Hannaford as to cross-border pursuits. Radio communication was considered fundamental to safe policing and there was a reasonable foreseeable risk that the officers might come to harm if they were unable to use the radio system. It was also reasonably

foreseeable that a lack of knowledge in police policies including cross-border pursuits would expose the officers to a risk of injury. Negligence in relation to these matters was established.

4. Mr Hannaford owed a duty to Mr Jausnik to drive safely, there being no inconsistency between the duty of a police officer to a passenger in the vehicle and the driver's duty as a police officer: *New South Wales* v *Tyszyk* [2008] NSWCA 107. This duty extended to protection against damages arising from pure mental harm under *Civil Law (Wrongs) Act 2002* (ACT) s 34(1).

5. Relevant aspects of Mr Hannaford's driving were identified as those which were alleged to be causally related to Mr Williams' collision. Mr Hannaford breached his duty to Mr Jausnik firstly by continuing to pursue Mr Williams when no contact had been made with the AFP and secondly by failing to terminate the pursuit when the danger of its continuation clearly outweighed the need to pursue the vehicle. No breach arose from the failure to obtain permission to enter into the ACT or to maintain the pursuit for a limited period. However, in the circumstances where there was difficulty making contact and when it became obvious that the vehicle was not intending to stop voluntarily, an officer acting reasonably would have terminated the pursuit.

6. Although the state and Mr Hannaford were found to be negligent it is not possible to find that the accident would not have occurred had there not been a breach of duty be the state or Mr Hannaford. It was not possible to determine that, had radio contact been made and appropriate procedures followed, the pursuit would have been terminated in time to avoid the collision. Nor was it possible to reach any conclusion as to what Mr Williams' behaviour would have been following a cessation of the pursuit. It therefore was not established on the balance of probability that either the state or Mr Hannaford are persons liable for the same damage.

7. The claim against both third parties failed.

8. If these conclusions are found to be wrong and the Nominal Defendant was able to prove that in the absence of the negligence on the part of Mr Hannaford the collision would not have occurred, the operation of s 21 of the *Civil Law (Wrongs) Act 2002* (ACT) in relation to Mr Hannaford's negligence and s 5 of the *Law Reform (Miscellaneous Provisions) Act 1946* (NSW) in relation to the state's negligence would come into operation and would lead to an exercise of apportionment between tortfeasors and a comparison of culpability. Consideration of the relative extent of departure from the standards of a reasonable person and the relative causal potency of the act in causing the damage, leads to an apportionment liability overwhelmingly to Mr Williams and hence the Nominal Defendant. It was the conduct of Mr Williams that caused the deaths of the three victims as well as himself and the injury to his passenger. The conduct of the state and Mr Hannaford was only indirectly a cause of harm to Mr Jausnik. The appropriate apportionment would be 92.5% to the Nominal Defendant, 5% to the state and 2.5% to Mr Hannaford.

[*Headnote by the Wolters Kluwer editors*]

P J Deakin QC, L P McFee (instructed by Minter Ellison) for the defendant.

G M Watson, W S Reynolds (instructed by Moray & Agnew) for the first third party.

J Sheller (instructed by HWL Ebsworth) for the Second third party.

M Rennie (instructed by NSW Crown Solicitor's Office) for New South Wales Commissioner of Police.

Before: Mossop AsJ.

New South Wales

[¶82-777] Tapp v Australian Bushmen's Campdraft & Rodeo Association Ltd

(2022) Aust Torts Reports ¶82-777
Medium neutral citation: [2022] HCA 11
High Court of Australia
6 April 2022

Recreational activity — Breach of duty of care — Causation — Obvious risk of dangerous recreational activity — Where appellant competing in campdraft competition — Where campdrafting a dangerous recreational activity — Where appellant's horse slipped and fell causing serious injury to appellant — Where 4 other contestants had falls prior to appellant's fall — Where experienced contestant warned organisers about condition of arena surface — Where organisers twice refused to stop competition — Whether respondent breached duty of care — Whether breach of duty of care caused appellant's injuries — Whether harm suffered by appellant result of materialisation of obvious risk of dangerous recreational activity — Civil Liability Act 2002 (NSW), ss 5B, 5C, 5D, 5F, 5L.

On 8 January 2011, 19-year-old Emily Tapp participated in a campdraft event at Ellerston, New South Wales. The event involved riders such as Ms Tapp rounding up cattle that had been placed in stations and then steering those cattle through a set of obstacles and fences. Ms Tapp was experienced at these events and travelled around the country over the summer in order to participate in them. Ms Tapp was also an experienced horse rider.

In the course of participating in the event, Ms Tapp fell from her horse and suffered a significant spinal injury in the form of incomplete T11 quadriplegia. She became wheelchair-bound as a consequence.

The event at Ellerston was organised by the Australian Bushmen's Campdraft and Rodeo Association Ltd (the Association). Both Ms Tapp and her sister completed the entry requirements for the event, which consisted of an application fee and completion of a Liability Waiver form. That form contained a clause headed "Exclusion of certain rights to sue". There was no issue that Ms Tapp signed this form and that she understood its significance.

Ms Tapp commenced proceedings in the Supreme Court of New South Wales against the Association, in negligence and claimed damages. Ms Tapp argued that the Association should have called off the event because the conditions at the time were inherently dangerous. She relied upon evidence that there had been at least 4 falls in the lead up to her particular event. The Association denied liability. It argued that it had not been under a duty to warn Ms Tapp of the obvious risks of dangerous recreational activities within the meaning of s 5L of the *Civil Liability Act 2002* (NSW). Further, if campdrafting was not regarded as a dangerous recreational activity, the Association had not been required to warn Ms Tapp of its obvious risks as by signing the waiver form, Ms Tapp had been warned of the risk of her injuries within the meaning of ss 5M and 5N of the Act.

Her Honour Lonergan J found that there was evidence that several other riders fell off their horses on Saturday, 8 January 2011 but made no finding as to the number of falls that occurred before Ms Tapp's incident. Her Honour noted that the only fall with respect to which there was admissible evidence as to the reason for the fall was Mr Shorten's, and he did not attribute the fall to a problem with the surface of the arena. The primary judge accepted Ms Tapp's evidence that she had been unaware that there had been any falls before her ride in the open event. There were no falls the following day, on 9 January 2011.

The primary judge found that campdrafting was a dangerous recreational activity. The risk of injury had been obvious to Ms Tapp and her injuries occurred through the materialisation of that risk. Section 5L of the Act applied to preclude the Association's liability. Even if campdrafting was not regarded as a "dangerous recreational activity" within the meaning of s 5L, the Association had no obligation to inform Ms Tapp of the risk of falling from her horse during the campdraft event because that risk was obvious. Liability was also precluded on that basis. The court dismissed Ms Tapp's claim: *Tapp* v *Australian Bushmen's Campdraft & Rodeo Association Ltd* (2019) Aust Torts Reports ¶82-505; [2019] NSWSC 1506.

Ms Tapp appealed the primary judge's findings. She argued on appeal that the primary judge erred in failing to find that the Association breached its duty of care to the appellant, and in finding that the injury she suffered was a result of the materialisation of an obvious risk of a dangerous recreational activity.

The court found no error in the primary judge's finding that it had not been shown in any of the respects pleaded by Ms Tapp that the Association breached its duty of care. As to whether the Association should have stopped the competition, it was not established, other than by evidence given in hindsight, that the surface of the arena had become unsafe or that the exercise of reasonable care in all the circumstances required the event to be stopped. The bare fact of the number of falls, in the absence of any evidence that those falls were causally related to any deterioration in the surface of the arena, did not establish that the exercise of reasonable care in all the circumstances required the event to be stopped. As to the obvious risk defence, the court found that even if the risk was correctly framed as being "the risk of injury as a result of falling from a horse that slipped by reason of the deterioration of the surface of the arena", the injury suffered by Ms Tapp was the manifestation of an obvious risk: *Tapp* v *Australian Bushmen's Campdraft & Rodeo Association Ltd* (2020) Aust Torts Reports ¶82-600.3; [2020] NSWCA 263.

Ms Tapp appealed to the High Court, following a successful special leave application (*Tapp* v *Australian Bushmen's Campdraft & Rodeo Association Ltd* [2021] HCATrans 74).

Held: appeal allowed.

Per Gordon, Edelman and Gleeson JJ:

1. As to breach of duty, the majority of the lower court found that without clear evidence as to the nature of the risk posed by the surface of the arena where Ms Tapp's horse fell, it was not possible to identify the risk of harm against which the Association should reasonably have taken precautions. The difficulty with that approach to characterisation of risk was that it required Ms Tapp to identify the risk by reference to the precise manner in which her injuries were sustained. That is inconsistent with the requirement deriving from s 5C(a) of the Act. A more accurate characterisation of the risk was that expressed in the dissenting judgment as "the risk of injury as a result of falling from a horse that slipped by reason of the deterioration of the surface of the arena". To adapt that description, consistently with the essential facts that established the risk for the purposes of the breach of duty, the risk should be characterised as the substantially elevated risk of physical injury by falling from a horse that slipped by reason of the deterioration of the surface of the arena. No more precision than that was necessary in characterising the relevant risk. [123]–[125]

2. Once the risk was identified at the correct level of generality, the factors which the court must consider under s 5B(2) of the Act all pointed to the conclusion that a reasonable person in the position of the Association would have taken the immediate precaution of stopping the event in response to the substantially elevated risk of contestants being injured from falling from a horse that slipped on the deteriorated surface of the arena. In short: (i) the relevant risk was substantially elevated, so that a reasonable person in the position of the Association could have foreseen a probability that harm would occur if the competition were not stopped until members of the Committee or MRC had taken precautions beginning with

inspecting the arena to be satisfied that the ground of the arena was reasonably safe; (ii) the likely seriousness of the harm was at the level of physical injury that could be catastrophic; (iii) the burden of taking precautions to avoid the risk of harm was the simple act of stopping the event to inspect the arena and consider the safety of the ground of the arena; and (iv) these matters could not be outweighed by the social utility of continuing the event so that contestants who had already competed on worse ground were not at a competitive disadvantage. [126], [127]

3. The lower court should have accepted that, by the time Ms Tapp competed in the Open Campdraft, as contestant 101, there was a substantially increased risk or probability of physical injury to her by reason of deterioration of the condition of the surface of the arena. [137]

4. Given the probability of harm, the potential magnitude of injury, the ease with which the event could have been stopped, and the minimal social disutility of disadvantage to contestants who participated in the Open Campdraft on 8 January 2011, the only available conclusion was that the event should have been stopped until members of the Committee or MRC on behalf of the Association inspected the arena and were satisfied that the ground of the arena was reasonably safe in that the risk of injury from falling from a horse that slipped on the ground of the arena was not substantially elevated. [139]

5. The Association breached its duty of care by failing to stop the competition in order to inspect the ground and to make "an informed decision ... as to whether it was safe to continue with the competition". The lower court erred in failing to find that the Association had breached its duty of care in that respect. [143]

6. As to whether Ms Tapp's fall would have occurred in any event if the competition had been stopped before she competed, and resumed so that she had competed the next day, the Association relied upon the conclusion by the trial judge that there was no evidence that ploughing the arena would have led to a different outcome. But that conclusion had been reached as a consequence of the trial judge's incorrect premise that the ground had not substantially deteriorated and that no breach of duty had been established. [148]

7. As to obvious risk, there were 3 reasons which, in combination, precluded any conclusion that the risk of injury as a result of falling from a horse that slipped by reason of substantial deterioration of the surface of the arena beyond the normal deterioration that might be expected would have been obvious to a reasonable person in Ms Tapp's position. Firstly, unlike the organisers of the competition on the Committee or MRC, Ms Tapp did not have the opportunity to examine the condition of the ground at all during the Open Campdraft, and particularly not in the hour before she competed, during which the other falls occurred. Secondly, a reasonable person in Ms Tapp's position would not have had any concerns about the condition of the ground from observations of other contestants or information about other contestants. Thirdly, decisions concerning the quality of the surface and how the surface was maintained were made by the Committee or MRC. A reasonable person in the position of Ms Tapp, who was preparing herself and her horse to compete in the hour before being called, would have relied upon the Committee or MRC for that assessment. Further, a reasonable person in Ms Tapp's position would, if they turned their mind to the issue at all, likely assumed the Committee or MRC had made an appropriate decision about the surface. [151]–[156]

Per Kiefel CJ and Keane J (dissenting):

1. The 2 issues raised on appeal were: firstly, whether Ms Tapp had established that the Association failed to take reasonable precautions against the risk of injury (and whether such a breach was a cause of her injuries); and secondly, if liability were otherwise established, whether her injuries resulted from the materialisation of an "obvious risk" such that s 5L of the *Civil Liability Act 2002* (NSW) (the Act) operated to deny liability on the part of the Association. [2]

2. The principal flaw in Ms Tapp's case was that she failed to prove the reason why her horse fell. The argument for Ms Tapp that, as a matter of common sense, the court should find that Ms Tapp's horse slipped because of deterioration in the surface of the arena over the course of the event, was an attempt to make a virtue of necessity. In considering a "common sense" submission as to the cause of a horse slipping in the course of a campdrafting event, the risk of a horse slipping as a result of losing its footing during a manoeuvre performed at speed was part and parcel of competitive campdrafting on even the most benign of surfaces. That risk may be elevated by a deterioration in the surface, however in approaching the question whether any particular fall occurred because of deterioration in the quality of the surface of the arena to the point where the surface became unsafe, it could not be speculated that deterioration in the surface was a more likely explanation than the materialisation of one or more of the other risks that were intrinsic to that form of recreation. Further, the decision of the Association, after Ms Tapp's fall, to suspend competition and to plough the surface of the arena before competition resumed on the Sunday could not be relied upon to inform either the Association's appreciation at the time of her fall of the extent of any deterioration in the surface, or the reasonableness of the precautions Ms Tapp contended should have been taken. Nor could the circumstance that no falls occurred on the day following Ms Tapp's fall, after the surface had been ploughed, be relied upon to overcome the primary judge's findings as to the factual deficit in the case advanced for Ms Tapp. [44]–[52]

3. Ms Tapp was unable to demonstrate that the Association ought reasonably to have taken the precaution of suspending the competition and ploughing the surface before allowing the event to continue. The question whether the Association breached its duty to Ms Tapp because it failed to suspend competition in order to plough the surface of the arena was a question that could not be approached on the basis that the only relevant consideration was to ensure the safety of competitors. If that were the only consideration, no campdrafting events would be permitted, because the risk of serious injury is intrinsic to the sport. The notion of reasonable precautions necessarily contemplates the balancing of countervailing considerations. In that vein, the decision of the Association fell to be made in a context in which competitors wanted to compete and were known to want to compete in their chosen form of recreation. In the context of the organisation and management of a campdrafting competition, a decision to allow the event to continue is not shown to be "wrong", much less negligently so, by pointing to the occurrence of a catastrophic injury without taking into account the willingness, indeed the eagerness, of competitors to engage in what is, on any view, a form of recreation fraught with risks of physical injury. It was difficult, given the tragic injury suffered by Ms Tapp, not to focus upon the circumstances of that tragedy. But one must not judge the wisdom of the Association's decision to continue the competition with the benefit of hindsight. Hindsight has the power to make an accidental injury appear both foreseeable and avoidable by the taking of precautions that now seem obvious. Hindsight may also cause one to focus on the particular risk of injury that ultimately materialised, thus losing sight of the potentially manifold risks intrinsic to the activity engaged in. [56]–[60]

4. A decision reflecting reasonable care for competitors required an assessment whether the level of risk posed by the state of the surface required the competition to be suspended. The decision made by the Association to continue the competition, viewed in the context in which it was made, does not appear to be unreasonable. It was also far from apparent to the Association's decision makers that it was the quality of the surface of the arena that was to blame for the falls which preceded Ms Tapp's fall, rather than any of the other manifold possibilities intrinsic to the dangerous activity. The absence of evidence at trial from any of

the other riders who fell as to their experience that the deteriorated surface caused their falls was emphatic confirmation that Ms Tapp's case was bound to fail for want of proof that deterioration in the surface caused her fall. [66]

[*Headnote by the Wolters Kluwer editors*]

DF Jackson QC with DF Villa SC and J Hillier (instructed by Commins Hendriks Solicitors) for the appellant.

JT Gleeson SC with DA Lloyd SC and KIH Lindeman (instructed by RGSLAW) for the respondent.

Before: Kiefel CJ, Keane, Gordon, Edelman and Gleeson JJ.

[¶82-771] Minister for the Environment v Sharma

(2022) Aust Torts Reports ¶82-771
Medium neutral citation: [2022] FCAFC 35
Federal Court of Australia, Full Court
15 March 2022

Novel duty of care — Representative proceedings — Duties of Minister for the Environment — Global warming — Statutory duties of Minister — Nature of judicial power — Public policy — Foreseeability — Control — Vulnerability — Determinacy — Whether Minister owed a duty of care when approving the extraction of coal from a coal mine — Whether recognition of duty of care impermissibly involved courts in legislative and executive decisions — Whether Minister had control, responsibility and knowledge in relation to foreseeable harm — Whether respondents were vulnerable to feared harm — Challenge to 5 findings of fact by primary judge concerning catastrophic risks of global warming caused by greenhouse gas emissions — Environment Protection and Biodiversity Conservation Act 1999 (Cth), ss 130, 133 — Civil Liability Act 2002 (NSW), ss 5B, 5C, 5D, 41, 42.

Vickery Coal Pty Ltd (Vickery) was a wholly owned subsidiary of Whitehaven Coal Pty Ltd (Vickery) which operated a coal mine near Gunnedah in New South Wales. In August 2020, Vickery sought approval for a substantial extension of the coal mine (the extension project) about 25 kilometres north of Gunnedah. However, a determination had been made under the *Environment Protection and Biodiversity Conservation Act 1999* (Cth) (EPBC Act) which affected the extension project. That determination had the effect of prohibiting the extension project unless the Commonwealth Minister for the Environment (the Minister) approved it under ss 130 and 133 of the EPBC Act.

The respondents were 8 Australian children who commenced representative proceedings pursuant to Div 9.2 of the *Federal Court Rules 2011* (Cth) against the Minister and Vickery. They claimed to represent children who ordinarily resided in Australia as well as "other represented children" who were identified as being children residing anywhere in the world. The respondents claimed that, if the extension project was approved, an additional 33 million tonnes of coal would be extracted from Vickery's coal mine which would in turn cause 100 million tonnes of carbon dioxide (CO2) to be emitted into the Earth's atmosphere when that coal was burned.

The respondents claimed that the Minister owed all children a duty of care to exercise her power under ss 130 and 133 of the EPBC Act with reasonable care so as not to cause them harm. On that basis, they argued that the Minister would fail to discharge that duty by exercising her discretion in favour of the approval of the extension project. That was because the respondents asserted that they would suffer harm if the extension project was approved, including mental or physical injury as well as economic and property loss. As such, the respondents sought declarations that a duty of care existed as well as injunctive relief to preclude the Minister from failing to discharge the duty.

The Minister did not dispute that climate change presented serious threats and challenges to the environment, the Australian community and the world generally. However, the Minister denied the existence of a duty of care as alleged and denied that injury to the children from the approval of the extension project was reasonably foreseeable. The Minister further argued that the relevant salient circumstances of the relationship between the parties pointed overwhelmingly against the recognition of the novel duty of care. In addition, the Minister argued that, if a duty of care did exist, there was no reasonable apprehension that the duty would be breached.

At first instance, Bromberg J noted that the Minister did not challenge the evidence adduced by the respondents concerning the existence of global warming and its causes. That included evidence about the emission of CO2 by coal plants and the causative effect of such emissions on global warming. His Honour also accepted the evidence about the harm that could occur to the children if such global warming continued to occur. However, Bromberg J then noted that the respondents were proposing a "novel" duty of care to protect them from such harm. It was therefore necessary to consider the "salient features" of the case to determine whether such a duty was to be recognised.

In assessing those salient features, Bromberg J firstly found that, given the state of the evidence, a reasonable person in the Minister's position would foresee that the respondents could suffer harm if the extension project was to be approved. His Honour further found that the Minister exercised "control" of the circumstances and that the respondents were in a position of vulnerability in that context. In addition, Bromberg J rejected the Minister's contentions that a duty of care would be incoherent with the EPBC Act given that "human safety" was an implied mandatory consideration under its terms. For these reasons, his Honour concluded that a duty was to be recognised.

On the question of whether the injunction was to be granted, Bromberg J held that it would effectively prevent the Minister from taking reasonable steps to address the foreseeability of risk. In other words, the injunction would stop the Minister from addressing that risk in considering whether or not to grant approval for the extension project. It remained open to the Minister to ensure that the duty would not be breached in that context. As such, although the respondents had succeeded in establishing the existence of a duty of care, they had not succeeded in demonstrating the need or appropriateness of injunctive relief.

The Minister appealed against the findings that she owed the children a duty of care when considering whether or not to grant approval for the extension project. The Minister argued that it was not appropriate to recognise such a duty because it was a context that specifically gave rise to issues of public policy, including economic, financial, social and political factors. The Minister argued that such a duty would be incoherent with the EPBC Act and that the elements of foreseeability, control, vulnerability and determinacy were also lacking. In addition, the Minister attacked several of Bromberg J's factual findings.

In seeking to uphold the finding that the Minister owed them the duty, the respondents argued that her exercise of discretion did not give rise to policy issues that were beyond the ambit of the judiciary. The case was instead said to simply require the application of well-accepted principles concerning the existence of a duty of care. It was further submitted that no incoherence was caused with the EPBC Act because the Minister was specifically required to take environmental considerations into account and was not excluded from civil liability. The primary judge's findings on foreseeability, control, vulnerability and determinacy were also said to disclose no error.

Held: appeal allowed; partied should seek to agree further orders necessary, including any appropriate orders concerning represented parties.

Per Allsop CJ:

1. The need to take account of "human safety" was not an implied mandatory consideration under the terms of the EPBC Act. Such an imperative was not consistent with the text, purpose and context of the statute. The need for "protection of the environment" had also not been a mandatory consideration. [214]–[217]

2. The EPBC Act did create a relationship between the Minister and people who would be affected by her decision on whether or not to approve the extension project. However, that relationship was not of a type that was susceptible to the common law of negligence given its inherently political nature. [218]–[232]

3. It could be accepted that the field of matters not amenable to the imposition of a duty of care at common law was narrow. However, it was also to be accepted that there would be some decisions of public authorities for which the law of negligence was an inapposite or unsuitable vehicle for examining the choices and judgements involved. [233]–[245]

4. The Minister's decision in the present case was to be regarded as a "core area of policy-making" that was "quasi-legislative or regulatory in nature". The natural places for the development of such policy and the making of decisions as to the implementation of such policy were the executive branch of government and the legislature. [246]–[266]

5. The posited duty would have also been incoherent and inconsistent with the EPBC Act and the legal and governmental framework of responsibility for the protection of the environment reflected therein. It would have created a form of mandatory consideration beyond the factors that were required to be taken into account. [267]–[272]

6. If considerations of policy and incoherence were not determinative of the question, then the non-recognition of a duty of care could also be based upon a consideration of the salient features of the case. In particular, the posited duty also failed for a want of reasonable foreseeability, control, vulnerability and determinacy. [273]–[343]

Per Beach J:

1. The primary judge did not err on the question of reasonable foreseeability because such reasonable foreseeability was established where the risk of harm was not remote. Taking into account the nature of evidence that was adduced and the need for courts to evolve to that type of evidence, the risk of harm was not remote in that sense. [423]–[442]

2. There was some degree of incoherence between the posited duty of care and the objectives of the EPBC Act, particularly because the statute was not concerned specifically with the issue of climate change. However, that degree of incoherence did not prevent recognition of a duty of care. [539]–[609]

3. It was true that there were policy questions involved in the Minister's determination as to whether the extension project was to be approved. However, the existence of those policy questions did not foreclose the existence of a duty of care because they could be adequately dealt with in the context of breach of duty. [610]–[633]

4. It was not to be accepted that the Minister did not have sufficient control over the circumstances to found a duty of care. Although other parties were to be involved in the extraction and processing of the coal, it was the very act of approval by the Minister that ignited the hypothesised causal chain. [634]–[668]

5. The primary judge's conclusions as to the vulnerability of the representative class could be partly supported. On the other hand, however, there was not a sufficient closeness and directness between the Minister's exercise of statutory power and the likely risk of harm to the respondents and the class that they represented. [669]–[701]

6. The other critical factor against recognition of a duty of care was that it would result in indeterminate liability. That was because the likely number of members of the claimant

class were not readily ascertainable at the time that the duty was being advanced. There was also no way of foreclosing that claimant class. [702]–[747]

Per Wheelahan J:

1. The possibility of personal injury to the respondents and those whom they represented as a consequence of climate change was not reasonably within the required focus of the controlling provisions of the EPBC Act for the purposes of the Minister's decision-making function. [837]–[852]

2. Issues pertaining to ecologically sustainable development were uniquely suited to elected representatives and executive governments responsible for law-making and policy-making. There would accordingly be incoherence between the suggested duty and the discharge of the Minister's statutory functions. [853]–[868]

3. It was not reasonably foreseeable that the approval of the extension to the coal mine would be a cause of personal injury to the respondents or those whom they represented, at least in the sense that reasonable foreseeability was understood for the purposes of the common law tort of negligence. [869]–[886]

[*Headnote by the Wolters Kluwer editors*]

Dr S Donaghue QC (Solicitor-General of the Commonwealth) with S Free SC and Z Maud (Australian Government Solicitor) for the appellant.

N Hutley SC with E Nekvapil, K Brazenor, S Brenker and N Petrie (Equity Generation Lawyers) for the respondents.

Before: Allsop CJ, Beach, Wheelahan JJ.

Wolters Kluwer Note: The full text of the judgment is accessible through the Federal Court of Australia, Full Court database on the AustLII website.

[¶82-721] Cox v Mid-Coast Council

(2021) Aust Torts Reports ¶82-721
Medium neutral citation: [2021] NSWCA 190
Supreme Court of New South Wales, Court of Appeal
31 August 2021

Public authorities — Duty of care — Breach of duty — Exclusion of liability — Dangerous recreational activities — Obvious risks — Characterisation of risks — Appeals — Respondent council approved a local festival on an area of that land for which it was responsible — Land was next to an airfield that Council operated and for which it had responsibility — Council also approved a Ferris wheel at that festival — Light aircraft collided with that Ferris wheel when attempting to land at airfield — Proceedings brought by appellant pilot against Council seeking damages for personal injuries — Primary Judge held that those injuries were an "obvious risk" of a dangerous recreational activity and so pilot was statutorily excluded from maintaining his claim — Pilot appeal to Court of Appeal — Civil Liability Act 2002 (NSW), ss 5K, 5L.

The Old Bar Airstrip (the Airstrip) at Old Bar in New South Wales was operated by the respondent, Mid-Coast Council (the Council) through a committee known as the Old Bar Heritage Airport Management Committee (the Airstrip Committee). In April 2011, the organisers of the Old Bar Festival (the Festival) applied to the Council to use the Council Park and Reserve, which included land adjacent to the airstrip, for the purposes of the Festival to be held on 1 and 2 October 2011. The operator of the Ferris wheel at the Festival also made an application to the Council to operate the Ferris wheel at the Festival. Both those applications were granted.

The appellant, Mr Paul Cox, was a part-time recreational pilot who had approximately 87 hours of flight experience after he obtained a recreational aviation licence in 2010. As part

of the Festival, he was invited to fly a light aircraft from Taree Airport to the Airstrip. He had experience at landing at the Airstrip but not during the Festival. Although the trip was initially postponed due to inclement weather, it ultimately proceeded after the clouds disbursed and the wind settled. However, on his initial approach to the Airstrip, Mr Cox was unable to land the aircraft. He therefore turned the aircraft around to make another approach. Soon thereafter, the aircraft struck the Ferris wheel.

Mr Cox subsequently sought damages from the Council in respect of personal injuries he claimed to have developed as a result of the collision. However, at first instance his Honour refused that claim on the basis that Mr Cox had been engaged in a ''dangerous recreational activity'' and was therefore excluded from claiming damages for an obvious risk by ss 5K and 5L of the *Civil Liability Act 2002* (NSW) (the CL Act): *Arndell BHT Arndell* v *Old Bar Beach Festival Incorporated*; *Cox* v *Mid-Coast Council* (2020) Aust Torts Reports ¶82-597; [2020] NSWSC 1710.

Mr Cox appealed. He claimed that the primary judge erred in failing to identify the risk of harm by reference to the Ferris wheel. He also claimed that the primary judge erred in finding that such a risk was an ''obvious risk'' of the recreational activity.

Held: appeal dismissed.

Payne JA (with whom Meagher JA agreed)

1. Mr Cox's contention that the primary judge's identification of the relevant risk required reference to the Ferris wheel imported hindsight into the statutory task by focussing upon the precise obstacle with which the aircraft actually collided. Such an approach to the formulation of risk had been consistently rejected by the Court of Appeal. [35]–[40]

2. The characterisation of the risk of harm which Mr Cox advanced was therefore too particular. The risk had to be expressed at a level of generality which preserved the intent of the CL Act in allocating where the burden fell for harm suffered by the manifestation of an obvious risk of a dangerous recreational activity. [41]–[49]

3. There was no error in the primary judge's approach to the meaning of ''obvious risk'' for the purposes of ss 5K and 5L of the CL Act. In particular, his Honour's reference to s 5F, and to the same meaning of ''obvious risk'' under both ss 5F and 5L, was a correct statement of law. [59]–[61]

4. In turn, the primary judge had been entitled to find that the relevant risk was ''obvious''. That was because it remained a pilot's duty to check an airfield for obstacles prior to take-off and landing. Had Mr Cox carried out that duty, the obstacle presented by the Ferris wheel would have been ''obvious'' within the meaning of ss 5K and 5L. [62]–[69]

Emmett AJA (who otherwise agreed with Payne JA)

5. The Civil Aviation Authority had published guidelines which made clear that pilots were required to ensure that the airfields which they used to take-off and land were free of obstacles. Mr Cox failed to follow these recommendations but, had he done so, the Ferris wheel with which he collided would have been obvious. [79]–[84]

[*Headnote by the Wolters Kluwer editors*]

CT Barry QC and R Royle (Shine Lawyers) for the appellant.

R Sheldon SC (Mills Oakley) for the respondent.

Before: Meagher JA, Payne JA and Emmett AJA.

[¶82-616] **Ethicon Sàrl v Gill**

(2021) Aust Torts Reports ¶82-616
Medium neutral citation: [2021] FCAFC 29
Federal Court of Australia, Full Court
5 March 2021

Medical negligence — Medical devices — Duty of care — Whether primary judge erred in finding appellants breached duty of care — Inadequate pre-market and post-market evaluations of safety of devices — Inadequate warnings of material risks of devices — Standard of care — Breach — Causation — Onus of proof — Civil Liability Act 2002 (WA), ss 5C, 5D — Wrongs Act 1958 (Vic), ss 51, 52.

Ethicon Sàrl and Ethicon Inc ("the Ethicon companies") manufactured 9 different surgical net-like mesh devices, 5 of which were used as surgical implants for women with stress urinary incontinence, and 4 were used as surgical implants for women with pelvic organ prolapse. The Ethicon companies supplied the mesh devices to Johnson & Johnson Medical Pty Ltd (JJM), which in turn promoted and supplied the Ethicon devices to Australian doctors and hospitals.

Kathryn Gill, Diane Dawson and Ann Sanders (the respondents) all underwent surgery, at different times, for the implantation of Ethicon mesh devices as part of treatment of stress urinary incontinence, vaginal prolapse and/or pelvic prolapse following childbirth. All respondents suffered severe and ongoing complications and side effects following the implantation of the mesh devices.

The respondents commenced a representative action against the Ethicon companies and JJM (the applicants) in the Federal Court of Australia, which included 7 claims: 4 under Commonwealth consumer protection laws and 3 at common law in negligence. All claims were denied by the applicants. The respondents argued that the appellants contravened relevant provisions of the Trade Practices Act and breached its duties of care in that it failed to take reasonable care to evaluate the safety of the devices both before and after they were taken to market, and claimed damages for the injuries they allegedly suffered as a result.

The appellants denied the allegations and argued that all surgical procedures present risks. They also pleaded a statutory defence, that the state of scientific or technical knowledge at the time the Ethicon devices were supplied was not such as to enable the defects to be discovered.

At the beginning of the trial, 700 women had registered as group members. The group was an open group. More than 90,000 devices were distributed in Australia.

Her Honour Katzmann J found in favour of the respondents. Her Honour found that the Ethicon companies as manufacturers were obliged to exercise reasonable care in the supply and marketing of the devices, and that the duty extended to providing accurate information about the performance and safety of the devices. That duty was a continuing obligation to evaluate their safety, keep abreast of information about the nature and extent of potential complications, and to convey that information to users of the devices. Further, the duty of care owed by JJM as the supplier but not the manufacturer, was to take reasonable steps to ensure that the information they conveyed about the devices was accurate, not misleading and sufficient to alert both medical practitioners and prospective patients about the true risks associated with the use of the devices. [3627], [3644]

Her Honour also found that the information about the potential risks in the instructions for use and promotional material provided by the appellants did not conform to the standard required of a reasonably prudent manufacturer or supplier in their position. It fell well short of capturing all known, let alone reasonably foreseeable, risks and was apt to mislead both doctors and patients about the safety and efficacy of the various devices. The risks were known, not insignificant and on the appellants' own admission, could cause significant and

serious harm if they eventuated. A far more cautious approach was warranted than the appellants took [3464]–[3879]: *Gill* v *Ethicon Sàrl & Ors (No 5)* (2019) Aust Torts Reports ¶82-500; [2019] FCA 1905.

Since the various claims were made in the alternative, the respondents were required to elect which remedy to take, in other words, which damages regime was to apply. Each of the respondents was to make an election as to whether she wished to receive damages under the Trade Practices Act or at common law. The law of Western Australia applied to the assessment of damages for the causes of action in negligence brought by Mrs Gill and Mrs Sanders. The law of Victoria applied to the claim for damages brought by Mrs Dawson. In *Gill* v *Ethicon Sàrl (No 6)* [2020] FCA 279, the primary judge quantified the damages payable to the respondents: $1,276,113 to Mrs Gill, $555,555 to Mrs Dawson and $757,372 to Mrs Sanders.

The appellants appealed the primary judge's findings. They challenged the trial judgment in which the primary judge held them liable for contraventions of the *Trade Practices Act 1974* (Cth), Sch 2 to the *Competition and Consumer Act 2010* (Cth), the Australian Consumer Law, and for negligence. As to the negligence findings, the appellants argued that the primary judge erred in finding that they breached their duty of care to warn in respect of each device, that the first appellant and second appellant breached their duty of care to take reasonable care to avoid injury to patients by finding that the appellants' pre-market and post-market evaluations of each of the devices was deficient, and in finding that causation had been established.

Held: appeal dismissed.

1. The proceedings were brought under Pt IVA of the *Federal Court of Australia Act 1976* (Cth) (the FCA Act) by 3 applicants, both on their own behalf and on behalf of other women who claim to have suffered complications from the implantation of one or other of the devices during the relevant period. The class of applicants is open and more than 90,000 of the devices have been supplied in Australia. [27]

Primary judge's key findings

2. The manufacturers had a duty to take reasonable care in the design, testing, evaluation, supply, and marketing of the devices. That duty extended to providing accurate information about the performance and safety of the devices, including warnings about potential complications and contraindications. The duty was not confined to the period before the devices were made or placed on the market, it was a continuing obligation to evaluate their safety and keep abreast of information about the nature and extent of potential complications and to convey that information to users of the devices. JJM was deemed to be a manufacturer for the purposes of the statutory claims but at common law it was a supplier. [279], [280]

3. With one qualification, JJM's duty of care was co-extensive with the duty of care owed by the manufacturers. All 3 appellants were obliged to exercise reasonable care in the supply and marketing of the devices. The exception related to the allegation that JJM had a duty to undertake clinical evaluations of the devices. Either as a matter of law or fact, the scope of JJM's duty did not extend that far. The standard of care expected of the manufacturer, or the supplier, was not affected by the fact that the devices were supplied through surgeons or following consultation with surgeons. [282], [283]

4. The pre-market evaluation of all of the devices was insufficient to discharge Ethicon's duty of care. All evinced a want of reasonable care. Ethicon failed to undertake post-market evaluation of the devices adequately and, in certain respects, at all. The post-market evaluation of all of the devices was deficient. It fell well below the level of care required of a reasonably prudent manufacturer. Ethicon supplied and marketed the devices without conducting sufficient post-market evaluations. The evaluations that were undertaken were

haphazard, often perfunctory, and passive. They did not conform to the standard of care expected of a reasonable person in the position of Ethicon in response to the foreseeable risks of injury and having regard to the gravity of the potential consequences. Reasonable care required warnings about the pleaded complications. A reasonably prudent manufacturer and supplier in the position of the appellants would have warned prospective users of all but one of the pleaded complications. [287]–[289]

5. Each of the appellants was negligent. The risks were known, not insignificant, and on Ethicon's own admission, serious harm could ensue if they eventuated. A far more cautious approach was warranted than the appellants took. [291]

Knowledge of risk

6. A preparedness to assume that pelvic surgeons had access to information other than the instructions for use (IFUs) and that "some" pelvic surgeons may be taken to have known of "most" of the pleaded complications was a long way from defeating the claims under statute and at common law. [405]

7. The primary judge found that the fact that pelvic surgeons may be taken to have known of a risk does not mean that the appellants were immune from statutory or common law liability for failing to warn of that risk. Such a finding needed to be understood in the context that the primary judge also accepted, correctly, that it was relevant that the devices were supplied to doctors and hospitals and not to patients directly. [409]

8. Beyond this class of case of an obvious risk, there were questions of fact relevant to each cause of action which must be answered on the facts and not at the level of principle. To the extent that the primary judge gave an in-principle answer to those issues, the court would disagree. Equally, the court did not agree with the primary judge that the applicable standard of care was unaffected by the fact that the devices were supplied to women via their pelvic surgeon. That fact must be relevant to the meaning of reasonable care (which is the relevant standard of care) in the circumstances and whether or not that standard had been breached. Thus, the independent duty of care the appellants owed to patients was necessarily affected by the fact that patients received the devices from a pelvic surgeon who had professional training, experience and knowledge and owed their patients a duty of care to exercise the skill and competence that an ordinary person having those special skills would exercise. Accepting that, however, was very different from the appellants' proposition, which was to the effect that the independent duty of care owed by pelvic surgeons to their patients effectively abrogated their own duty of care in respect of the safety of their devices. [420]

9. That said, the court does not accept that the mere fact that pelvic surgeons could have obtained information about all of the pleaded complications the devices could cause from medical literature (if it were the fact, which it is not) meant that the appellants could not be liable for such a risk which was not disclosed by it to a learned intermediary or the ultimate user. Still less can the liability of a manufacturer/supplier either under statute or at common law depend on the potentially idiosyncratic belief of a manufacturer/supplier about what the learned intermediary knew about the product, should have known about the product, or could have known had they made further inquiry. [421]

10. The weight of the evidence amply supported the inference that pelvic surgeons in general did not know of the pleaded complications (nor even that they could have known of them until many years after the devices were on the market and the problems with the devices became manifest). The fact that the primary judge accepted that some pelvic surgeons may be taken to have known of many, if not most, of the pleaded complications was not inconsistent with the conclusion which the primary judge must be taken to have reached that it should be inferred that pelvic surgeons generally did not in fact know of the pleaded complications. [422]

11. The primary judge did not err in inferring that at all material times pelvic surgeons in general did not know about the pleaded complications, nor in failing to conclude that the pelvic surgeons knew about the pleaded complications at all material times. On the evidence, the inference that she drew, that pelvic surgeons in general did not know about the pleaded complications, was correct. [478]

12. The fact that at all material times the devices presented a risk of harm through the pleaded complications, and that the appellants provided no or no adequate information, advice or warnings in relation to that risk, meant that at all material times the devices were defective. [657]

Failure to warn

13. The appellants submitted that it could not be the case that they were bound to inform patients directly of the pleaded complications if pelvic surgeons knew about them. It may be accepted that it would have been sufficient for the appellants to have warned pelvic surgeons, rather than patients directly, about the pleaded complications. But the evidence showed that the appellants did not do so. [710]

14. The question of what a reasonable person would do in response to the reasonably foreseeable risk was relevant to the requirement of the standard of care (reasonableness) in the particular circumstances, and thus breach of the duty of care. On a fair reading of the primary judge's reasons in context, the court does not consider that she was applying a standard of care other than objective reasonableness in the particular circumstances. The primary judge's reference to the level of caution which a reasonable manufacturer of a permanent implant would exercise being "high" is nothing more than a reflection of the fact that the objective standard of reasonableness which might be required in any particular case was related to the probability and nature of the risk involved. That reasoning was orthodox. [712], [713]

15. The appellants said that the requisite warning was one that was sufficient to permit the recipient of the warning — the treating surgeons with the necessary clinical experience and expertise — properly to engage in the informed consent process with the particular patient. However, pelvic surgeons in the present case could not properly engage in the informed consent process because they did not know about the pleaded complications. [724]

Failing adequately to conduct pre-market and post-market testing

16. The fact that the TGA did not require that the manufacturer of a medical device undertake independent pre-market testing of the safety and efficacy of a medical device with a CE marking prior to the TGA registering the device on the Australian Register of Therapeutic Goods (ARTG) does not mean that:

a. there was no evidence demonstrating that there was insufficient clinical or other evaluation of the safety and efficacy of the devices in the Australian regulatory context, or

b. the primary judge's findings that the appellants breached their duty of care to consumers by failing adequately to conduct pre-market evaluations must be set aside. [749]

17. The fact that the TGA did not impose separate requirements for registration of the devices on the ARTG does not mean that the pre-marketing evaluations of the first and second appellants could not involve breach of a duty of care to Australian consumers to ensure that there had been adequate pre-market testing of the devices before they were sold into the Australian market. Nor could it be said that there was no evidence capable of establishing breach of such a duty of care merely because there were not separate Australian regulatory requirements. [754]

18. There was ample evidence from which the primary judge could be (and was) satisfied as to the manifest inadequacy of the pre-market and post-market testing of the devices. [763]

Causation

19. The appellants could not import into or supply within Australia the devices unless they were registered on the ARTGT. JJM, as the Australian sponsor of the devices, had to apply for registration on the ARTG and certify certain matters including that the device complied with the essential principles as set out in the Medical Devices Regulations. The primary judge identified the essential principles. If the device had a CE marking the TGA did not conduct an independent assessment but allowed the device to be registered on the basis of the CE marking. The devices were registered on the ARTG on the basis of the CE marking. On the primary judge's findings, the CE marking could not have been placed on any of the devices other than because of the appellants' negligence. The proper inference to be drawn from these circumstances, which the primary judge drew, was that but for the appellants' negligence the devices would not have been supplied in Australia in the way they were in fact supplied. [830]

20. The primary judge found that had non-negligent warnings about the pleaded complications been given, none of the respondents would have consented to implantation of the device that was implanted in them. The primary judge also found that it was the devices that caused the compensable injuries. That was sufficient for the conclusion that the requirement of causation was satisfied. That conclusion was not undermined by the submissions of the appellants to the contrary. It cannot be accepted that the primary judge erred in finding that the appellants' negligence in not providing the necessary warnings with the devices caused the injuries to the representative respondents. [862], [868]

[*Headnote by the Wolters Kluwer editors*]

B Walker SC with K Morgan and D Wong (Clayton Utz) for the appellants.

A Bannon SC with A Naylor, C Colquhoun and Z Hillman (Shine Lawyers) for the respondents.

Before: Jagot, Murphy and Lee JJ.

[¶82-600] Capar v SPG Investments Pty Ltd t/as Lidcombe Power Centre

(2020) Aust Torts Reports ¶82-600
Medium neutral citation: [2020] NSWCA 354
Supreme Court of New South Wales, Court of Appeal
22 December 2020

Negligence — Breach of duty — Shopping centre — Intruder enters shopping centre via gap in roller door — Security guard — Voluntary assumption of risk — Duty of care — Causation — Contributory negligence — Damages — Psychiatric injury — Normal fortitude — Whether person of normal fortitude might in the circumstances of the case suffer psychiatric harm — Civil Liability Act 2002 (NSW), ss 5B, 5D, 5R, 5S, 32.

The appellant, Mr Gengiz Capar, was employed as a security guard at the Lidcombe Power Centre in New South Wales (the premises). The first respondent, SPG Investments Pty Ltd trading as Lidcombe Power Centre (SPG), was the owner of the premises at the relevant time. The second respondent, Business Protection Group Pty Ltd (BPG), provided security services for SPG at the premises. The third respondent, the Worker's Compensation Nominal Insurer (the nominal insurer), was the insurer of Dynamite Security Protection Services Pty Ltd (Dynamite), the entity that employed Mr Capar and provided his services to SPG. By the time of the initial proceedings, Dynamite had been de-registered, but its interests were represented by the nominal insurer.

In February 2010, Mr Capar was carrying out his duties at the premises when an alarm sounded. After inspecting the premises, he found that a trolley had been smashed through the glass fronting of one of the shops. He called his supervisor, who told him to call the police. He did so, but nothing further came of their investigation. The following day, Mr Capar and his

supervisor reviewed the CCTV footage which had been taken at the time of the alarm sounding, which showed that 2 people gained entry to the premises through a gap near the roller shutter over one of the sets of fire stairs.

In March 2010, Mr Capar was again on night duty at the premises. While sitting in the control room during a meal break, he noticed an intruder on the CCTV monitor outside the premises. The intruder ran towards one end of the premises, before disappearing out of the range of the nearest CCTV camera. Mr Capar decided to leave the control room to investigate whether the intruder had gained access to the premises. He made his way to level one of the premises and waited there for a short time. The intruder then appeared in front of Mr Capar, in possession of an axe. At that point, Mr Capar identified himself as a security guard. In response, the intruder said to him: "I'm going to kill you". Mr Capar immediately ran back to the control room and locked himself inside before calling the police. The police attended and the intruder was later apprehended.

As a result of this incident, Mr Capar suffered post-traumatic stress disorder and claimed that he had been rendered permanently unfit for any form of employment.

Mr Capar commenced proceedings in the Supreme Court of New South Wales against SPG, BPG and the Nominal Insurer, in negligence and claimed damages. He claimed that SPG was liable as the owner and occupier of the premises, that BPG was liable by virtue of the contract it had with SPG, and that the nominal insurer was liable as the insurer for Dynamite which had owed him a duty as his employer.

Each of the respondents denied liability. They argued that Mr Capar had acted in complete disregard of his training by pursuing the intruder rather than calling for help. On that basis, they relied upon s 32 of the *Civil Liability Act 2002* (NSW) (the CL Act) applied to exclude the existence of a duty of care to prevent mental harm to Mr Capar. In the alternative, SPG and BPG filed cross-claims against each other and both of them filed additional cross-claims against the nominal insurer.

The primary judge found that Mr Capar's decision to pursue the intruder was found to have been directly contrary to the instructions that he had been given in the various manuals and supporting documents, namely that in such a situation he was to "back off", remain in the secure confines of the control room and call the police. The primary judge also found that given the way in which Mr Capar acted in complete disregard of his training, it was not reasonably foreseeable to either the first or second respondents that the intruder might have threatened him in the manner in which he did. Section 32 of the CL Act applied to exclude them from owing Mr Capar a duty of care in relation to the mental harm. Further, the scope of the duty of the first respondent as occupier of the premises did not extend to preventing harm caused by an unlawful entrant. If s 32 of the CL Act had not applied, Mr Capar would also have failed on the question of breach of duty on the basis that the obligations imposed upon the first and second respondents, as confined by s 3B of the CL Act, had been fulfilled by the steps that they had taken in training Mr Capar what to do if he was confronted. The primary judge dismissed Mr Capar's claim: *Capar* v *SPG Investments Pty Ltd t/a Lidcombe Power Centre & Ors (No 5)* (2019) Aust Torts Reports ¶82-447; [2019] NSWSC 507.

Mr Capar appealed the primary judge's findings. He argued that the primary judge erred in findings as to the duty of care owed and breach of that duty, and that Mr Capar was solely responsible for the occasioning of this injury.

Held: appeal allowed.

Per Basten JA (with whom McCallum and Emmett AJA (in part) agreed):

1. The CL Act neither abolished nor codified common law principles with respect to assumption of risk; rather, ss 5F and 5G appear to have made quite specific changes to one aspect of the doctrine, namely awareness of risk. [39]

2. To the extent that the finding of the trial judge that the appellant was solely responsible for his own misfortune involved application of the doctrine of voluntary assumption of risk, the finding should be rejected. To the extent that the appellant encountered danger in the course of his employment as the result of negligence on the part of the respondents, he cannot be said to have voluntarily consented to such a risk of harm. The security guard who is shot and killed by an armed robber, in circumstances where his or her employer has negligently failed to supply appropriate protection, cannot be said to have voluntarily consented to the risk of being murdered. If there was a defence of ‘‘voluntary assumption of risk’’ it was not engaged in such cases. [60], [61]

3. The appellant's conduct followed the broad description of appropriate steps to be taken in the precise situation which eventuated on 17 March. Even more importantly, the existence of clause 35 anticipated that a security guard might find himself or herself in such circumstances. Secondly, the intimation in the trial judge's findings that a security guard was expected to play an entirely passive role, avoiding any situation in which he might confront an intruder, cannot be reconciled with the functions described in the Site Operations Manual. Thirdly, the evidence of what the appellant did on 10 February, on instructions and without criticism from management who would have viewed the incident report, was inconsistent with the trial judge's view of a security officer's functions, based on a semantic analysis of limited parts of the instruction manuals. Finally, the emails from management on the morning of 17 March demonstrated no criticism of the appellant's conduct on the previous night; indeed the contrary. Nor did any respondent call any witness to suggest that the appellant had acted in contravention of proper practice, or contrary to expectations of management. [85]–[88]

4. The findings at [109] of the primary judgment must be rejected. The appellant, it should be found, acted appropriately. [89]

Duty of care

5. SPG owed a duty of care to the appellant. That conclusion should be accepted, as a matter of law. The duty was to take reasonable care for the safety of occupants. That duty included providing a secure perimeter during hours when the building was not open to the public. Whether particular steps were required in relation to the access obtained by the intruder over the roller door was a factual matter to be considered in determining whether there had been any breach of duty to those who were required to work on the premises, including a security guard employed to work alone after hours. [104], [106]

6. As to BPG, there was ample evidence to support the finding that BPG took responsibility for training security staff and defining the operations to be carried out, as it was the subcontractor of the owner. The trial judge was correct to conclude that BPG owed a duty of care to security staff, including the appellant, with respect to the operations at the Lidcombe Power Centre.

Breach of duty of care

7. Even if SPG had not actually been aware of the incident in February 2010 and the mechanism by which the intruders obtained entry, they ought to have been aware of the absence of a physical barrier preventing entry over the roller door. There was a breach of duty on the part of SPG towards a class of persons which included the appellant. [147], [148]

8. BPG had no power itself to rectify the weakness in the building security. However, reasonable precautions required more than a single email on the morning the weakness was identified as an ‘‘issue’’. BPG ought reasonably to have undertaken a risk assessment to determine what steps were necessary to alleviate or mitigate the risk. In the absence of evidence from any of the respondents to indicate that any action was taken at all, after the sending of the email at 11.58 am on 10 February, there was a failure on the part of BPG to take reasonable steps in the exercise of its duty of care. BPG was in breach of its duty of care to the appellant. [152]

9. There was no doubt that Dynamite was well aware of what happened on 10 February 2010. There was no evidence from any person on behalf of Dynamite. There was no other source of evidence identified in this Court which might have suggested that Dynamite took any steps at all with respect to the risk identified by the 10 February break in. There was no basis to consider that the appellant's employer had any lesser an obligation in respect of a duty to protect him from violent intruders than did BPG. If BPG was in breach of its duty, which the trial judge considered was analogous to that of an employer, Dynamite was also in breach. [155]

Causation

10. The question of causation may be dealt with on a common basis with respect to all 3 respondents. The trial judge did not deal with this issue, having found either no duty of care owed, or, if a duty were owed, no breach. On the appellant's case, the question of causation was straightforward. If steps had been taken to prevent the intruder obtaining access to the Centre over the roller door, the confrontation would not have occurred and the injury would not have been suffered. That position should be accepted. There was no reason to deny the proposition that causation was established on the evidence. [156]–[170]

Relief

11. The court can undertake the task of assessing damages on the basis of the existing evidential material, both documentary and in the transcript. That exercise can be undertaken without reliance on challenged evidence of the appellant. This court should dispose of the proceedings. As to future economic loss, there was no doubt that such employment would put him at risk of either witnessing or being subjected to traumatic incidents. It follows that there was a significant possibility that the appellant would at some stage have suffered a further trigger of the kind to which he was undoubtedly susceptible, resulting in unemployability. Damages for future economic loss (and past economic loss) ought to be adjusted by 50%. As to non-economic loss, the trial judge allowed an amount calculated as 22% of a most extreme case. However, on the assumption that the trial judge underestimated the seriousness of the contribution of the March 2010 incident to the appellant's mental health, that figure should be increased to 30% of a most extreme case. [216], [221]

12. The appeal should be allowed and the judgment below set aside. Each respondent owed (or represented a party which owed), and was in breach of, a duty to the appellant to take reasonable care for his safety whilst working as a security guard at the premises. The various breaches of duty contributed to the psychological harm suffered by the appellant as a result of being threatened by the intruder on 10 March 2010. The appellant was not contributorily negligent. He was entitled to recover damages from each respondent. [226]

Per Emmett AJA (dissenting in part):

1. There was no breach of any duty owed by SPG, BPG or Dynamite to the appellant. [233]

2. The primary question was whether the duty of care owed to the appellant by any of SPG, BPG and Dynamite extended to preventing unauthorised entry into the premises after hours by an intruder who might, by his actions, cause injury to the appellant. [245]

3. It may be that SPG owed a contractual obligation to its tenants to afford security. That, however, was beside the point. The question was whether SPG owed a duty to the appellant, a security guard employed by Dynamite, whose services were provided to BPG, which had contracted to provide security services to SPG. The object of the appellant's presence in the premises was to observe the premises and, in the event of unauthorised intrusion, to report that circumstance to the police. Clearly, the very fact that BPG was retained by SPG to provide security guards indicates an expectation that there may be intruders attempting to gain access to the premises. It would be curious, therefore, for SPG, as occupier of the premises, to be held to owe a duty to a security guard, whose function was

to report intruders, to take steps to ensure that there were no intruders. SPG did not owe to the appellant the duty formulated above. [248], [249]

4. The claim against BPG was based on the assertion that the appellant was not provided with a safe system of work. The system under which the appellant was required to work enabled him, by means of security cameras, to observe the intruder on the morning of 17 March 2010. The appellant's duties did not require him to leave the security room. Had he remained there, there was no reason to doubt that he would have been perfectly safe and would not have been threatened. Nevertheless, the appellant left the comfort of the security room in order to ascertain whether or not the person that he had observed on the security camera had in fact gained access to the premises. He was not required by his system of work to do so. There was no failure by BPG or Dynamite to provide the appellant with a safe system of work. [251]

[*Headnote by the Wolters Kluwer editors*]

D Campbell SC and E Young (Premier Lawyers) for the appellant.

DD Feller SC (Vardanega Roberts) for the first respondent.

R Cheney SC (Clyde & Co) for the second respondent.

S Flett and S Blount (Sparke Helmore) for the third respondent.

Before: Basten, McCallum JJA and Emmett AJA.

[¶82-580] Coffs Harbour City Council v Polglase

(2020) Aust Torts Reports ¶82-580
Medium neutral citation: [2020] NSWCA 265
Supreme Court of New South Wales, Court of Appeal
23 October 2020

Negligence — Catastrophic injuries — Liability — Public authorities — Duty of care — Breach of duty — Fences and railings — Foreseeable danger — Duty of guardians — Appeal — First respondent was 5-year-old child who suffered catastrophic injuries after falling through railings of a jetty while in company of his grandparents — Warning sign did not provide a statutory defence because it did not warn of specific dangers to children — Civil Liability Act 2002 (NSW), ss 5M, 5O and 42.

On 30 September 2011, the first respondent, Mr Tedmund Polglase (Tedmund), who was then 5 years of age, was in the company of his grandparents, the third and fourth respondents, Mrs Betty Whitton (Mrs Whitton) and Mr David Whitton (Mr Whitton). That afternoon they visited the Coffs Harbour Jetty (the jetty) situated at Coffs Harbour in the State of New South Wales. The jetty extended out into the sea that rose and fell with the tide. It followed that, at any given time, there could be wet sand directly underneath the jetty rather than water. The distance between that wet sand and the jetty was approximately 4 metres. A steel guard rail ran along the length of the jetty. It consisted of 2 horizontal rails that were supported by intermittent vertical posts.

Mr and Mrs Whitton walked with Tedmund along the jetty for approximately 50 metres from its entrance. At that point, they paused to look at the sea and some swimmers. As they did this, Tedmund was holding the middle railing and looking through the gap between the middle railing and the top railing. Mr and Mrs Whitton then turned to go and took a few steps. Tedmund fell from the jetty and landed on the wet sand below. He suffered severe injuries as a result, including a brain injury.

Tedmund by his tutor Mr Jeffrey Polglase commenced proceedings in the Supreme Court of New South Wales against the Coffs Harbour City Council (the Council), the Coffs Coast State Park Trust (the Trust) and the State of New South Wales (the State). The Trust was appointed the trustee of the relevant area in February 2003 but at all material times the

Council was the appointed manager for the Trust. The State had financed and been involved in a restoration of the jetty (including the railing) between 1995 and 1997. Mr and Mrs Whitton were subsequently sued by both the Council and Tedmund on the ground that they had been negligent in their care of him.

At first instance, the primary judge found in favour of Tedmund against the Council and the Trust and dismissed the claim against the State and Mr and Mrs Whitton. As against the Council and the Trust, the primary judge found that responsibility for the jetty following the restoration had been handed from the State to the Council and the Trust and that from that point, the Council and the Trust had been put on notice about the danger of the railings because of other incidents in which children had been seriously injured. In addition, the precautions that the Council could have taken were found not to have been disproportionate to its financial means: *Polglase by his tutor Jeffrey Polglase* v *Coffs Harbour City Council (No 2)* (2019) Aust Torts Reports ¶82-506.1; [2019] NSWSC 1848.

The Council and the Trust appealed the primary judge's findings. They argued that the primary judge erred in finding that:

- the Council and the Trust had breached their duty to Tedmund by failing to install additional railings or a mesh infill to prevent young children from falling from the jetty;
- a warning sign placed at the entry to the jetty did not constitute a risk warning for the purposes of s 5M of the *Civil Liability Act 2002* (NSW) (the CL Act);
- the State had not been liable to Tedmund even though it had been responsible for restoring the jetty and had been its former occupier; and
- Mr and Mrs Whitton were not liable to Tedmund for failing to take proper care of him immediately before the accident occurred.

Held: appeal dismissed.

Per Leeming JA (with whom Basten and Macfarlan JJA agreed):

1. The standard of care imposed upon the Council was not absolute and some risk was to be borne by persons using the jetty. In addition, it was to be accepted that the railing on the jetty had been designed according to existing safety standards and taking into account the need to preserve the jetty as a heritage site. [106]–[108]

2. However, the Council and the Trust had been put on notice that the design of the railing created risks to small children and that risk had eventuated with serious consequences. The costs of addressing the risk, for example, by installing a mesh infill or using strands of wire, had been minimal. In those circumstances, the finding on breach of duty was to be upheld. [109], [110]

3. For a risk warning to satisfy the requirements of s 5M of the CL Act, it had to warn of risks which included the particular risk concerned and it also had to warn of the general nature of the particular risk. In this case, the sign relied upon by the Council and the Trust did not satisfy those requirements because it simply generally warned of the risks of falling from the jetty. [111]–[120]

4. Up to 2002 when the State handed over responsibility for the jetty to the Council and the Trust, there had been one incident when a child fell from the jetty but was not seriously injured. After 2007, by contrast, there had been 3 incidents leading up to the plaintiff's accident, including one incident in which a child had suffered significant injuries. These were the key findings upon which the position of the State, on one hand, and the Council and the Trust, on the other, could be distinguished. After repeated safety incidents, a reasonable person would have expected the entity responsible for the jetty to take action. Hence, there was no error in the primary judge's finding that the State was not liable. [145]–[151]

5. As to the liability of Mr and Mrs Whitton, a reasonable person in their position would not necessarily have firmly held Tedmund's hand or ensured that it was impossible for him suddenly to approach and pass through the railing. The primary judge's finding that they had not breached their duty was to be upheld. [152]–[162]

[*Headnote by the Wolters Kluwer editors*]

R Sheldon SC with S Walsh (Mills Oakley) for the first and second appellants.

R McIlwaine SC with R Quickenden (Whitelaw McDonald) for the first respondent.

N Chen SC with H Chiu (Wotton + Kearney) for the second respondent.

M Hutchings with G Keesing (Sparke Helmore Lawyers) for the third and fourth respondents.

Before: Basten, Macfarlan and Leeming JJA.

[¶82-570] Plaintiff A and B v Bird; Plaintiff C v Bird; Plaintiff D v Bird

(2020) Aust Torts Reports ¶82-570
Medium neutral citation: [2020] NSWSC 1379
Supreme Court of New South Wales
9 October 2020

Torts — Intentional torts — Personal injury — Historic sexual abuse of children being cared for at a childcare centre — Whether assaults occurred — Vicarious liability —Volunteers — Whether first defendant a volunteer or employee — Negligence — Whether duty to children breached — Whether reasonable steps to avoid risk of harm to children could have been taken — Compliance with regulatory requirements — Whether child protection policy in operation — Whether supervision was adequate — Whether duty owed to mothers of child plaintiffs — Nature of psychological injuries suffered — Whether duty breached — Whether causation established — Evidence — Civil standard of proof — Witness evidence — Evidence of children's disclosures — Reliability of evidence where children were not cross-examined — Civil Liability Act 2002 (NSW), ss 3, 5D, 5E, 6E–6H, 13, 15, 21, 27, 31–33.

Little Pigeon Pty Ltd (Little Pigeon) owned the Footprints childcare centre (Footprints). Mr Bird owned 1% of Little Pigeon's shares and Mr Bird's daughter, Ms Clancy owned the remaining 99% of Little Pigeon's shares. Mr Bird worked every day at Footprints as a volunteer. Little Pigeon was the licensee of Footprints.

Plaintiffs B and D started attending Footprints in 2008 when they were aged two, until 2010 when they were removed after Mr Bird was arrested and charged with two offences of sexual abuse involving another child (child 1) who had made disclosures about him. Plaintiffs B and D and four other children later also made disclosures about Mr Bird. While police investigations resulted in further criminal charges being laid against Mr Bird in relation to plaintiff B and another child, none were laid in relation to plaintiff D. The Department of Public Prosecutions did not pursue any of the charges to trial.

After his arrest, Mr Bird gave a recorded police interview in which he made numerous admissions about his access to and interaction with children at Footprints, particularly in relation to child 1 who was the subject of the charges laid against him. What he recounted involved various types of inappropriate and sexualised conduct. [16]

Plaintiffs B and D, as well as plaintiffs A and C who are B and D's mothers, respectively, commenced proceedings in the Supreme Court of New South Wales against Mr Bird, Ms Clancy and Little Pigeon, in negligence, assault and battery and breach of contract and claimed damages, including aggravated and exemplary damages. In addition to the claim against Mr Bird, the plaintiffs also claimed that Little Pigeon and Ms Clancy were vicariously liable for Mr Bird's acts and that they were all also negligent.

At the time of the trial, plaintiffs B and D had no memory of what had happened and therefore they could not be cross examined. However, that did not preclude evidence of their disclosures being received.

Held: judgment in favour of the plaintiffs.

Evidence

1. During his recorded police interview, Mr Bird made numerous admissions about his access to and interaction with children at Footprints and what he recounted involved various types of inappropriate conduct. Early in the interview, when asked about child 1, Mr Bird acknowledged that on arrest he had been told that the reason was for allegations of indecent assault upon child 1 and he said that he knew her. He also said, among many other things, that he had rubbed child 1's back or patted her bottom, which he volunteered "may be what people could classify as assault". [16], [17]

2. There was no issue that Mr Bird's admissions were admissible against him. Little Pigeon conceded that Mr Bird's admissions were admissible against it. Whether they were admissible against Ms Clancy remained in issue. [20]

3. Ms Clancy was not only Little Pigeon's 99% shareholder and its controlling mind, on her evidence she also had the regulatory responsibilities of both the licensee and of Footprint's authorised supervisor. It was Ms Clancy who sought approval in 2008 for Mr Bird to be involved in the management of the centre; who directed Mr Bird to conduct himself with affection towards the children, as if he were their grandfather; and who, it may be inferred, was the author of the documents in which Mr Bird's role in the centre was disclosed to be as part of its management team. In all of the circumstances, Mr Bird's admissions were admissible against Ms Clancy. [27], [28]

4. The admissibility of evidence of plaintiffs B and D's disclosures about Mr Bird in 2010 and 2011 to their mothers (plaintiffs A and C); their electronically recorded police interviews; and the disclosures which four other children had made about Mr Bird in their police interviews, remained in issue. The plaintiffs relied on the disputed acts which the four young children, when aged two, three and four, had disclosed to their mothers and police, together with Mr Bird's own admissions about his acts towards children at the centre, to establish his tendency to act in the notified ways. There were similarities and differences between what each child had disclosed. But a common feature was that each child's disclosure involved Mr Bird, a man of mature years, touching them opportunistically in sexually inappropriate ways at times when his actions at this highly regulated workplace entailed a very high risk of detection. It was these features which made the disputed evidence significantly probative of Mr Bird having assaulted plaintiffs B and D, in the ways they had disclosed. [107]–[110]

5. The restriction on the receipt of tendency evidence imposed by s101 of the *Evidence Act 1995* (NSW) in criminal proceedings, when tendency evidence is sought to be adduced about a defendant by the prosecution, does not apply to civil proceedings. The plaintiffs did not need to establish that the probative value of the disputed evidence outweighed the danger of unfair prejudice to the defendants. [111]

6. That there were issues as to the children's understanding of the concepts of truth and lies at the time they made their disclosures and that they could not be cross-examined did not detract from the conclusion that having regard to other evidence adduced or to be adduced, the disputed evidence did have significant probative value and was thus admissible as tendency evidence. [112]

Intentional tort

7. The plaintiffs did meet the onus which fell upon them to establish, on the balance of probabilities, that Mr Bird did assault plaintiffs B and D. [206]

8. Because plaintiffs B and D could not be cross-examined, very careful consideration had to be given to the evidence of their disclosures. But a very important consideration in

determining whether their disclosures could be accepted as true and the onus satisfied was Mr Bird's own admissions. They established that the way in which he admitted he touched children to whom he had access at the centre was not only inappropriate but had involved assaults. Thereby he corroborated important aspects of the children's disclosures. It followed that their disclosures were not inherently unlikely. [213]

9. Consistent with Mr Bird being a part owner of Little Pigeon, part of the management team and the playground supervisor, there was no evidence that anyone was responsible either for accompanying Mr Bird or supervising him. Instead, he was treated in the same way as other staff members, when he had contact with children. That the result was that Mr Bird was neither always accompanied when in the presence of children, nor adequately supervised, was well established by what Mr Bird told police about young girls flashing their private parts at him in the yard. He said that he always dealt with this simply by telling them that young ladies do not do that. He did not report this unusual behaviour to anyone else, so that it was never dealt with, as Ms Clancy said that it should have been. The proper inference was that Mr Bird was not accompanied or supervised, as he needed to be, when in the presence of children. If he had been, another member of staff would have observed the repeated conduct he described, and it would have been reported and dealt with. On all of the evidence, there was in reality no supervision of Mr Bird's contact with children. The mere presence of other staff members in his vicinity was not only insufficient to deter him from acting as he did, it was also insufficient for his acts to be observed and reported to Department of Community Services, as they should have been. [263]–[266], [304]

10. The evidence established that Mr Bird did assault plaintiff B, having repeatedly kissed her, including with an open mouth and pulled down her pants, as she disclosed. [326]

11. The plaintiffs established that plaintiff D was assaulted in the way which she disclosed. [397]

12. The *Civil Liability Act 2002* (NSW) (the Act) does not apply to the claims in respect of assault. It was established that Mr Bird intentionally assaulted plaintiffs B and D that the plaintiffs have proven the intentional torts they alleged, on the balance of probabilities. There was no issue about causation in relation to those claims. [408]–[410]

Vicarious liability

13. The defendants argued that Mr Bird was a volunteer for whom the other defendants were not vicariously liable. The plaintiffs argued that even if it was concluded that Mr Bird was not an employee, in his circumstances Little Pigeon was vicariously liable for his acts, as it would have been if he had been an employee. Sections 6G and 6H of the Act now make provision for vicarious liability for child abuse perpetrated by employees and individuals akin to employees, in specified circumstances. On the evidence, Mr Bird would fall within that definition. Section 6F imposes a duty to take reasonable precautions to prevent an individual associated with the organisation from perpetrating child abuse in connection with the organisation's responsibility for the child. But those provisions did not apply in this case, given that the events in question occurred before these provisions took effect. [412], [413], [416]

14. The evidence established that in reality Mr Bird was an employee, even though he was not paid wages for his work and was represented to be a volunteer. The facts would permit the conclusion that Little Pigeon was vicariously liable for Mr Bird's acts, even if he provided his services to Little Pigeon as a volunteer, rather than as an employee. [418], [424]

15. The considerable authority which Mr Bird was given at the centre, which permitted him to have the same close contact which other staff employed there had with children; the control which Little Pigeon had and Ms Clancy exercised over all that he did; his integration into the business; how he was represented to others as being an integral part of its operations and how he was supervised in the same way as other staff, rather than being accompanied in

the way the regulations required volunteers to be accompanied, must result in the conclusion that in truth he was an employee, not a volunteer. [446]

16. Little Pigeon was vicariously liable for Mr Bird's wrongful acts. The evidence established that what Little Pigeon and Ms Clancy did both created and enhanced the risk of abuse which materialised, when Mr Bird conducted himself as he admitted. [450], [458]

Plaintiffs B and D's negligence claim

17. There was no issue that plaintiffs B and D were owed a duty of care. The duty was not to ensure against injury but to take reasonable care to prevent it, requiring the taking of reasonable steps which should reasonably have been foreseen. The plaintiffs relied on Mr Bird's background, lack of training or qualifications, the access he was given to the children, and how he was supervised to establish that he posed a risk of harm. Taking into account the requirements of s 5B and 5C of the Act, the evidence established that Mr Bird did pose such a risk and that it was a foreseeable risk, which was not insignificant and in the circumstances a reasonable person in the defendants' position would have taken available precautions. [459]–[461]

18. Whether the duty had been breached turned on what precautions had been taken and what precautions a reasonable person in Little Pigeon and Ms Clancy's position would have taken. On all of the evidence, the duty owed to plaintiffs B and D was breached. [462]

19. The evidence established that all plaintiffs had proven that the defendants' negligence was a necessary condition of the harm which they each suffered and that it was appropriate for the scope of their liability to extend to the harm which they caused. The plaintiffs established factual causation, namely that the negligence caused the harm which plaintiffs B and D suffered and that it was appropriate for the scope of their liability to extend to the harm which they so caused. [481], [482]

Plaintiffs A and C's negligence claim

20. Whether plaintiffs A and C were owed a duty of care was in issue. That must be determined in accordance with s 32(1) of the Act, which provided that a duty of care was not owed to another person to take care not to cause mental harm "unless the defendant ought to have foreseen that a person of normal fortitude might, in the circumstances of the case, suffer a recognised psychiatric illness if reasonable care were not taken". In issue was whether the defendants ought to have foreseen that a person of normal fortitude might, in the circumstances of both plaintiffs A and C, suffer a recognised psychiatric illness, if reasonable care were not taken. [483], [486]

21. As to plaintiff A, despite her prior history, Mr Bird's arrest for offences against another child and plaintiff B's disclosures as to what he had done to her and their aftermath did result in mental harm, which the defendants ought to have foreseen that a person of normal fortitude might suffer if they did not take reasonable care. Section 32 was satisfied and plaintiff A was owed a duty of care. [498], [499]

22. As to plaintiff C, the evidence established that plaintiff C suffered a psychiatric illness in circumstances in which the defendants ought to have foreseen that a person of normal fortitude might suffer such harm, if they did not take reasonable care. Plaintiff C was also owed a duty of care. [506], [507]

23. The duty owed to plaintiffs A and C was breached. What the evidence established about the failure to ensure that the regulatory requirements were observed, the child protection policy was in effective operation and Mr Bird was adequately supervised, established breach of the duty plaintiffs A and C were owed. It was reasonably foreseeable that mothers such as plaintiffs A and C who left their vulnerable children in the defendants' care would be at risk of injury if precautions were not taken. Further, that a reasonable person in their position would have ensured that they were. [509], [510]

24. Plaintiffs A and C established causation. In both plaintiffs A and C's cases the evidence established that the breach of the duties, which they were owed, did make a material contribution to their injuries, which was also reasonably foreseeable. Further, it was reasonable for Little Pigeon and Ms Clancy, its controlling mind, to be expected to foresee that their approach to the regulatory requirements, Mr Bird's work and supervision and the implementation of the child protection policy carried a risk of harm to plaintiffs A and C, of the kind that resulted. [512]–[514]

25. Also, plaintiffs A and C established their contractual claims, but no additional damages flow. [526]

Damages

26. The Act did not apply to the assessment of damages for plaintiffs B and D as a result of Mr Bird's assaults. [528]

27. Plaintiff A's damages were assessed in the total sum of $994,097.09. [529]–[633]

28. Plaintiff B's damages were assessed in the total sum of $465,000, including exemplary damages of $70,000. [634]–[679]

29. Plaintiff C's damages were assessed in the total sum of $512,582.89. [680]–[716]

30. Plaintiff D's damages were assessed in the total sum of $455,000, including exemplary damages of $70,000. [717]–[741]

[*Headnote by the Wolters Kluwer editors*]

C Barry QC with M Tanevski and M Hamdan (Shine Lawyers) for the plaintiffs.

C Heazlewood (EMP Michael) for the first defendant.

A Horvath with R McEwen (Norton Rose Fullbright) for the second and third defendants.

Before: Schmidt AJ.

[¶82-537] SW v Khaja

(2020) Aust Torts Reports ¶82-537
Medium neutral citation: [2020] NSWCA 128
Supreme Court of New South Wales, Court of Appeal
14 July 2020

Negligence — Motor vehicle accident — Passenger falling from moving taxi — Central factual contest as to whether she was engaged in joint criminal enterprise of attempted armed robbery of the driver — Where appellant conceded that it was open to find she had possession of a knife but denied using it and denied any robbery — Whether evidence supports the finding that the appellant did attempt to rob the driver with the knife — Prohibition on awarding damages by operation of s 54 — Civil Liability Act 2002 (NSW), ss 5D(1), 52, 53, 54 .

On the evening of 28 November 2015, being SW's 15th birthday, she met with three friends and booked a taxi. When the taxi driven by Mr Khaja arrived, SW sat in the front seat next to the driver while her three friends got into the back seat. Before the vehicle came to a stop, the passengers began undoing their seatbelts. The three rear passengers then got out. In the course of exiting, it is alleged that SW produced a knife and demanded money in an attempt to rob the taxi driver.

The taxi was fitted with CCTV. While the taxi was still moving and the passenger door open, with SW having undone her seatbelt, Mr Khaja's right hand can be seen on the taxi CCTV footage on SW's right upper arm and there appears to be a struggle as she goes out the open door. The taxi was then moving at approximately 27 km/h. The taxi crossed to the wrong side of the road and mounted the kerb, where it struck a small electric box. SW, who was out of the taxi at this time, was found on the footpath, also on the wrong side of the road. The other three taxi occupants attempted to drag SW from the place where she was lying but,

when they could not do so, they fled the scene. A number of local residents went to the assistance of SW and the police arrived at the scene very quickly. A kitchen knife fitting the description was located by the police at the scene of the accident. SW was taken to hospital by ambulance as she suffered catastrophic injuries. She was rendered a paraplegic as a result of the accident.

SW commenced proceedings in the District Court of New South Wales against Mr Khaja in negligence and claimed damages. She alleged that Mr Khaja was negligent in pushing SW out of a moving vehicle. SW denied that she had a kitchen knife, or that she used it, or that she made any attempt to rob the taxi driver. [26]

Mr Khaja denied liability. He argued that SW was engaged in an illegal enterprise and, on that basis, s 54(1) of the *Civil Liability Act 2002* (NSW) precluded an award of damages. He further argued that he was acting in self-defence.

The primary judge found that the evidence established that SW was engaged in an illegal enterprise, namely the commission of robbery involving the use of a knife, in circumstances satisfying all of the criteria in *R* v *Henry* (1999) 46 NSWLR 346. Her Honour found that there was no duty of care owed to SW in circumstances where SW was using a knife to try to rob Mr Khaja and he was responding by trying to push her away or out of the vehicle: *SW* v *MK (No. 5)* (2019) Aust Torts Reports ¶82-454; [2019] NSWDC 242.

SW appealed the primary judge's findings. She argued on appeal that the primary judge erred in finding that SW attempted to rob Mr Khaja with a knife. SW conceded on appeal that there was sufficient evidence to support a finding that she had possession of a knife. However, she challenged the finding that she used the knife to rob Mr Khaja. [66]

Held: appeal dismissed.

Per McCallum JA (with whom Emmett AJA and Simpson AJA agreed):

1. After a careful and thorough analysis of all the evidence, the primary judge found that SW was engaged in an illegal enterprise, namely the commission of robbery involving the use of a knife. [47]

2. The primary judge was satisfied that Mr Khaja pushed SW away from himself in order to defend himself. While it followed that he pushed her in the direction of the open door while the taxi was moving, the critical issue was whether that was done in response to being threatened with a knife, in which event it took on a completely different complexion. The primary judge found that Mr Khaja owed no duty of care to SW in circumstances where the evidence established that SW was using a knife to try to rob Mr Khaja and he was responding by trying to push her away or out of the vehicle. [49], [50]

3. It was correct that the primary judge did not explicitly address the second element of s 54(1) of the *Civil Liability Act 2002* (NSW). It does not necessarily follow that her Honour overlooked that issue. In addressing the test in s 5D(1)(a), her Honour had found that SW's commission of the offence of armed robbery was "the dominant and immediate cause" of her harm. In that context, a finding in terms of s 54(1)(b) that SW's criminal conduct "contributed materially" to her harm was so obvious that it went without saying. That is the only reasonable conclusion that could be reached on the findings made by the primary judge as to the commission of the offence. [82]

4. It followed inexorably from her Honour's findings that s 54 precluded any award of damages. [85]

Per Emmett AJA:

1. The pivotal grounds of appeal relied upon by SW are that any illegal conduct on her part ceased when she attempted to alight from the taxicab while it was stationary and that Mr Khaja intentionally pushed her out of the moving taxicab. The primary judge made no error in reaching her conclusion that SW never wavered from her intention to commit the offence

of robbery and her finding that Mr Khaja did not intentionally push her out of a moving motor vehicle in circumstances other than in self-defence. [131]

[*Headnote by the Wolters Kluwer editors*]

RS McIlwaine SC with N D Compton (Stacks Goudkamp Lawyers) for the appellant.

P Deakin QC with A Parker (McInnes Wilson Lawyers NSW) for the respondent.

Before: McCallum JA, Emmett AJA and Simpson AJA.

[¶82-357] Smith by his tutor Debra Smith v South Western Sydney Local Health Network

(2017) Aust Torts Reports ¶82-357
Medium neutral citation: [2017] NSWCA 123
Supreme Court of New South Wales Court of Appeal
Judgment delivered 31 May 2017

Appeal and new trial — Appeal — New point raised on appeal not taken below — Where appellant attempted suicide at home while on a period of leave from a mental health facility — Where primary judge found respondent had breached its duty of care by failing to provide adequate advice to the appellant and his parents that alcohol and contact with his ex-fiancée were stressors to be avoided, and if his parents were concerned about his condition to telephone the respondent for advice or return the appellant to hospital — Where appellant sought to reformulate the content of the duty of care on appeal — Where alleged breach of duty involved the failure to advise the appellant's parents to immediately return the appellant to hospital if the appellant was exposed at all to either stressor — Whether appellant could rely on new case on appeal — Whether cross-examination by the respondent likely to be different — Whether appellant had otherwise demonstrated exceptional circumstances justifying the court entertaining the new point.

Torts — Negligence — Essentials of action for negligence — Where appellant attempted suicide at home while on a period of leave from a mental health facility — Causation — Whether respondent's breach of duty as found by the primary judge caused the appellant to attempt suicide — Where appellant advanced alternative counterfactuals based on evidence of what the appellant's mother would have done in a hypothetical situation — Where primary judge found that no real weight could be given to such evidence — Whether appellate court should interfere with the primary judge's assessment of such evidence — Whether appellant's consumption of two beers and text messages with a friend that related to his ex-fiancée were causally connected with his later decision to attempt to commit suicide — Whether factual findings open to primary judge — Civil Liability Act 2002 (NSW), ss 5B, 5D, 43A.

In April 2008, Mr Daniel Smith consulted his GP, Dr Vo, and complained of depression, crying and insomnia and that he was drinking heavily. Dr Vo diagnosed depression and anxiety and prescribed Valium. A few days later, Mr Smith took a large number of Valium tablets. He was taken to Campbelltown Hospital where the psychiatric registrar regarded it as a suicide attempt. Mr Smith was started on anti-depressant medication and was discharged the following day.

A few months later, on 4 November 2008, Mr Smith was found hanging in the garage by his neck. CPR was commenced immediately and Mr Smith was taken by ambulance to Liverpool Hospital in a coma. He remained in intensive care for a number of days. He was referred for psychiatric review and was transferred to the Mental Health Unit at Liverpool Hospital where he was involuntarily admitted as a mentally disordered person pursuant to the *Mental Health Act 2007*.

On 11 November 2008, Mr Smith was reviewed in hospital and a risk assessment was carried out which assessed his suicide risk as low. The next day, on 12 November 2008, Mr

Smith was granted leave over the weekend and went home with his parents. At about 10.30 pm that same evening, Mr Smith was found hanging by a yellow strap tied around his neck. He was rushed to Campbelltown Hospital where he was resuscitated. He suffered a hypoxic brain injury and is now confined to a wheelchair with permanent injuries.

Mr Smith commenced proceedings in the District Court of New South Wales against the South Western Sydney Local Health District (the Health District), in negligence and claimed damages. He claimed that the Health District, which was responsible for the conduct of staff at Campbelltown Hospital, was negligent in granting him leave in November 2008 from the mental health unit at Campbelltown Hospital, and that had he remained in the hospital, he would not have attempted suicide and he would not have sustained injury.

His Honour Garling J found that the decision to grant leave was not unreasonable as Mr Smith had been adequately assessed as having a low suicide risk and could not have been detained as an involuntary patient for an unlimited period of time. His Honour found that the Health District's failure to warn Mr Smith's parents about the stressors which needed to be avoided, namely that he should avoid drinking alcohol and should not make contact with his former girlfriend Ms Scott, did in fact constitute a breach of duty but that such breach did not, in any way, give rise to the decision made by Mr Smith to attempt to take his own life; there was no causal link and nothing which the parents could have done that would have prevented Mr Smith from attempting taking his own life. Accordingly, Garling J dismissed Mr Smith's claim against the Health District.

Mr Smith appealed the primary judge's findings. He argued that the primary judge erred in finding no causal connection between Mr Smith's behaviour of consuming alcohol and contacting regarding his former girlfriend and his suicide attempt.

***Held:* appeal dismissed.**

Per Gleeson JA (with whom Meagher and Payne JJA agreed):

1. It was open to the primary judge to find that Mr Smith was not affected by alcohol at the time of the third suicide attempt on 16 November 2018. Mr Smith's submission on appeal that there is evidence of the link between the consumption of alcohol and the attempted suicide on 16 November 2018 is rejected. [139]

2. Further, it was open to the primary judge to find that the exchange of text messages with Mr Campion had not caused any upset to Mr Smith and were not causally connected with his later attempted suicide. [150]

3. Mr Smith has not demonstrated error in the primary judge's findings on causation.

[*Headnote by the Wolters Kluwer editors*]

Mr D Higgs, SC with Dr E Peden and Ms V Thomas (instructed by Marsdens Law Group) for the appellant.

Mr R Cheney SC with Mr H Chiu (instructed by Tress Cox Lawyers) for the respondent.

Before: Meagher, Gleeson and Payne JJA.

[¶82-345] State of New South Wales v DC & Anor

(2017) Aust Torts Reports ¶82-345
Medium neutral citation: [2017] HCA 22
High Court of Australia
Judgment delivered 14 June 2017

Negligence — Duty of care — Statutory power to report abuse of child to police — Where duty of care in exercise of statutory powers conceded — Where scope or extent of duty disputed — Where primary judge found that no authority acting reasonably could regard failure to report abuse to police as reasonable exercise of statutory powers in present case — Where State conceded that only reasonable exercise of statutory powers in some cases may be to report abuse to police — Whether appropriate in light of concessions to consider scope or extent of duty — Special leave to appeal revoked — Civil Liability Act 2002 (NSW), s 43A.

Tort — Vicarious liability — Where State conceded vicarious liability for breach of duty of care — Where statute providing for vicarious liability of Crown not in force — Where concession may not have reflected applicable law at relevant times — Special leave to appeal revoked — Law Reform (Vicarious Liability) Act 1983 (NSW), s 8.

Words and phrases — "duty of care", "scope or extent of duty", "statutory discretionary power", "vicarious liability".

TB and DC are sisters and were both child victims of long-term sexual and physical abuse by their stepfather between 1974 and 1983. The stepfather was known to have a criminal record for prior sexual assaults, was on bail for a charge of sexually assaulting his son's girlfriend, and had also had been imprisoned for previous sexual offences.

The sisters both attended Bankstown High School. They confided in a teacher at the school about the abuse, and the teacher notified the Department of Youth and Community Services of the abuse on 20 April 1983. The District Officer spoke to the teacher at the high school and formed the view that TB and DC's health, welfare and safety were endangered. The sisters were "apprehended" by the District Officer on 21 April 1983, on the basis that they were neglected children. They were taken to a shelter.

On 15 September 1983, the District Officer spoke to the stepfather, who admitted to sexually assaulting both TB and DC. In 1984, by order of the Children's Court, TB and DC were placed in foster care. The Department did not report the abuse to the police.

The stepfather was ultimately prosecuted in 2005 on an indictment containing nine offences; four of the counts related to TB and five to DC. The stepfather eventually pleaded guilty to all charges and was sentenced to 10 years imprisonment, with a non-parole period of four years.

TB and DC commenced proceedings in 2008, 25 years after the events occurred, against the State of New South Wales (the Department of Youth and Community Services) and the District Officer involved, Caroline Quinn. The proceedings were summarily dismissed in 2009 as showing no reasonable cause of action. An appeal from that decision to the New South Wales Court of Appeal was allowed on 22 February 2010. On 1 March 2012, after a three-day hearing, his Honour Harrison J made orders permitting the proceedings to continue.

The hearing proceeded before his Honour Campbell J.

TB and DC claimed damages for personal injury and mental harm caused by what they alleged was the continuation of the sexual and physical abuse by the stepfather, after the Department was notified of the abuse. They alleged that the Department and the Department's District Officer owed them a duty of care, to take reasonable care to avoid each of them being exposed to the ongoing risk of physical and mental harm from continuing abuse by their stepfather. They claimed that although the Department investigated their complaints and took proceedings in the Children's Court, it failed to report the abuse to the

police; had it been reported to the police, the stepfather would have been arrested, charged and denied bail, with the outcome being that he would not have been able to continue his abuse of them.

The Department denied that it owed any duty to either of TB or DC to use reasonable care in the exercise of its statutory powers, and argued that there was no evidence of ongoing abuse after it was notified. The Department also argued that, while accepting the physical injury and serious mental harm suffered by the sisters, any ongoing abuse, which it did not accept had occurred, would have made no difference to the outcome suffered by TB and DC as victims of repeated abuse over many years before the Department was first notified of their situation.

His Honour Campbell J found that in all likelihood the Department did not notify the police of the abuse, but that in any event his Honour was not satisfied on the balance of probabilities that the stepfather continued to abuse TB and DC after it was reported to the Department. His Honour found that the Department owed each of TB and DC a duty to use reasonable care in the exercise of its powers, and that the Department breached its duty of care by omitting to notify the police of the abuse, which it was required to do. However, on the basis of the finding that the abuse did not continue after the Department was notified, his Honour found that the breach by the Department was not a necessary condition of the harm suffered by TB and DC.

TB and DC appealed the primary judge's findings. The court found that, contrary to the primary judge's findings, the evidence did establish that the abuse continued after the notification. On that basis, the Department breached its duty in failing to protect TB and DC from further abuse, and notification of the abuse to the police was required in order to discharge the duty of care. Accordingly, the court upheld the appeal and awarded damages of $939,000 to TB and $536,000 to DC.

By grant of special leave, the State appealed to the High Court. On 10 May 2017, the High Court revoked special leave in relation to one of the grounds of appeal, namely the vicarious liability of the State (ground 3 of the notice of appeal). After revoking special leave in relation to ground 3, the court reserved its decision on the question whether special leave to appeal in relation to ground 2 of the notice of appeal, namely as to the extent or scope of duty, should be revoked until after hearing argument.

Held: special leave to appeal in relation to ground 2 of the notice of appeal dated 23 February 2017 revoked.

Per Kiefel CJ, Bell, Gageler, Keane and Gordon JJ:

1. The State did not dispute that, in the exercise of its statutory powers under s 148B(5) of the *Child Welfare Act 1939* (NSW), a common law duty was owed by the State to the sisters. The grounds of the State's appeal to the High Court encompassed, first, the extent or scope of that duty and, second, if that duty was breached, whether the State was vicariously liable. [15], [16]

2. The State accepted that there was a common law duty to use reasonable care in the exercise of the powers conferred by s 148B(5) of the CW Act for the protection of children at risk. In relation to the scope or extent of that common law duty, the State further accepted, during the course of argument, that there will be cases where, in the circumstances, the only reasonable exercise of the powers conferred by s 148B(5) would be to report the matter to the police. [20]

3. The primary judge held that failure to report the abuse to the police constituted a breach of duty. Having regard to the course taken by the State at trial, and in the appeals to the Court of Appeal and to this Court, this case is not an appropriate vehicle for considering the scope or extent of the common law duty owed in the exercise of the powers under the CW Act. [23]

4. Special leave to appeal in relation to ground 2 should be revoked.

[*Headnote by the Wolters Kluwer editors*]

N J Williams SC with I L Harvey and L A Coleman for the appellant (instructed by Crown Solicitor (NSW)).

A S Morrison SC with J R K Pryde and N F Morrissey for the respondents (instructed by Graham Jones Lawyers).

Before: Kiefel CJ, Bell, Gageler, Keane and Gordon JJ.

[¶82-188/1] Davis v Swift

(2014) Aust Torts Reports 82-188/1
Medium neutral citation: [2014] NSWCA 458
Supreme Court of New South Wales, Court of Appeal
Judgment delivered 22 December 2014

Torts — Negligence — Whether breach of duty of care — Whether contributory negligence — No issue of principle.

Torts — Motor accidents — "Blameless accident" — Where accident or injury not caused by driver or owner's negligence — Where contributory negligence — Apportionment of responsibility — Motor Accidents Compensation Act 1999 (NSW), s 7B, 7F, 138.

Torts — Damages — Assessment of damages — No issue of principle.

On 20 March 2009, Carolyn Davis was injured when a motor vehicle driven by Deborah Swift ran over her right foot as Ms Davis was attempting to cross Vincent Street in Cessnock. Ms Davis stepped off the kerb in front of Ms Swift's parked vehicle and walked to the middle of the road. At that point, the traffic travelling in the opposite direction made it unsafe to proceed. Ms Davis ran or stepped backwards very quickly into the path of Ms Swift's vehicle.

In the seconds before this happened, Ms Swift was preparing to leave the kerb. She looked over her shoulder and then forward. As she did, she turned the steering wheel to the right and slowly began to drive from the kerb and collided with Ms Davis, catching her right foot under the front driver's side wheel.

Ms Davis commenced proceedings in the District Court against Ms Swift, in negligence and claimed damages. In the alternative she alleged that her injuries were the result of a "*blameless motor accident*" within Div 1 of Pt 1.2 of the *Motor Accident Compensation Act 1999* (NSW) (MAC Act).

The primary judge found in favour of Ms Swift, that it was a "*blameless accident*" and assessed contributory negligence at 100%.

Ms Davis appealed. She argued on appeal that Ms Swift breached her duty of care by failing to keep a proper look out, and that the primary judge erred in holding that if the accident was a "*blameless accident*" that the contributory negligence should be assessed at 100%.

Held: appeal allowed.

Per Meagher JA (with whom Leeming JA and Adamson J agreed):

1. The primary judge did not err in not inferring fault on the part of the Ms Swift, the respondent. The evidence did not justify a finding that from the respondent's position in the driver's seat had she looked forwards, backwards and forwards as she asserted, she must have seen the appellant in time to take some action to avoid colliding with her.

2. In *Axiak* v *Ingram* [2012] NSWCA 311, it was held that a "*blameless*" accident includes one where there has been contributory negligence on the part of the injured person. The closing words of the definition of blameless accident — "*and not caused by the fault of*

***any other person*''** — **refer only to tortious conduct of a person other than the injured person. That is principally because ''*fault*'' is defined in s 3 as meaning ''*negligence or any other tort*''. It follows that a ''*blameless accident*'' can include one in which there has been contributory negligence of the injured person.**

3. Section 7F preserves the application of a reduction to damages for injuries resulting from a ''*blameless motor accident*''. As neither party submitted that *Axiak* was wrongly decided, any appeal must be based on whether the primary judge erred by not applying the approach laid down in that case.

4. In describing the appellant's conduct as the ''*sole cause of the accident*'', the primary judge took into account an impermissible consideration. Such a statement could only be relevant to identifying culpable conduct which caused the accident and her injuries, and this approach was rejected in *Axiak*.

5. This error by the primary judge makes re-assessment of the reduction of damages by reason of contributory negligence necessary. The appellant's behaviour involved a significant departure from the standard of care expected. However, in the range of possible departures from that standard of care, the appellant's conduct is not an example of a worst possible case. Her damages should be reduced by 80%.

Per Adamson J (dissenting in part):

1. There was no error in the primary judge's finding that Ms Swift had not been shown to be at fault.

2. The effect of the construction of s 7A in *Axiak* was to obliterate any statutory distinction between contributory negligence which was causal of the event itself, and contributory negligence which aggravated the damages but was not causative. Allowing access to damages under Div 1 Pt 1.2 as ''*blameless accidents*'' for injured persons irrespective of conduct which may have been causal.

3. Contributory negligence under s 7F includes conduct by the appellant which is causal. The causal nature of the contributory negligent therefore can be taken into account in determining what damages are ''*just and equitable*'' under s 138(3) of the MAC Act.

4. The primary judge did not err in the finding of contributory negligence of 100%. By describing the appellants conduct as the ''*sole cause of the accident*'', it should be understood that the primary judge was referring to Ms Davis' conduct as amounting to the only conduct that involved culpability. It is self-evident that the accident would not have happened if Ms Swift had not performed the manoeuvre of pulling out from the kerb at the precise time when the Ms Davis stepped backwards. To that extent, Ms Swift's conduct was a cause.

[*Headnote by the Wolters Kluwer editors*]

R McIlwaine SC with M R Quickenden (instructed by Brazel Moore) for the appellant.

P R Cummings SC (instructed by Moray & Agnew) for the respondent.

Before: Meagher,Leeming JJA and Adamson J.

[¶82-188] Hunter and New England Area Local Health District v Mckenna

(2014) Aust Torts Reports ¶82-188
Medium neutral citation: [2014] HCA 44
High Court of Australia
Judgment delivered 12 November 2014

Negligence — Duty of care — Statutory duties — Mental Health Act 1990 (NSW) provided for admission and detention of mentally ill persons in hospital — Act prohibited detention or continuation of detention of mentally ill person in hospital unless medical superintendent formed opinion that no other care of less restrictive kind appropriate and reasonably available — Alleged negligence of hospital and medical staff in discharging mentally ill person — Whether hospital and medical staff owed common law duty of care to protect other persons against harm caused by mentally ill person upon discharge — Whether duties under Act inconsistent with common law duty of care — Civil Liability Act 2002 (NSW), ss 5B, 5D, 5O, 43A, 50 — Mental Health Act 1990 (NSW).

On 20 July 2004, Stephen Rose was concerned about the mental health of his friend, William Pettigrove, and arranged for him to be taken by ambulance to Manning Base Hospital in Taree (Hospital). Following a medical assessment, Mr Pettigrove was compulsorily detained under the *Mental Health Act 1990* (NSW) (MH Act). The following day, and after a subsequent assessment by Dr Coombes, a psychiatric doctor working at the Hospital, the Hospital discharged Mr Pettigrove into the care of Mr Rose to enable them to travel by car to Mr Pettigrove's mother's house in Victoria. During the trip Mr Pettigrove strangled and killed Mr Rose. The plaintiffs, Mr Rose's mother and sisters (relatives), claimed damages for psychiatric injury resulting from nervous shock caused by the negligence of the Hunter and New England Local Health District (Health Authority) that was responsible for the conduct of the Hospital and those working within it. According to Mr Rose's relatives, the Hospital owed it a duty of care which was breached when it discharged Mr Pettigrove into Mr Rose's custody. The discharging of Mr Pettigrove from the Hospital, of itself, was not negligent. Rather, the relatives argued that placing Mr Pettigrove into Mr Rose's care for the road trip was the act of negligence.

The primary judge concluded that there had been no breach of duty and entered judgment for the Health Authority. Those conclusions were reached on the application of the *Civil Liability Act 2002* (NSW) (CLA). Section 5B(1) of the CLA was engaged because it was not shown that a reasonable person in Dr Coombes' position would have concluded that there was a not insignificant risk of Mr Pettigrove behaving as he did. His Honour further found that the Health Authority was afforded the protection of s 5O of the CLA and that Dr Coombes had acted in a manner (at the time the service was provided) that was widely accepted in Australia by peer professional opinion as competent professional practice.

The relatives appealed to the Supreme Court of New South Wales, Court of Appeal. The Health Authority contended that judgment was properly entered in its favour because the Hospital and Dr Coombes owed no relevant duty of care to the relatives because it did not owe Mr Rose a duty to take reasonable care to avoid Mr Pettigrove inflicting physical injury on Mr Rose. Allowing the appeal, Macfarlan JA (with whom Beazley P agreed) held that the Hospital owed a duty of care to take reasonable care to prevent Mr Pettigrove from causing physical harm to Mr Rose, given that the Hospital had direct dealings with Mr Rose, including releasing Mr Pettigrove into his care, and had control over the source of risk to Mr Rose. The plaintiffs established negligence on the part of Dr Coombes, and therefore on the part of the Hospital, in discharging Mr Pettigrove. There was a foreseeable and not insignificant risk of serious harm being occasioned to Mr Rose. The Hospital did not respond to that risk by taking the precaution of continuing to detain Mr Pettigrove. That precaution would have been taken by a reasonable person in the Hospital's position. In relation to causation, the plaintiffs established that the injuries that Mr Rose, and therefore they,

suffered were causally related to Dr Coombes' negligence. For the purposes of s 5D of the CLA, the Hospital's breach was a necessary condition of the harm and it was appropriate that liability extend to this harm.

The Health Authority appealed to the High Court alleging that the Court of Appeal was wrong to hold that it owed a duty of care to Mr Rose and his relatives. It also raised issues about the application of s 5B of the CLA and breach of duty, s 50 of the CLA and competent professional practice; along with s 43A of the CLA and the exercise of special statutory powers. At the hearing of the appeals, the High Court required both parties to make oral submissions about only the question of duty of care.

Held: appeal allowed.

Per French CJ, Hayne, Bell, Gageler and Keane JJ

1. In relation to the question of to whom the relevant duty was owed, it was not necessary to decide whether the Court of Appeal was right to conclude that, because the Hospital and Dr Coombes owed Mr Rose a duty to take reasonable care to prevent Mr Pettigrove from inflicting physical harm on him, they also owed the relatives a duty to take reasonable care to prevent psychiatric injury sustained on learning that Mr Pettigrove had killed Mr Rose.

2. It was also not necessary to consider the extent and potential indeterminacy of the liability which imposing the alleged duty of care would entail.

3. There were also difficulties in determining the existence of a duty of care. The relatives' claims presented issues about the nature of harm, about the exercise of statutory powers and discretions, about indeterminacy of class and about coherence. On this occasion, the statutory power consideration was determinative.

4. The relatives sought to distinguish the act of placing Mr Pettigrove into Mr Rose's care from the decision to discharge Mr Pettigrove. It was to be greatly doubted that such a distinction could be made in this case. In any event, there was still a need to identify the duty which it was alleged was owed to the relatives: a duty to take reasonable care when deciding that the powers given by the MH Act, which had been used to detain Mr Pettigrove, should no longer be used to prevent him leaving the Hospital.

5. Identifying whether there was such a duty required consideration of the MH Act. That Act prohibited detention, or the continuation of detention, unless the medical superintendent of the hospital formed the opinion that no other less restrictive care was appropriate and reasonably available.

6. It would be inconsistent with the provisions of the MH Act for a duty of care to the relatives to exist. The core of the relatives' complaint was that each was injured because a decision was made not to continue to detain a mentally ill person. But those who made that decision had other duties prescribed by the MH Act.

7. There arose an inconsistency of obligations and as explained in the High Court decision of *Sullivan* v *Moody* (2001) Aust Torts Reports ¶81-622; (2001) 207 CLR 562, if a suggested duty of care would give rise to inconsistent obligations, that would ordinarily be a reason for denying that the duty exists.

8. If a hospital or doctor were to owe to those with whom a mentally ill person may later come in contact, a duty to take reasonable care to protect those others from risk of physical harm done by the mentally ill person, the hospital or doctor would be required to ask whether that risk was foreseeable and not insignificant and then take whatever steps a reasonable person would take in response to that risk.

9. The powers, duties and responsibilities of doctors and hospitals respecting the involuntary admission and detention of mentally ill persons were prescribed by the MH Act. There arose an inconsistency between those provisions and the finding of a common law duty of care alleged by the relatives. The Hospital and Dr Coombes did not owe the relatives a relevant duty of care.

[*Headnote by the Wolters Kluwer editors*]

R J Cheney SC with N E Chen (instructed by TressCox Lawyers) for the appellant.

B M Toomey QC with G R Graham (instructed by T D Kelly & Co) for the respondents.

Before: French CJ, Hayne, Bell, Gageler and Keane JJ.

[¶82-168] Taylor v The Owners — Strata Plan No 11564 & ORS

(2014) Aust Torts Reports ¶82-168;
Medium neutral citation: [2014] HCA 9
High Court of Australia
Judgment delivered 2 April 2014

Statutes — Statutory construction — Whether Court of Appeal erred in construction of Civil Liability Act 2002 (NSW), s 12(2) — Whether Civil Liability Act 2002 (NSW), s 12(2) limits awards of damages under Compensation to Relatives Act 1897 (NSW), s 3, 4 — Whether s 12(2) limitation applies to deceased's gross weekly earnings — Civil Liability Act 2002 (NSW), s 12(1), 12(2) — Compensation to Relatives Act 1897 (NSW), s 3, 4.

Mrs Taylor was the widow of the late Mr Taylor. Mr Taylor was killed when an awning outside a shop collapsed on him. Mrs Taylor commenced proceedings in the Supreme Court of New South Wales claiming damages under s 3 and 4 of the *Compensation to Relatives Act 1897* (NSW) (CR Act). The action was a representative proceeding brought for the benefit of Mrs Taylor and any entitled children of the deceased. The deceased was a land surveyor in private practice. Had the deceased lived, he would have earned income substantially in excess of three times the amount of average weekly earnings. Mrs Taylor claimed damages for the loss of benefits that she and the children expected to have received had the deceased lived, derived from his personal exertion, investment, creation and maintenance of capital assets and services. No component of the damages claimed was based upon any loss of Mrs Taylor's, or the children's, earnings.

A preliminary question in the Supreme Court proceedings asked whether any such award of damages would be limited by s 12(2) of the *Civil Liability Act 2002* (NSW) (CL Act). Section 12(2) of the CL Act directed a court, when awarding damages relating to the death of or injury to a person, to disregard the amounts (if any) by which "the claimant's" gross weekly earnings would, but for the injury or death, have exceeded three times the amount of average weekly earnings at the date of the award (the s 12(2) limitation). The s 12(2) limitation applied to awards of damages for *inter alia* "the loss of expectation of financial support". The latter expression was apt to describe an award of damages under the CR Act.

The primary judge identified the purpose of s 12 of the CL Act as being to limit claims for tortiously caused damage and to restrict financial loss claims for high earning individuals. His Honour determined that it was consonant with the purpose of the scheme to apply the s 12(2) limitation to the deceased's income. He held that in order to give the provision operative effect in the case of an award for the loss of expectation of financial support, "claimant" in s 12(2) was to be construed as meaning "the deceased upon whose earnings the claim depends".

The primary judge therefore gave an answer to the preliminary question which was that, insofar as it included damages for the loss of an expectation of the financial support provided by the late Mr Taylor, the claim was to be determined in accordance with s 12(2) of the CL

Act by the Supreme Court disregarding the amount (if any) by which the late Mr Taylor's gross weekly earnings would (but for his death) have exceeded an amount that was three times the amount of average weekly earnings at the date of the award: see *Taylor* v *The Owners — Strata Plan No 11564* [2012] NSWSC 842.

The primary judge's decision was upheld by majority in the Court of Appeal. The court stated that the ordinary meaning of "claimant" was someone who made a claim or entered a claim or one who had a claim upon anything. The court observed that the person killed by the defendant's wrongful conduct giving rise to a CR Act claim was neither the person who made the claim nor the person who was entitled to do so. The Court of Appeal concluded that the literal meaning of s 12(2) did not apply the limitation to the gross weekly earnings of the deceased.

Justice McColl, writing for the majority of the Court of Appeal, considered that the primary judge was right to find that a literal construction of s 12(2) produced a result that was inconsistent with the provision's purpose. Her Honour adopted a purposive construction then read s 12(2) as if it contained additional words that provided that the court was to disregard the amount by which "the claimant's *or* deceased person's gross weekly earnings" would (but for the injury or death) have exceeded an amount that was three times the amount of average weekly earnings at the date of the award: see *Taylor* v *The Owners — Strata Plan No 11564* [2013] NSWCA 55.

The primary judge and McColl JA each adopted a purposive construction but differed with respect to the words to be added with the result that they gave differing operation to the s 12(2) limitation. Unlike the construction proposed by the primary judge, McColl JA's construction did not result in the s 12(2) limitation having no application to the claimant's gross weekly earnings in a CR Act action in which the court had regard to those earnings.

Mrs Taylor was then granted special leave to appeal to the High Court of Australia. The active respondents to the appeal were the Owners — Strata Plan No 11564, Ms Lamond, Mr G Sunn, Mr C Sunn, and Manly Council (the active respondents). The issue presented by the appeal was whether, in the case of an award of damages for the loss of expectation of financial support, the s 12(2) limitation was to be construed as applying to the deceased's gross weekly earnings.

Mrs Taylor submitted that McColl JA erred by not giving s 12(2) its ordinary grammatical meaning. She submitted that her Honour exceeded the proper limits of statutory implication by re-writing s 12(2). The alternative grammatical meaning, for which Mrs Taylor contended, involved reading "the claimant's gross weekly earnings" as meaning the gross weekly earnings of the person who happened to be the claimant.

The active respondents submitted that the restrictions on "reading in" words to a statutory text applied in a case in which the court was asked to add words that were quite beyond any tenable view of the contextual meaning. They contended that "claimant" in s 12(2) had the contextual meaning of "the impaired person": an expression that accorded with the conceptual basis of the three awards that were the subject of the s 12(2) limitation. The active respondents also embraced a further construction of s 12(2) posited on acceptance of s 12(1)(c) as being confined to direct financial support. The phrase "the claimant's gross weekly earnings", they submitted, was to be understood as meaning the gross weekly earnings on which the claimant relied.

Manly Council supported McColl JA's construction of s 12(2), contending that the addition of the words "or deceased person's" after "claimant's" was the correction of an obvious drafting error.

Held: appeal allowed.

Per French CJ, Crennan and Bell JJ:

1. The question whether the court was justified in reading a statutory provision as if it contained additional words or omitted words involved a judgment of matters of degree. That judgment was readily answered in favour of addition or omission in the case of simple, grammatical, drafting errors which if uncorrected would defeat the object of the provision. It was answered against a construction that filled gaps in legislation or made an insertion which was "too big, or too much at variance with the language in fact used by the legislature".

2. On no view could the deceased have been "the claimant" in s 12(2). To read s 12, in the case of an award under s 12(1)(c), as applying the s 12(2) limitation to the deceased's gross weekly earnings could not be reconciled with the language that the parliament had enacted. The phrase "the claimant's gross weekly earnings" was incapable of identifying the gross weekly earnings of the deceased.

3. The purpose of s 12 may have been identified as the limitation of the component of the award that was assessed by reference to a claimant's high earnings, in claims for personal injury damages brought by or on behalf of high-earning individuals. The fact that the occasions for the application of the s 12(2) limitation in CR Act awards may have been infrequent was not a reason for identifying some different legislative purpose outside the terms of the statute.

4. For these reasons the appeal was allowed and the answer to the separate question should have been "...No, the operation of s 12(2) of the *Civil Liability Act 2002* (NSW) does not limit the first plaintiff's claim for damages pursuant to s 3 and 4 of the *Compensation to Relatives Act 1897* (NSW) as pleaded on behalf of herself and any other entitled relatives of the late Mr Craig Taylor in that it does not require the court to disregard the amount by which the gross weekly earnings of Mr Craig Taylor would, but for his death, have exceeded an amount that is three times the average weekly earnings at the date of the award".

Per Gageler and Keane JJ:

1. Mrs Taylor's appeal from the judgment of the Court of Appeal should have been dismissed.

2. The structure of s 12, within the context of Pt 2 of the CL Act, was a significant guide to the construction of s 12(2). Section 12(1) identified three categories of personal injury damages. Section 12(2) then set out a rule which bound a court awarding personal injury damages within each of those categories. That structure made clear that the targets of the rule set out in s 12(2) were awards of damages within each of the three categories of personal injury damages identified in s 12(1). The express statutory identification of those targets left no room for the invocation of any presumption against statutory interference with the common law or statutory rights which would be vindicated by such awards of damages, even assuming that such a presumption might otherwise have scope for operation.

3. Unless s 12 was to miss one or more of its legislatively defined targets entirely, s 12(2) must have been construed to allow the rule it set out to operate in respect of at least some awards of damages within each of the three categories of personal injury damages identified in s 12(1).

4. The construction of s 12(2) adopted by the majority in the Court of Appeal cohered with the statutory object of subjecting an award of damages of the kind identified in (c) of s 12(1) to the rule set out in s 12(2). But it was a very strained construction. The statutory object was equally achieved if "the claimant's gross weekly earnings" was read as meaning the gross weekly earnings on which the claimant relied, as "claimant", in making the claim for damages that was the subject of an award of damages. And the text of s 12(2) was less strained.

5. To read "the claimant's gross weekly earnings" as meaning the gross weekly earnings on which the person making the claim for damages relied gave the rule in s 12(2) work to do

in respect of an award of damages falling within (c) of s 12(1) in exactly the same way as it gave that rule work to do in respect of an award of damages falling within (a) and (b) of s 12(1).

6. The claimant in relation to an award of damages falling within (c) of s 12(1) may have (but need not have) been one of the relatives of the deceased for whose benefit the action was brought and may simply have been the executor or administrator. To establish the claimed loss of expectation of financial support which was the subject of the award, such a claimant relied on the gross weekly earnings of the deceased. The preferred construction of s 12(2) was therefore to construe s 12(2)'s reference to "the claimant's gross weekly earnings" as a reference to the gross weekly earnings on which the claimant relied in the claim for damages that was the subject of an award of damages.

7. The problem with Mrs Taylor's submitted grammatical meaning that "the claimant's gross weekly earnings" meant the gross weekly earnings of the person who happened to be the claimant was that the gross weekly earnings of the claimant could then never bear on the loss of expectation of financial support to be quantified in an award of damages falling within (c) of s 12(1). While it would leave s 12(2) with work to do in respect of awards of damages falling within (a) and (b) of s 12(1), the meaning would deprive s 12(2) of any work to do in respect of any award of damages falling within (c) of s 12(1). The meaning would have rendered (c) of s 12(1) a statutory curiosity: a target which could never have been hit.

[*Headnote by the Wolters Kluwer editors*]

J Poulos QC with V M Heath (instructed by Craddock Murray Neumann) for the appellant.

P W Taylor SC with A C Scotting (instructed by Meridian Lawyers) for the first to fourth respondents.

S R Donaldson SC with S P W Glascott (instructed by DLA Piper Australia) for the sixth respondent.

Before: French CJ, Crennan, Bell, Gaegler and Keane JJ.

[¶82-131] Wallace v Kam

(2013) Aust Torts Reports ¶82-131
Medium neutral citation: [2013] HCA 19
High Court of Australia
Judgment delivered 8 May 2013

Negligence — Causation — Medical practitioner — Where medical practitioner failed to warn patient of two distinct material risks inherent in surgical procedure — Where only one risk eventuated — Where patient would have chosen not to undergo surgical procedure if warned of both risks — Where patient would have chosen to undergo surgical procedure if warned only of risk that eventuated — Whether failure to warn of both material risks was a necessary condition of injury caused by the risk that eventuated — Whether appropriate for scope of medical practitioner's liability to extend to that injury — Civil Liability Act 2002 (NSW), s 5D.

Mr Wallace sought medical assistance in relation to a condition of his lumbar spine. Dr Kam, a neurosurgeon, performed a surgical procedure on him. The surgical procedure had inherent risks. One risk was of temporary local damage to nerves within his thighs, described as "bilateral femoral neurapraxia", resulting from lying face down on the operating table for an extended period. Another, distinct risk was a one-in-twenty chance of permanent and catastrophic paralysis resulting from damage to his spinal nerves. The surgical procedure was unsuccessful: the condition of Mr Wallace's lumbar spine did not improve. The first risk materialised: Mr Wallace sustained neurapraxia which left him in severe pain for some time. The second risk did not.

Mr Wallace claimed damages from Dr Kam for the neurapraxia he sustained. Mr Wallace's claim in the Supreme Court of New South Wales was that Dr Kam negligently failed to warn him of risks including the risk of neurapraxia and the risk of paralysis and that, had he been warned of either risk, he would have chosen not to undergo the surgical procedure and would therefore not have sustained the neurapraxia.

The claim was dismissed by the trial judge Harrison J. He found that Dr Kam negligently failed to warn Mr Wallace of the risk of neurapraxia. But he also found that Mr Wallace would have chosen to undergo the surgical procedure even if warned of the risk of neurapraxia. He concluded, for that reason, that Dr Kam's negligent failure to warn Mr Wallace of the risk of neurapraxia was not a necessary condition of the occurrence of the neurapraxia. He declined to make any finding about whether Dr Kam negligently failed to warn Mr Wallace of the risk of paralysis, and about what Mr Wallace would have done if warned of the risk of paralysis, on the basis that the "legal cause" of the neurapraxia "could never be the failure to warn of some other risk that did not materialise".

Mr Wallace appealed to the Court of Appeal (Allsop P, Beazley and Basten JJA). He argued that Harrison J erred in holding that the legal cause of the neurapraxia could not be the failure to warn of the risk of paralysis. The Court of Appeal tested that argument by assuming that Dr Kam negligently failed to warn Mr Wallace of the risk of paralysis and that, if warned of that risk, Mr Wallace would not have undergone the surgical procedure. Was Dr Kam, on that assumption, liable for the neurapraxia?

The Court of Appeal divided in answering that question. The majority, Allsop P and Basten JA, answered it in the negative. The appeal was therefore dismissed. Beazley JA answered it in the affirmative and would have ordered a new trial. Mr Wallace appealed to the High Court of Australia.

Held: appeal dismissed with costs.

1. A component of the single comprehensive duty of a medical practitioner to a patient is ordinarily to warn the patient of "material risks" of physical injury inherent in a proposed treatment. A risk of physical injury inherent in a proposed treatment is material if it is a risk to which a reasonable person in the position of the patient would be likely to attach significance, or if it is a risk to which the medical practitioner knows or ought reasonably to know the particular patient would be likely to attach significance in choosing whether or not to undergo a proposed treatment (at [8]).

2. The common law duty of a medical practitioner is therefore ordinarily breached where the medical practitioner fails to exercise reasonable care and skill to warn a patient of any material risk of physical injury inherent in a proposed treatment. However, consistent with the underlying purpose of the imposition of the duty to warn, the damage suffered by the patient that the common law makes compensable, is not impairment of the patient's right to choose. Nor is the compensable damage exposure of the patient to an undisclosed risk. The compensable damage is, rather, limited to the occurrence and consequences of physical injury sustained by the patient as a result of the medical treatment that is carried out following the making by the patient of a choice to undergo the treatment (at [9]).

3. For particular physical injury sustained by a patient as a result of medical treatment the patient has chosen to have carried out to be compensable, it must be determined to have been caused by the particular failure of the medical practitioner to exercise reasonable care and skill to warn the patient of one or more material risks inherent in that treatment (at [10]).

4. The critical question, as the Court of Appeal recognised and on which it divided, is the scope of liability question posed by s 5D(1)(b). Is it appropriate for the scope of Dr Kam's liability to extend to the physical injury in fact sustained by Mr Wallace in circumstances where Mr Wallace would not have chosen to undergo the surgical procedure had he been

properly warned of all material risks but where he would have chosen to undergo the surgical procedure had he been warned only of the risk that in fact materialised? (at [30]).

5. The ultimately persuasive force of the proposition that Mr Wallace should not be compensated for the materialisation of a risk he would have been prepared to accept, lies in its recognition of the distinct nature of the material risks about which Dr Kam failed to warn Mr Wallace and in relating Mr Wallace's acceptance of the risk that came home to the policy underlying Dr Kam's duty to warn Mr Wallace of all material risks (at [32]).

6. To fail to warn the patient of one risk while informing the patient of another may still in such a case be to expose the patient to a level of risk of physical injury occurring that is unacceptable to the patient. But the risk of physical injury that comes home in such a case is not necessarily the risk of physical injury that is unacceptable to the patient (at [35]).

7. Consideration of a case involving the materialisation of one of a number of distinct risks of different physical injuries makes it necessary to return to the nature of the duty and the policy that underlies its imposition. The duty of a medical practitioner to warn the patient of material risks inherent in a proposed treatment is imposed by reference to the underlying common law right of the patient to choose whether or not to undergo a proposed treatment. The underlying policy is to protect the patient from the occurrence of physical injury the risk of which is unacceptable to the patient. It is appropriate that the scope of liability for breach of the duty reflect that underlying policy (at [36]).

8. Dr Kam is not liable to Mr Wallace for impairment of Mr Wallace's right to choose whether or not to undergo the surgical procedure and is not liable to Mr Wallace for exposing him to an unacceptable risk of catastrophic paralysis. He can be liable, if at all, for the neurapraxia Mr Wallace sustained. Mr Wallace is not to be compensated for the occurrence of physical injury the risk of which he was prepared to accept (at [39]).

9. The distinct nature of the risks of neurapraxia and paralysis, and the willingness of Mr Wallace to accept the risk of neurapraxia, therefore combine to support the shorthand holding of Harrison J that any failure of Dr Kam to warn Mr Wallace of the risk of paralysis could not be the "legal cause" of the neurapraxia that materialised (at [40]).

[*Headnote by the Wolters Kluwer editors*]

PW Bates with PG White (instructed by Gerard Malouf & Partners) for the appellant.

DJ Higgs SC with EM Peden (instructed by TressCox Lawyers) for the respondent.

Before: French CJ, Crennan, Kiefel, Gageler and Keane JJ.

[¶82-123/1] **Axiak v Ingram**

(2012) Aust Torts Reports ¶82-123/1
Medium neutral citation: [2012] NSWCA 311
Supreme Court of New South Wales Court of Appeal
Judgment delivered 27 September 2012

Motor accident — Motor accident not caused by the fault of the respondent — Construction of Part 1.2 of the Motor Accidents Compensation Act 1999 (NSW) — Whether appellants are entitled to damages under Div 1 of Pt 1.2 of the Act — Whether accident was a "blameless motor accident" within the meaning of the definition of that expression in s 7A of the Act — Meaning of the word "fault" in the definition of "blameless motor accident" — Construction of the definition of "fault" and whether it includes the non-tortious negligence of the injured party — Whether a restrictive construction of "fault" would be inconsistent with the use of the word "fault" in other provisions of the Act — Whether the primary judge was correct in her assessment of the degree of the first appellant's contributory negligence — Costs — Motor Accidents Compensation Act 1999 (NSW), s 7A.

On June 2008, Alana Axiak, who was 14 years of age at the time, was returning home from school in a school bus. She was accompanied by her sister, Mikaela, who was 12 years at the time. The bus stopped opposite the family home to allow the girls to disembark.

After alighting the bus, the two girls darted behind the back of the bus. They were running, with Alana proceeding first, followed by Mikaela.

Matthew Ingram was driving from the opposite direction. On rounding a curve in the road, he saw the bus and slowed from the speed limit of 80 kph down to 40 kph. He was unable to see the girls as they were obscured by the bus, and his first view of them was when they emerged from behind the bus. Mr Ingram attempted to brake but he could not get his foot onto the break before Alana collided with the vehicle. Alana, who was slightly ahead, ran straight in front of his car and was struck, suffering serious injury.

Alana, through her tutor, commenced proceedings in the Supreme Court of New South Wales, in negligence and claimed damages. Her sister Mikaela and Mr Michael Axiak (the father) each instituted separate proceedings seeking damages for nervous shock.

Alana's statement of claim did not include any allegation of fault on the part of the driver but rather alleged that the accident was a "*blameless motor accident*" within the meaning of the definition of that expression in s 7A of the *Motor Accidents Compensation Act 1999* (NSW). She also argued that, even if her contributory negligence caused the accident, this did not disentitle her to recover modified common law damages for future economic loss and non-economic loss under Div 1 Pt 1.2 of the Act. Mr Ingram alleged that the accident was caused by the fault of Alana in that, by running across the road without first checking for oncoming vehicles, she failed to take reasonable care for her own safety, that Alana was contributorily negligent and was at fault in that her conduct was the sole cause of the accident.

There was no issue that the accident was not caused by the fault of Mr Ingram, being the driver of the motor vehicle. The issue that arose was whether the motor vehicle accident was caused by "*the fault of any other person*" and whether the term "fault" is to be confined to tortious negligence or to encompass contributory negligence.

Her Honour Adamson J found that the term did include contributory negligence and that the accident was caused by the "fault" of Alana. Her conduct in running across the road from behind the bus, without ensuring that there was no vehicle travelling in the opposite direction, was the sole cause of the accident and she was guilty of contributory negligence. Her Honour found that even if the claim succeeded, Alana's claim would be reduced by 100% as a result of a process of comparative culpability, the consequence being that the claim failed in its entirety and as such so did the claims of Mikaela and Michael Axiak.

Alana appealed the primary judge's findings. She argued on appeal that the primary judge erred by; failing to accord to the word "fault" in s 7A its defined meaning in s 3 of "negligence or any other tort"; failing to take account of s 7F which makes specific provision in relation to contributory negligence generally; and by failing to give effect to the totality of the definition of "fault" and, in particular, for the words "any other tort". She argued that the use of the word "other" was a clear reference back to the word "negligence" and thereby evinced an intention that the "negligence" referred to in the definition was used in the sense of a tort and not to contributory negligence which is not a tort.

Mr Ingram sought to uphold the primary judge's construction of the word "fault" as including "contributory negligence" upon the ground that an unduly restrictive construction would defeat the purpose of what was a no-fault scheme and would be inconsistent with the use of the word "fault" in other provisions such as in s 7K(1).

Held: appeal allowed.

Per Tobias AJA (with whom Beazley JA and Sackville AJA agreed):

1. The purpose of Pt 1.2 was to provide a "no-fault" scheme for persons, be they adults or children, who sustained injuries in a motor accident in respect of which, but for the scheme, the injured person would not have a cause of action to recover damages for those injuries. There is no difficulty in understanding the scheme as one which seeks to provide a right of recovery to persons injured in motor vehicle accidents where the accident is "blameless" in the sense that fault cannot be sheeted home to any person such as to support a cause of action at law.

2. "*Fault*" under s 3 of the Act is defined as "*negligence or any other tort*". It is the expression "*or any other tort*" that distinguishes the present case from that of *Insurance Commission of Western Australia* v *Leigh & Anor* [2001] WASCA 232. The words "*or any other tort*" can only refer to any tort other than the tort of negligence.

3. Once it is accepted that the expression "*fault of any other person*" refers only to the tortious conduct of that person, it must follow that the "*person*" referred to cannot include the injured person whose "*fault*" in the form of non-tortious contributory negligence is excluded from the definition of "*blameless motor accident*" in s 7A.

4. It is true that a construction of s 7A is inconsistent with the use of the word "*fault*" in s 7K(1) where it can only refer to a child's contributory negligence in the conventional sense. This is an anomaly.

5. Subject only to the anomaly of s 7K(1), it follows that the primary judge was in error in construing the word "*negligence*" in the definition of "*fault*" for the purposes of s 7A as including non-tortious negligence such as the first appellant's contributory negligence.

6. Even if the claim succeeds, s 7F requires consideration of whether there should be a reduction of the first appellant's damages by reason of her contributory negligence, noting that any such reduction cannot apply to those heads of damage referred to in s 7J(3). It would follow that the only heads of damage affected by s 7F are those of future economic loss and non-economic loss.

7. The exercise of making comparisons of culpability and the relevant importance of the acts of the parties in causing the personal injury as called for in *Prodrebersek* v *Australian Iron and Steel Pty Ltd* (1985) 59 ALJR 492 have no application to a case such as the present. Division 1 of Pt 1.2 of the Act proceeds upon the assumption that the defendant driver is not at fault.

8. It follows that the concept of "*contributory negligence*" in s 7F of the Act has to be applied in a different manner. This can be done consistently with the objectives of the legislation by inquiring how far the plaintiff has departed from the standard of care he/she is required to observe in the interests of his/her own safety. The degree contributory negligence can, in a case such as the present, only be assessed upon the basis of a value judgment as to the extent to which her conduct failed to conform to the standard of care expected of a 14-year-old girl in her position.

9. Taking into account all of the circumstances to which reference has been made, the first appellant's damages should be reduced due to her contributory negligence by 50 percent. Mikaela and Michael Axiak are also entitled to succeed subject to the same reduction.

[*Headnote by the Wolters Kluwer editors*]

R Sheldon SC with P J Nolan (instructed by Stacks Goudkamp) for the appellants.

K Rewell SC (instructed by Curwoods Lawyers) for the respondent.

Before: Beazley JA, Sackville and Tobias AJJA.

[¶82-099] Strong v Woolworths Limited

(2012) Aust Torts Reports ¶82-099;
Medium neutral citation: [2012] HCA 5
High Court of Australia
Judgment delivered 7 March 2012

Torts — Negligence — Breach of duty — Damage — Causation — Slip case — Shopping centre — Failure to clean — Onus of proof — Balance of probabilities — Discharge of onus — Appellant slipped and fell on a greasy chip when visiting first respondent's retail premises — First respondent accepted that it had breached its duty to appellant by failing to provide more regular cleaning services — Appellant thus commenced proceedings claiming that first respondent's negligence had caused her to fall — First respondent defended proceedings on basis that more frequent cleaning services would not necessarily have prevented the accident because the chip may have only recently fallen — Primary judge held that Woolworths had been negligent — First respondent appealed to Court of Appeal — Appeal allowed on basis that it was more probable than not that chip had fallen shortly before accident and that more regular cleaning would therefore not have prevented it — Appellant granted leave to appeal by High Court — Whether appellant was under an onus to prove when chip had fallen on floor — Whether there had to be direct evidence of when chip had fallen — Whether time that chip had fallen could be inferred from evidence on balance of probabilities — Civil Liability Act 2002 (NSW), s 5D(1)(a).

Some time prior to the incident in question, the appellant, Ms Kathryn Strong had her right leg amputated below the knee. She consequently required a crutch to walk. In September 2004, Ms Strong visited the Centro Taree Shopping Centre (the Centre) with her friend and daughter. The first respondent, Woolworths Ltd trading as Big W (Woolworths), conducted a Woolworths and an adjoining Big W at the Centre. Woolworths leased those premises from the second respondent, CPT Manager Limited (CPT), the centre's owner. According to the terms of that lease, Woolworths had the exclusive right to conduct "sidewalk sales" in an area that extended 11 metres around the Big W entrance doors into the common area towards the food court. Two shoulder-high pot plant stands were positioned on either side of the sidewalk sales area. During the course of her visit, Ms Strong moved towards that area in order to inspect the pot plants. As she did so, the tip of her crutch came into contact with a chip, or with grease deposited by the chip, and the crutch slipped out from under her, causing her to fall. Shortly thereafter, Ms Strong saw a grease mark on the floor at the point where the crutch had slipped. Her daughter described the grease stain as being "as big as a hand". The daughter and the friend each claimed to have seen a chip on the ground.

At all relevant times, CPT, or a company associated with it, had a contract with a cleaning services company. The contract specified that the premises were to be maintained so that the floors "were free of any rubbish and or spillages". The maximum time between cleaning inspections for the "mall/common areas" was stipulated to be 15 minutes. Ms Kathryn Walker was employed as a cleaner by the cleaning services company. Ms Walker, who was on lunch break at the time of Ms Strong's fall, was responsible for cleaning the common area but this did not extend to the sidewalk sales area. A second cleaner, who was simultaneously on duty, was required to clean the food court area, the public toilets and to respond to calls to clean up spillages. Security staff patrolled the Centre continuously and would contact the cleaner by two-way radio if a spillage was detected. In addition, Big W employed a person to act as a "people greeter", to welcome people coming into the store, to check the bags of those leaving it and to keep an eye out for spillages within the sidewalk sales area. All other Big W employees were trained to be vigilant for spillages. Despite these contingencies, Woolworths acknowledged that it did not have any system in place on the day of the incident for the periodic inspection and necessary cleaning of the sidewalk sales area.

Ms Strong then commenced proceedings against Woolworths in the District Court. In that context, Woolworths was said to have been negligent in failing to institute and maintain a proper cleaning system to detect spillages and foreign objects in and around the plant trolleys. At first instance, the primary judge held that Woolworths was the occupier of the sidewalk sales area and that it owed a duty of care to persons coming within it. His Honour then accepted the claim that Woolworths had been negligent in not removing the chip and the grease from the floor. Judgment was accordingly entered for Ms Strong. Woolworths then appealed to the Court of Appeal. In that respect, Woolworths did not contest that it had been negligent because it had not complied with the agreed standard of providing cleaners at least every 20 minutes. Woolworths instead focused upon causation. More particularly, it contended that, even if it had a checking and cleaning system in place that complied with that standard, there was no evidence that the accident would not have happened anyway. That was because it was not clear that the chip and the grease had not fallen to the ground immediately before the accident. The Court of Appeal thus concluded that Ms Strong had not satisfied s 5D(1)(a) of the *Civil Liability Act 2002* (NSW) (the Act), which required that the negligence was a ''necessary condition of the occurrence of the particular harm''. Ms Strong then appealed to the High Court, with leave being granted to argue that same issue of causation.

Held: appeal allowed.

Per French CJ, Gummow, Crennan and Bell JJ

1. A necessary condition of the occurrence of the particular harm was a condition that had to be present for the occurrence of that harm. However, there could conceivably be more than one set of conditions necessary for the occurrence of particular harm in any set of circumstances.

2. It followed that a defendant's negligent act or omission which was necessary to complete a set of conditions that were jointly sufficient to account for the occurrence of the harm would meet the test of factual causation stipulated by s 5D(1)(a) of the Act.

3. In the present case, Ms Strong was required to prove that, had a system of periodic inspection and cleaning of the sidewalk sales area been employed on the day of her fall, it was likely that the chip would have been detected and removed before she approached the entrance to Big W.

4. However, it was not necessary for Ms Strong to adduce some evidence permitting an inference to be drawn concerning when the chip had been dropped on the floor. Ms Strong could instead discharge the onus by reference to the probabilities that were established on the evidence.

5. In the present case, the probabilities favoured the conclusion that the chip had been dropped more than 20 minutes before the fall rather than less than 20 minutes before the fall. The probabilities were hence that, if Woolworths had implemented a proper cleaning system, the accident would not have occurred.

6. It therefore followed that, on the balance of probabilities, the admitted negligence of Woolworths caused the damage accruing to Ms Strong for the purposes of s 5D(1)(a) of the Act. As such, the Court of Appeal erred and the decision of the District Court was to be restored.

Per Heydon J (in dissent)

7. Assuming that Woolworths breached its duty by not providing cleaning services for the area every 20 minutes, it was not for it to demonstrate that the chip fell less than 20 minutes before the accident. It was for Ms Strong to prove that it fell more than 20 minutes beforehand.

8. The problem for Ms Strong was that there was no direct evidence either way. Nor was there much circumstantial evidence concerning the temperature or state of the chip. That made it hard to draw circumstantial inferences about when the chip may have fallen.

9. The considerations that Woolworths relied upon to suggest that the chip had fallen less than 20 minutes before the accident were not persuasive. But on the other hand, the factors that Ms Strong cited to support the inference that the chip had fallen more than 20 minutes before the accident were also not convincing.

10. Woolworths therefore could not be held liable. That flowed simply from the location of the legal burden of proof and the inherent difficulty which a plaintiff in a slipping case faced where the standard of care called only for periodical inspections rather than constant vigilance.

[*Headnote by the Wolters Kluwer editors*]

BM Toomey QC with TJJ Willis and EG Romaniuk for the appellant (instructed by Leitch Hasson Dent Lawyers).

JE Maconachie QC with P Biggins for the first respondent (instructed by Bartier Perry Solicitors).

Before: French CJ, Gummow, Heydon, Crennan and Bell JJ.

[¶82-060] Wicks v State Rail Authority of New South Wales; Sheehan v State Rail Authority of New South Wales

(2010) Aust Torts Reports ¶82-060;
Medium neutral citation: [2010] HCA 22
High Court of Australia
Judgment delivered 16 June 2010

Torts — Negligence — Duty of care — Nervous shock — Whether state rail authority liable for psychological injuries suffered by rescue workers attending scene of train crash — Effect of Civil Liability Act 2002 (NSW), s 30(2) — Whether appellants witnessed persons being killed, injured or put in peril — Civil Liability Act 2002 (NSW), s 30(2).

In January 2003, a passenger train operated by the respondent (State Rail) derailed at high speed, killing seven passengers and injuring many more. State Rail admitted that it was negligent in the operation of the derailed train. The appellant in each appeal (Mr Wicks and Mr Sheehan respectively) was, at the time of the accident, a member of the New South Wales Police Force. They were among the first to arrive at the scene of the accident, and spent many hours assisting the injured and attempting to free those still trapped in the wreckage. They each sued State Rail in negligence, alleging that as a consequence of being present at the crash site and witnessing the resulting scenes of carnage they suffered various psychological injuries, including post traumatic stress syndrome and nervous shock.

State Rail argued that it was not liable to the appellants because of the operation of s 30(2) of the *Civil Liability Act 2002* (NSW) (the Act). Section 30(2) provides that "the plaintiff is not entitled to recover damages for pure mental harm unless: (a) the plaintiff witnessed, at the scene, the victim being killed, injured or put in peril ...". Emphasising the effect of the term "being", State Rail submitted that the section operated to exclude recovery unless the plaintiff had observed an event unfolding which led to another's death, injury or being put in peril. Further, the plaintiff must be able to demonstrate that the psychiatric injury was occasioned by observation of what was happening to a particular victim.

The trial judge made no finding as to whether State Rail owed each appellant a duty of care or whether the appellants had suffered a recognised psychiatric illness; however, it was held that neither appellant had established their entitlement to recover under s 30(2) of the

Act. The NSW Court of Appeal dismissed the appeals against the trial judge's findings, and the appellants were given special leave to bring the matter before the High Court.

Held: appeal allowed.

Per French CJ, Gummow, Hayne, Heydon, Crennan, Kiefel and Bell JJ

1. The issue should be resolved in favour of the appellants, and each matter remitted to the Court of Appeal of New South Wales for its further consideration on the issues of duty of care and whether or not the appellants suffered recognised psychiatric injuries as a result of State Rail's negligence.

2. By enquiring whether s 30(2)(a) of the Act is engaged, without first deciding whether State Rail owed a relevant duty of care, the lower courts failed to consider an important anterior question. However, while it would be open to this court to decide the issue of duty of care without the need to remit the matter, it is not desirable to do so in view of the parties' express submissions that the matter ought not to be decided in the present appeal.

3. Assuming that State Rail did owe the appellants a duty to take reasonable care not to cause mental harm, the determining issue is whether pursuant to s 30(1) the claims of the appellants arose "wholly or partly from mental or nervous shock in connection with another person ... being killed, injured or put in peril" by the negligence of State Rail.

4. As regards the element of mental shock, there can be little doubt that those who came upon the scene of the derailment were confronted with a scene that would cause a sudden and disturbing impression on the mind or feelings, an impression that would have continued as witnesses took in more of the scene and set about their tasks.

5. As far as the requirement that a claimant witness another person or other persons "being killed, injured or put in peril", it would be incorrect to read s 30(2) as assuming that death, injury or peril are events that begin and end in short time frame. In the present case, it could be inferred that some who suffered physical trauma in the derailment suffered further injury as they were removed from the wrecked carriages, or that they continued to suffer psychiatric injuries after the appellants' arrival on the scene.

6. Even if neither of these inferences were drawn, the fact remained that the appellants had witnessed surviving passengers "being ... put in peril" in the aftermath of the crash. The expression should be given the meaning which the words ordinarily convey: a person is put in peril when put at risk, and until the person ceases to be at risk he or she is "being put in peril" within the meaning of s 30(2).

7. Section 30 does not require that a psychiatric injury be attributed to the observation of a particular victim. The reference in s 30(1) to "another person (the victim)" should be read as "another person or persons (as the case requires)", and the reference to "victim" in s 30(2)(a) is to be read as a reference to one or more of those persons.

[*Headnote by the Wolters Kluwer editors*]

BJ Gross QC with KO Earl for the appellant in both matters (instructed by Baker & Edmunds).

JT Gleeson SC with PM Morris and BA Arste for the respondent in both matters (instructed by DLA Phillips Fox Lawyers).

Before: French CJ, Gummow, Hayne, Heydon, Crennan, Kiefel and Bell JJ.

[¶82-057] Tabet v Gett

(2010) Aust Torts Reports ¶82-057;
Medium neutral citation: [2010] HCA 12
High Court of Australia
Judgment delivered 21 April 2010

Negligence — Loss of chance of better outcome — Entitlement to damages — Assessment of value of lost chance — Application to medical negligence claims — Whether law of tort recognises or should recognise loss of chance of better outcome as damage giving rise to liability in negligence — Relevance of policy considerations concerning extension of liability in medical negligence cases — Words and phrases — ''balance of probabilities'', ''damage'', ''gist of the action'', ''loss of chance of a better outcome'', ''standard of proof''.

In January 1991, Ms Reema Tabet (the appellant) was six years old. Following a history of headaches, nausea and vomiting, she suffered a seizure in that month. After a CT and ECG scan were performed, she was diagnosed as suffering from a brain tumour. The appellant then received treatment, including an operation to have the tumour removed. However, she subsequently suffered irreversible brain damage, partly as a result of the seizure, partly from the tumour (which had been growing for over two years), and partly from the operative procedure and other treatment (which was not said to be in any way negligently performed). Dr Maurice Gett (the respondent) was the specialist paediatrician who had primary care of the respondent.

By her tutor, the appellant commenced proceedings in the Supreme Court against the respondent claiming that his treatment of her had been negligent. The central allegation was that the CT scan should have been performed earlier. In that regard, it was claimed that if it had been performed earlier, the appellant would have had a better medical outcome. Her claim was one in negligence and did not include a claim in contract.

At first instance, Studdert J found that the respondent was negligent in failing to order a CT scan earlier than he had done. More specifically, his Honour found that the appellant would have had a chance of a better medical outcome had the CT scan been performed earlier. Apart from that, Studdert J held that the respondent had not acted negligently. In assessing damages, his Honour held that the appellant's total damages amounted to $6,092,586. His Honour then held that the appellant's decline from the point when the CT scan should have been performed contributed 25% to her total damages. That represented a sum of $1,523,146. Of that 25%, 40% was found to be referable to her loss of a chance of a better medical outcome. In other words, there had been a 40% chance of preventing the damage that did occur. That 40% of $1,523,146 represented a sum of $610,000. On that basis, Studdert J ordered that the respondent pay the appellant damages in the sum of $610,000 plus interest.

The respondent appealed against that conclusion. The Court of Appeal allowed the appeal. It held that awarding damages for loss of a chance of a better medical outcome altered the principle of causation. That was because the plaintiff did not need to prove on the balance of probabilities that the damage was caused by the breach of duty. *Rufo* v *Hosking* [2004] NSWCA 391 and the decisions that preceded it were ''plainly wrong''. The court also held that the notion of damages for loss of chance not only departed from conventional principles of tort law but formed no part of recognised streams of authority. Such a fundamental change to the law of torts with respect to proof of causation was a matter of policy for the High Court only. In the absence of such a High Court authority, damages were only to be awarded if the court was satisfied on the balance of probabilities that the breach of duty by the tortfeasor materially contributed to the harm. If the court was so satisfied, then the tortfeasor would be held liable for the whole of the harm so caused.

In conclusion, the Court of Appeal found in favour of the respondent and held that the negligence that had been found against the respondent had not been shown to be causative of any loss. For that reason, no damages should have been awarded against him in respect of the damage suffered as a result of that negligence.

The appellant was granted special leave and appealed to the High Court of Australia. The question was whether the common law of Australia should recognise the loss of a chance of a better outcome, in cases where medical negligence has been found, as actionable damage.

Held: appeal dismissed with costs.

Per Kiefel J (with whom Hayne, Bell and Crennan JJ agreed)

1. The common law requires proof, by the person seeking the compensation, that the negligent act or omission caused the loss or injury constituting the damage. All that is necessary is that, according to the course of common experience, the more probable inference appearing from the evidence is that a defendant's negligence caused the injury or harm.

2. Expressing what is said to have been lost as the loss of a chance diverts attention from the proper connection between fault and damage. It is artificial and breaks the causal link. The question of whether harm or damage has been suffered is bound up in the question of causation. *LaFerrière* v *Lawson* [1991] 1 SCR 541 applied.

3. The general standard of proof required by the common law and applied to causation is relatively low. It does not require certainty or precision. It requires that a judge be persuaded that something was probably a cause of the harm the plaintiff suffered.

4. It would require strong policy considerations to alter the present requirement of proof of causation. None are evident. The argument that there should be compensation where breach of duty is proved simply denies proof of damage as necessary to an action in negligence.

5. The requirement of causation is not overcome by redefining the mere possibility, that such damage as did occur might not eventuate, as a chance and then saying that it is lost when the damage actually occurs.

Per Gummow ACJ

6. In personal injury cases the law of negligence as understood in the common law of Australia does not entertain an action for recovery when the damage, for which compensation is awarded consequent upon breach of duty, is characterised as the loss of a chance of a better outcome of the character found by the trial judge in this case.

7. The traditional approach in personal injury cases, of an "all or nothing" outcome on the balance of probabilities, represents the striking by the law of a balance between the competing interests of the parties, and the substitution of the loss of a chance as the actionable damage represents a shift in that balance towards claimants.

8. The determination of the existence and content of a duty of care is not assisted by looking first to the harm sustained by the plaintiff and then reasoning, as it were, retrospectively (*Vairy* v *Wyong Shire Council* applied). Nor is it appropriate to reason that, duty and breach being established, the plaintiff who on the balance of probabilities cannot establish actionable damage nevertheless must have a remedy.

Per Heydon J

9. The question of law between the parties is no longer live and decisive. The question has become hypothetical in the sense that an assumption it rests on has turned out to be incorrect. There is no answer to the question posed which will produce any consequences for the parties. The only significance of an answer would lie in what future courts would make of it. They are likely to treat it not as a decision, but only as dictum. Therefore there is no utility in seeking to answer the question.

Per Hayne and Bell JJ

10. The language of loss of chance should not be permitted to obscure the need to identify whether a plaintiff has proved that the defendant's negligence was more probably than not a cause of damage (in the sense of detrimental difference). The language of possibilities (language that underlies the notion of loss of chance) should not be permitted to obscure the need to consider whether the possible adverse outcome has in fact come home, or will more probably than not do so.

[*Headnote by the Wolters Kluwer editors*]

BW Walkerr SC with JLA Lonergan and J Chambers for the appellant (instructed by Slater & Gordon Lawyers).

NJ Young QC with JK Kirk and KC Morgan for the respondent (instructed by Blake Dawson Lawyers).

Before: Gummow ACJ, Hayne, Heydon, Crennan, Kiefel and Bell JJ.

[¶82-042] Adeels Palace Pty Ltd v Moubarak; Adeels Palace Pty Ltd v Bou Najem

(2009) Aust Torts Reports ¶82-042;
Medium neutral citation: [2009] HCA 48
High Court of Australia
Judgment delivered 10 November 2009

Torts — Negligence — Civil liability — Duty of care — Breach of duty — Causation — Criminal conduct — Proprietor's duties — Respondents in both appeals were at a restaurant owned by the appellant on New Years Eve — Fight broke out in restaurant and respondents both became involved — Another person in restaurant briefly went outside to get a gun and then returned inside — Gunman subsequently shot both appellants — Respondents commenced proceedings against appellant claiming breach of its duty to them — Claims upheld at first instance and by Court of Appeal — Appellant granted special leave to appeal to High Court — Whether appellant owed duty to respondents — Whether appellant not required to protect respondents from criminal conduct — Whether any relevant duty was breached — Whether breach of any relevant duty led to respondents' injuries — Modbury Triangle Shopping Centre Pty Ltd v *Anzil (2000) 205 CLR 254 — Civil Liability Act 2002 (NSW), s 5B, 5C, 5D, 5E — Liquor Act 1982 (NSW), s 2A, 103, 125.*

The appellant in each appeal (Adeels Palace) conducted a reception and restaurant business at premises in Punchbowl, New South Wales. The premises were licensed under the Liquor Act 1982 (NSW) (the Liquor Act). An "On Licence (Restaurant)" licence permitted the service of alcohol on the premises on any day, between midday and 4.00 am on the day following. A condition of the licence limited the seating capacity of the premises to restaurant seating for 295 persons. The local council authorised the use of the premises as a place of public entertainment between midday and 4.00 am on the next day but limited the capacity of the premises to 283 persons. At the times relevant to these matters, a director of Adeels Palace was the licensee.

On New Years Eve of 2002, Adeels Palace was open for business and full. Admission to the premises, collected at the door, cost $60 per person which included food but not alcoholic drinks. There was a band; there were singers and entertainers; patrons could dance. Seating was at long tables. The bar was open. Waiters brought drinks to the tables.

At about 2.30 am there was a dispute between some women dancing on the dance floor. That led to a general confrontation in which punches, chairs, plates and bottles were thrown. One man involved in the fight was hit in the face, drawing blood. He left the restaurant and returned soon after with a gun. Someone called out "Gun, gun, run away". The respondent

in the second appeal, Mr Bou Najem, followed that instruction. More specifically, he ran into the restaurant's kitchen but slipped over. The gunman then came in. As Mr Bou Najem tried to get up, the gunman pointed the gun at him. Mr Bou Najem pleaded with him not to shoot, but he did shoot, wounding Mr Bou Najem in the leg. The gunman then left the kitchen and went back into the restaurant itself. There he found the man who had struck him in the face during the course of the fight, namely, the respondent in the first appeal, Mr Moubarak. The gunman shot Mr Moubarak in the stomach and then left the premises.

Mr Bou Najem and Mr Moubarak subsequently brought proceedings in the District Court of New South Wales against Adeels Palace claiming damages for personal injury. Each of them alleged that they had suffered injury as a result of Adeels Palace's negligence in not providing any or any sufficient security during the function on New Year's Eve. In the District Court, the two actions were heard together, and each of Mr Bou Najem and Mr Moubarak obtained judgments for damages. Adeels Palace then appealed to the Court of Appeal of New South Wales but the two appeals were unanimously dismissed.

By special leave, Adeels Palace then appealed to the High Court. In that context, Adeels Palace disputed that it owed each Mr Bou Najem and Mr Moubarak a duty of care to prevent harm of the kind suffered. That claim was advanced on the basis that Adeels Palace owed no duty to those attending its premises to prevent criminal conduct by third parties. Such a duty was said to be inconsistent with the decision of the High Court in *Modbury Triangle Shopping Centre Pty Ltd* v *Anzil* (2000) 205 CLR 254. In addition, Adeels Palace claimed that, even if that duty had been breached, that breach had not been a cause of the damage suffered within the terms of the Civil Liability Act 2001 (NSW).

Held: appeals allowed.

Per French CJ, Gummow, Hayne, Heydon and Crennan JJ

Duty of care

1. Contrary to the submissions on behalf of Adeels Palace, the High Court's decision in Modbury did not dictate the conclusion that Adeels Palace owed no relevant duty of care to persons in the position of Mr Bou Najem and Mr Moubarak in the present case.

2. The duty alleged in Modbury was said to be founded only on the defendant's position as occupier of the land controlling the physical state of the land. What was said in Modbury had to be understood as responding to those arguments and did not extend into any generally applicable principle.

3. Adeels Palace did owe each of Mr Bou Najem and Mr Moubarak a duty to take reasonable care to prevent injury to patrons from the violent, quarrelsome or disorderly conduct of other persons. That duty was consistent with the duty imposed by statute upon the licensee and was a duty enforceable by criminal processes.

4. Although it was a duty directed to controlling the conduct of others (for the avoidance of injury to other patrons) it was chiefly a duty to take reasonable care in the conduct of activities on licensed premises, particularly with regard to allowing persons to enter or remain on those premises.

Breach of duty

5. The failure to provide bouncers or crowd controllers was not a breach of the relevant duty of care for the purposes of the Civil Liability Act unless the risk to be foreseen was a risk of a kind that called for those measures as a matter of reasonable precaution.

6. In the circumstances, the failure of Adeels Palace to provide licensed personnel to act as crowd controllers or bouncers at the door of the premises (in addition to whomever Adeels Palace used to take the cost of admission from patrons at the door) was not a breach of the duty of care owed by Adeels Palace to its patrons.

Causation

7. Security personnel may have been able to deter or prevent re-entry by the drunk or angry patron. There was, however, no basis on the evidence for concluding that security staff at the entrance to the restaurant would have deterred or prevented the re-entry to the premises of a man armed with a gun intent on revenge.

8. In addition, the evidence at trial did not show that the presence of security personnel would have deterred the re-entry of the gunman. That conclusion could have been reached only if it was assumed that the gunman would have acted rationally, which was not a justifiable inference in the circumstances.

[*Headnote by the Wolters Kluwer editors*]

JE Sexton SC with MJ Gollan for the appellant (instructed by Lee & Lyons Lawyers).

BM Toomey QC with DR Campbell SC and DC Morgan for the respondent in S191/2009 (instructed by Leitch Hasson Dent Solicitors).

SG Campbell SC with JW Catsanos for the respondent in S192/2009 (instructed by Sanford Legal).

Before: French CJ, Gummow, Hayne, Heydon and Crennan JJ.

[¶81-888] Cox v State of New South Wales

(2007) Aust Torts Reports ¶81-888;
Medium neutral citation: [2007] NSWSC 471
Supreme Court of New South Wales
Judgment delivered 14 May 2007

Negligence — duty of care — causation — psychiatric injury — plaintiff bullied in primary school — bullying reported to school authorities by plaintiff's mother — damages — relevance of plaintiff's mother's psychiatric condition — s 5D(1)(a) of the Civil Liability Act 2002 (NSW).

The plaintiff, Benjamin Cox, commenced proceedings seeking damages for psychiatric injuries he claimed to have suffered as a consequence of being bullied at a primary school administered by the defendant. The bullying was said to have occurred in 1994 and 1995 while the plaintiff was in kindergarten and year one at Woodberry Public School. The bullying complained of was carried out entirely by one student and was quite severe in nature. It involved both physical and verbal threats and acts, including an attempt to strangle the plaintiff along with an attempt to shove a jumper down his throat, which saw him lose a tooth.

The plaintiff's behaviour underwent noticeable changes as a result of the bullying. He began to suffer headaches and nightmares and commenced refusing to attend school. He became unwilling to use public change rooms or toilets when he was involved in rugby on the weekends. Upon ascertaining in 1994 that her son was being bullied at school, the plaintiff's mother informed a teacher at the school. It was alleged that the teacher agreed to "keep an eye on" the plaintiff. The plaintiff's behaviour continued to deteriorate and his mother subsequently complained to the school's principal and deputy principal, together with two administrative officers employed by the NSW Department of Education. Despite his mother's notification of various authority figures the plaintiff continued to be bullied when he attended school, which had continued detrimental effects on his behaviour and mental health. Consequently, in September 1995, his mother with drew him from the school.

While the plaintiff subsequently completed his primary schooling, he refused to attend high school and consequently his education progressed no further. The medical opinions in regard to the plaintiff's condition were not unanimous; however it was widely accepted that he suffered severe to acute Separation Anxiety Disorder, possibly in tandem with Post-

Traumatic Stress Disorder and Depression. The plaintiff's mother had a history of depressive illness and it was suggested at trial that the plaintiff was predisposed to developing similar disorders himself.

At trial it was not in dispute that the defendant owed a duty of care to the plaintiff. The plaintiff sought to establish, by way of expert evidence, that the defendant had breached its duty of care. In turn, the defendant sought to argue that the plaintiff's alleged vulnerability to mental illness was such that the plaintiff's condition was apt to occur as a result of the ordinary stresses of life, rather than being a result of the defendant's negligence. Consequently, according to the defendant, the plaintiff was unable to satisfy the factual causation test established in s 5D(1)(a) of the Civil Liability Act 2002 (NSW).

***Held:* Verdict for the plaintiff**

Per Simpson J:

1. While the evidence indicated that the plaintiff had some vulnerability to depressive illness, it did not go so far as to establish that this vulnerability would be exposed as a consequence of the ordinary stresses of life.

2. It is incorrect to assume that s 5D(1)(a) of the Civil Liability Act operates to protect a tortfeasor from the consequences of their actions in circumstances where the plaintiff has some inherent vulnerability to harm.

3. The correct formulation of s 5D(1)(a) is whether the tortfeasor's negligence, if established, was a necessary condition for the occurrence of the particular harm said to have occurred. It is not essential, for the section's purposes, that the negligence established be the sole cause of that harm.

4. The severity of the plaintiff's non-economic loss should be assessed at 50% of a most extreme case. His adolescence has been largely destroyed and his adult life is unlikely to fair any better. He has little to no chance of gaining employment, is unable to form romantic or platonic relationships, has no friends and is likely to suffer anxiety and depression for the remainder of his life.

[*Headnote by the Wolters Kluwer editors*]

D Wheelahan QC with P Biggins for the plaintiff (instructed by Whitelaw McDonald).

R Sheldon for the defendant (instructed by Makinson d'Apice).

Before: Simpson J.

Northern Territory

[¶82-705] Campbell v Northern Territory of Australia (No 3)

(2021) Aust Torts Reports ¶82-705
Medium neutral citation: [2021] FCA 1089
Federal Court of Australia
9 September 2021

Negligence — Breach of statutory duty — False imprisonment — Use of force — Battery — Assault — Custodial centres — Detainees — Defences — Independent statutory authority — Good faith exercise of powers — Time limitations — Youth Justice Act 2005 (NT), ss 153(5), 215(2), 215A and 215B.

The applicant, Mr Marley Campbell (Mr Campbell), was a member of the Kngwarraye and Aranda People who was born in August 1994 in Alice Springs. In May 2009, when he was 14 years old, Mr Campbell began a series of juvenile custodial sentences for offences committed in the Northern Territory. In particular, from April 2011 to July 2012, Mr Campbell served custodial sentences at the Alice Springs Youth Detention Centre (ASYDC), the Don Dale Youth Detention Centre in Darwin (Don Dale) and the Darwin Correctional Centre in Berrimah (the DCC). He served these sentences for a range of offences including stealing in company, causing bodily harm and robbery.

Mr Campbell made a number of claims about how he was treated during this period of detention from April 2011 to July 2012. In particular, he claimed that on the night of 7–8 April 2011, he was subject to a period of unlawful isolation at the ASYDC. More particularly, he claimed that, after lockdown at ASYDC on the night of 7–8 April 2011, he was removed from his room and was held in an "isolation cell". Mr Campbell claimed that that placement constituted false imprisonment because it had not been authorised under s 153(5) of the *Youth Justice Act 2005* (NT) (the YJ Act) which only allowed the Superintendent of the ASYDC to isolate detainees in prescribed circumstances.

On 15 October 2011, Mr Campbell was transferred from ASYDC to Don Dale and was kept there almost continuously until 9 July 2012. He claimed that this period of detention constituted a breach of the duty of care owed to him by the first respondent, the Northern Territory (the Territory) and the second respondent, the Superintendent of the Don Dale Youth Detention Centre (the Superintendent). He made this claim on the basis that he had been induced to volunteer for transfer from ASYDC to Don Dale in order to solve overcrowding at ASYDC but that he was told that he would be transferred back in 2 weeks. He further claimed to have suffered mental harm by reason of being kept at Don Dale.

Mr Campbell further claimed that he was falsely imprisoned at Don Dale on 27 December 2011 and between 2 to 9 January 2012 because neither isolation was authorised under the YJ Act. During this period, he was also transferred to the DCC where spit hoods were used to cover his face and head. The use of these spit hoods was said by Mr Campbell to constitute a battery, assault and a breach of the duty of care owed to him by the Territory and the Superintendent. Mr Campbell also made claims that he was subject to unreasonable force when he was handcuffed and restrained at Don Dale on 29 May 2012 and that such conduct also amounted to battery and assault.

In a separate claim, Mr Campbell alleged that, throughout his detention, he had suffered from an impairment of his eyesight but that there had been no testing of his visual acuity and so his impaired vision had been undetected and untreated. He alleged that the Territory, in failing to test his visual acuity, had therefore breached the duty of care it owed to him. In response, the Territory and the Superintendent denied this claim and all the other claims Mr Campbell had made. In general, they pleaded that all aspects of Mr Campbell's detention had

been reasonably justified, including periods in isolation and uses of restraints including spit hoods. They also raised 3 substantive defences:

- **The Territory claimed that, because superintendents exercised an independent statutory discretion in the management of detention centres, the Territory could not be liable, whether directly or vicariously, in relation to the claims made by Mr Campbell.**
- **Under s 215(2) of the YJ Act, the Superintendent had an immunity from action for acts which were performed in good faith and that provision applied to all the conduct which Mr Campbell had pleaded.**
- **Mr Campbell's claims were time-barred because ss 215A and 215B of the YJ Act provided that no proceedings were to be commenced in relation to an act done or omitted to be done by a person under the YJ Act more than 6 months after the act was done or the omission occurred.**

Held: application dismissed.

General principles

1. It was accepted that the Territory and the Superintendent owed a non-delegable duty of care to Mr Campbell to exercise reasonable care for his health and safety while he was held in detention. However, that duty was to be framed in terms that were consistent with the statutory scheme set out in the YJ Act. [232]–[239]

2. In addition, the *parens patriae* jurisdiction of the Courts, which imposed an obligation to protect young people from serious harm, informed the content of the duty. That jurisdiction derived from the direct responsibility of the Crown for those who could not look after themselves. [240]–[244]

3. An analysis of the objectives set out in the YJ Act revealed a range of imperatives. Superintendents were entitled to exercise discretion in the exercise of the responsibilities imposed on them under the statute. The best interests of the individual detainee were an important matter in that respect, but they are not the sole consideration. [245]–[257]

Mr Campbell's specific claims of false imprisonment, breach of duty, battery and assault

4. The evidence about the night of 7–8 April 2011 established that the purpose of placing Mr Campbell into isolation had been to avoid a conflict between he and another detainee. As such, the isolation had been for "the good order" of the ASYDC within the meaning of s 153(5) of the YJ Act and so unlawful imprisonment had not occurred. [113]–[161]

5. Mr Campbell had not identified exactly how the Territory and the Superintendent had breached the duty of care they owed him when he was transferred to Don Dale in October 2011. He may have had a sense of grievance about not being transferred back given the representations that were made to him, but that did not constitute a breach of duty. [282]–[290], [662]–[671]

6. In December 2011 and up to 2 January 2012, Mr Campbell engaged in conduct, in particular threats and aggressive behaviour, that made it especially appropriate for him to be isolated from other detainees in. It followed that his isolation at that time had been authorised under the YJ Act and so false imprisonment had not occurred. [364]–[408]

7. In relation to Mr Campbell's isolation at Don Dale between 2 to 9 January 2012, no evidence had been adduced to establish why that isolation had been necessary and the only evidence available suggested that Mr Campbell's behaviour had improved. His claim of false imprisonment had been made out for this isolation period. [409]–[473]

8. It was clear that Mr Campbell found the use of the spit hoods unpleasant and humiliating. However, the torts of assault and battery could only be made out if there was no lawful purpose for the force applied. Given Mr Campbell's preceding conduct, use of the spit hoods had been justified and so assault and battery were not established. [506]–[542]

9. Mr Campbell alleged that the spit hoods caused him discomfort including difficulty in breathing and mental harm "arising from that physical harm". However, these alleged injuries were not substantiated on the evidence and so he had also not established negligence in relation to the use of the spit hoods. [543]–[545]

10. With respect to Mr Campbell's claims about how he had been treated in May 2012, an assessment of the evidence demonstrated that any force that had been applied to him had been reasonable. He had therefore not made out his claims in assault and battery or in breach of duty. [546]–[635]

11. Mr Campbell was seen at Don Dale's medical clinic on several occasions and had ample opportunity to raise concerns about his vision but he had not done so. It also had not been established that he had suffered any damage as a consequence of the Territory's alleged failure to provide him with a visual acuity assessment. [697]–[707]

The defences of the Territory and the Superintendent

12. While the YJ Act vested specific responsibilities in superintendents, it did not indicate either explicitly or implicitly that those functions were to be discharged independently of the management, direction and control of the executive. It followed that the Territory could be held liable for the torts alleged by Mr Campbell. [775]–[806]

13. The good faith defence provided to the Superintendent under s 215(2) of the YJ Act did not apply to the conduct which led to Mr Campbell's isolation at Don Dale between 2 to 9 January 2012. It had not been shown why it had been necessary to detain Mr Campbell at that time and so it could not be presumed that the Superintendent had acted in good faith. [817]–[832]

14. Section 215B(1) of the YJ Act was the applicable iteration of the time bar which had been in force and continued to be in force. It followed that, without an extension of time (which was not pursued by Mr Campbell), all of his tort claims were statute-barred. That include his otherwise successful claim of false imprisonment in relation to the period 2 to 9 January 2012. [856]–[898]

[*Headnote by the Wolters Kluwer editors*]

P Tierney with A Perigo (Ken Cush & Associates) for the applicant.

D McLure SC with T Moses (Solicitor for the Northern Territory) for the respondents.

Before: White J.

Wolters Kluwer note: The full text of the judgment is accessible through the Federal Court of Australia database on the AustLII website.

[¶82-451] JB & Ors v Northern Territory of Australia

(2019) Aust Torts Reports ¶82-451
Medium neutral citation: [2019] NTCA 1
Supreme Court of the Norther Territory, Court of Appeal
18 February 2019

Torts — Appeal — Battery — Deployment of CS gas — Reasonable and necessary to discharge CS gas — Emergency situation — Youths handcuffed in van while being transferred to adult prison — Use of handcuffs authorised by superintendent — Youth ground stabilised for 15 minutes or thereabouts and restraints applied — Conduct of youth justice officers reasonable and necessary — Self-defence — Use of restraints to maintain order in an emergency situation — Appeals dismissed.

On 21 August 2014, an incident occurred at the Behavioural Management Unit (BMU) of Don Dale Youth Detention Centre. Five detainees in the Unit became increasingly aggressive and violent towards staff and began to smash windows and doors in the Unit. One of the boys, Jack Roper, had escaped from his cell and armed himself with a heavy fire extinguisher and

was threatening to arm the Youth Justice Officers who were trying to return him to his cell. Two of the other detainees, EA and JB, smashed a hole in their door and using a broken light bracket began to chip bits of render off the walls and throw them at staff. In order to de-escalate the situation, the Centre's supervisor, Commissioner Middlebrook agreed to deploy CS gas into the MBU to subdue Jack Roper. As a result of the disturbance and the damage caused to the BMU, the five detainees were removed and transferred to Berrimah Correctional Centre, an adult correctional facility, where they were detained for four days before being transferred to Holtze Correctional Centre.

Four of the five detainees (known as LO, EA, JB and KB) commenced proceedings in the Supreme Court of the Northern Territory against the Northern Territory claiming damages for assault and battery, but not personal injury, as a result of the incident of 21 August 2014 and subsequent events at Berrimah and Holtze. Collectively the detainees claimed assault and battery arising from seven different incidents: the incident at Don Dale on 21 August 2014 culminating in the release of CS gas into the BMU; their transfer from Don Dale to Berrimah in handcuffs, on the night of 21 August 2014; on 22 August 2014 when EA, JB and KW were taken to a medical appointment handcuffed, shackled and wearing spit hoods; an alleged assault on LO where he was grabbed by the throat and shouted at so that spit landed on his face by a prison guard at Berrimah on 23 August 2014; the transfer of all four plaintiffs from Berrimah to Holtze on 25 August 2014 handcuffed, shackled and wearing spit hoods and two alleged assaults and batteries of EA by Youth Justice Officers on 5 and 6 April 2015 where EA was held down and handcuffed.

The Territory accepted that the decision to transport the plaintiffs handcuffed shackled and wearing spit hoods on 22 August and 25 August was not reasonable or necessary and admitted liability for battery in relation to those incidents. In relation to the incident of the night of 21 August, the Territory claimed that the decision to deploy CS gas and the decision to transport the detainees handcuffed behind their backs to Berrimah was reasonable and necessary in the circumstances. In relation to the alleged assault on 23 August, the Territory denied LO's version of events and claimed that only minimal force was used and that it was reasonable and necessary in the circumstance. In relation to the alleged assaults on EA, the Territory claimed that on both occasions, the force used was reasonable and necessary in the circumstances.

In relation to damages, the plaintiffs claimed general, aggravated and exemplary damages. As a preliminary point, the Territory claimed that both aggravated and exemplary damages were precluded by s 19 of the *Personal Injuries (Liabilities and Damages) Act 2003*. The section provided that aggravated or exemplary damages must not be awarded in respect of a personal injury (as defined). The defendant's relied upon *New South Wales* v *Williamson* (2012) 248 CLR 417 to support a submission that damages for battery were damages for personal injury. However, in each statement of claim, the plaintiffs had not claimed to have suffered any injury as a result of the various batteries and assaults rather pleading they had each suffered extreme distress, humiliation, discomfort and pain.

The court found in favour of EA, JB and KW on the claim for damages for the acts of battery consisting of placing a spit hood on each of those plaintiffs, placing leg shackles on each of those plaintiffs and handcuffing each of those plaintiffs with their hands behind their backs, rather than in front on their way to the medical area at Berrimah on 22 August 2014. The court also found in favour of EA, JB, LO and KW on their claim for damages for the acts of battery consisting of placing a spit hood on each of those plaintiffs and placing leg shackles on each of those plaintiffs when travelling to Holtze on 25 August 2014. Otherwise, the court found in favour of the Territory on the balance of the claims for assault and battery, in particular battery arising out of the use of CS gas at the detention centre on 21 August 2014, and assault and battery for being handcuffed behind their backs while being transported from the detention centre to Berrimah Correctional Centre on 21 August 2014.

The appellants appealed the primary judge's specific findings as to battery arising out of the use of CS gas at the detention centre on 21 August 2014, and assault and battery for being handcuffed behind their backs while being transported from the detention centre to Berrimah Correctional Centre on 21 August 2014.

Held: appeals dismissed.

Per Southwood J and Graham AJ (with whom Riley AJ agreed):

1. The appellants submitted that the use of the CS gas at the detention centre on 21 August 2014 was unlawful because (i) it was an offence contrary to s 6 of the *Weapons Control Act*, and (ii) the trial Judge erred in finding that the exemption under s 12(2) of the *Weapons Control Act* applied to the prison officer's use of the CS gas. Under ground 4, the appellants contend that the trial Judge erred in holding that the power of the superintendent under s 152(1) of the *Youth Justice Act* (to do what was necessary and convenient for the performance of his functions under the Act) was *not* limited by s 153(3)(b) of the Act (which excluded enforced dosing with a medicine, drug or other substance for the purpose of maintaining discipline). [94]

2. The appellants have misinterpreted the relevant provisions of the *Weapons Control Act*, the *Prisons (Correctional Services) Act* and the *Youth Justice Act*. The interpretation and application of the relevant statutory provisions adopted by her Honour the trial Judge was correct. [109]

3. As a matter of common sense, it is apparent that Prisoner Office Flavell did not deploy the CS gas to discipline Jake Roper but to momentarily restrain him in order to restore order and ensure the safe custody of detainees and the protection of all persons within the precincts of the detention centre. This is made abundantly clear by the proclamation that was made by Prison Officer Lovegrove. [129]

4. From time to time, CS gas is deployed in emergency situations in prisons and detention centres across Australia to *restrain* an unruly detainee and restore order and protect detainees and others within the precincts of those institutions. As was conceded by the appellants, such an action would ordinarily fall within the scope of the powers granted by s 151(3)(c) and s 152(1) of the *Youth Justice Act* but for the interpretation they give to s 153(3)(b) of the Act, and their submission that the deployment of the CS gas was a disciplinary act. As is apparent from what we have stated, we do not consider the deployment of the CS gas to be a disciplinary act. Further, while s 153(2) and (3) of the Act regulate what may be done when a superintendent is exercising his disciplinary powers, and s 153(4) and (5) regulate the circumstances in which handcuffs may be used to restrain detainees and place them in isolation, none of those provisions regulate the superintendents' actions when he is otherwise exercising his powers under s 151(3)(c) and s 152(1) of the Act. The superintendent had power under s 152(1) of the *Youth Justice Act* to deploy the CS gas on 21 August 2014 provided it was reasonable and necessary to do so for the purposes of s 151(3)(c) of the Act. He was not prevented from doing so by s 152(1) of the *Youth Justice Act*. However, independent of the *Youth Justice Act*, s 6 of the *Weapons Control Act* prevented him from doing so personally but only because he was not a prescribed person under s 12(1) of that Act. Whereas Prison Officer Flavell was a prescribed person and was exempted from the application of s 6 of the *Weapons Control Act*. [130]

5. The use of the canister to deploy the CS gas by Prison Officer Flavell was necessary and reasonable conduct which was undertaken to maintain order and ensure the safe custody of the detainees at the detention centre and the protection of all persons in the detention centre. Prison Officer Flavell was acting within the scope of the power granted to the superintendent under s 152(1) of the *Youth Justice Act* and within the powers delegated to him under s 157(2) of the Act. Prison Officer Flavell was acting within the scope of his duties as a prisoner officer when he deployed the CS gas which was supplied to him by his employer for the purposes of assisting in an emergency situation at the detention centre. [135]

6. Under ground 3 of the appeal, the appellants submitted that for the respondent to be able to rely on s 157(2) of the *Youth Justice Act* as the basis of the prison officers' lawful authority to deploy the CS gas and handcuff the appellants on 21 August 2014, the respondent must establish that the powers under s 157(2) of the Act were invoked. The respondent failed to do so because there is no evidence about a call from the superintendent for assistance from the prison officers who deployed the CS gas and handcuffed the appellants. The appellants submitted that, in the circumstances, the precondition to the exercise of power under s 157(2) of the Act — prison officers being called upon by the superintendent to assist — was not made out. This ground of appeal also fails. There was evidence that the superintendent called upon the prison officers to assist. [144]–[145]

7. As to ground 5 of the appeal, that there was a lack of statutory authority for the application of handcuffs to the appellants while being transported by prison van from the detention centre to Berrimah Correctional Centre on 21 August 2014, the court accepts the respondent's submission. [159]

8. It was well established that the appellants were handcuffed under the powers granted by s 152(1) and s 157(2) of the *Youth Justice Act* for the purpose of restoring order and ensuring their safety and the safety of others and that thereafter the handcuffs were not removed when the appellants were to be transferred in the van to the Berrimah Correctional Centre. Due to the circumstances in which the handcuffing occurred, the resolution of this aspect of the appeal is not contingent on it being established that the superintendent's approval under s 155 of the *Youth Justice Act* preceded the handcuffing. The critical factor is that the superintendent's approval preceded the transfer of the appellants to the Berrimah Correctional Centre. For the reasons, we have stated above we find that it did. [174]

[*Headnote by the Wolters Kluwer editors*]

B Walker SC with K Foley (North Australian Aboriginal Justice Agency) for the Appellants.

D McLure SC with T Moses (Solicitor for the Northern Territory) for the Respondent.

Before: Southwood J, Riley AJ and Graham AJ.

[¶82-410] Street v Arafura Helicopters Pty Ltd t/as Alice Springs Helicopters

(2018) Aust Torts Reports ¶82-410
Medium neutral citation: [2018] NTCA 11
Supreme Court of the Northern Territory Court of Appeal
16 August 2018

AVIATION — Civil Aviation — Claim for damages caused by injury arising out of helicopter accident — Limitation period — Right of person to damages extinguished — Appeal dismissed — Civil Aviation (Carriers' Liability) Act 1959 (Cth), s 34

PRACTICE AND PROCEDURE — Supreme Court procedure — Period of limitation — When proceedings "brought" for purposes of limitation period — Originating motion — Writs — Whether date of filing is the date the documents are received or date they are accepted as filed by the proper officer — unnecessary to decide — Proper officer did not in fact accept the documents lodged — Appeal dismissed — Civil Aviation (Carriers' Liability) Act 1959 (Cth), s 34.

On 12 November 2013, Ryan Street was a passenger in a Bell 206 helicopter operated by Arafura Helicopters Pty Ltd t/as Alice Springs Helicopters and flown by a pilot employed by Arafura. About one hour into the flight, the pilot told Mr Street that the helicopter was going down and that he should brace for impact. The helicopter hit the ground and Mr Street suffered serious injuries.

Mr Street commenced proceedings in the Supreme Court of the Northern Territory against Arafura, in negligence and claimed damages. Arafura denied liability. It also argued

that liability had been extinguished under s 34 of the *Civil Aviation (Carriers' Liability) Act 1959* (Cth) because the claim was not brought within two years after the date of the accident.

It was common ground that the material date for the purpose of the application of s 34 was 12 November 2013 so that the two-year period expired at midnight on 12 November 2015.

Following a change in legal representation, on 18 December 2015, Mr Street's new solicitors filed an originating process that was in accordance with the Supreme Court Rules and was accepted by the Supreme Court Registry. The issue became whether the originating process could be backdated to an earlier date, and therefore within the limitation period.

His Honour Southwood J noted that the jurisdiction of the Supreme Court is invoked when a Writ is delivered to the Alice Springs Supreme Court Registry and is accepted by a Proper Officer of the Court. On the evidence, this only occurred on 18 December 2015 (five weeks after the limitation period). None of the documents filed before that date were accepted by the Registrar. Accordingly, Southwood J found that Mr Street's claim was extinguished by the operation of s 34 of the Civil Aviation (Carriers' Liability) Act.

Mr Street appealed the primary judge's findings. He argued that it is the date of lodgement of the Writ or originating motion at the registry and not the date of acceptance which determines when a proceeding is commenced, and accordingly within the limitation period.

***Held:* appeal dismissed**

Per Kelly, Barr and Hiley JJ:

1. The primary judge was correct in determining that the Proper Officer did not accept the documents for filing, and it cannot be inferred that the documents were accepted for filing when they were returned to the lodging party and an email sent advising that the documents had been rejected. [59]

2. The primary judge was correct to find that the first document to be delivered to the registry and accepted for filing was the writ which was filed on 18 December 2015, and out of time. [62]

3. The primary judge was correct to hold that while the registry in the Supreme Court in Alice Springs had a practice of backdating originating process that had not been formatted correctly, and did so in this case, there is no power to do so.

[*Headnote by the Wolters Kluwer editors*]

N Christrup (HWL Ebsworth) for the appellant.

A Wyvill SC with M Littlejohn (Piper Ellis) for the respondent.

Before: Kelly, Barr and Hiley JJ.

[¶82-240] Alcan Gove Pty Ltd v Zabic

(2015) Aust Torts Reports ¶82-240

Medium neutral citation: [2015] HCA 33

High Court of Australia

Judgment delivered 07 October 2015

Limitation of actions — When cause of action accrues — Negligence — Damage — Statute abolished cause of action unless accrued before 1 January 1987 — Whether compensable damage suffered upon changes to mesothelial cells following exposure to asbestos — Whether mesothelioma inevitable — Relevance of hindsight — Whether "trigger" for development of disease endogenous or exogenous.

Torts — Negligence — Damage — Dust diseases — Mesothelioma — Whether changes to mesothelial cells compensable damage — Workers Rehabilitation and Compensation Act (NT), ss 52, 189.

Mr Zorko Zabic was employed by Alcan Gove Pty Ltd as a manual labourer at its alumina refinery from 1974–1977. Mr Zabic regularly carried out repairs and maintenance of the network of pipelines at the refinery, which were insulated with asbestos lagging. Mr Zabic removed asbestos lagging from pipes on hundreds of occasions during the period 1974–1977 and ingested asbestos dust and fibres. In November 2013, Mr Zabic began to experience chest pain and shortness of breath. A few months later, in January 2014, he was diagnosed with malignant mesothelioma.

Mr Zabic commenced proceedings in the Supreme Court of the Northern Territory against Alcan in negligence and claimed damages. He argued that Alcan was negligent in exposing him to asbestos dust and fibres when it knew of the dangers, and failed to take any precautions for his safety. Mr Zabic also argued that the cause of action arose with the inhalation of the asbestos dust, (in 1974–1977) which caused changes to the mesothelial cells, as opposed to when the symptoms of mesothelioma developed (in 2013) and on that basis arose before the commencement of the *Workers Rehabilitation and Compensation Act 1986* (NT) (the Act).

Although Alcan admitted that Mr Zabic's malignant mesothelioma was an injury within the meaning of the Act and relevantly, a disease arising out of Mr Zabic's employment with Alcan, it argued that Mr Zabic's action was statute barred and was not preserved by s 189 of the Act. It argued that Mr Zabic did not suffer compensable damage until the onset of the malignancy process, most likely in 2009 and on that basis, the claim was statute barred because the cause of action did not arise before the commencement of the Act, namely 1 January 1987.

The primary judge, his Honour Barr J, found that although Alcan was negligent and Alcan's breach of duty of care caused Mr Zabic's malignant mesothelioma, the claim was statute barred pursuant to s 52 of the Act, on the basis that the cause of action arose with the onset of the malignancy process, which was after 1 January 1987, and was not preserved by s 189 of the Act. His Honour found that the cause of action arose at the malignant transformation stage, and not at the time of Mr Zabic's ingestion of the asbestos fibres and when changes to the mesothelial cells commenced. The initial mesothelial cell changes were not compensable damage. His Honour found that Mr Zabic had not suffered compensable damage until well after 1987 and that his claim was statute barred.

Mr Zabic appealed the primary judge's findings. The Supreme Court of the Northern Territory Court of Appeal upheld the medical evidence, which established that exposure to asbestos caused changes in Mr Zabic's mesothelial cells at the time of ingestion, well prior to 1987, and found that those changes were the start of a process that resulted in Mr Zabic suffering from malignant mesothelioma. The changes to the mesothelial cells, which constituted damage that was material had a causative relationship to the subsequent symptoms and suffering of malignant mesothelioma.

The court found that the cause of action and the compensable damage arose in 1974 when the asbestos fibres were first ingested and caused changes in Mr Zabic's mesothelial cells, and not when he developed malignant mesothelioma (most likely in 2009). On the basis that the cause of action arose in 1974 and prior to the commencement of the Act, the court upheld Mr Zabic's appeal and found that the claim was *not* statute barred. The court also noted that hindsight is permitted in determining when a cause of action accrues, and that injury or damage can be material although it is unknown or symptomless.

By grant of special leave, Alcan appealed to the High Court. Alcan relied on the decision of *Orica Ltd* v *CGU Insurance Ltd* (2003) 59 NSWLR 14 and argued that the risk of

mesothelioma is not compensable damage, and that any departure from such a view would likely be productive of widespread ramifications.

Held: **appeal dismissed with costs.**

Per French CJ, Kiefel, Bell, Keane and Nettle JJ:

1. The Court of Appeal was correct in finding that it was possible, with the benefit of hindsight, to say that the damage done to the mesothelial cells was compensable damage sufficient to found a cause of action, and the subsequent development of malignant mesothelioma was part of the damage in the accrued cause of action.

2. Mr Zabic's mesothelial cells were so damaged shortly after inhalation of asbestos fibres between 1974–1977 and inevitably lead to the eventual onset of the malignant mesothelioma and on that basis, the initial cell changes amounted to compensable damage.

3. The question was whether it could be inferred in hindsight that a cause of action had accrued before it could have been detected. On the evidence, there was no reason in fact why it could not be inferred that there were initial molecular changes in the mesothelial cells which preceded the appearance of symptoms of mesothelioma, and that those initial changes led to mesothelioma.

4. The cause of action in negligence accrued when the initial mesothelial cell changes occurred (and prior to the relevant date of 1 January 1987) and damages for the mesothelioma from which Mr Zabic now suffered are recoverable in that cause of action.

5. Initial cell changes do not develop into mesothelioma without a trigger and, based on the expert evidence, once the initial mesothelial cell changes had occurred the trigger already existed or was bound to occur. The Court of Appeal was correct in finding that the trigger was endogenous.

[*Headnote by the Wolters Kluwer editors*]

G Watson SC with J Sheller (instructed by Bartier Perry) for the appellant.

B Walker SC with G Little SC (instructed by Shine Lawyers) for the respondent.

Before: French CJ, Kiefel, Bell, Keane and Nettle JJ.

[¶81-966] Imbree v Mcneilly; Mcneilly v Imbree

(2008) Aust Torts Reports ¶81-966;
Medium neutral citation: [2008] HCA 40
High Court of Australia
Judgment delivered 28 August 2008

Torts — Negligence — Standard of care — Where passenger undertakes to supervise inexperienced driver — Whether standard of care owed by inexperienced driver to supervising passenger is lower than that owed by a reasonably competent driver — Whether authority of Cook v Cook (1986) 162 CLR 376 still stands — Relevance of compulsory third party insurance in defining standard of care.

The appellant, Paul Anthony Imbree, suffered serious injuries when the vehicle in which he was a passenger overturned on a gravel road in the Northern Territory. At the time of the accident, he was supervising the driving of the first respondent, Jesse McNeilly. The appellant was aware of the fact that the first respondent, who was sixteen years old, had little driving experience and did not hold either a driving licence or a learner's permit.

The appellant brought proceedings against the first respondent as driver and the second respondent as owner of the vehicle. The trial judge, having rejected the respondents' contention that the appellant had voluntarily assumed the risk of injury, found in favour of the appellant. However, the award of more than $9.5 million in damages was reduced by 30% on account of contributory negligence.

On appeal (*McNeiily* v *Imbree* (2007) Aust Torts Reports ¶81-895), the NSW Court of Appeal applied the principle established in *Cook* v *Cook* (1986) 162 CLR 376, that where an unlicensed learner driver is driving a vehicle under the supervision of a passenger who is fully aware of the driver's inexperience, the duty of care owed to such a passenger was limited to that reasonably to be expected of an unqualified and inexperienced driver in the circumstances. The majority (Beazley and Basten JJA; Tobias J dissenting) found that the driver had breached this standard of care, though the court went on to hold that the appellant's contribution for contributory negligence should be assessed as two-thirds.

On appeal to the High Court, the appellant submitted that Cook v Cook should be overruled, and that the first respondent owed the same objective standard of care as that of a licensed driver. On this objective standard, the apportionment of responsibility calculated by the Court of Appeal was a distortion.

Held: Appeal allowed.

Per Gummow, Hayne and Kiefel JJ (with whom Gleeson CJ, Kirby and Crennan JJ agreed)

1. The standard of care which a learner driver owes a supervising passenger is the same as that of any other person driving a motor vehicle: to take reasonable care to avoid injury to others. The standard is that of the "reasonable driver": Cook v Cook overruled.

2. Basic considerations of principle require that the distinction drawn in Cook v Cook should no longer be treated as expressing any distinct principle in the law of negligence. A plaintiff may occupy the position of a supervising passenger, a regular passenger with no supervisory role, or another road user; in all cases, however, the plaintiff is entitled to expect that the learner driver will take reasonable care in operating the vehicle.

3. A plaintiff's awareness that the defendant's driving may not meet the standard of the reasonable person may constitute a step toward demonstrating voluntary assumption of risk, but it is neither sufficient nor conclusive of itself.

4. A plaintiff's actual knowledge that a defendant may not use reasonable care goes to issues of contributory negligence. It is not a basis for concluding that some lesser standard should be applied to the duty of care owed by the defendant to the plaintiff.

5. The appellant's failure to advise the first respondent to do nothing sudden when driving on a dirt road amounted to a want of care for his own safety.

6. The issue of apportionment for contributory negligence depends upon the extent to which the departure from what was required of the appellant and the first respondent caused or contributed to the appellant's damage. In attributing an apportionment of two-thirds, the Court of Appeal had measured the responsibility of the first respondent against a lesser standard of care than that of the reasonable driver.

7. It was appropriate to substitute an apportionment of 30% contributory negligence to the appellant.

Per Gleeson CJ

8. A driver being supervised by another does not owe a lower standard of care to the supervisor than to anybody else, though as a matter of logic the supervisor may be more likely than others to be affected by contributory negligence.

Per Gleeson CJ (Kirby J disagreeing)

9. The issue of the standard of care owed by an inexperienced driver to a supervising passenger is one of common law principle. The existence of a scheme of compulsory third party insurance is not directly relevant in resolving this issue.

Per Kirby J

10. The existence of a statutory framework establishing a compulsory scheme of third party insurance for drivers of motor vehicles was a relevant consideration in determining the scope of the first respondent's common law liability.

11. The reliance of Cook v Cook on the now superseded criterion of "proximity", together with the existence of compulsory motor vehicle third party insurance, justifies a departure from the individual culpability principle established by Cook, and the adoption instead of a single, universal and objective standard of care for drivers of motor vehicles.

Per Heydon J

12. The Court of Appeal had failed to show any error on the part of the primary judge to warrant an alteration in the extent of contribution for contributory negligence. The orders of the primary judge apportioning 30% contributory negligence to the appellant should therefore be restored.

13. As it was not necessary to consider the correctness of Cook v Cook from the point of view of liability in this case, opinion on this point should be reserved.

[*Headnote by the Wolters Kluwer editors*]

AS Morrison SC with MR Hall and AJ Stone for the appellant (instructed by Abrahms Turner Whelan Family Lawyers).

KP Rewell SC with MA Cleary for the respondent (instructed by TL Lawyers).

Before: Gleeson CJ, Gummow, Kirby, Hayne, Heydon, Crennan and Kiefel JJ.

Queensland

[¶82-696] Medlin v Nominal Defendant

(2021) Aust Torts Reports ¶82-696
Medium neutral citation: [2021] QSC 186
Supreme Court of Queensland
5 August 2021

Motor vehicle accident — Unidentified drivers — Nominal defendant — Disputed versions of events — Onus of proof — Credibility of witnesses — Expert evidence — Plaintiff suffered personal injuries when vehicle he was driving crashed into a vehicle ahead of him — Reason for collision was disputed — Plaintiff claimed that an unidentified red vehicle was driving ahead of him and swerved left just prior to collision — Proceedings were commenced by plaintiff against Nominal Defendant in lieu of unidentified driver of red car — Nominal defendant pleaded that there had been no red car immediately prior to collision — Plaintiff bore onus of proof of establishing existence of red car — No other witness attested to seeing red car prior to collision — Civil Liability Act 2003 (Qld), ss 11, 22, 23, 24 — Motor Accidents Insurance Act 1994, ss 31, 33, 37.

On 1 December 2014, a vehicle being driven by the plaintiff, Mr Darren Medlin (Mr Medlin), was involved in a collision with the vehicle being driven by Mr Hayden Finn (Mr Finn). The collision occurred on a 2-lane road near Yeppoon in Queensland. Mr Finn's vehicle was stationary in his lane as he waited for a break in the oncoming traffic to make a right-hand turn into an adjacent property. Mr Medlin was travelling behind Mr Finn and initially did not see his stationary vehicle. As a consequence, the 2 vehicles collided and Mr Medlin suffered serious injuries. Mr Finn, and his mother (Ms Finn) who was travelling in the vehicle with him, were also injured.

While those aspects of the accident were undisputed, the explanation for why Mr Medlin had not seen Mr Finn's vehicle at an earlier point was contentious. Mr Medlin claimed that, just before the collision had occurred, he had been travelling behind an unidentified red car. He further claimed that the red car "suddenly, and without warning, sharply swerved to its left, off the roadway". It was only then that Mr Medlin saw the stationary vehicle of Mr Finn which was waiting to make a right-hand turn. But by that time it was too late to avoid the collision. The unidentified red car did not stop at the scene but instead continued along the road beyond Mr Finn's vehicle.

Mr Medlin commenced proceedings in the Supreme Court of Queensland against the Nominal Defendant claiming that the driver of the unidentified red car had been negligent and had been responsible for the collision. The Nominal Defendant denied liability on the basis that there had been no red car involved in the incident. In that regard, the Nominal Defendant placed particular reliance on the evidence given by Mr Finn and Ms Finn, both of whom were adamant that there had been no red car travelling behind them just prior to the collision. The Nominal Defendant also claimed that, even if there had been a red car involved, it had not been established that its driver's negligence was a cause of the accident.

Held: judgment for defendant.

1. Mr Medlin was an honest witness overall although his evidence suffered from reconstruction based on what he thought he would have done, rather than him recalling what had occurred. On some details of what happened he was vague and there were also some inconsistencies between his evidence and his statement to police in December 2014. [29]–[32]

2. Ms Finn attested that it was her practice to look in the passenger side rear view mirror whenever they were turning into the property. That was because both she and Mr Finn were

aware of the dangers posed by making the right-hand turn. She was consistent in her evidence that the only car she had seen behind them was Mr Medlin's vehicle. [39]–[54]

3. Mr Finn also attested that he had been looking in the driver's rear-view mirror immediately before the collision occurred, although he was also keeping an eye on oncoming traffic as he waited for an opportunity to turn. Mr Finn had also been consistent in his evidence that he only ever saw Mr Medlin's vehicle. [55]–[62]

4. The collision was witnessed by another motorist, Mr Adrian Evans, who was passed by Mr Medlin's vehicle. When that happened, Mr Evans considered that the vehicle was going very fast because he himself was going at the speed limit of 100 kmph. Just before the collision occurred, Mr Evans did not see any red car. [71]–[100]

5. The evidence of the attending police officer did not shed any light on the question of whether a red car had obscured Mr Medlin's view immediately prior to the collision. In addition, expert reports (which were filed by both parties) were equivocal because they did not purport to determine the existence of the red car. [102]–[109]

6. Mr Medlin bore the onus of proving the case that he had pleaded on the balance of probabilities, including the existence of the red car. In that context, the issue was not simply whether witnesses were honest (given that all witnesses in the proceeding had generally been honest) but also the extent to which they were reliable. [110]–[111]

7. The evidence did not establish the existence of a red car on the balance of probabilities. The only person who claimed to have seen it immediately before the collision was Mr Medlin. While that may have been his honest belief, the more likely explanation was that the memory of the red car amounted to a reconstruction on his part. [112]–[133]

8. If a red car had suddenly swerved just prior to the collision, it was highly likely that it would have been seen by other witnesses. Although some allowance was to be given for the fact that Mr and Ms Finn were pursuing separate claims again Mr Medlin, it was inconceivable that no other witness would have seen it. Mr Medlin had therefore not proved his pleaded case. [134]–[142]

[*Headnote by the Wolters Kluwer editors*]

MT O'Sullivan (Shine Lawyers) for the plaintiff.

GO'Driscoll (Jensen McConaghy Lawyers) for the defendant.

Before: Brown J.

[¶82-625] Mallonland Pty Ltd & Anor v Advanta Seeds Pty Ltd

(2021) Aust Torts Reports ¶82-625
Medium neutral citation: [2021] QSC 74
Supreme Court of Queensland
9 April 2021

Pure economic loss — Negligent acts, omissions or misrepresentations — Duty of care — Where the plaintiffs grew grain sorghum as part of their farming businesses — Where the defendant carried on business producing and selling seeds for commercial planting, including grain sorghum seed — Contaminated seed — Whether, "but for" the defendant's failures, growers would have avoided the loss suffered — Limitation of actions — Civil Liability Act 2002 (NSW), ss 5B, 5C, 5D — Civil Liability Act 2003 (Qld), ss 9, 10, 11 — Civil Proceedings Act 2011 (Qld), ss 103V, 103W, 103X — Limitation Act 1969 (NSW), s 14 — Limitation of Actions Act 1974 (Qld), s 10.

The plaintiffs, Mallonland Pty Ltd (as trustee for the Andrew Jenner Family Trust) ("Mallonland") and ME & JL Nitschke Pty Ltd (as trustee for the Nitschke Family Trust) ("ME & JL") grew crops, including grain sorghum, as part of their farming businesses.

The defendant, Advanta Seeds Pty Ltd carried on business selling seeds it produced for commercial planting by farmers, including grain sorghum seed. It was a subsidiary of a multi-national company.

Mallonland grew grain sorghum in the summer of 2010–11 from seed produced by the defendant and acquired from a distributor to whom the defendant supplied the seed for on-sale. In late 2010, Mallonland purchased ten 20 kg bags of contaminated seed from a distributor of the defendant's products and planted the contaminated seed on the Jenner properties. In late 2011, Mallonland purchased seven 20 kg bags of uncontaminated seed from the defendant's distributor and planted from both the contaminated seed and the uncontaminated seed on the Jenner properties in the same areas.

From May 2012, an off-type species of sorghum plant, referred to as "shattercane", grew on the Jenner properties. From the end of 2012, Mallonland ceased growing sorghum on the affected areas of the Jenner properties (apart from 36 hectares in the 2014–15 summer season).

ME & JL planted approximately 100 hectares of area with contaminated seed in September 2010. In early September 2011, ME & JL purchased seed of a different variety from the distributor and planted a 2011–12 summer season sorghum crop. In around December 2011 or January 2012, it was noticed that off-type plants were growing between the rows and it was believed that they must have come from the planting in the previous 2010–11 summer season.

The plaintiffs commenced representative proceedings against the defendant and alleged that the seed they purchased was contaminated with seed of another subspecies and that the contamination occurred because of the negligence of the defendant in producing the seed sold in 2010 for the 2010–11 summer season. Alternatively, they claimed that the defendant engaged in misleading or deceptive conduct in connection with the supply of that seed. The representative proceeding was tried under Pt 13A of the *Civil Proceedings Act 2010* (Qld).

The defendant admitted that it produced 5 relevant batches of seed for the 2010–11 summer season that contained .03% Australian grassy off-type sorghum or "shattercane". However, the defendant denied the existence of any duty of care owed to any of the plaintiffs or any group member. It argued that there was no reasonably foreseeable risk of economic loss to the plaintiffs or any group members prior to in or about February 2011, that the label attached to each bag of seed stated the contents of each bag, that the terms on the bag stated the purchasing grower's rights and the defendant's obligations in respect thereof, and there was not an established category or any other circumstance going to policy to ground the existence of a duty of care. The defendant relied on the terms on the bags to exclude a duty of care in negligence to the plaintiffs and group members.

Held: plaintiffs' claim dismissed.

1. The issues of fact raise and inform a question of law as to whether the defendant owed a duty of care in negligence to any of the plaintiffs and group members to avoid the risk of economic loss of the kind claimed by the plaintiffs and group members in relation to the supply of the contaminated seed. A critical aspect of the issues was the contractual matrix in which the disputed duty of care was said to arise. [109]

2. The defendant did not sell seed directly to growers. Seeds were sold or supplied to distributors who were also referred to as resellers, suppliers or agents. There were hundreds of such distributors around Australia who sold the defendant's seeds. Some were independently owned businesses and others were nationally owned by companies. The defendant supplied the seed to distributors in 2 categories — by straight out sale or on consignment. [110]

3. The defendant alleged that terms were marked on the bags of contaminated seed including conditions of sale and use. The defendant did not allege or submit that by a plaintiff or group member opening the bag and using the seed, a contract was made between the

plaintiff or group member and the defendant under which the plaintiff or group member agreed to those terms and conditions. But it relied on the terms on the bags to exclude a duty of care in negligence to the plaintiffs and group members. The defendant alleged that each of the bags of contaminated seed (and other grain sorghum seed sold by the defendant) bore the terms. On the evidence, it was more likely than not that the contaminated seed bags did bear the terms alleged. The terms on the bag were not proved to be terms of the contract of sale of the contaminated seed by a distributor to any of the plaintiffs or group members. [126]–[140]

4. The unusual aspect of this case in relation to the organising principles of the tort of negligence was that the alleged duty of care was one to avoid economic loss owed by a producer or manufacturer of goods to an end user where the producer or manufacturer was not in a direct contractual relationship with the end user. Liability of a producer or manufacturer of goods to an end user in negligence for physical loss or damage has been a central concern of the law of negligence. But when it comes to loss or damage constituted by economic loss only, the path to liability in negligence has been more difficult: *Brookfield Multiplex Ltd* v *Owners Corporation Strata Plan 61288 & Anor* (2014) 254 CLR 185; *Barclay* v *Penberthy* (2012) 246 CLR 258; *Woolcock Street Investments Pty Ltd* v *CDG Pty Ltd* (2004) 216 CLR 515; *Perre* v *Apand Pty Ltd* (1999) 198 CLR 180. [141], [142]

5. It may be unrealistic, in many consumer-like transactions constituting a sale (and purchase) of or supply (and acquisition) of goods, to expect that the buyer from a producer or distributor of a thing is in a bargaining position to extract a warranty from the seller against a defect in the quality of the goods purchased that would protect against economic loss, that is not provided for by statute. Similarly, a retailer may be unlikely to agree to provide a contractual warranty to the buyer against the risk of such loss based on the quality of the goods if it cannot extract for itself, as buyer, a similar warranty from the producer or distributor as seller. An everyday commercial transaction of sale of goods, like the purchase of seed for agriculture by a grower from a distributor, may test the logical utility or limits of the concept of vulnerability as a salient factor in determining whether a duty of care is owed by the producer of seed to the grower as end user against economic loss if the seed is contaminated. [189]–[191]

Duty of care

6. The defendant's submission that the terms on the bag operated as a disclaimer of an assumption of responsibility to negate the existence of a duty of care to avoid economic loss that the seed supplied would be free of contamination by shattercane or grassy off-types should be accepted. [204], [205]

7. The plaintiffs did not establish that, for the tort of negligence, the defendant owed a duty of care to the plaintiffs to take reasonable care to avoid the risk of economic loss of increased expenses of farming operations and decreased revenue from sorghum sales if seed was contaminated by shattercane or other off-type grassy sorghum plants. [206]

Negligence — breach of duty

8. The plaintiffs alleged that the defendant failed to take reasonable precautions to avoid the risk of harm to the plaintiffs and group members through the sale of seed that was contaminated with off-type plant seeds. [333]–[337]

9. It was not in dispute that the relevant 2010–11 summer season seed batches were contaminated with seed from an off-type plant, although the precise classification of that plant and the extent of the contamination were disputed questions. The precise source of the contamination was also disputed. The more likely inference was that the contamination occurred in the 2010 production of seed for the 2010–11 summer season seed. That seed was produced by Cavaso Farming. Assuming there was no external source of contamination of the 2010 seed produced by Cavaso Farming after harvest, the relevant hypothesis was that the Cavaso Farming seed production crop included plants that were of the off-type or were fertilised by pollen from an off-type plant that resulted in contaminated seed in the relevant

2010 seed batches. Further, the inference that followed was that the rogueing of the early 2010 Cavaso Farming production was not carried out carefully enough to prevent the contamination of the 2010–11 summer season seed that did occur. Even though there was an absence of specific evidence of failure by the defendant's staff to follow the rogueing protocols provided for in the Seed Production Manual, the better inference to draw on the whole of the evidence was that there was a failure to exercise a reasonable standard of care by the defendant in rogueing the early 2010 Cavaso Farming seed production crop. [338]–[353]

10. A ''grow out'' is an expression that refers to planting and growing a sample of seed from a production batch to assess whether, inter alia, the batch is contaminated with off-type or weed seed. Until 2006, the defendant conducted grow outs of samples of the sorghum seed it produced for commercial sale as part of its usual business practices. From 2006, the defendant discontinued that practice. After the 2010–11 and 2011–12 summer seasons, which were the subject of this case, the defendant reintroduced the practice of conducting grow outs of samples of the sorghum seed it produced for commercial sale. Under ss 9 and 10 of the *Civil Liability Act 2003* (Qld) and their equivalents in New South Wales, the fact of the change in practice by the defendant was not an admission. Nevertheless, the fact that grow outs were conducted before 2006 and that they were reintroduced as a result of the change in policy introduced in or about 2011, together with the feasibility and cost of the practice of a commercial grow out procedure, lead to a finding that the defendant failed to act with reasonable care in failing to conduct a commercial grow out of the contaminated seed in the winter of 2010 before it was sent to market and sold for the 2010–11 summer season. [355]–[367]

Alternative finding

11. Assuming (against the contrary finding) that the defendant owed a duty of care in negligence to the plaintiffs and group members and having regard to the finding that the defendant breached the standard of care in negligence for such a duty by failing to conduct a grow out, the next question was whether the breach of duty was causative of the harm to the plaintiffs and sample group members. The determination of that question for the tort of negligence required the court to consider the elements of factual causation and scope of liability. [476]

12. Factual causation was proved by the plaintiffs in respect of the plaintiffs and the sample group members. Had the defendant conducted a grow out of the contaminated seed after production of that seed, it was more likely than not that the contamination would have been revealed and the defendant would not have supplied that seed into the market and would have recalled any of the relevant batches that may already have been sent to distributors before the plaintiffs or sample group members had planted that seed. [479]

13. Assuming (against the contrary finding) that the defendant owed a duty of care in negligence to the plaintiffs and group members and having regard to the finding that the defendant breached the standard of care in negligence for such a duty by failing to rogue the Cavaso Farming production block, it followed that the plaintiffs and sample group members suffered loss or damage from that breach of duty, because had the rogueing been carried out with proper skill and care it was more likely than not that the contamination would not have occurred. [480]

[*Headnote by the Wolters Kluwer editors*]

D Campbell QC, N Andreatidis QC and B Hall (Creevey Russell Lawyers) for the plaintiffs.

P Dunning QC, G Beacham QC, E Goodwin, L Judd, M Barnes and M Brooks (Creevey Russell Lawyers) for the defendant.

Before: Jackson J.

Wolters Kluwer Note: The full text of the judgment is accessible through the Supreme Court of Queensland database on the AustLII website.

[¶82-553] Queensland v Masson

(2020) Aust Torts Reports ¶82-553

Medium neutral citation: [2020] HCA 28

High Court of Australia

13 August 2020

Negligence — Standard of care — Breach — Where woman suffering severe asthma attack treated by ambulance officers including intensive care paramedic — Where intensive care paramedic elected to administer intravenous (IV) salbutamol rather than IV adrenaline in initial phase of treatment due to woman's high heart rate and high blood pressure — Where Clinical Practice Manual (CPM) required that ambulance officers "consider" IV adrenaline — Whether decision to administer IV salbutamol contrary to CPM — Whether treatment fell below standard of care expected of ordinary skilled intensive care paramedic — Whether trial judge's finding that intensive care paramedic made clinical judgment to administer adrenaline "contrary to compelling inferences" or "glaringly improbable" — Whether administration of IV salbutamol supported by responsible body of opinion within medical profession.

On 21 July 2002, 25-year-old Jennifer Masson, who was a chronic asthmatic, drove to the home of her friend Jonathon Turner in Brinsmead, Cairns. On walking into the house, she was wheezing badly and announced she was returning to her car, apparently to look for her Ventolin puffer. When she returned to the house, she asked Mr Turner to take her to the hospital. As they walked outside, Ms Masson collapsed on the front lawn. Another friend who was present telephoned for an ambulance and Mr Turner performed mouth-to-mouth resuscitation.

Ambulance officers arrived six minutes after the call. Ms Masson was noted to be in respiratory arrest and hypoxic. The ambulance officer, Mr Peters, applied an intravenous (IV) cannula and one minute after arrival he commenced administering IV salbutamol. Ms Masson was loaded into the ambulance to be transported to hospital. However, during the ambulance ride, cardiac arrest was imminent, so Mr Peters administered 300 micrograms of adrenaline. Ms Masson suffered severe hypoxic brain damage as a result of oxygen deprivation. It was not in dispute that this was caused as a result of events prior to her arrival at hospital. She was catastrophically brain damaged and remained in around-the-clock care for more than 13 years up until her death in 2016.

Ms Masson's estate commenced proceedings in the Supreme Court of Queensland against the State of Queensland, in negligence and claimed damages. It argued that the deprivation of oxygen giving rise to the hypoxic brain injury occurred in the course of her treatment by the ambulance officers because adrenaline was not administered during the initial phase of her treatment at the scene. The State denied liability. It argued that Ms Masson's severe hypoxic brain damage had already irreversibly occurred prior to intervention by the ambulance officers. Quantum was agreed at $3m prior to trial.

The trial judge noted that proof of causation required evidence that timely administration of adrenaline would have prevented Ms Masson's brain damage, and that she was not already hypoxic. It was accepted that adrenaline was more prevalent in treating asthmatics in 2002. However, there had been a shift towards salbutamol, particularly, as in this case, where the use of adrenaline with Ms Masson's high blood pressure may have caused her heart to stop.

The trial judge found that adrenaline was considered in the early stages of treatment but was ruled out because of Ms Masson's high heart rate and blood pressure. This was a reasonable response to the risks at the time, where paramedics faced the dilemma that adrenaline could, in this case, worsen Ms Masson's condition. Salbutamol provided an alternative which did not carry the same risk. Administering salbutamol did not fall below the paramedic's standard of care and was not contrary to the Queensland Ambulance Service Clinical Practice Manual (the CPM). Accordingly, the trial judge dismissed the claim: *Masson* v *State of Queensland* (2018) Aust Torts Reports ¶82-399; [2018] QSC 162.

Ms Masson's estate appealed the trial judge's findings. It argued on appeal that the trial judge erred by reasoning that the paramedic Mr Peters was not negligent because the patient was treated in a way that accorded with "a responsible body of opinion in the medical profession". In effect, it was argued that the trial judge failed to consider whether reasonable care had been exercised, as distinct from whether there was a body of medical opinion which would have supported it. [137]

The court noted that the difference between the care and skill to be expected of an ambulance officer and that to be expected from a specialist in emergency medicine is significant in a number of ways. Further, because of the more limited education, training and experience of ambulance officers, compared with medical specialists, it would not be consistent with the exercise of reasonable care and skill for an ambulance officer to depart from the guidance of the CPM. The court found that a departure from that guidance, with the grave risk that the patient would not avoid serious injury or death, could not be easily justified upon the basis that the officer believed that there was a responsible body of medical opinion which supported that course. [148], [149]

The court found that there was no basis, consistent with the exercise of reasonable care and skill by Mr Peters as an ambulance officer, for him to use what he ought to have understood was a less effective drug for a patient in this critical condition. The existence of potential side effects, from the perspective of an ambulance officer instructed by the CPM, was not a justification for instead using salbutamol. The trial judge ought to have held that Mr Peters was negligent in not administrating adrenaline at the outset. The court upheld the estate's appeal: *Masson* v *State of Queensland* (2019) Aust Torts Reports ¶82-450; [2019] QCA 80.

The State was granted leave to appeal to the High Court of Australia. The State argued that the Court of Appeal departed from settled principle by treating the CPM as determinative of the standard of care. It was also contended that the Court of Appeal was wrong to overturn the trial judge's findings that: (i) Mr Peters considered the administration of adrenaline in accordance with the CPM; and (ii) in 2002, there was a responsible body of opinion within the medical profession supporting the administration of salbutamol to a patient in Ms Masson's condition. [7]

Held: appeal allowed.

Per Kiefel CJ, Bell and Keane JJ:

1. The standard of care expected of Mr Peters was that of the ordinary skilled intensive care paramedic operating in the field in circumstances of urgency. The Court of Appeal correctly observed that intensive care paramedics cannot be expected to make fine professional judgments of a kind that require the education, training and experience of a medical specialist. This is not to say, however, that an intensive care paramedic is not expected to exercise clinical judgment. The guidance in the CPM is posited upon the assumption that ambulance officers will exercise clinical judgment and that officers may depart from its guidelines where the departure is justified and is in the best interests of the patient. [10]

2. The Court of Appeal was wrong to say that had there been a body of opinion that adrenaline should not be given to a patient in Ms Masson's condition with a high heart rate and high blood pressure, and had Mr Peters been aware of that opinion and acted upon it, where adrenaline was the drug indicated in the CPM, then by reason of that guidance he would have failed to take reasonable care. The CPM was not expressed to be, and was not, determinative of the range of reasonable responses for an intensive care paramedic treating an asthmatic patient in imminent arrest who presented with Ms Masson's symptoms. [11]

3. Contrary to the Court of Appeal's analysis, there was ample evidence to support the trial judge's finding that, in 2002, a responsible body of opinion within the medical profession favoured the administration of IV salbutamol in the initial stage of treatment for a patient in Ms Masson's overall condition, with her high heart rate and high blood pressure. [71]

4. The asthma flowchart prompted consideration of adrenaline but did not require its administration. The decision Mr Peters made in the face of Ms Masson's high heart rate and high blood pressure, to administer IV salbutamol, was supported by a responsible body of medical opinion. In the circumstances, the trial judge's conclusion that Mr Peters' treatment of Ms Masson did not fall below the standard of care expected of an ordinary skilled intensive care paramedic was clearly correct. [79]

Per Nettle and Gordon JJ:

1. The asthma flowchart was one aspect of the CPM, of which another, as has been seen, was the warning that the use of adrenaline may lead to hypertension, stroke, heart attack or life-threatening arrhythmias. And, as the expert evidence established, that was especially so in the presence of an already elevated heart rate and elevated blood pressure. Consequently, as the primary judge concluded, in determining the pharmacological component of the broader treatment to be administered, Mr Peters was presented with the dilemma that, because Ms Masson was tachycardic and hypertensive, the administration of the drug ordinarily favoured for administration to a patient in extremis, namely, adrenaline, would carry a real risk of worsening Ms Masson's condition. [108]

2. A body of professional opinion does not need to align to majority opinion in order to be regarded a responsible body of professional opinion; and, for the same reasons, a body of opinion does not need to be premised on the same assumptions as underscore the majority opinion in order to be regarded a responsible body of opinion. Consequently, the body of medical opinion adhering to the view that the risks posed by the use of adrenaline justified the use of salbutamol was well capable of amounting to a responsible body of opinion, whether or not it proceeded from the premise that adrenaline was a superior bronchodilator. It might have been different if it had been established as a fact that adrenaline was superior to salbutamol in achieving fast and effective bronchodilation. Conceivably — although, even then, not necessarily — the establishment of that proposition might have so cast doubt on opinion premised upon its denial as to render that opinion unrespectable. But that was not the case here. The uncontested evidence was that there was no evidence that adrenaline was superior to salbutamol in achieving fast and effective dilation. [134]

3. In order for the estate to establish negligence, it needed to prove, on the balance of probabilities, that Mr Peters' clinical judgment fell below that standard. As the primary judge held, it did not. The estate proved on the balance of probabilities that the majority of specialist emergency physicians operating in hospital emergency rooms in 2002 would have chosen adrenaline from the outset. But, as has been explained, the fact that the majority of specialist emergency practitioners may have chosen adrenaline from the outset does not mean that the minority who would have chosen salbutamol as first preference would have been regarded as negligent; still less that an emergency paramedic operating in the field without the assistance and certitude of the facilities of an emergency room would be so regarded. [137]

4. The overall effect of the evidence led before the primary judge was that a responsible body of opinion in the medical profession in 2002 supported the view that Ms Masson's high heart rate and blood pressure in the context of her overall condition provided a medically sound basis to prefer salbutamol to adrenaline at the time of initial treatment. In the urgent reality with which Mr Peters was presented, he was faced with the dilemma of choosing between the administration of adrenaline, which he correctly understood would carry a real risk of worsening the patient's condition, and salbutamol, which did not carry that risk. Consistently with a responsible body of medical opinion, he chose the latter, and such evidence as there was of practice among paramedics was that it was not an inappropriate decision. No breach of duty of care was established. [139]

[*Headnote by the Wolters Kluwer editors*]

SL Doyle QC with RN Traves QC and CJ Fitzpatrick (Crown Solicitor (Qld)) for the appellant.

BW Walker SC with DR Campbell SC and AS Katsikalis (RMB Lawyers) for the respondent.

Before: Kiefel CJ, Bell, Keane, Nettle and Gordon JJ.

[¶82-544] Sochorova v Durairaj & Anor

(2020) Aust Torts Reports ¶82-544

Medium neutral citation: [2020] QCA 158

Supreme Court of Queensland, Court of Appeal

28 July 2020 (on the papers)

Torts — Negligence — Standard of care — Scope of duty and subsequent breach — Where the appellant suffered a stroke and, while in the Cairns Base Hospital receiving treatment, she suffered a further stroke — Where the appellant claims damages against the operator of the hospital and the principal treating doctor — Where the appellant submits that the further strokes were caused by the respondents administering thrombolysis — Whether it was negligent of the respondents to administer the treatments — Whether it was correct for the trial judge to conclude that the treatments administered to the appellant were appropriate — Whether the treatments caused the further strokes which damaged the right side of the appellant's brain and caused significant disabilities — Whether it was correct for the trial judge to conclude that the treatments did not cause the appellant's additional strokes — Civil Liability Act 2003 (Qld), s 21 — Uniform Civil Procedure Rules 1999 (Qld), rr 427, 681.

On 29 July 2018, 84-year-old Ms Sochorova was admitted to Cairns Base Hospital, which was run by the Cairns and Hinterland Hospital and Health Service. She was in poor health. Ms Sochorova already had a history of suffering strokes, including two previous admissions of her to Cairns Hospital for strokes, in 2013 and 2014, respectively. Three days prior to Ms Sochorova's admission to hospital on 29 July 2018 she ceased taking her anticoagulant medication, which was done on the advice of a doctor in preparation for her undergoing a biopsy.

Dr Durairaj, a qualified stroke specialist, examined Ms Sochorova in emergency. His assessment revealed a National Institute of Health stroke score of 10, indicating the stroke was severe. She underwent a thrombolysis procedure and was later taken to the stroke ward. Ms Sochorova suffered a second stroke, which coincided with her deterioration between about 11.30 pm and midnight. After being maintained in the hospital for about a month, Ms Sochorova then went into full-time care at a Bupa Aged Care Home and continued to require significant care.

Ms Sochorova, who was represented by her brother Mr Joseph Moder, commenced proceedings in the Supreme Court of Queensland against Dr Durairaj and the Cairns and Hinterland Hospital and Health Service, in negligence and claimed damages. She alleged that the hospital was negligent in administering thrombolysis and in failing to warn of the risks associated with thrombolysis. Had such a warning been given, Mr Moder would have disallowed the procedure, thus avoiding the alleged causation of the subsequent second stroke.

His Honour Henry J found that Ms Sochorova's serious deficits resulted from her stroke symptoms progressing despite, not because of, the administration of thrombolysis, and there was no evidence that the thrombolysis caused the strokes: *Sochorova* v *Durairaj & Anor* (2019) Aust Torts Reports ¶82-493; [2019] QSC 251.

Ms Sochorova appealed the primary judge's decision.

Held: appeal dismissed.

Per Davis J (with whom Boddice J and Sofronoff P agreed):

1. In her outline of argument, Ms Sochorova raised various arguments against factual findings made at the trial. There was no submission that his Honour made any error of law. The appeal was against factual findings which were based on uncontradicted expert evidence. [35], [36]

2. There were two issues in this case. First, whether it was negligent of the respondents to administer the treatments and, second, whether the treatments caused the further strokes that damaged the right side of Ms Sochorova's brain and caused left-sided disabilities. She had to prove that the treatments ought not to have been given and that the treatments caused the further strokes. [72]

3. The primary judge did not err in accepting the expert opinion that there was no evidence that the thrombolysis procedure or, indeed, the administration of prothrombinex caused those strokes.

4. The primary judge's findings were all supported by evidence which his Honour was entitled to accept. After reviewing the evidence, there was nothing suggestive of error. [76]

Per Boddice J:

1. A real review of the evidence and of the trial judge's reasons for judgment supported a conclusion that the treatment administered to the appellant was appropriate and that treatment did not cause Ms Sochorova's additional strokes. The findings of fact were consistent with the evidence accepted at trial and none of those findings of fact were wrong or contrary to the available inferences. [3], [4]

[*Headnote by the Wolters Kluwer editors*]

J Moder (the brother and holder of power of attorney of the appellant) for the appellant.

M Hickey (Minter Ellison) for the first and second respondents.

Before: Sofronoff P, Boddice and Davis JJ (on the papers).

Wolters Kluwer Note: The full text of the judgment is accessible through the Supreme Court of Queensland, Court of Appeal database on the AustLII website.

[¶82-547] Goondiwindi Regional Council v Tait

(2020) Aust Torts Reports ¶82-547
Medium neutral citation: [2020] QCA 119
Supreme Court of Queensland, Court of Appeal
5 June 2020

Torts — Negligence — Road traffic accident — Defects in roads — Obligations of statutory authorities — Inspection — Repair — Actual state of knowledge — Content of duty — Failure to warn — Causation — Contributory negligence — Respondent was seriously injured when motorcycle she was riding struck a pothole — Appellant Council was statutory authority responsible for maintaining road — Council was aware of potholes in road but temporary warning signs that it had erected had fallen over — Primary judge held that Council had failed to discharge a duty of care to warn about potholes and that its state of knowledge meant that statutory exclusion of liability did not apply — Council appeal — Primary judge had been entitled to find that Council's state of knowledge gave rise to a duty of care to warn respondent — Findings made by primary judge sustained conclusions that Council had failed to discharge that duty and that such failures led to respondent's injuries — Civil Liability Act 2003 (Qld), s 37.

On 25 September 2016, the respondent, Ms Paula Tait (Ms Tait), was riding her motorcycle with a group of fellow bike riders in a southerly direction on the Leichhardt Highway through the Mittengang Creek Floodway. The floodway was located at Billa Billa, on the Leichhardt Highway, about 47 km north of Goondiwindi in Queensland. She struck a large pothole and sustained serious injuries as a consequence of falling from her motorcycle.

Ms Tait commenced proceedings in the Supreme Court of Queensland against the appellant, Goondiwindi Regional Council (the Council), for damages as a result of the injuries she sustained. The Council was the local government authority with control over roads in its district. As such, it had responsibility for maintaining the section of road where Ms Tait fell as part of its contractual arrangement with the State of Queensland under a contract known as a Road Maintenance Performance Contract (RMPC).

The relevant section of the highway was a two-lane undivided bitumen-sealed road. Because it was a floodway, certain signs and markers were in place. Depth markers and "Floodway" signs, with temporary flaps stating "Water Over Road", were installed on both approaches to the floodway. Between 13 and 20 September 2016 there was considerable rainfall which brought widespread flooding to the area of the floodway.

The flooding caused damage to the road's surface and that damage was noted by the Council's road maintenance patching crew in the days leading up to 25 September 2016. However, because the road was still wet, the crew decided not to fix the resulting potholes. They instead put temporary signage in the vicinity. That signage stated "Rough Surface" and advised approaching motorists to "Reduce Speed".

As Ms Tait approached the area on 25 September 2016, she saw the "Floodway" signs but not the temporary signs — that was because they had fallen over in the bad weather conditions. One of the other riders in the group hit the potholes and veered out of control and impeded Ms Tait's vision. She then hit the potholes and fell off her bike. There was no issue that at the time of the accident Ms Tait was travelling within the speed limit.

The primary judge found that the terms of the RMPC required the Council to fix defects in the road. The Council sought to rely on s 37(1) of the *Civil Liability Act 2003* (Qld) (the CL Act), which provided that a public authority was not to be held liable in any proceeding for failing to repair, or failing to inspect, a road.

The primary judge applied s 37(2) of the CL Act, which stated that s 37(1) did not apply "if at the time of the alleged failure the authority had actual knowledge of the particular risk". The primary judge found that the Council did have actual knowledge and that therefore the Council ought to be held liable for its failure to properly erect warning signs.

The Council appealed the primary judge's findings. The Council argued on appeal that the primary judge had not made findings to sustain the state of actual knowledge required for a duty of care to arise. It also argued that the primary judge made no finding as to whether the duty to warn was limited by the terms of the RMPC or was instead a freestanding duty arising independently of that contract. The Council also raised issues about causation and contributory negligence.

Held: appeal dismissed.

Per Morrison JA (with whom McMurdo JA and Burns J agreed):

1. The primary judge's finding that a duty of care arose in the circumstances was not based on the RMPC documents alone, but rather on a combination of the obligations in the RMPC and the actions and knowledge of the Council's workers in the days leading up to 25 September 2016. [86]–[90]

2. The findings concerning the Council's state of knowledge at the relevant time included findings that there was pavement damage on the floodway, that the sealed bitumen surface had begun to strip, and that potholes were beginning to develop in that area. These could sustain a conclusion that the Council had actual knowledge of the risk. [91]–[96]

3. The content of the duty identified by the primary judge was essentially a duty to warn. That is, the primary judge had found that, having identified defects in the road that could not yet be repaired because of the wet conditions, the Council had been under a duty to ensure that motorists were properly warned. [97]–[102]

4. Those erecting the temporary signs knew there were no sandbags to hold the signs in place yet did nothing to secure the signs with the result that they soon fell over in the stormy conditions. The patching crew was aware that this could happen but did nothing to find alternatives to sandbags. [103]–[106]

5. The primary judge had been entitled to rely upon the evidence given by other riders in the group that Ms Tait was a careful rider who would have slowed down had the signs been visible. As such, there was a basis for the primary judge to find that causation had been established. [107]–[110]

6. There was no foundation for any finding of contributory negligence. The group of riders, including Ms Tait, had been riding well within the speed limit at the time of the accident and were all experienced road riders. They had also been riding in a staggered formation to reduce the risk of accidents occurring. [111]–[117]

[*Headnote by the Wolters Kluwer editors*]

KN Wilson QC (King & Company Solicitors) for the appellant.

SC Holt QC with RJ Lynch (Shine Lawyers) for the respondent.

Before: Morrison and McMurdo JJA, Burns J.

Wolters Kluwer Note: The full text of the judgment is accessible through the Supreme Court of Queensland, Court of Appeal database on the AustLII website.

[¶82-538] **HAP2 Pty Ltd v Bankier**

(2020) Aust Torts Reports ¶82-538
Medium neutral citation: [2020] QCA 152
Supreme Court of Queensland, Court of Appeal
21 July 2020

Torts — Negligence — Economic or financial loss — Careless advice, statements and non-disclosure — Professional advisers — Respondent was seriously injured in a car accident in 1997 when she was 16 years old — Respondent was awarded almost $2m in damages for her losses and injuries — Respondent sought financial advice about investing the damages from the appellant — Respondent had made significant withdrawals from her capital to fund her lifestyle and business enterprises — Trial judge concluded that the appellant had a duty to warn the respondent about the risks of depleting her damages award to an extent that the sum left would no longer serve her needs by overspending — Trial judge found that the appellant had failed to give appropriate warnings to the respondent — Appellant submits that the trial judge should have found that such a risk should have been obvious to the respondent — Appellant submits that to find such a duty would wrongly involve characterising the retainer as one that involved more than "a portfolio review service" — Whether the trial judge erred in finding that the appellant had a duty to warn the respondent about material risks — Civil Liability Act 2003 (Qld), ss 11, 15 — Civil Proceedings Act 2011 (Qld), ss 58, 59 — Corporations Act 2001 (Cth), ss 945A, 945B, 953B — Limitation of Actions Act 1974 (Qld), s 10 — Uniform Civil Procedure Rules 1999 (Qld), rr 283, 289.

Ms Michelle Bankier was involved in a car accident in 1997 when she was 16 years old and suffered severe injuries as a result, including spinal damage and short bowel syndrome as a consequence of intestinal trauma. She commenced proceedings in the District Court of New South Wales in 2002, with the court awarding her approximately $2m in damages.

Following the court award, Ms Bankier engaged Mr Anthony Avery, who conducted a business as a financial planner, for advice on how to manage her finances prospectively. Mr Avery operated through his company, Avery Financial Planning Pty Ltd, which was the corporate predecessor to HAP2 Pty Ltd (HAP 2). Once deductions were made for various expenses, the amount that Ms Bankier had available for investment at the time she engaged Mr Avery was $1,184,600. On the basis of advice that Mr Avery gave, Ms Bankier invested the sum of $1,132,109 in a share portfolio. She also periodically requested that Mr Avery take out amounts so that she could fund businesses she was attempting to start. None of those businesses were successful, at least partly because of limitations caused by her injuries.

Although Mr Avery valued Ms Bankier's share portfolio in June 2006 at $1,565,200, by the end of 2008 he informed her that its value had dropped to around $700,000. Over the course of the following year, that value decreased even further consistently with the global financial crisis. In June 2010, Ms Bankier ended Mr Avery's appointment as her financial adviser.

Ms Bankier commenced proceedings in the Supreme Court of Queensland against HAP 2, claiming that Mr Avery was negligent in that he breached his duty of care owed to Ms Bankier by not warning her against spending money in excess of her estimated living expenses; borrowing money for investments; and trying to start a business.

HAP 2 denied liability. Mr Avery claimed that he had made a number of attempts to warn Ms Bankier about the implications of taking money out of her investments and spending it in excess of their agreed budget and that whenever he warned her about the risks Ms Bankier said that she felt that it was worth doing, given that she was investing in a business. Mr Avery also argued that even if it was found that he did not give Ms Bankier appropriate warnings or that those warnings were deficient, giving them would not have ultimately changed the situation in which she lost a large amount of her compensation award.

His Honour Martin J found that in discharging his duty to Ms Bankier, Mr Avery was obliged to have a detailed knowledge of her circumstances and he should have read, or otherwise sought advice on, the District Court's decision. Mr Avery was, in the circumstances, under a duty to give warnings to Ms Bankier against particular expenditures. Had Mr Avery warned her of those risks, then Ms Bankier would have altered her ways and curbed her expenditures. His Honour found in favour of Ms Bankier: *Bankier* v *HAP2 Pty Ltd* (2019) Aust Torts Reports ¶82-448; [2019] QSC 101.

HAP2 appealed the trial judge's findings. HAP2 argued on appeal that the trial judge erred in finding that Mr Avery had a duty to warn Ms Bankier about the risks of depleting her damages award to an extent that the sum left would no longer serve her needs by overspending and that his Honour should have found that such a risk should have been obvious to Ms Bankier. HAP2 also argued that the trial judge erred in finding that Mr Avery had failed to give appropriate warnings because he had in fact done so, and also erred in finding that, had Mr Avery given appropriate warnings, Ms Bankier would have heeded his advice and would not have incurred the losses.

Held: appeal dismissed.

Per Sofronoff P (with whom Morrison and Philippides JJA agreed):

1. At the trial, the relevant legal principles were not in issue and it was common ground that Mr Avery owed Ms Bankier a duty of care. [59]

2. The law imposes a duty upon those who engage upon a calling, profession or business that requires the application of skill and competence not possessed by the ordinary person to exercise that standard of skill and competence generally possessed and applied by persons engaged in such calling, profession or business. A person who carries on a business which involves the giving of advice of a kind which calls for special skill and competence thereby represents to the recipient of advice that the adviser claims to possess, and will apply, that degree of skill and competence that is generally possessed and exercised by people in the business of giving such advice. It has also been established that in the case of a financial adviser part of this duty is a duty to warn the client about material risks of which the adviser is aware, or of which the adviser should have been aware, but of which the client is unaware. A material risk, in this context, is one to which a reasonable person in the client's position would attach significance if warned of it. [62], [63]

3. The trial judge found that Ms Bankier did not understand that her actual expenditures, for which she requested a liquidation of assets or for which she requested transfers of funds by Mr Avery, would diminish her capital so as to render it insufficient to fund the expenses that she would incur by reason of her injuries and which she could not otherwise pay for by personal exertion. Nor did she understand that borrowing money in order to purchase an investment would have, or could have, the same effect because of the need to pay interest. Those findings about Ms Bankier's lack of appreciation were amply justified by the evidence and were correct. The trial judge's finding that Mr Avery knew that Ms Bankier had "no or limited exposure to financial dealings involving the investment of money" was also correct. [71]

4. The trial judge did not err in finding that Mr Avery had a duty to warn about the proposed withdrawals of sums from investments for Ms Bankier's proposed expenditures. This was not a duty to oversee a client's spending. The duty was to warn a client about the imminent dangers that would be caused by the client's proposed interference in the adviser's investment plan by the withdrawal of capital in amounts that the adviser knew will be significant in their effect. It was something that Mr Avery must have known would or might cause his plan to fail and that he should have appreciated that his client did not know. [74]–[77]

5. Mr Avery knew or he ought to have known the limits of Ms Bankier's understanding about her proposed use of money. It followed that Mr Avery was under a duty to advise Ms Bankier in plain terms about what would happen if she insisted upon doing the things that she did. [83]

[*Headnote by the Wolters Kluwer editors*]

S Couper QC with S Eggins (Moray & Agnew) for the appellant.

DJ Campbell QC with BA Hall (Shine Lawyers) for the respondent.

Before: Sofronoff P, Morrison and Philippides JJA.

Wolters Kluwer Note: The full text of the judgment is accessible through the Supreme Court of Queensland, Court of Appeal database on the AustLII website.

[¶82-469] Lee v Lee

(2019) Aust Torts Reports ¶82-469
Medium neutral citation: [2019] HCA 28
High Court of Australia
4 September 2019

Insurance law — Motor vehicles — Personal injury — Where appellant injured in motor vehicle collision — Where appellant gave evidence father driving vehicle at time of collision — Where appellant alleged injuries caused by negligence of father — Where appellant's blood located on driver's airbag — Where expert evidence relating to possible source of blood — Where expert evidence relating to seatbelt and airbag design — Where trial judge concluded appellant driving vehicle — Where Court of Appeal dismissed appeal — Whether trial judge's findings glaringly improbable or contrary to compelling inferences — Appeal — Rehearing — Where trial judge drew inferences and made findings of fact based on lay and expert evidence — Where Court of Appeal found inferences wrong in material respects — Whether Court of Appeal erred in failing to conclude trial judge misused advantage as trial judge — Whether Court of Appeal failed to conduct "real review" of evidence given and trial judge's reasons for judgment — Words and phrases — "contrary to compelling inferences", "glaringly improbable", "real review", "trial judge's advantage".

On 25 September 2013, 17-year-old Lien-Yang Lee sustained severe spinal injuries in a car accident on North Stradbroke Island, which rendered him a partial tetraplegic. Lien-Yang and his family had travelled to Stradbroke Island in Queensland. At approximately 12.30 pm, as the family was driving down Tazi Road, a collision occurred when the family's Tarago travelled on to the wrong side of the road and collided head-on with a Nissan Patrol driven by David Hannam. Lien-Yang maintained that his father, Chin-Fu, was the driver of the Tarago, that his mother, Chao-Ling, was the front seat passenger, and that their three sons including Lien-Yang were all back seat passengers.

Police and ambulance attended the scene shortly after the accident. The investigating police officer formed the view that Lien-Yang himself was driving the Tarago. Lien-Yang was unlicensed and had not yet obtained his learner's permit.

Lien-Yang commenced proceedings in the Supreme Court of Queensland against his father, in negligence and claimed damages. He alleged that his father was driving the vehicle when it collided with the other vehicle and that the accident was caused by the negligence of his father as driver. The insurer, RACQ Insurance Limited, denied liability. It argued that Lien-Yang himself was driving the Tarago and that by doing so without being the holder of a driver's licence or learner's permit, he was wholly responsible for his injuries, or 100% contributorily negligent.

His Honour Boddice J found that Lien-Yang was the driver of the Tarago, that he was not wearing a seat belt, and that the catastrophic spinal injury was a hyperextension injury

sustained by his contact, at force and unrestrained, with a deployed airbag. Boddice J dismissed Lien-Yang's claim: *Lee* v *Lee* (2017) Aust Torts Reports ¶82-328; [2017] QSC 42.

Lien-Yang and his parents appealed the primary judge's findings. The parties agreed that the accident was caused solely by the negligence of the driver of the Toyota. The only issue was the identity of the driver, whether it was Lien-Yang's father who had been driving the Toyota, or Lien-Yang himself. The court found no error in the primary judge's findings and that, based on the evidence, Lien-Yang was driving the Tarago at the time of the accident. Accordingly, the court dismissed Lien-Yang's appeal, with costs: *Lee* v *Lee* (2018) Aust Torts Reports ¶82-393; [2019] QCA 104.

Lien-Yang and his parents appealed to the High Court of Australia. The court noted that the first ground of appeal challenged the adequacy of the Court of Appeal's reasons, arguing that McMurdo JA failed to engage with a critical argument based on unchallenged expert evidence on which Lien-Yang relied. The second ground of appeal challenged the Court of Appeal's restraint in the face of the trial judge's ''advantage'' in circumstances in which it is argued that the finding that Lien-Yang was the driver of the vehicle was contrary to the compelling inferences from uncontroverted evidence. [27]

Held:

B61 of 2018 — *Lien-Yang Lee v Chin-Fu Lee & Ors*

1. The appeal is allowed.

2. The third respondent is to pay the appellant's costs.

3. The order of the Court of Appeal of the Supreme Court of Queensland made on 1 June 2018 is set aside and in lieu thereof, it is ordered that:

(a) the appeal to the Court of Appeal is allowed and the orders of the trial judge made on 23 March 2017 are set aside

(b) judgment for the appellant on his claim against the third respondent in the sum of $3,350,000.00 (clear of rehabilitation expenses by the third respondent pursuant to the Motor Accident Insurance Act 1994 (Qld)), with the date of judgment to take effect pursuant to r 660(3) of the Uniform Civil Procedure Rules 1999 (Qld) on 23 March 2017

(c) the counterclaim of the third respondent against the appellant is dismissed

(d) the third respondent pays the appellant's costs of and incidental to his claim on the indemnity basis, and

(e) the third respondent pay the appellant's costs of and incidental to the third respondent's counterclaim and of the appeal to the Court of Appeal on the standard basis.

B62 of 2018 — *Chao-Ling Hsu v RACQ Insurance Limited*

1. The appeal is allowed with costs.

2. The order of the Court of Appeal of the Supreme Court of Queensland made on 1 June 2018 is set aside and in lieu thereof, it is ordered that:

(a) the appeal to the Court of Appeal is allowed

(b) the orders of the trial judge dated 23 March 2017 are set aside and in lieu thereof judgment for the appellant on the respondent's counterclaim against the appellant

(c) the respondent pays the appellant's costs of the counterclaim on the standard basis, and

(d) the respondent pays the appellant's costs of the appeal to the Court of Appeal on the standard basis.

B63 of 2018 — *Chin-Fu Lee v RACQ Insurance Limited*

1. The appeal is allowed with costs.

2. The order of the Court of Appeal of the Supreme Court of Queensland made on 1 June 2018 is set aside and in lieu thereof, it is ordered that:

(a) the appeal to the Court of Appeal is allowed

(b) the orders of the trial judge dated 23 March 2017 are set aside and in lieu thereof judgment for the appellant on the respondent's counterclaim against the appellant

(c) the respondent pays the appellant's costs of the counterclaim on the standard basis, and

(d) the respondent pays the appellant's costs of the appeal to the Court of Appeal on the standard basis.

Per Kiefel CJ:

1. Given the finding made by his Honour McMurdo JA, that it was improbable that the father could have moved the appellant from the driver's seat to the rear seat in the time available, it is not obvious that the DNA evidence compelled a conclusion that the appellant was present in the driver's seat. If the DNA evidence was the only other evidence to be taken into account, it was not a matter of choosing which of the two hypotheses it raised was the more probable in isolation from that earlier finding. Each hypothesis would have to be considered in light of the level of certainty which attended that finding. [9]

2. There were other matters which it was necessary to consider but which were not taken into account. It is by this means that the Court of Appeal fell into error. These matters affected the weight which could be given to the DNA evidence and effectively forestalled any consideration of the two hypotheses. [10]

3. The finding concerning the use of the seatbelt and Dr Grigg's evidence of the seatbelt's operation rendered the DNA evidence of little, if any, value. The RACQ could not make out its case that the appellant was the driver. Nothing remained to prevent the Court of Appeal acting upon the foreshadowed conclusion that the appellant's case was made out. [13]

Per Bell, Gageler, Nettle and Edelman JJ:

1. It was an error for the Court of Appeal to dismiss the appeals in this "*very closely balanced*" case on the footing that the trial judge's *decision* was neither glaringly improbable nor contrary to compelling inferences. It was the duty of the Court of Appeal to decide for itself which of the two hypotheses was the more probable. It was the duty of the Court of Appeal to persist in its task of "*weighing* [the] *conflicting evidence and drawing its own inferences and conclusions*" (*Dearman* v *Dearman* (1908) 7 CLR 549 at 564; [1908] HCA 84, quoting *The Glannibanta* (1876) 1 PD 283 at 287; *Fox* v *Percy* (2003) 214 CLR 118 at 127 [25]), and, ultimately, to decide for itself which of the two hypotheses was the more probable. It did not. [56]

2. It is not correct to argue, as the RACQ does, that it was incumbent on the appellant to establish how his blood came to be on the airbag. The question is whether it is more probable than not that the father was the driver. As McMurdo JA reasoned, the fact that Lien-Yang was located in the rear passenger seat within 90 seconds of the collision is a circumstance powerfully in favour of the conclusion that he was not the driver. [59]

3. Further, in determining whether Lien-Yang proved upon the balance of probabilities that the father was driving the Toyota at the time of the collision, all the circumstances must be taken into account, namely; the father appears to have been cooperative at the scene; about an hour after the collision he stated that he was the driver. The presence of Lien-Yang's blood on the airbag gave rise to the hypothesis upon which the RACQ's case relied, that in less than 90 seconds the father pulled the paralysed Lien-Yang from the driver's seat and positioned him in the rear passenger seat in which he, the father, had been sitting. That hypothesis is, to a high degree, improbable. [63]

4. How Lien-Yang's blood came to be on the airbag is unknown. However, in light of the finding that the driver was restrained by the seatbelt, the likelihood that it was the product of direct contact with Lien-Yang's bleeding face cannot be accounted greater than the likelihood that it was transferred from the father's hands. [64]

5. McMurdo JA's tentative conclusion that it is much more likely that the father was the driver is correct for the reasons that his Honour gave. It is not a conclusion that is weakened, much less contradicted, by the presence of the appellant's blood on the airbag given Dr Grigg's unchallenged evidence of the operation of the seatbelt and the airbag. [65]

[*Headnote by the Wolters Kluwer editors*]

GW Diehm QC with MM Callaghan (Slater & Gordon Lawyers) for the appellant in B61/2018.

JMN Hewson (VBR Lawyers) for the first respondent in B61/2018 and the appellant in B63/2018.

M Grant-Taylor QC with JMN Hewson (Littles Lawyers) for the second respondent in B61/2018 and the appellant in B62/2018.

RJ Douglas QC with BF Charrington (Gilchrist Connell Lawyers) for the third respondent in B61/2018 and the respondent in B62/2018 and B63/2018.

Before: Kiefel CJ, Bell, Gageler, Nettle and Edelman JJ.

[¶82-359] Foster v Carter & Anor

(2017) Aust Torts Reports ¶82-359
Medium neutral citation: [2017] QSC 135
Supreme Court of Queensland
Judgment delivered 28 June 2017

Damages — Measure and remoteness of damages in actions for tort — Measure of damages — Personal injuries — General principles — Where the plaintiff was injured in the course of her employment as a bus driver when the defendant's vehicle collided with the rear of her bus after the defendant lost control of his vehicle — Where the defendants admit liability for the accident — Whether damages should be assessed at common law or under the Civil Liability Act 2003 (Qld) — Whether the plaintiff's employment was a significant contributing factor to the injuries.

Damages — Measure and remoteness of damages in actions for tort — Measure of damages — Personal injuries — Loss of earnings and earning capacity — Where the plaintiff suffered physical injuries, including cervical spine and lumbar spine injuries, and psychological injuries — Where damages assessed pursuant to the Civil Liability Act 2003 (Qld) — Where assessment of damages for the diminution in earning capacity was in issue — Civil Liability Act 2003 (Qld), ss 5, 59, 60, 61, 62.

On 2 September 2014, 50-year-old Karen Foster was driving a bus in the course of her full-time employment towards a roundabout, when a Holden Commodore vehicle driven by Jade Carter drove through the roundabout, went out of control and collided with the rear of the bus before ricocheting onto the median strip.

Ms Foster sustained a neck and back injury as a result of the accident and as she held the steering wheel trying to control the bus to make sure it did not come out of control. The impact was recorded on CCTV footage in the bus which revealed that rather than the heavy impact alleged by Ms Foster that shunted the bus at least "half a metre" sideways. The video showed her moving slightly in her seat and steering the bus closer to the curb before stopping. Ms Foster visited her GP frequently over the following weeks and was referred to physiotherapy and hydrotherapy. Ms Foster already had a significant prior shoulder injury and some spinal degeneration.

Ms Foster commenced proceedings in the Supreme Court of Queensland against Ms Carter, in negligence and claimed damages. Although Ms Foster received workers'

compensation payments, she contended for damages at common law rather than as confined by the *Civil Liability Act 2003* (Qld) (CLA) and argued that she fell within the CLA, s 5(1)(b) exception.

Ms Carter admitted liability for the accident, however, quantum was in dispute as to whether damages were to be assessed at common law or under the CLA. Ms Carter also disputed Ms Foster's injuries sustained in the accident, in particular the nature and extent of the physical injuries sustained and the consequences of the injuries for her employability.

***Held:* judgment for the plaintiff against the defendant in the sum of $539,765.**

Per Mullins J:

1. Ms Foster argued that employment was a factually significant factor because she was a bus driver and that was the reason she was driving the bus. Ms Carter argued that there was no evidence that "*the exigencies or activities of the plaintiff's employment made a significant contribution to the occurrence of the injury*".

2. Ms Foster was only driving the bus as it approached the roundabout where the accident occurred, because of her employment. Connection between the time and place of the accident and employment is not sufficient, however, to satisfy the test for an injury pursuant to s 32 of the *Workers' Compensation and Rehabilitation Act 2003* (Qld) (WCRA). Ms Foster's statement of claim is a classic pleading for a claim for personal injuries sustained in a motor vehicle accident. It is pleaded that she was driving the subject bus at the time of the accident, but there is no pleading of any circumstances that can be characterised as "*the exigencies of the employment of the worker by the employer*".

3. The fact that Ms Foster was in receipt of workers' compensation benefits after the accident does not determine the question of whether the injury to her fell within s 32 of the WCRA. Accordingly, the CLA applies to Ms Foster's claim for damages. [69]

4. Damages are assessed in the total sum of $539,765.00, including $21,280.00 for general damages as a common law assessment was not open due to the damages being limited by the CLA.

[*Headnote by the Wolters Kluwer editors*]

G F Crow QC (instructed by Schultz Toomey O'Brien Lawyer) for the plaintiff.

K S Howe (instructed by Quinlan Miller & Treston) for the defendant.

Before: Mullins J.

[¶82-342] Captain v Wosomo

(2017) Aust Torts Reports ¶82-342
Medium neutral citation: [2017] QSC 86
Supreme Court of Queensland
Judgment delivered 17 May 2017

Torts — Negligence — Miscellaneous defences — Illegality of plaintiff's activity — Obvious risks of dangerous recreational activities — Effect of civil liability legislation — Injuries to passengers — Defences of volenti non fit injuria, no breach of duty, and contributory negligence — Failure to wear a seat belt — Where the plaintiff had participated in the theft of a vehicle — Where the plaintiff was a passenger in the stolen vehicle driven by the defendant — Where the vehicle crashed and the plaintiff sustained severe head injuries — Whether the plaintiff had effectively withdrawn from the joint criminal activity prior to the accident — Whether a duty of care was owed by the defendant to the plaintiff — Whether s 45(1) of the Civil Liability Act 2003 applies to exempt the defendant from civil liability — Whether an exemption from civil liability would be "harsh" and "unjust" under s 45(2) — Whether the plaintiff voluntarily assumed risk — Whether the plaintiff's injuries were an obvious risk of a dangerous recreational activity — Whether the plaintiff was contributorily negligent by reason of failure to wear a seatbelt — Civil Liability Act 2003, s 45(1), (2).

Traffic law — Offences — Particular offences — Offences relating to use of vehicle without consent of owner or person in possession — Offences — Where the plaintiff and defendant were jointly engaged in an unlawful use of a vehicle under s 408A, Criminal Code (Qld) — Whether the plaintiff had withdrawn from the joint illegal enterprise at the time the incident occurred — Criminal Code (Qld), s 408A.

At approximately 1.40 am on 8 February 2013, Alifaio Captain, Willie Wosomo and their two friends jointly stole a dual cab Toyota Hilux utility vehicle (the vehicle) from its owner's driveway and took it for a joyride. Mr Wosomo was driving the vehicle. Mr Captain was 14 years old and Mr Wosomo was 16 years old at the time. Mr Wosomo lost control of the vehicle and crashed into a light pole in Gulliver Street, Aitkenvale, just off the intersection with Ross River Road. Mr Captain was the front seat passenger and suffered severe head injuries as a result of the collision. He is significantly disabled and requires 24-hour care and attention.

Moments before the collision, some of the passengers, possibly including Mr Captain, had yelled at Mr Wosomo to slow down.

Mr Captain commenced proceedings against Mr Wosomo in the Supreme Court of Queensland, in negligence and claimed damages. The parties agreed that by reason of their involvement in a joint illegal enterprise, no duty of care was initially owed by Mr Wosomo. However, Mr Captain argued that he had withdrawn from the joint illegal enterprise at the point Mr Wosomo had been asked to slow down. Mr Captain conceded on the facts of the case that criminals not to be awarded damages pursuant to s 45 of the *Civil Liability Act 2003* (Qld) ("CLA") but argued that by the time of the accident, he had effectively withdrawn from the joint criminal activity. In the alternative, he argued that if it does fall under the exclusion in s 45(1), the court should be satisfied that, in the circumstances of this case, the application of that exclusion would operate harshly and unjustly and the court should order an assessment of damages.

Mr Wosomo argued that, in the circumstances, there was no duty owed by him to Mr Captain, and denied that any of the other boys in the vehicle told him to slow down. He also argued that Mr Captain was contributorily negligent in failing to wear a seatbelt at the time of the accident.

***Held:* plaintiff's claim is dismissed.**

Per Daubney J:

1. On the authority of *Miller* v *Miller* (2011) 242 CLR 446, when a plaintiff and defendant are engaged in illegal activity, the defendant does not owe a duty of care to the plaintiff where upholding such a duty is inconsistent with the statutory purpose of prohibiting the criminal activity. The question before the court was whether on the facts of this case Mr Captain had withdrawn from the joint illegal enterprise at the time the accident occurred. If a plaintiff unequivocally withdraws from a joint criminal activity before an accident occurs, the duty of care owed by the defendant survives.

2. On the evidence, at the time of the accident, the parties were jointly engaged in a criminal activity. Accordingly, Mr Wosomo did not owe a duty of care to Mr Captain in circumstances where they were, at the time of the accident, jointly engaged in a criminal activity.

3. The phrase "*harshly and unjustly*" is a composite phrase intended to convey that the potential carve out from the s 45(1) exclusion is reserved to those cases, and only those cases, in which both conditions are found to be present. Both of the words "harshly" and "unjustly" are ordinary words of plain meaning, and it is not necessary to put any further gloss on them.

4. The fact that Mr Captain was not complicit in the offence of dangerous driving does not mean that he was not complicit in the offence of unlawful use of the vehicle. That was the

circumstance which invoked the s 45(1) exclusion of the CLA. The fact that he was not guilty of some other offence does not render operation of the exclusion either harsh or unjust.

5. Mr Captain had not withdrawn from illegal activity when Mr Wosomo was implored to slow down. The unequivocal notice of the withdrawal must be communicated before the duty will be re-instated. Mr Captain would need to establish something more than a mere mental change of intention and that he took such action as he could reasonably take to undo the effect of his previous encouragement or participation. None of those elements were satisfied and accordingly, no duty of care was owed by Mr Wosomo.

6. The defence of voluntary assumption of risk is rejected, as even if Mr Captain was aware of the risk of Mr Wosomo driving dangerously, there was no evidence to suggest that Mr Captain was consciously placing himself in harm's way.

7. Mr Wosomo sought to invoke the defence of "*dangerous recreational activities*" under s 18 and 19 of the CLA. This was premised on a finding that after stealing the car, Mr Captain and the other boys were going joyriding. The direct and express application of s 45 of the CLA would exclude the application of s 18 and 19 in the CLA to the particular facts of this case.

[*Headnote by the Wolters Kluwer editors*]

M E Eliadis (instructed by Shine Lawyers) for the plaintiff.

G F Crow QC (instructed by Jensen McConaghy Solicitors) for the defendants.

Before: Daubney J.

[¶82-322-1] Silwood v Chandler

(2016) Aust Torts Reports ¶82-322-1
Medium neutral citation: [2016] QCA 273
Supreme Court of Queensland, Court of Appeal
28 October 2016

Occupiers liability — Respondent suffered injury when she slipped on wet tiled steps at the home of the appellant — Trial judge found the appellant liable in negligence — Appellant challenged the trial judge's findings of foreseeability of risk and want of reasonable care, submitting that these findings were affected by hindsight bias — Appellant challenged findings of causation — Civil Liability Act 2003 (Qld), s 9.

Ms Kayleen Chandler and Mr Clive Silwood were the parents of a child born in August 2008. Although Ms Chandler and Mr Silwood had previously been in a relationship, it had ended by the time the child was born. Two weeks after the birth, Ms Chandler visited Mr Silwood's house after it was agreed that he would look after the child for the night. Ms Chandler had consumed some alcohol. On her arrival at Mr Silwood's house at about 8.30 pm, with the baby and her older daughter in her car, she pulled up on the driveway, got out of the car and walked to the front door. She saw no lights inside the house nor was there any outside light. When Ms Chandler put her right foot on the lower step, she felt herself slide forward. In trying to stop herself from falling, she put her outstretched arms through the bottom glass panel of the door, injuring her right arm and severing an artery which bled profusely.

The stairs were wet. Earlier in the evening, on arriving home from work Mr Silwood had noticed some bat droppings on the front wall of the house and so he had hosed next to the front door.

Ms Chandler commenced proceedings in the Supreme Court of Queensland against Mr Silwood, in negligence and claimed damages. There was no dispute as to quantum (which was agreed at $650,000), but liability was denied. Ms Chandler alleged that Mr Silwood, as owner and occupier of the house, was negligent in that he failed to switch on the outside light, failed

to warn Ms Chandler that the area could be wet or slippery and failed to ensure that the area was dry. Mr Silwood denied the allegations and also alleged that the incident was the result of Ms Chandler's inebriation and carelessness. He also alleged contributory negligence of at least 50%. Mr Silwood conceded that he had not turned on the front outside light.

The primary judge found that the steps were almost certainly still damp when Ms Chandler arrived and it would have been apparent to Mr Silwood that the steps would remain wet for some time and could be hazardous in that state. The risk of injury to Ms Chandler was foreseeable. Mr Silwood knew that she was coming to the house that night. The risk of her falling on the stairs and hurting herself was not insignificant. It was compounded by the fact that the stairs were in darkness. A reasonable person in Mr Silwood's position would have made sure the stairs were dry or at least warned Ms Chandler in their telephone conversation that they might be wet and should be taken with care. The failure to take those steps was a breach of his duty to her: *Chandler* v *Silwood* (2016) Aust Torts Reports ¶82-267; [2016] QSC 90.

Mr Silwood appealed. He argued that the primary judge erred in finding that Ms Chandler slipped as a result of the steps being wet, and in finding that he breached his duty of care by failing to have made sure the steps were dry, or warning Ms Chandler that the steps might be wet and should be taken with care, or have made sure that the light in the vicinity of the steps was on.

Held: appeal dismissed.

1. The primary judge's findings of fact were thoroughly explained and well justified. Those facts were: the steps were wet; Mr Silwood had made them wet by hosing the wall above them; the steps were slippery when wet if approached at an angle; Mr Silwood knew Ms Chandler would be using the steps that night. Unsurprisingly, Ms Chandler slipped on the steps. Had Mr Silwood thought about it he would have realised that the steps were wet and slippery. A reasonable response to that situation was to dry the steps, to warn Ms Chandler of the risk, or at least to have illuminated the steps so that she would have some prospect of seeing that they were wet and therefore potentially slippery. [30]

2. Applying the law to the facts as found, the risk of a person slipping on the wet steps and being injured was foreseeable and not insignificant and so a reasonable person would have taken the precautions suggested by the primary judge given the probability of the harm of slipping, the seriousness of the harm that could result from slipping and how easy it would have been to obviate the risk of harm. [31]

3. The findings made by the judge were in accordance with the evidence. The law was correctly applied to the findings of fact. [32]

[*Headnote by the Wolters Kluwer editors*]

GW Diehm QC and KS Howe (Barry Nilsson) for the appellant.

K Fleming QC and G Hampson (O'Donnell Legal) for the respondent.

Before: McMurdo P, Gotterson JA, Atkinson J.

[¶82-277] Robinson Helicopter Company Inc v McdermottRobinson Helicopter Company Inc v Mcdermott

(2016) Aust Torts Reports ¶82-266
Medium neutral citation: [2016] HCA 22
High Court of Australia
Judgment delivered 8 June 2016

Torts — Negligence — Personal injury — Breach of duty of care — Duty to take precautions against risk — Where first respondent seriously injured in crash of helicopter manufactured by appellant — Where crash resulted from defect caused by third party — Where helicopter subject to multiple routine inspections but defect not detected — Whether appellant's maintenance manual for helicopter provided sufficient instruction to facilitate detection of defect — Whether appellant breached duty of care.

Torts — Negligence — Causation — Where majority of Court of Appeal found multiple possible causes of damage suffered Whether open to majority of Court of Appeal to find one particular possibility more likely to have occurred than other possibilities — Whether causation established by failure to take precautions against risk other than that which in fact occurred. Appeal — Rehearing — Where primary judge drew inferences and made findings of fact based on lay and expert evidence — Whether majority of Court of Appeal erred by overturning primary judge's findings of fact. Words and phrases — "causation", "contrary to compelling inferences", "glaringly improbable", "incontrovertible facts or uncontested testimony", "real review" — Civil Liability Act 2003 (Qld), ss 9, 12.

On 30 May 2004, Graham McDermott was a passenger in a Robinson R22 helicopter, manufactured by the Robinson Helicopter Company Inc, from which he was inspecting fences on a cattle station in the Northern Territory. During the course of the flight, the helicopter crashed. The pilot, Kevin Norton was killed and Mr McDermott was catastrophically injured.

The crash occurred when a critical part of the helicopter's drive mechanism, called a forward flex plate, failed. One of the four bolts securing the flex plate was incorrectly assembled and was not tightened. Over time, two cracks developed that eventually caused a piece to come away, resulting in a loss of power to the rotor blade and control of the helicopter, causing it to be brought down quickly.

The flex plate and associated parts had been removed and reassembled on 17 February 2004. After reassembly, but before the crash, the flex plate had been subject to two 100 hourly inspections on 27 March 2004 and 12 May 2004.

The helicopter maintenance manual specified that a secondary locking mechanism, a palnut, must be placed on Bolt 4 and that after the installation of the palnut, a torque stripe be applied across both Bolt 4 and the palnut. It specified that the torque stripe be applied in a stripe across both the nut and exposed bolt thread so that a visual inspection of the torque stripe would show any bolt rotation.

Neither of the two Licensed Aircraft Maintenance Engineers (LAMEs) who carried out the last two 100 hourly inspections, nor the pilots who examined the flex plate during at least 28 visual inspections prior to flying the helicopter, noticed anything about the torque stripe which caused them to be concerned about the integrity of Bolt 4.

The manual did not make it clear that during a periodic service that a visual inspection of torque stripes may not be sufficient to indicate whether critical fasteners like Bolt 4 were correctly assembled.

Mr McDermott commenced proceedings in the Supreme Court of Queensland against the manufacturer of the helicopter, Robinson, alleging that it was negligent. He argued that the Robinson's manual failed to specify and require an adequate inspection procedure; had an adequate procedure been established, the defect that led to the accident would have been

detected and rectified and the accident would have been prevented. He also argued that the manual failed to require that the tightness of the four bolts through the flex plate should be checked by a method more stringent than simply looking at marks on the bolts.

The primary judge, his Honour Lyons J, noted that the manual required the LAME to examine the condition of the torque stripe for Bolt 4, and that the relevant provisions of the manual gave adequate instruction for the inspection of the flex plate bolts. Reliance upon the torque stripes as an indicator of the condition of the bolts was sufficient. His Honour found that Robinson took reasonable care to address the risk of failure of the flex plate from an inadequately torqued bolt, and that Robinson did not breach its duty of care. Mr McDermott's claim was dismissed.

Mr McDermott sought leave to appeal. He argued that the primary judge erred in finding that the manual was adequate; had a further, simple instruction to use a torque wrench or spanner to verify whether a bolt was loose been included in the manual, the incorrectly assembled Bolt 4 would have been detected, the bolt reassembled and the accident avoided. He also argued that the torque stripe was an unreliable indicator of whether the bolt was loosened.

His Honour Wilson J, with whom her Honour McMurdo J agreed, found that there was no evidence to support the earlier finding that no torque stripe had been applied to Bolt 4 and was, therefore, missing at the time of inspection. The evidence did point to a finding that whatever the actual state of the torque stripe, it was not such as to alert any of the LAME to the fact that the bolt was loose and rotating. Further, the stripes were not a trustworthy or reliable indicator of the security of the bolts and reliance on the stripes, for inspection purposes, was insufficient. Also, reliance in the manual on torque stripes as a method of verifying security was inadequate.

His Honour Holmes JA (dissenting) found that even if a less than complete torque stripe was inspected, it did not necessarily mean that the bolt was moving; it might have simply deteriorated. His Honour found that the instructions in the manual were adequate.

The majority found that Robinson was liable in negligence. Its manual was not adequate as it did not make it clear that a visual inspection of torque stripes may not be sufficient to indicate whether critical fasteners, such as Bolt 4, were correctly assembled. Nor did the manual specify that a deteriorated torque stripe might indicate looseness of a critical bolt. The majority upheld Mr McDermott's appeal.

By grant of special leave, Robinson appealed to the High Court. It argued that the court erred in rejecting the primary judge's finding that it was likely that there was no torque stripe on Bolt 4 when the relevant 100 hourly inspections were carried out. It also argued that the court erred in finding that because the manual did not specify the LAMEs to apply a torque wrench to Bolt 4 during the inspections, Robinson had breached its duty of care to Mr McDermott.

Mr McDermott argued that the court was correct in finding that a torque stripe could not be regarded as a sufficient indicator that a bolt was incorrectly torqued, and was correct in finding that Robinson was negligent in failing to include an express instruction in the manual that Bolt 4 be verified with a torque or wrench during 100 hourly inspections, and that failing to do so caused the crash. Mr McDermott also emphasised what the majority of the court of appeal identified as errors in the primary judge's reasoning in what were said to be two inconsistent findings.

Held: appeal allowed with costs.

Per French CJ, Bell, Keane, Nettle and Gordon JJ:

1. It was not disputed that the flex plate failed and the crash occurred because, contrary to instructions given in the manual, one of the four bolts securing the flex plate was incorrectly assembled and was not tightened to the requisite degree. Robinson did not cause

the defect and it was not known whom did. "*The focus of these proceedings, however, was not so much on when and how the defect arose as upon whether the manual provided sufficient instruction to facilitate detection of the defect at subsequent inspections.*"

2. The evidence was sufficient to found the primary judge's inference that it was likely that a torque stripe was not applied to Bolt 4 when it was incorrectly assembled, and therefore open to the primary judge to find that if a LAME had examined Bolt 4 in accordance with the manual he/she would have understood that it was necessary to check it with a torque wrench or spanner in order to gauge whether further examination was required.

3. There was no contradiction in the primary judge's findings firstly that it was probable that a torque stripe was not applied when Bolt 4 was incorrectly assembled and secondly, if the LAMEs had examined Bolt 4 the condition of the torque stripe would have indicated that Bolt 4 had rotated. The primary judge made the later finding in the context of a later submission by Robinson that it was probable that palnuts were missing from some of the flex plate bolts when the 100 hourly inspections were carried out and the LAMEs were negligent in failing to detect their absence. The primary judge's later finding was made in that context, and that in order to deal with that later submission, it was necessary for the primary judge to assume that the torque stripe was present.

4. The majority of the court of appeal erred in their interpretation of the evidence and in overturning the primary judge's findings of fact and causation.

5. The primary judge was correct to find that whatever other inadequacies there might or might not have been in the manual, it was not shown to have been inadequate to convey to the LAMEs that Bolt 4 needed attention, and was correct to hold that "*it was not shown that the contents of the Manual fell short of what was required to discharge Robinson's duty of care in the circumstances of this case*".

[*Headnote by the Wolters Kluwer editors*]

S Doyle QC with M Hickey (instructed by Meridian Lawyers) for the appellant.

W Sofronoff QC with M Eliadis and C George (instructed by Shine Lawyers) for the respondent.

Before: French CJ, Bell, Keane, Nettle and Gordon JJ.

[¶82-266] Whittington v Smeaton

(2016) Aust Torts Reports ¶82-277
Medium neutral citation: [2016] ACTSC 76
Supreme Court of the Australian Capital Territory
Judgment delivered 18 April 2016

Torts — Negligence — Personal injury — Injury sustained after falling off a jet ski — Whether defendants in breach of duty to take precautions against risk of harm — Civil Liability Act 2003 (Qld), s 9 — Whether the injury was an obvious risk of a dangerous recreational activity — Riding as observer on a jet ski towing a waterskier found to be a recreational activity — Assessment of whether or not activity is dangerous turns on particular circumstances of the case — Harm suffered must have been an obvious risk — Obvious to a reasonable person in plaintiff's position — Activity found not to be dangerous — Harm suffered not a manifestation of an obvious risk — Civil Liability Act 2003 (Qld), ss 9, 11, 13, 18, 19.

Insurance — Exemption clause in insurance policy contract — Insurance Contracts Act 1984 (Cth), s 54 — Power to refuse to pay claim by reason of act of insured — Act must be capable of being reasonably regarded as being capable of causing or contributing to a loss — Low threshold test — Insurer not able to refuse to pay where no part of the loss that gave rise to the claim was caused by act — Absence of licence not found to have caused any part of the loss giving rise to the claim.

On 27 November 2010 Nathan Whittington was having lunch with a friend, Scott Smeaton. There was a discussion with Scott about going waterskiing. Scott contacted his brother, Todd, who owned a jet ski. Mr Whittington and Scott then went down to the Ross River reserve and met Todd. As Mr Whittington agreed to be a "spotter". His role as a spotter was to sit on the back of the jet ski facing the waterskier and recognise hand signals given by the waterskier and convey them to the driver, to notify the driver if the skier fell off, and pull the towrope out of the water.

Initially Todd drove the jet ski and Scott skied behind. Scott, who was barefoot skiing, was having some difficulty so they went to shore where the skier and driver swapped roles. They set off again, with Scott driving and Todd skiing. Todd then fell off. Mr Whittington notified Scott and told him that Todd had fallen off. Scott then started turning the jet ski to the left. Mr Whittington leaned forward to take the slack out of the towrope and at that point the jet ski hit the wake of another boat. The wake led the jet ski to became unstable and caused Mr Whittington to fall off. He fell into the water and his leg became tangled in the towrope and his foot was traumatically amputated.

Mr Whittington sued both Scott and Todd in the Supreme Court of the Australian Capital Territory, in negligence and claimed damages. Scott and Todd both pleaded an immunity from liability under the *Civil Liability Act 2003* (Qld) (the Act) on the basis of a materialisation of an obvious risk of a dangerous recreational activity. Scott and Todd also joined as a third party Allianz Insurance Australia Limited. Allianz had denied liability to Todd under a policy of insurance that he had taken out because Scott, who was driving the jet ski at the time, was not licensed to drive it.

Mr Whittington alleged that Scott and Todd failed to properly instruct him in relation to his responsibilities relating to the towrope, failed to instruct him how to brace himself when sitting in a rearward position, failed to give notice that the jet ski was about to cross the wake of another boat and failed to avoid unnecessary sudden movements of the jet ski that might make him unstable on the jet ski.

Both Scott and Todd admitted the existence of a duty of care but denied that they had breached their duty of care. However they pleaded an immunity from liability, pursuant to the provisions of the *Civil Liability Act 2003* (QLD), in particular s 19, which protects a defendant from harm suffered as a result of the materialisation of an obvious risk of a dangerous recreational activity.

Allianz denied the claim on the basis of an exclusion clause within the policy, that Todd knew that Scott did not have a license. Scott and Todd relied upon s 54 of the *Insurance Contracts Act 1984* (Cth), that Allianz may not refuse to pay a claim, as no part of the loss was caused by the act of Scott in driving the jet ski while unlicensed.

***Held:* judgment in favour of the plaintiff against the defendants, judgment in favour of the defendants against the third party.**

Per Mossop AsJ:

1. The risk of harm was identified as the risk that a rearward facing passenger might become unbalanced or dislodged from the jet ski and suffer injury. That risk of harm was foreseeable and was not insignificant.

2. A reasonable person in the position of the brothers would have taken precautions against the risk, and the failure to take the precautions identified was a necessary condition of the occurrence of the harm.

3. As to the defence relating to the materialisation of an obvious risk created by a dangerous recreational activity, the brothers bear the onus of establishing the elements of the immunity, with the first matter to be determined was whether or not Mr Whittington

engaged in a dangerous recreational activity. A person in the position of Mr Whittington, riding the jet ski was not an activity with a significant risk of harm. It was therefore not a dangerous recreational activity. Further, the risk that materialised was a risk which was far from obvious. The harm that suffered was not the result of the materialisation of an obvious risk of that activity.

4. In relation to Allianz, the obtaining of a license would not have made any difference to the loss suffered by Mr Whittington. No part of Mr Whittington's loss was caused by the unlicensed driving of the jet ski. On the basis of s 54 of the Insurance Contracts Act, Allianz may not refuse to pay the claim by reason of that Act.

5. Mr Whittington's claim is upheld, and the claim against Allianz, with damages agreed in the total sum of $800,000.

[*Headnote by the Wolters Kluwer editors*]

Mr A Black SC with Mr J Wilson (instructed by Stacks Southern Lawyers) for the plaintiff.

Mr G Smith (instructed by Johnston Legal) for the defendants.

Mr D Lloyd (instructed by McCullough Robertson Lawyers) for the third party.

Before: Mossop AsJ.

[¶82-191] Mules v Ferguson

(2015) Aust Torts Reports ¶82-191
Medium neutral citation: [2015] QCA 005
Supreme Court of Queensland
Judgment delivered 06 February 2015

Professions and trades — Healthcare professionals — Medical practitioners — Liability in tort — General principles — Where the appellant was diagnosed on 26 September 2008 with cryptococcal meningitis, sustaining personal injuries — Loss of sight and hearing — Where the appellant brought an action in negligence against her general practitioner claiming the doctor did not undertake a proper examination or make proper enquiries as to the appellant's reported symptoms so as to exclude this disease — Where the appellant contended that had the doctor acted competently, the respondent would have referred the appellant for tests and treatment so that the disease was diagnosed and treated before she suffered her grievous injuries — Where, after an 11-day trial, the primary judge assessed the appellant's damages at over $6.7m but dismissed her claim — Where the central focus on appeal was whether the appellant ought to have been referred for specialist assessment by the respondent at the time of her consultations on 18 or 19 of September, and whether such a referral would have led to a diagnosis and commencement of treatment before the onset of the appellant's catastrophic injuries — Whether there was evidence the appellant had an observable restricted range of movement of the neck by 18 September 2008 — Whether testing movement in all directions during a physical examination was likely to have revealed difficulty in movement such as to warrant further investigation by means of specialist referral — Whether the appeal should be allowed.

Torts — Negligence — Applicability and effect in actions for negligence — Where s 22 of the Civil Liability Act 2003 (Qld) provides a defence to a breach of duty if the medical practitioner establishes he or she acted in a way which was widely accepted by peer professional opinion by a significant number of professionals in that field — Where the trial judge found that the respondent's conduct at the consultations on 18 and 19 September 2008 met this standard — Where the trial judge's finding was based on an acceptance of the opinions of two general practitioners that the respondent's management of the appellant's case was consistent with a reasonable standard of general practice — Where the opinions of the two general practitioners were based on facts consistent with the respondent's version of events — Where the facts as found by the trial judge were not entirely consistent with the respondent's version of events — Whether the respondent had discharged her onus under the Act — Civil Liability Act 2003 (Qld), s 22.

Ms Mules sustained devastating personal injuries, including the loss of her sight and hearing, after contracting cryptococcal meningitis in or about September 2008. Ms Mules consulted her general practitioner Dr Ferguson in June 2008, complaining of rushes of blood to the head and dizzy spells. The symptoms continued and by September 2008, she had also developed an extremely sore neck and was experiencing intermittent headaches. She consulted Dr Ferguson on 12 September complaining of worsening neck pain over the past six weeks. She again saw Dr Fegurson on 18 September and indicated her symptoms had "increased immensely". A physical examination was not conducted but Ms Mules was referred for a CT scan which showed five bulging discs in her cervical spine. She again presented to Dr Ferguson on 19 September for the results of the scan accompanied by her mother who had moved in to help her then 43-year-old daughter. She was prescribed medication for her alleged musculo-skeletal disorder and advised to go to bed for a week.

On 24 September, Ms Mules was suffering extreme pain in her neck and dizziness and was taken by ambulance to Cairns Base Hospital. She was diagnosed with a possible early chest infection and was discharged. On 25 September, Ms Mules was driven to Dr Ferguson's rooms by her mother who described her worsening pain and distress. Dr Ferguson referred Ms Mules to Cairns Private Hospital. By 26 September, Ms Mules was suffering from profound deafness, both pupils were sluggish and a lumbar puncture was positive for cryptococcal meningitis.

Ms Mules commenced proceedings against Dr Ferguson in negligence for failing to properly conduct an examination of Ms Mules, failing to recognise symptoms of her condition and failing to appropriately refer Ms Mules for specialist assessment or to her local hospital for further assessment.

Dr Ferguson contended that she had not been negligent and said even if she had referred Ms Mules at an earlier time, diagnosis and commencement of the necessary treatment could not have occurred any earlier as Ms Mules' condition on presentation up until 25 September 2008 meant it would be several days before diagnosis of cryptococcal meningitis could have been made. Further, Dr Ferguson argued that her conduct was consistent with widely accepted practice by professional peer opinion such that there was no breach of duty by reason of s 22 of the *Civil Liability Act 2003* (Qld).

His Honour found that Dr Ferguson failed to act with reasonable care and skill in not physically examining Ms Mules' neck and enquiring about the progress of her previously recorded symptoms of headache and facial flushing. However, his Honour found that breach did not cause Ms Mules' injuries. Such an examination and enquiries would not have detected anything to prompt Dr Ferguson, exercising reasonable care, to recognise the potential presence of a serious central nervous system condition, such as cryptococcal meningitis, rather than the musculo-skeletal disorder from which Ms Mules was apparently suffering, and respond differently.

The primary judge assessed damages as over $6.7m but dismissed Ms Mules' case on the basis that she failed to prove a causative breach of duty. His Honour also found that Dr Ferguson's conduct was lawful as it came within the defence provision of s 22 of the *Civil Liability Act 2003* (Qld).

Ms Mules appealed. The central focus on appeal was whether Ms Mules ought to have been referred for specialist assessment by Dr Ferguson at the time of her consultations on 18 or 19 September, and whether such a referral would have led to a diagnosis and commencement of treatment before the onset of Ms Mules' catastrophic injuries. Ms Mules contended the primary judge erred first, in finding that Dr Ferguson's breach of care was not causative of her injuries and, second, in finding that the doctor had a defence under s 22.

Dr Ferguson in a notice of contention argued first, that the judge erred in finding any breach of duty on her part and second, that, had Dr Ferguson referred Ms Mules to a specialist on 18 or 19 September, it was unlikely that cryptococcal meningitis would have been diagnosed and treated so that Ms Mules would have suffered her grievous injuries in any case.

Held: **appeal allowed.**

Per McMurdo P (agreeing with Boddice J):

1. A thorough review of the evidence of the chiropractor and the physiotherapist did not support the conclusion that had Dr Ferguson examined Ms Mules' neck by performing the chin on chest test on 18 or 19 September, she would not have detected neck stiffness suggestive of meningeal irritation. Rather, such an examination was likely to have revealed an inability to place her chin on her chest.

2. Ms Mules' history of worsening symptoms, prolonged distress and deteriorating condition since 5 September required Dr Ferguson, acting reasonably, to refer Ms Mules to a neurologist or specialist physician so as to exclude the possibility of her having the insidious and most serious disease of cryptococcal meningitis.

3. Ms Mules was plainly keen to alleviate her prolonged distress and had conscientiously attended various medical and health practitioners since 5 September. She would have attended a specialist by Monday 22 September and her meningitis would likely have been diagnosed and treated by 23 September, preventing the grievous injuries she suffered.

Per Applegarth J (in dissent):

1. A critical issue on the appeal is whether the primary judge erred in concluding that a physical examination on 18/19 September would not have detected neck stiffness suggestive of meningeal irritation and would not have caused Dr Ferguson to suspect the presence of a symptom with a cause any more sinister than a musculo-skeletal cause.

2. The trial judge's finding was not based on a misapprehension of evidence about neck stiffness. The trial judge considered in commendable detail the range of expert evidence and found that Ms Mules presented on 18 and 19 September with a reduced range of movement of her neck. The finding was properly made and supported by the evidence.

3. The evidence left open the possibility that a physical examination, including passive flexion, may not have allowed Ms Mules' chin to touch her chest. However on the causal breach issue, that *possibility* was not enough to discharge Ms Mules' onus of proving what a physical examination of her neck and further inquiry about her headache *probably* would have detected.

4. With respect to Ms Mules' headaches, there was no sound basis for disturbing the primary judge's assessment of the evidence that at the relevant time Ms Mules was experiencing intermittent headache associated with neck pain and inconsistent with the type of headache associated with cryptococcal meningitis.

5. The simple analgesia that had been recommended on 12 September may not have been adequate to treat Ms Mules' neck pain and associated symptoms. But this did not mean that her headaches were other than intermittent. It did not suggest that her pain and her restricted neck movement had other than a musculo-skeletal cause.

6. Although there was a breach of duty in failing to conduct a physical examination of Ms Mules' neck on 18 or 19 September, Ms Mules' case on causation failed for lack of sufficient evidence to conclude that had a physical examination of the neck, in conjunction with enquiry about headaches and facial flushing, been undertaken it would have made a difference to the tragic outcome which befell Ms Mules.

7. The evidence of Dr Kable and Dr Turnbull nor the evidence as a whole, warranted the conclusion that Dr Ferguson had discharged her onus in establishing a defence under s 22 of the *Civil Liability Act 2003* (Qld).

8. Based on the symptoms which the primary judge found Ms Mules had on 18 September, Dr Turnbull's evidence supported the conclusion that a physical examination should have been undertaken as a standard practice upon someone with neck pain, and also upon someone who presented with other symptoms as found by the primary judge.

9. Dr Kable's evidence was not persuasive as to why a physical examination would not have been undertaken on someone who presented with neck pain and stiffness.

10. The defence to a breach of duty claim was not established but had it been, s 22(5) would not have operated to exclude it. The relevant breach of duty and liability arose in this case in connection with a failure to examine and a failure to inquire which in turn were alleged to result in a failure to recognise a potentially serious condition and refer Ms Mules to a specialist for urgent assessment. This was not a case in which the posited liability arising from those breaches arose in connection with the giving of (or the failure) to give a warning, advice or other information.

11. Ms Mules failed to establish that the proven breaches caused her injury and loss and the appeal should be dismissed.

Per Boddice J:

1. Contrary to the conclusion of the trial judge that there was no observable neck stiffness or lack of movement prior to 25 September, there was evidence Ms Mules had an observable restricted range of movement of the neck by 18 September. Having regard to the fact that Ms Mules had cryptococcal meningitis, the trial judge erred in concluding a physical examination preformed on 18 or 19 September would not have caused Dr Ferguson to suspect the presence of a symptom with a cause any more sinister than a musculo-skeletal cause.

2. A medical practitioner would have performed the physical examination that would have been undertaken. If carried out in accordance with the medical practitioner's duty to exercise reasonable care and skill, it would have involved testing movement in all directions. That would have included the cardinal test of the chin to the chest. That test might not have definitively indicated the presence of meningeal infection, but it is likely to have revealed difficulty in movement such as to warrant further investigation by means of a specialist referral.

3. Further enquiries as to the location of the headaches would have revealed the headaches were associated with neck pain which is an indicator of the presence of the condition.

4. The evidence in respect of an observable restriction in Ms Mules' range of movement and the existence of headaches, in the context of a deteriorating condition, supported a conclusion that if Dr Ferguson, exercising reasonable care and skill, had undertaken a physical examination of Ms Mules' neck and made appropriate enquiries as to the location, duration, frequency and severity of her headaches at the consultations on 18 and 19 September, she would have concluded that Ms Mules had symptoms consistent with the possibility of meningeal infection.

5. Such a conclusion ought to have resulted in Dr Ferguson, acting in accordance with her duty of care, referring Ms Mules for investigation either to a specialist or to her local hospital. The trial judge's findings that such a referral was likely to have led to Ms Mules' condition being diagnosed and treatment commenced on or before 23 September, with the consequence that Ms Mules would not have suffered her catastrophic injuries, were open on the evidence.

6. The trial judge's finding that Dr Ferguson's conduct on 18 and 19 September fell within the s 22 defence was based on an acceptance of the opinions of two experienced general

practitioners, Dr Kable and Dr Turnbull. However, their opinions were based on facts consistent with Dr Ferguson's version of events. The facts as found by the trial judge were not entirely consistent with Dr Ferguson's version of events.

7. The trial judge found by 18 September, Ms Mules' condition had deteriorated; not only was there a reduced range of movement, there was a complaint of dizziness for the first time and ongoing headaches. The trial judge failed to have regard to those symptoms when finding that Dr Kable and Dr Turnbull's opinions were that Dr Ferguson's consultations were consistent with a reasonable standard of general practice. There was no evidence upon which the trial judge could be satisfied that Dr Ferguson had discharged her onus under s 22.

[*Headnote by the Wolters Kluwer editors*]

S Doyle QC, with R Lynch and A Katsikalis (instructed by Shine Lawyers), for the appellant.

G Diehm QC with J Trevino (instructed by K & L Gates), for the respondent.

Before: Applegarth and Boddice JJ and McMurdo P.

[¶82-141] Lamble v Howl at the Moon Broadbeach Pty Ltd

(2013) Aust Torts Reports ¶82-141
Medium neutral citation: [2013] QSC 244
Supreme Court of Queensland
Judgment delivered 9 September 2013

Torts — Negligence — Vicarious liability — Employee of nightclub assaulted patron plaintiff — Whether employee authorised to perform security-related duties — Whether significant connection between employee's unauthorised act and his employment — Whether unauthorised act done in furtherance of employer's interests — Where plaintiff suffered other, unrelated injuries following the assault — Whether other injuries significant and relevant to apportionment and measurement of damages — Civil Liability Act 2003 (Qld), s 4; 9(1)(b).

Mr Cerantonio was employed as a barman by Howl at the Moon Broadbeach Pty Ltd (Howl). Mr Cerantonio hit the plaintiff, Mr Lamble, with a metal rubbish collector while Mr Lamble was standing on the periphery of a fight involving a manager of the Howl nightclub and other unruly patrons. Mr Lamble suffered significant head injuries.

Before the assault Mr Lamble had worked as a roof labourer. After the assault, Mr Lamble experienced chronic neck and back pain, migraines and suffered from depression and anxiety. He sought psychiatric treatment for suicidal thoughts and also experienced financial difficulties and separated from his wife. After Mr Lamble was involved in a motor vehicle accident in 2010, the lower back pain he experienced after the assault became worse.

Mr Lamble brought an action in trespass against Howl, claiming that it was vicariously liable for the actions of its employee and that Howl had breached its duty to him as an occupier at common law and under statute by virtue of s 9(1)(b) of the *Civil Liability Act 2003* (Qld).

Howl's defence to the claim of vicarious liability was that Mr Cerantonio, in assaulting Mr Lamble, had not acted within the scope of his authority as a bartender. It was submitted that Mr Cerantonio had been instructed orally and in writing not to become involved in crowd control, fights, the commission of assaults or security issues. Howl then submitted that if it had breached an independent duty owed to Mr Lamble, Mr Lamble had voluntarily involved himself in the scuffle outside the bar where it was foreseeable that an excessive act from another participant could cause injury and sought a finding of contributory negligence.

Mr Lamble contended that contributory negligence was not available as a defence to an action for trespass to the person and that the Civil Liability Act did not apply in respect of that cause of action because it did not involve a breach of duty as set forth in s 4. It was also submitted that the additional injuries sustained in the subsequent motor vehicle accident

should have been viewed as having caused a negative impact upon whatever opportunity Mr Lamble had of returning to some form of work after the assault. Mr Lamble then submitted that a reasonable way to factor in the motor vehicle-based injuries was to allow a discount for contingencies, in respect of past and future economic loss.

Held: verdict for the plaintiff.

Per Douglas J

Vicarious liability

1. The mere fact that Mr Cerantonio's conditions of employment may have provided that he should have deferred to security staff did not mean that what he did was not in the course of his employment, especially when no security staff were available. The fact that Mr Lamble was not actively involved in the struggle when he was hit did not lead to the conclusion that this was an independently aggressive act by Mr Cerantonio.

2. Mr Cerantonio's actions were carried out in intended or ostensible pursuit of Howl's interests in protecting the manager. He was not engaged in a frolic of his own. Alternatively, there was a sufficiently close connection between what he did and his employment to make it just that Howl should be liable for Mr Lamble's injury. Even though what Mr Cerantonio did was inappropriate, it did not take it out of the category of case where he was defending his employer's interests. Howl had an interest in preserving order outside its premises as well as in preserving its manager's welfare. Howl was, therefore, vicariously liable in negligence for Mr Cerantonio's actions towards Mr Lamble.

Direct liability

3. It was probable that there was some oral instruction to Mr Cerantonio not to behave in the manner in which he did and to leave security issues to the security staff. However, there was no evidence that the manager's actions in escorting the unruly patron from the premises himself rather than using security staff should have been treated as a general revocation of the earlier advice to bar staff. It may have provided some implicit encouragement to Mr Cerantonio's behaviour in coming to the manager's aid but it did not revoke the general instruction.

Contributory negligence

4. As no breach of an independent duty owed by Howl was established, no occasion arose to determine this issue.

Damages

5. When Mr Lamble's psychiatric disability was coupled with the consequences of the physical injuries he suffered, his overall disability stemming from the attack could be assessed as very serious. His psychiatric disability provided the major component of his disability. It seemed likely that the assault was the serious contributor to his psychiatric problems. It was also likely that the neck injury he suffered was more significant than the subsequent back injury from the motor vehicle accident. His earning capacity was also substantially destroyed by the assault.

6. The motor vehicle accident added to the injury caused by the assault. It did not prevent the harm caused by the assault from continuing to affect the earning capacity, pain and suffering and the loss of amenities already sustained by Mr Lamble. The additional injuries were a contingency which had actually happened. The bulk of the damage had been done, however, before the motor vehicle accident.

[*Headnote by the Wolters Kluwer editors*]

G Diehm SC with B Munro (instructed by Shine Lawyers) for the plaintiff.

D Atkinson (instructed by Barry Nilsson) for the defendant.

Before: Douglas J.

[¶81-989] Pollard v Trude

(2008) Aust Torts Reports ¶81-989;

Medium neutral citation: [2008] QCA 421

Queensland Court of Appeal

Judgment delivered 23 December 2008

Torts — Duty of care — Breach of duty — Warnings — Golf injury — Appellant was injured when struck by a golf ball which respondent had hit — Respondent called out "watch it" or "watch out" after hitting ball — Appellant looked towards ball as a consequence of that call — Proceedings commenced by appellant against respondent claiming damages for consequential injuries — Appellant claimed that respondent had been under a duty to call "fore" after hitting the ball — Primary judge held that respondent had fully discharged his duties by calling "watch it" or "watch out" — Appellant appealed to Court of Appeal — Whether respondent had been obliged to call "fore" — Whether respondent had breached his duty to appellant — Civil Liability Act 2003 (Qld), ss 9, 13, 14, 15, 16.

The appellant (Dr Pollard) was playing golf with the respondent (Mr Trude) as part of a club competition with two others. In the course of one of the holes, Dr Pollard was up ahead of Mr Trude on the fairway searching for his ball in some trees. While Dr Pollard was doing that, Mr Trude took his shot. Mr Trude did not mean to hit his ball in Dr Pollard's direction at that time but did so inadvertently. Soon after hitting the ball, Mr Trude called out "Watch it, Errol" or "Watch out, Errol" (Dr Pollard's first name was Erroll). That call caused Dr Pollard to turn in the direction of where Mr Trude had hit the ball from. As he so turned, the ball which Mr Trude had hit ricocheted off a tree and struck Dr Pollard just above the right eye.

Proceedings were subsequently commenced by Dr Pollard against Mr Trude in respect of his consequential injuries. At first instance, those proceedings were unsuccessful. The primary judge held that Mr Trude's call of "Watch it, Errol" or "Watch out, Errol" was meant as a warning and not as a request to Dr Pollard to see where the ball ended up. In that context, the primary judge rejected the notion that only a call of "fore" could be regarded as a warning. For that reason, Mr Trude was found to have done all that he reasonably could have done to warn Dr Pollard of the unexpectedly mis-hit ball heading towards him.

Dr Pollard then appealed to the Court of Appeal. In essence, the issue in the appeal was whether Mr Trude's duty of care to Dr Pollard had obliged him to give a particular type of warning before he played his shot. More specifically, the issue was whether, in order to discharge his duty of care, Mr Trude had been obliged to shout out "fore" rather than "Watch it" or "Watch out".

***Held:* appeal dismissed.**

Per McMurdo P

1. The primary judge was correct to conclude that Mr Trude's call of "Watch it, Errol" or "Watch out, Errol" was meant as a warning and not as a request to Dr Pollard to see where the ball ended up. It followed that Mr Trude had taken steps to warn Dr Pollard of the imminent danger.

2. Mr Trude did all that could reasonably be expected to warn Dr Pollard of the unexpectedly mis-hit ball heading towards him. It had just been unfortunate that, on hearing the warning, Dr Pollard, instead of covering his head and face with his hands, turned in the direction of the call.

Per Holmes JA (with whom White AJA agreed)

3. A call of "fore" might have been warranted had Mr Trude mis-hit the ball directly towards Dr Pollard. However, Mr Trude's state of information was that his ball was travelling, several metres up, into a tree on the edge of a grove where Dr Pollard was standing.

4. In hindsight, "fore" might have been the call better designed to produce a quicker and more effective reaction to danger (because it might have produced some protection of the face). The shout of "Watch it, Errol" or "Watch out, Errol" was nevertheless a reasonable response in the circumstances.

5. Mr Trude's call was especially reasonable when it was considered that a warning only became necessary once the ball entered the trees where Dr Pollard was. It was unlikely that there could have been more than a second or two from then until the ball actually ricocheted and hit Dr Pollard.

[*Headnote by the Wolters Kluwer editors*]

R Wensley QC for the appellant (instructed by McInnes Wilson).

R Douglas SC with S Cilento for the respondent (instructed by Minter Ellison).

Before: McMurdo P, Holmes JA and White AJA.

South Australia

[¶82-789] Plumridge v Pandelis

(2022) Aust Torts Reports ¶82-789
Medium neutral citation: [2022] SADC 42
District Court of South Australia
11 April 2022

Motor accident — Assessment of damages — Interaction of common law and statutory damages — Civil liability legislation modifications — Civil Liability Act 1936 (SA), ss 3, 35, 51, 52, 53, 54, 55, 56A, 76 — Civil Liability Regulations 2013 (SA), ss 14, 23.

Injured cyclist awarded more than $270,000

A young woman who was injured when she was knocked off her bike while riding to work, has successfully sued the defendant driver in negligence and been awarded damages of more than $270,000 in damages, with no reduction for contributory negligence. Liability was admitted and the matter proceeded to hearing as to quantum only. The court noted that the claim concerned an assessment of damages under the *Civil Liability Act 1936* and the Civil Liability Regulations 2013 in circumstances where the provisions of the Act and the Regulations relevant to the case had not been judicially considered. The court found that the plaintiff suffered both physical and psychological injuries attributable to the accident and rejected the defendant driver's claim that the plaintiff exaggerated the extent of her claimed injuries and the level of adverse impact. Damages were assessed in the total sum of $271,864, including $5,200 for non-economic loss.

Before: Thomas J.

Wolters Kluwer Note: The full text of the judgment is accessible through the District Court of South Australia database on the AustLII website.

[¶82-556] Sloan v Service Stream Ltd

(2020) Aust Torts Reports ¶82-556
Medium neutral citation: [2020] SADC 98
District Court of South Australia
28 July 2020

Torts — Negligence — Contributory negligence — Essentials of action for negligence — Damage — Causation — Measure and remoteness of damages in actions for tort — Personal injuries — Loss of earnings and earning capacity — Civil Liability Act 1936 (SA), ss 31, 32, 34, 35, 36, 39,44,52,54,58 — Law Reform (Contributory Negligence and Apportionment of Liability) Act 2001 (SA), ss 3, 7 — Workers Rehabilitation & Compensation Act 1986 (SA), ss 35, 36 — Return to Work Act 2014 (SA), s 66.

At approximately 11 am on 13 March 2013, 41-year-old Eugene Sloan was undertaking pit and pipe installation work for Service Stream Ltd (Service Stream), under a labour hire contract with Mr Sloan's employer, Skilled Group Ltd (Skilled). Mr Sloan claimed to have suffered an injury to his lower back when he attempted to lift a "P9 pit" that weighed approximately 60 kg with two other workers.

Mr Sloan had previously injured his lower back at work in 2009, 2011 and on 7 January 2013. At the time Mr Sloan applied for employment with Skilled, he was certified unfit for work and was in receipt of workers compensation benefits. However, he did not disclose this, or any prior work-related back injury, in his application with Skilled.

Mr Sloan commenced proceedings in the District Court of South Australia against Service Stream, in negligence and claimed damages. He argued that Service Stream was

negligent in failing to provide appropriate training or instruction with respect to the lifting of the pit and/or appropriate assistance to enable the pit to be safely lifted; failing to establish, implement, provide and/or maintain a safe and appropriate system of work for the lifting of the pit; and failing to take all reasonable care to avoid reasonably foreseeable injury where Service Stream knew or ought to have known of the risk of injury arising from lifting the pit. [211], [212]

Service Stream denied liability and argued that any disability and/or incapacity suffered by Mr Sloan was the result of a pre-existing medical condition. Service Stream also argued that Mr Sloan was contributorily negligent in failing to disclose his prior back injuries to Skilled (and therefore Service Stream), engaging in employment which he knew required him to engage in heavy manual lifting in light of his history of prior back injury, and the manner in which he lifted the pit. [222], [223]

Held: judgment in favour of the plaintiff.

1. Mr Sloan bore the burden of proving a breach of duty by Service Stream on the balance of probabilities. As such, Mr Sloan carried the onus of proving that a reasonable person in the position of Service Stream would have taken precautions against the risk of harm. It was not for Service Stream to prove that such precautions were not necessary. [227]

2. Mr Sloan made a deliberate decision to withhold from Skilled (and therefore Service Stream) all information relating to his previous back injuries. He did not disclose to Skilled (and therefore Service Stream) that he had suffered any prior back injury; that he had ever had difficulties with his back, or with bending and twisting or with lifting, carrying or moving weights; and that he had any pre-existing injuries, diseases or medical conditions that could be affected by manual handling tasks, despite having knowledge of the disc injury he suffered at L5/S1. [325]

3. Mr Sloan was given no specific instruction or training by the Service Stream as to how to lift a P9 pit. Rather, he was expected to learn how to do so "on the job" by watching and learning. [329]

4. The evidence established that at the time of the incident Service Stream knew, or ought reasonably to have known, that the P9 pits weighed between 60 and 72 kg and were not only heavy, but awkward to lift because of their size and shape, and that Mr Sloan had received no specific training or instruction as to how to properly lift a P9 pit. [362]

5. Despite the fact that Service Stream knew nothing of Mr Sloan's prior back injuries, Service Stream knew, or ought reasonably to have known, that there was a foreseeable risk of injury in the event that P9 pits were not manually handled correctly and that such risk was not insignificant. [363]–[365]

6. Service Stream was negligent in that it failed to provide and maintain a safe system of work and failed to provide information, training, instruction or supervision necessary to prevent injury to Mr Sloan. [369]

7. As to contributory negligence, Mr Sloan must have known that in attempting to lift the pit in this manner, he was exposing himself to a significant risk of suffering an injury to his lower back. That risk was greater to Mr Sloan than to a physically fit person in the position of Mr Sloan, and only he knew that to be the case, given his failure to reveal the fact of his prior back injuries and/or condition (namely the existence of the disc bulge at L5/S1) to Service Stream. Mr Sloan's negligence caused or contributed to the incident. Liability is apportioned 60/40% as against Service Stream. [378], [379]

8. For the purposes of s 34(1)(a) of the *Civil Liability Act 1936* (SA), Service Stream's negligence, insofar as it caused or contributed to the incident, was a necessary condition of the occurrence of "harm" to Mr Sloan. [686]

9. Damages were assessed in the total sum of $80,355.06, reduced to $48,213.04 on account of a 40% reduction for contributory negligence.

[*Headnote by the Wolters Kluwer editors*]

A Siow (Di Sotto Lawyers) for the plaintiff.

M Tilley (HWL Ebsworth Lawyers) for the defendant.

Before: Schammer J.

Wolters Kluwer Note: The full text of the judgment is accessible through the District Court of South Australia database on the AustLII website.

[¶82-482] Clare & Gilbert Valleys Council v Kruse

(2019) Aust Torts Reports ¶82-482
Medium neutral citation: [2019] SASCFC 106
Supreme Court of South Australia, Full Court
6 September 2019

Torts — Negligence — Motor vehicles — Public roads — Maintenance of roads — Reduced visibility — Warning and danger signs — Council responsibilities — Breach of duty — Causation — Contributory negligence — Apportionment — Appeals — Respondent's car collided with a grader undertaking road maintenance — Grader was being driven by employee of appellant Council — Visibility at time of collision had been reduced because road at that point was gravel and a dust cloud had formed around vehicles — Trial Judge found that Council had been negligent in failing to adequately warn motorists but that respondent was also liable for contributory negligence — Liability apportioned at 50% to each party — Council appealed — Held: appeal dismissed — Council failed to take proper steps to ensure motorists were properly warned of upcoming hazard — Trial Judge's apportionment of liability was within reasonable range — Civil Liability Act 1936 (SA) s 31, 32, 34 and 50.

On 1 March 2011, the respondent, Mr Brenton Kruse, was driving his car behind a semi-trailer along Main Road 45 in Steelton in South Australia. The road was initially made of bitumen but then changed to gravel. The semi-trailer suddenly created a dust cloud, severely restricting Mr Kruse's vision. As Mr Kruse drove through an intersection, his vehicle collided with a grader and he was injured as a result. That grader was being operated by an employee of the Clare & Gilbert Valleys Council (the Council) in the course of performing maintenance on the road. That job required the grader to be driven from time to time on the incorrect side of the road. At the time of the collision, the grader was moving towards the oncoming traffic at a slow speed and Mr Kruse's car was on the correct side of the road.

Mr Kruse commenced proceedings in the District Court of South Australia against the Council, in negligence and claimed damages. He alleged that the grading operation was being conducted negligently in that there were insufficient warning signs or markings. He contended that those requirements had been particularly necessary in light of the fact that the road at that point was gravel and that it was foreseeable that a cloud of dust would be created by traffic heading towards the grader.

The parties agreed as to quantum and liability was the only issue at trial. On that question, the trial Judge found in favour of Mr Kruse, that the Council was negligent, but also found that Mr Kruse was guilty of contributory negligence given that he had been driving ''blind'' at the time of the collision. Liability was apportioned on the basis that both parties were 50% responsible.

The Council appealed the primary judge's findings.

***Held:* appeal dismissed.**

Per Blue, Lovell and Hinton JJ:

1. Standards and industry practice could be a guide in determining what was reasonable in the conduct of a particular trade, business, profession or activity. However, when the risk of injury was high, the potential effect of injury was serious and the cost of eliminating the risk of injury was small, it was unlikely that such practice would negate a finding of negligence. [33]–[35]

2. However, even if standards and industry practice were applicable, it had to be shown that they were actually applied in the circumstances. In this case, there was no evidence that the employee driving the grader ever performed the risk assessment that was required by the standards that the Council relied upon. [36]–[53].

3. It followed that the Council did not use more warning signs because it had carried out a risk assessment of what was actually needed, but simply because it was not its usual practice to place additional signage when that type of grading was being carried out. The Council did not comply with the standard of care imposed upon it. [54]–[60]

4. Had the Council carried out a proper risk assessment, it would have been bound to conclude that the road surface was such that dust from its surface presented a foreseeable risk of causing visibility problems for traffic passing the grader. In turn, the need for additional warning signage would have become apparent. [61]–[73]

5. A sign restricting the speed of vehicles as they approached the grader would have reduced the dust. The failure to restrict the speed of vehicles was causative of the dust and therefore the collision. These conclusions had been open to the trial Judge and hence causation had also been established. [74]–[101]

6. In considering the apportionment of responsibility, it was to be borne in mind that Mr Kruse's visibility was also reduced behind him. He therefore could not have stopped completely without risking a collision. Mr Kruse bore some responsibility for what happened. In the circumstances, 50% apportionment had been appropriate. [102]–[123].

[*Headnote by the Wolters Kluwer editors*]

A Harris QC and P Bullock (Wallmans Lawyers) for the appellant.

F Nelson QC (Steven M Clarke Pty Ltd) for the respondent.

Before: Blue, Lovell and Hinton JJ.

Wolters Kluwer Note: The full text of the judgment is accessible through the Supreme Court of South Australia Full Court database on the AustLII website at www.austlii.edu.au

---

[¶82-388] Amaca Pty Ltd v Latz

(2018) Aust Torts Reports ¶82-388
Medium neutral citation: [2018] HCA 22
High Court of Australia
13 June 2018

Negligence — Personal injury — Damages — Assessment of present value of future loss — Where claimant diagnosed with terminal malignant mesothelioma postretirement — Where claimant's life expectancy reduced — Where claimant receiving superannuation pension under Superannuation Act 1988 (SA) and age pension under Social Security Act 1991 (Cth) — Whether superannuation pension entitlement which would have been received during remainder of preillness life expectancy compensable loss — Whether age pension entitlement which would have been received during remainder of pre-illness life expectancy compensable loss — Whether reversionary pension payable under s 38(1)(a) of Superannuation Act to partner on claimant's death should be deducted from damages award.

This case is two appeals from the Full Court of the Supreme Court of South Australia ('Full Court').

Mr Latz is a retiree who is dying from acute mesothelioma (lung cancer), diagnosed in 2016, and caused by the negligence of Amaca Pty Ltd ('Amaca'). In the mid 1970's, Mr Latz inhaled asbestos while cutting and installing fencing manufactured by Amaca. Mr Latz' life expectancy has been reduced by over 16 years. Mr Latz receives the age pension under Part 2.2 of the *Social Security Act 1991* (Cth) ('SSA') and a superannuation pension under the *Superannuation Act 1988* (SA) ('SA').

The Full Court held that the value of age pension and superannuation payments that Mr Latz *could* have received had his life expectancy not been reduced, was a compensable loss. Amaca appeals this finding. The damages awarded to Mr Latz were reduced to account for a reversionary pension payable upon his death, to Mr Latz' partner, Ms Taplin, pursuant to s 38(1)(a) of the SA. Mr Latz appeals this finding.

Held: Matter No A8/2018 – Appeal allowed in part; Matter No A7/2018 – Appeal dismissed.

Per Kiefel CJ and Keane J (dissenting):

1. The Full Court's finding was novel. Amaca's argument that Mr Latz's loss of pension and superannuation payments was not the result of any loss of earning capacity and hence does not constitute actual financial loss, ought to be accepted. Entitlement to superannuation benefits was 'earned' by Mr Latz prior to any impact to his earning capacity, whilst the age pension is a gratuitous statutory benefit. The Full Court failed to distinguish between income actively earned and income passively received from a pension or superannuation.

2. The compensatory principle, that a plaintiff be placed in the position they would have been had they not suffered negligence, is well-established. However, this applies to compensable damage. The accepted heads of loss are non-pecuniary losses for loss of amenities of life, loss of earning capacity – not the loss of earnings themselves, and actual financial loss sustained by reason of the injury: *CSR Ltd* v *Eddy* [2005] HCA 64. Liability for economic loss should not be expanded beyond these heads of damage.

3. The potentially long interval between mesothelioma infection and symptoms does not detract from the nature of the loss when it *is* sustained and on what basis that loss is compensable.

4. In assessing damages for loss of earning capacity, the court must have regard to the probable length of a plaintiff's working life had they not been injured, and not merely their probable life expectancy as a result of the injury. Loss of the enjoyment of a passive income by a plaintiff's untimely death is not a compensable economic loss. If such loss is compensable at all, it is only a modest aspect of the loss of amenities of life. Because he retired prior to 'injury', Mr Latz suffered no loss of earning capacity, whilst his age pension accrues regardless.

Per Bell, Gageler, Nettle, Gordon and Edelman JJ:

5. Any compensation to Mr Latz is for actual loss, guided by the compensatory principle. Mr Latz is entitled to damages for loss of earning capacity for those years in which he otherwise would have been earning income. Because Superannuation benefits are remunerative, they form part of an assessment of loss of earning capacity. However, the loss is not the loss of opportunity to enjoy the asset; rather it is the diminution in value of the asset.

6. Mr Latz has suffered a quantifiable loss which has a present value. The value of Mr Latz's capital asset, being his superannuation payment, has been diminished by Amaca's negligence. But for Amaca's negligence, Mr Latz's rights under the SA would have been more valuable. Mr Latz's superannuation is intrinsically linked to his earning capacity. There is no

principled basis for denying Mr Latz compensation for lost superannuation benefit, solely because his illness only materialised after his retirement. Amaca cannot avoid liability by arguing that Mr Latz's earning capacity was not impacted by their negligence.

7. In contrast, Mr Latz's aged pension is not intrinsically linked to earning capacity or remuneration. This payment is not a future income stream to which Mr Latz is entitled; rather it ceases on his death. As such, it should not be included in the damages payable to Mr Latz. The assessment of damages must also account for any asset value which remains following a plaintiff's death, in this case the reversionary interest payable to Ms Taplin. Hence Mr Latz's appeal against reduction of the damages, by reason of that amount, is rejected.

[*Headnote by the Wolters Kluwer editors*]

JT Gleeson SC with DF Villa and CG Winnett for the Appellant in Matter A8/2018 and the Respondent in Matter A7/2018.

DF Jackson QC with S Tzouganatos for the Respondent in Matter A8/2018 and the Appellant in Matter A7/2018.

Before: Kiefel CJ, Bell, Gageler, Keane, Nettle, Gordon and Edelman JJ.

[¶82-216] King v Philcox

(2015) Aust Torts Reports ¶82-216
Medium neutral citation: [2015] HCA 19
High Court of Australia
Judgment delivered 10 June 2015

Negligence — Duty of care — Mental harm — Motor accident — Civil Liability Act 1936 (SA) — Appellant negligently drove motor vehicle resulting in death of passenger — Respondent witnessed aftermath — Respondent later realised brother died in accident — Whether appellant as driver owed duty of care to passenger's brother not to cause mental harm — Whether mental harm to brother of person killed foreseeable under s 33 of Civil Liability Act — Whether sibling relationship relevant to foreseeability — Damages for mental harm — Civil Liability Act 1936 (SA) — Whether respondent present at scene of accident when accident occurred — Whether accident includes aftermath. Words and phrases — "accident", "duty of care", "incident", "present at the scene of the accident when the accident occurred", "proximity", "reasonably foreseeable" — Civil Liability Act 1936 (SA), s 33, 53(1)(a).

On 12 April 2005, Scott Philcox was a passenger in a motor vehicle driven by George King in a suburb of Adelaide. As a result of Mr King's negligence, the vehicle collided with another at an intersection. Scott Philcox was fatally injured and died a short time after impact while trapped in the vehicle. Ryan Philcox, the plaintiff in the proceedings, was the brother of Scott who died in the accident. He drove past the accident site on a number of occasions without realising that it was his brother who was trapped and dying. He nevertheless clearly saw the wreckage of the car and inferred that its front passenger would have been fatally wounded. It was not until later that night that Mr Philcox's parents informed him that his brother had been killed in a car accident at the location that he witnessed. Only at that point did he make the connection. Subsequently, he developed a major depressive disorder. He then sought damages for pure mental harm from the defendant, George King, who admitted negligence in causing the accident.

Mr Philcox's evidence, in particular, his evidence of five occasions on which he drove through or turned left at the intersection and his evidence of how he learned of his brother's death was accepted by the district court judge. Mr King owed Mr Philcox a duty to take reasonable care not to cause him mental harm. A reasonable person in Mr King's position would have foreseen that a person of normal fortitude in Mr Philcox's position might suffer a

psychiatric illness as a result of the sudden shock upon seeing or hearing of his brother's death. Mr Philcox was found to have suffered mental harm within the meaning of s 33 of the *Civil Liability Act 1936* (SA) (CL Act). That mental harm consisted of a recognised psychiatric illness as a result of the shock upon receiving the news. Despite these findings in relation to duty and breach, the trial judge held that Mr Philcox could not recover damages as he did not witness, at the scene of the accident, his brother being killed, injured or put in peril and was therefore not present at the scene of the accident when the accident occurred which were the requirements of s 53 CL Act. Section 53(1) of the CL Act states that damages may only be awarded for mental harm if the injured person:

(a) was physically injured in the accident or was present at the scene of the accident when the accident occurred, or

(b) is a parent, spouse, domestic partner or child of a person killed, injured or endangered in the accident.

Mr Philcox appealed those findings to the Full Court of the Supreme Court of South Australia. Mr King filed a notice of alternative contention challenging the primary judge's finding that he owed Mr Philcox a duty of care. That notice was briefly dismissed by Gray J, who wrote the leading judgment (with which Sulan and Parker JJ agreed).

Despite the s 53 restriction, the Full Court of the Supreme Court of South Australia (Full Court) found that Mr Philcox had been present at the scene of the accident when the accident occurred and that he thereby satisfied the condition for recovery of damages for pure mental harm. Presence at the aftermath of an accident was considered sufficient. The Full Court was satisfied that there was a direct temporal link between the motor vehicle accident death and the development of the condition of a major depressive disorder. The Full Court held that the primary judge had found, and found correctly, that Mr King owed Mr Philcox a duty of care. It also held, however, that the primary judge erred in finding that Mr Philcox was not present at the scene of the accident when it occurred. Mr Philcox's appeal was allowed and the Full Court awarded him damages in the sum of $69,212.75.

Mr King appealed arguing that both the judge at first instance and the Full Court on appeal had erred in holding that he did owe Mr Philcox a duty of care. Further, even if a duty of care existed, Mr King argued that Mr Philcox could not recover damages because of the operation of s 53. Mr Philcox was not present at the scene of the accident when the accident occurred, nor was he a parent, spouse, domestic partner or child of a person killed, injured or endangered in the accident. Neither of the arms of s 53 was satisfied.

Held: appeal allowed.

Per French CJ, Kiefel and Gageler JJ:

1. It is s 33 of the CL Act that controls the extent of the duty of care to avoid causing mental harm, and, as in the common law, the existence of a duty of care not to cause another person pure mental harm is dependent upon a number of variables which inform the foreseeability of risk.

2. Section 33 does not prescribe any particular pre-existing relationship. It does not require the plaintiff to have witnessed at the scene a person being killed, injured or put in peril. It does not require a sudden shock. It does require that the defendant has in contemplation a person of normal fortitude in the plaintiff's position.

3. Having regard to the variables which can be taken into account for the purpose of determining the existence of the duty of care, it cannot be said that the conclusion reached by the Full Court in this case was wrong.

4. This court has previously held that a duty of care is owed to a parent, spouse, child, fellow employee or rescuer of a victim. That is not to say that it is not owed to the

sibling of a victim. Section 33 includes as one of the variables the nature of the relationship between the plaintiff and the person killed, injured or put in peril.

5. **The question of causation is not raised by the grounds of appeal in the case. It follows that if Mr King owed Mr Philcox the relevant duty of care, it was breached by his negligent driving which had the consequence that Mr Philcox suffered recognised psychiatric illness.**
6. **The application of s 53(1)(a) and the text of the particular section does not support the extended notion of "[presence] at the scene of the accident when the accident occurred" for which Mr Philcox contends.**
7. **According to the ordinary English usage, he drove past "the scene of the accident" several times. Even if, on that basis, he could be taken to be "present at the scene of the accident", he was not "present at the scene of the accident when the accident occurred".**
8. **Despite the existence of a duty of care and its breach, and resulting mental harm to Mr Philcox, his claim is defeated by the explicit language of the condition imposed by s 53(1)(a) and the Full Court erred in its construction and application of s 53 (1)(a) in this case.**

Per Keane J:

1. **Because Mr Philcox was not a parent, spouse or child of the deceased, s 53 (1)(a) prevented him from recovering damages for the mental harm he was caused by Mr King's negligent driving unless he was "present at the scene of the accident when the accident occurred". This was so, even though Mr King had, by his negligent driving, breached his duty of care to Mr Philcox.**
2. **Mr Philcox was not "present at the scene of accident when the accident occurred" for two independent reasons. Firstly, being in the same locale as the accident isn't sufficient to satisfy s 53(1)(a). Secondly, even if Mr Philcox was present at the scene of the accident, he was not present *when the accident occurred.***
3. **To say, as the Full Court did, that an "accident ... encompasses events at the scene after its occurrence" is to expressly depart from the language of s 53(1)(a). Events that take place after an accident has occurred have not taken place "when the accident occurred".**
4. **Given the unmistaken intention of s 53(1)(a) to cut back common law rights on a selective basis, it would be out of place to insist upon an artificial construction in order to preserve common law rights. In any event, it is to strain too far against the plain meaning of s 53(1)(a) to say that "an accident" is "synonymous" with its aftermath.**

Per Nettle J:

1. **Section 53(1) is considered to exclude the aftermath of an accident and so confines the class of eligible claimants for pure mental harm suffered as a result of an accident to claimants present at the scene of the accident at the relevant time or, if not present, to parents, spouses and children of persons killed or injured as a result of the accident. Mr Philcox sat outside those requirements.**

[*Headnote by the Wolters Kluwer editors*]

Appearances: M C Livesey QC with B J Doyle for the appellant (instructed by Finlaysons Lawyers).

P A Heywood-Smith QC with G Stathopoulos for the respondent (instructed by SE Lawyers).

Before: French CJ, Kiefel, Gegeler, Keane and Nettle JJ.

[¶82-250] Allen v Chadwick

(2016) Aust Torts Reports ¶82-250

Medium neutral citation: [2015] HCA 47

High Court of Australia

Judgment delivered 9 December 2015

Torts — Negligence — Contributory negligence — Section 47 of Civil Liability Act 1936 (SA) presumes contributory negligence of injured person who relied on care and skill of intoxicated person and who was aware or ought to have been aware that other person was intoxicated — Section 47(2)(b) establishes exception where injured person could not reasonably be expected to have avoided risk — Where respondent travelled in car with intoxicated driver and suffered serious injuries — Whether respondent could reasonably be expected to have avoided risk — Proper construction of s 47(2)(b) — Relevance of respondent's capacity to make reasonable assessment of relative risks — Relevance of subjective characteristics — Section 49 presumes contributory negligence where person injured in motor vehicle accident not wearing seatbelt — Where respondent was not wearing seatbelt and suffered serious injuries in motor vehicle accident — Whether appellant's erratic driving prevented respondent from fastening seatbelt — Whether factual findings overturned on appeal — Relevance of "act of a stranger" defence — "Act of a stranger", "could not reasonably be expected to have avoided the risk", "reasonable assessment of risk" — Civil Liability Act 1936 (SA), ss 3, 44(1), 47, 49.

At the time of the accident, Ms Chadwick (the plaintiff and respondent) was a 21-year-old pregnant woman who had a five-year-old daughter with her de facto partner Mr Allen (the defendant and appellant). She suffered catastrophic injuries in a motor vehicle accident when the car she was a backseat passenger in rolled, throwing her clear of the vehicle. Shortly before the accident, Ms Chadwick had been driving the motor vehicle while Mr Allen, and his friend, were passengers. Just outside the township, Ms Chadwick stopped her car to go to the toilet on the side of the road. When she left the car, Mr Allen assumed the driver's seat even though he was drunk. When Ms Chadwick returned to the car, Mr Allen was in the driver's seat. Ms Chadwick remonstrated with him and told him not to drive. She gave evidence that he replied, "Get the fuck in the car" or words to that effect.

Despite knowing that Mr Allen had been drinking, Ms Chadwick got into the backseat of the station wagon and Mr Allen commenced driving. Ms Chadwick failed to fasten her seatbelt or appreciate that she was in close proximity to her hotel. Later, while driving out of the township, Mr Allen accelerated rapidly and failed to take a right-hand curve. Ms Chadwick was thrown out of the backseat of the station wagon. Mr Allen was subsequently found to have had a blood alcohol level of 0.22 grams of alcohol per millilitre of blood at the time of the accident.

The primary judge concluded that, shortly after Ms Chadwick entered the rear passenger seat of the vehicle, Mr Allen lost control of the vehicle. As a result, Ms Chadwick was thrown from the vehicle and sustained acute spinal cord injuries. The judge had regard to the level of intoxication of Mr Allen and the evidence of the relevant expert witnesses in concluding that these events were caused by the gross negligence of Mr Allen.

Ms Chadwick's damages were assessed at $2,392,486.65. The judge made a reduction of 25% for contributory negligence on account of Ms Chadwick's failure to wear a seatbelt, pursuant to s 49 of the *Civil Liability Act 1936* (SA).

The primary liability issues at trial were:

- **whether when Ms Chadwick entered the vehicle, she did so in circumstances that attracted the mandatory statutory reduction on account of contributory negligence of 50% under s 47(5) of the Civil Liability Act, due to the driver being intoxicated with a blood alcohol concentration exceeding 0.15 grams in 100 millilitres of blood, and**

- whether Ms Chadwick's failure to wear a seatbelt at the time of the accident constituted a breach of the *Road Traffic Act 1961* (SA) so as to attract the mandated statutory reduction of 25% pursuant to s 49.

In relation to the first issue, the judge concluded that, viewed objectively, Ms Chadwick had little choice but to enter the vehicle in the particular circumstances, and that, on balance, no person in the precarious situation in which Ms Chadwick found herself could reasonably be expected to have any practical alternative in the matter other than to get into the backseat of the vehicle. This finding was challenged by Mr Allen on appeal.

In relation to the second issue, the judge concluded that, on balance, Ms Chadwick had sufficient opportunity to fasten her seatbelt but did not do so. As a consequence, the mandated statutory reduction of 25% applied. This is the finding that Ms Chadwick challenged on the cross-appeal.

Mr Allen complained on appeal that the judge should have found Ms Chadwick guilty of a further act of contributory negligence in that she relied on the care and skill of Mr Allen whom she was, or ought to have been, aware was intoxicated at the time of the accident. It was contended that, in these circumstances, the judge should have further reduced Ms Chadwick's award of damages by 50% in accordance with the terms of s 47 of the Civil Liability Act (SA).

The major liability issues for the appeal court to consider were:

- whether the judge erred in finding that the plaintiff could not reasonably be expected to have avoided the risk of being a passenger in a vehicle driven by an intoxicated person
- whether the judge erred in reducing the damages award by 25% on account of the plaintiff's failure to wear a seatbelt.

The Full Court of the Supreme Court of South Australia ruled that having regard to the objective circumstances facing the plaintiff, the judge was correct to conclude that she could not reasonably be expected to have avoided the risk of re-entering the vehicle. Additionally, the judge erred in reducing the plaintiff's damages by 25% on account of her failure to wear a seatbelt. The mandatory statutory reduction under s 49 of the Civil Liability Act will not apply where a plaintiff's failure to wear a seatbelt occurred in circumstances of involuntariness or as a result of the unlawful act of another person, as was the case in Ms Chadwick's situation. Accordingly, s 49 did not apply and the finding of contribution was set aside.

Mr Allen appealed to the High Court of Australia. The appeal to the High Court of Australia focused on whether a reasonable person in the position of Ms Chadwick would or ought to have known that Mr Allen was intoxicated and would have relied on him to drive (s 47(2)(b) issue), and whether Ms Chadwick had an opportunity to fasten her seatbelt (s 49 issue).

Held: appeal allowed in part.

Per French CJ, Keifel, Bell, Keane and Gordon JJ:

In relation to the s 47(2)(b) issue

1. Given the facts of the case Ms Chadwick could not reasonably have been expected to have avoided the risk of travelling with Mr Allen.

2. The evaluation which s 47(2)(b) contemplates is an evaluation of relative risk in a given situation by the exercise of reasonable powers of observation and appreciation of one's environment, as well as the exercise of a reasonable choice between alternative courses of action.

3. Once it is accepted that, as the trial judge found, Ms Chadwick did not know where she was, then the availability of a relatively low-risk alternative to travelling back to the hotel in the vehicle with Mr Allen was not reasonably apparent.

4. The trial judge found as a fact that Ms Chadwick did not know where she was, and did not appreciate how close she was to the township and the hotel; and it could not be said that her imperfect understanding of her situation was unreasonable.

In relation to the s 49 issue

5. The question was not whether Ms Chadwick's failure to fasten her seatbelt was an understandable, or even a reasonable, response to Mr Allen's driving. The question was whether she was prevented by Mr Allen from fastening her seatbelt.

6. There was no reason to interfere with the trial judge's finding of fact that Mr Allen's driving did not prevent Ms Chadwick from fastening her seatbelt.

7. The Full Court did not explain how it was that the trial judge erred in concluding that the manner of Mr Allen's driving did not actually prevent her from fastening her seatbelt at some time from when she entered the car until the occurrence of the accident.

8. The trial judge did not accept Ms Chadwick's account that the accident occurred "a matter of seconds" after she got into the back seat of the car. The account was inconsistent with evidence of the route travelled by the car while it was being driven by Mr Allen. That evidence established that there were at least two opportunities to engage the seatbelt as the car was driven on the straight sections of Main Street.

9. Ms Chadwick bore the onus of proof on this issue, and in this regard her account failed to satisfy the trial judge. His Honour was sceptical of Ms Chadwick's evidence generally; and there were good reasons not to accept Ms Chadwick's account in relation to the seatbelt issue.

10. Mr Allen's appeal should be allowed in relation to the s 49 issue with Ms Chadwick's award of damages reduced from $1,776,542.36 to $1,223,287.74.

[*Headnote by the Wolters Kluwer editors*]

M C Livesey QC with B J Doyle (instructed by Hunt & Hunt Solicitors) appeared for the appellant.

R J Whitington QC with J M Atkins and B J Krupka (instructed by Meller Olsson Lawyers) for the respondent.

Before: French CJ, Keifel, Bell, Keane and Gordon JJ.

[¶82-235] Anwar v Mondello Farms Pty Ltd

(2015) Aust Torts Reports ¶82-235
Medium neutral citation: [2015] SASCFC 109
Supreme Court of South Australia Full Court
Judgment delivered 10 August 2015

Torts — Negligence — Essentials of action for negligence — Damage — Causation.

Torts — Negligence — Essentials of action for negligence — Duty of care — Reasonable foreseeability of damage.

Torts — Negligence — Essentials of action for negligence — Where nervous shock or mental disorder.

Damages — Measure and remoteness of damages in actions for tort — remoteness and causation — pre-accident condition of plaintiff.

Appeal and new trial — Appeal — General principles — Civil Liability Act 1936 (SA), s 33.

Sayed Anwar was an Afghani refugee who arrived in Australia with his family in 2003. In 2005, Mr Anwar obtained employment as a process line stacker in a potato packing plant operated by Mondello Farms Pty Ltd (Mondello). His duties consisted of removing 20 kg bags of potatoes from a conveyor belt and placing them on a pallet. On 11 April 2005, about one week after Mr Anwar started work at Mondello, he suffered an injury when his hand became trapped in the conveyor belt. His hand was trapped for approximately 10 minutes and could

only be freed with the use of tools. As a result, Mr Anwar suffered a debridement injury, with the skin on the back of his hand being burnt and stripped off. He required plastic surgery and underwent a skin graft. Five months after the incident, Mr Anwar developed symptoms of stress and anxiety. He suffered a psychotic episode in September 2005 and was at that time diagnosed as suffering from schizophrenia and type two diabetes. Mr Anwar had not worked since the incident.

Mr Anwar commenced proceedings in the District Court of South Australia against Mondello, in negligence and claimed damages. His Honour Cuthbertson J found Mondello liable in negligence and breach of statutory duty. His Honour also found that Mr Anwar's schizophrenia was caused by the hand injury and that the schizophrenia was the main cause of Mr Anwar's inability to work. He reasoned that the case involved consequential, rather than pure, mental harm on the basis that Mr Anwar's schizophrenia was a consequence of suffering a bodily injury. However, Cuthbertson J also found that Mondello did *not* owe Mr Anwar a duty of care under s 33 of the *Civil Liability Act 1936* (SA) (the Act), that Mondello did not owe a duty to take care not to cause Mr Anwar mental harm, and that Mondello did not know and could not reasonably have known Mr Anwar was a person of less than normal fortitude.

Damages were awarded only in respect of the physical hand injury and were assessed at $18,042.30. His Honour undertook a notional assessment of damages, in the event that he was wrong in the application of s 33 of the Act and that a duty of care existed, and assessed total damages in the sum of $1.6m. His Honour also noted the high likelihood that Mr Anwar would have developed schizophrenia in any event and irrespective of the injury to his hand and reduced damages by 30%.

Mr Anwar appealed on the basis that the primary judge erred in his construction and application of s 33 of the Act. He argued that the primary judge erred by concentrating on whether Mondello should have foreseen Mr Anwar's schizophrenia rather than foreseeing the development of a psychiatric illness of any kind. He also argued that the primary judge erred in finding that the development of a psychiatric illness was not reasonably foreseeable because it was highly unlikely.

Both Mr Anwar and Mondello also appealed the primary judge's notional assessment of damages and the finding of a 30% reduction for the probability that Mr Anwar would have developed schizophrenia in any event and regardless of Mondello's negligence. Mr Anwar argued that the primary judge's conclusions were contrary to the evidence and that Mondello had not proved that the onset of schizophrenia was inevitable. Mondello argued that the primary judge should have made a greater reduction and in the realm of 50%.

***Held:* appeal allowed.**

Per Kourakis CJ:

1. There is a significant difference between pure mental harm and consequential harm over and above the statutory distinction made by the Act.

Per Gray J (dissenting as to damages only):

1. The primary judge correctly reasoned that the case involved consequential, rather than pure, mental harm as Mr Anwar's schizophrenia was a consequence of suffering bodily injury.

2. A reasonable person in the position of Mondello would understand that a person of normal fortitude in Mr Anwar's position would find the experience of being trapped in industrial machinery to be terrifying. While the development of mental harm might be unlikely, it was not far fetched or fanciful.

3. The primary judge erred in finding that a reasonable person in the position of Mondello would not have foreseen that a person of normal fortitude in the position of Mr Anwar might suffer mental harm, and on that basis Mondello owed Mr Anwar a duty to take care not to cause him mental harm.

4. The evidence established that Mr Anwar would have developed schizophrenia irrespective of the hand injury. It was appropriate for the primary judge to make an allowance on a contingency basis, and a reduction of 30% was open in the circumstances and that the primary judge's findings on damages should not be disturbed.

Per Stanley J:

1. While a reasonable person in the position of Mondello would not have foreseen that a person of normal fortitude might in the circumstances suffer schizophrenia, that was irrelevant; the question was the foreseeability of suffering any psychiatric illness.

2. There was no error in the primary judge's findings and conclusion on causation. But for the accident, Mr Anwar would not have suffered schizophrenia when he did. The operation of s 33 of the Act narrows the circumstances in which a defendant is to be held liable for the infliction of consequential mental harm. The enquiry is to be directed to foreseeability. The primary judge erred in concluding that a reasonable person in Mondello's position would not have foreseen a psychiatric illness in consequence of the injury. Mondello did owe a duty to Mr Anwar to take care not to cause him mental harm.

3. The reduction in damages by 30% was manifestly inadequate and the primary judge should have discounted the damages for future losses by 50%.

[*Headnote by the Wolters Kluwer editors*]

M Livesey QC with A Lindsay (instructed by Palios, Meegan & Nicholson) for the appellant.

A Harris QC with T Besanko (instucted by Gilchrist Connell) for the respondent.

Before: Kourakis CJ, Gray and Stanley JJ.

CCH Note: The full text of the judgment is accessible through the Supreme Court of South Australia database on the *AustLII* website at www.austlii.edu.au/cgi-bin/download.cgi/au/cases/sa/SASCFC/2015/109.

[¶82-100] Motor Accident Commission v Curzons

(2012) Aust Torts Reports ¶82-100;
Medium neutral citation: [2012] SASCFC 22
Supreme Court of Australia Full Court
Judgment delivered on 15 March 2012

Torts — Negligence — Contributory negligence — Appeal from decision of district court judge awarding plaintiff damages for injuries suffered as a result of being struck by a vehicle driven by defendant — Whether judge erred in assessing contribution of plaintiff at 25% — Plaintiff in state of extreme intoxication, leading to significant impairment of faculties — Comparison of relative culpability of plaintiff and driver of vehicle — Appeal allowed to apportion damages at 50% on account of contributory negligence — Miscellaneous defences — Illegality of plaintiff's activity — Whether plaintiff's conduct constituted an indictable offence under s 19 and 29 of the Criminal Law Consolidation Act 1935 (SA), excluding liability of defendant pursuant to s 43 of the Civil Liability Act 1936 (SA) — Judge provided clear reasons for why the defendant had not satisfied the onus of proof that the plaintiff's conduct constituted an indictable offence — Findings of judge concerning liability confirmed — Damages — Measure and remoteness of damages in actions for tort — Measure of damages — Personal injuries — Loss of earnings and earning capacity — Legal principles — Criminal Law Consolidation Act 1935 (SA), s 19 and 29 — Civil Liability Act 1936 (SA), s 43.

Anthony Curzons, the plaintiff and respondent, sustained injuries at around 5 am on 8 October 2004 when he was hit by a car driven by Mark Boyce who fled the scene of the accident. As a consequence Mr Curzons sued the Motor Accident Commission, the defendant and appellant. At about 11 pm on 7 October 2004 Mr Curzons and his friends, Michael Olds

and Jason Nuitta, finished work and proceeded to a hotel in Gawler and afterwards to the Eureka Tavern at Salisbury. Mr Curzons and Mr Nuitta consumed a number of alcoholic beverages. Mr Olds was the designated driver and drank less. Paul Jefferson and two young women, Sarah and Reagan, arrived after Mr Curzons and his friends and were shortly joined by Mr Boyce, another friend of Mr Jefferson. The two groups met and began talking and drinking together.

An argument between Mr Curzons and Mr Jefferson ensued. Mr Jefferson attempted to punch Mr Curzons but was restrained by a security guard and removed from the Eureka Tavern. Both groups left soon after and departed in separate vehicles. Mr Boyce drove Mr Jefferson's vehicle while Mr Jefferson was in the passenger seat and Mr Olds drove his own vehicle, with Mr Curzons in the backseat.

Both vehicles travelled towards the Salisbury Highway. They stopped alongside each other at traffic lights at the intersection of Gawler Street and the Salisbury Highway. The argument that commenced at the Tavern resumed. Mr Curzons was sitting on the edge of the rear passenger window brandishing an iron bar. Mr Nuitta was also sitting on the window sill next to the front passenger seat. They were yelling and screaming. The vehicles then travelled north on Salisbury Highway and stopped at another set of traffic lights. Mr Curzons and Mr Nuitta got out of Mr Olds' vehicle and Mr Nuitta went to Mr Boyce's car window and proceeded to attack him with the iron bar. Mr Boyce's window was smashed and the iron bar ended up on the road when Mr Boyce drove off towards the traffic island on John Rice Avenue. Before getting back into Mr Olds' vehicle which proceeded to follow Mr Boyce's vehicle to the traffic island, Mr Nuitta or Mr Curzons retrieved the iron bar and also collected items capable of being used as weapons or missiles from the boot of Mr Olds' vehicle. Once both vehicles were at the traffic island they began circling it with one of the occupants of Mr Olds' vehicle throwing the iron bar. Mr Jefferson jumped out of the window of the vehicle driven by Mr Boyce and picked up the iron bar. Mr Jefferson threw the iron bar at Mr Olds' vehicle. Mr Boyce did another lap of the traffic island then slowed down to allow Mr Jefferson to climb back into the vehicle through the window. At this time Mr Olds drove his vehicle to the opposite side of the traffic island to that of Mr Boyce's vehicle and Mr Curzons and Mr Nuitta got out of Mr Olds' vehicle with Mr Curzons leaving his left rear passenger side door open.

Mr Curzons ran to retrieve the iron bar that had been earlier thrown by Mr Jefferson and returned to Mr Olds' vehicle. While Mr Curzons was still on the road Mr Boyce performed a U-turn, sped up and proceeded towards Mr Olds' vehicle. He swerved around Mr Olds' vehicle and in the process struck Mr Curzons while he was about to climb back into Mr Olds' vehicle.

The District Court found that Mr Boyce had driven negligently and awarded Mr Curzons damages but reduced those for contributory negligence by the statutory minimum of 25%. The trial judge found that Mr Boyce, immediately before the collision, must have seen at the very least that the rear passenger side door was open. In those circumstances Mr Boyce must have known that it was likely that Mr Curzons or Mr Nuitta were outside of the car and possibly on the road. There was a significant and foreseeable risk of injury, such that a reasonable person would have taken precautions as there was a higher probability of serious harm being caused unless such precautions were taken. The trial judge concluded that Mr Boyce owed a duty of care to other users of the road, that he had breached that duty, and that his breach of duty contributed materially to the plaintiff's injuries.

The Motor Accident Commission appealed to the Full Court of the South Australian Supreme Court arguing that:

(i) the trial judge, by rejecting the defence of *volenti non fit injuria* had failed to have adequate regard to the fact that Mr Curzons was engaged in conduct which actively incited Mr Boyce's negligent conduct

(ii) the trial judge's apportionment was erroneous and that Mr Curzons should bear a substantially greater proportion than 25%

(iii) s 43 of the *Civil Liability Act 1936* (SA) excluded liability for criminal conduct and as Mr Curzons had committed an indictable offence in breach of s 19 and 29 of the *Criminal Law Consolidation Act 1935* (SA) at the same time as the negligent acts of Mr Boyce, liability for damages was excluded

(iv) the evidence did not support the conclusions of the trial judge with respect to the damages awarded for past and future loss of earning capacity and past gratuitous services.

Held: appeal allowed Per Gray J, (Sullan and David JJ agreeing).

1. There was no reason to reject the trial judge's conclusion that a reasonable person in Mr Curzons' position, being aware that the vehicles had been pursuing each other, would have reasonably thought that he could get across the road and retrieve the iron bar before Mr Boyce's vehicle came around the southern end of the traffic island. Thus, the trial judge was correct to conclude Mr Curzons had not taken an obvious risk.

2. It followed that the trial judge's findings did not support a conclusion that Mr Curzons was inciting Mr Boyce to drive the vehicle negligently as was argued by the Motor Accident Commission on appeal. Consequently, the trial judge was correct in concluding that the defence of *volenti non fit injuria* should fail.

3. In order to accurately compare the culpability of Mr Curzons and Mr Boyce and the relative importance of the acts of each of them in causing Mr Curzons' injuries, the trial judge had to assess their degrees of departure from the standard of care of the reasonable person in possession of all information which each of them had, or ought reasonably to have had, at the time of the collision.

4. The evidence established that Mr Curzons was extremely intoxicated at the time of the collision. Mr Boyce was sober and was well aware that Mr Curzons was intoxicated. An apportionment of 50% fairly reflected the respective culpabilities. Mr Curzons was not only intoxicated but he was creating a situation of danger and the trial judge did not adequately assess the respective culpabilities.

5. Section 43 of the Civil Liability Act operated to exclude liability for criminal conduct but recognised the serious consequences that may follow by requiring proof beyond reasonable doubt. Further, s 43(1)(a) introduced the word "while", suggesting the relevant criminal conduct was to be contemporaneous with the act of negligence.

6. Consequently the Motor Accident Commission had to prove beyond reasonable doubt that at the time of Mr Boyce's negligent act and the collision, Mr Curzons was threatening to cause harm to an occupant of Mr Boyce's vehicle. The trial judge found that at the time of Mr Boyce's negligent act, Mr Curzons was attempting to get back into Mr Olds' vehicle. Additionally the Motor Accident Commission had not excluded the reasonable hypothesis that as far as Mr Curzons and his friends were concerned the incident was over and they were about to drive away having retrieved the iron bar.

7. The evidence justified an award for future loss of earning capacity assessed at $375,000 rather than the trial judge's award of $450,000. An assessment of the pre-trial net loss should have been made at $60,000 rather than the trial judge's assessment of $90,000. Mr

Curzons' tax returns disclosed the plaintiff's pre-injury earnings that demonstrated that the trial judge's approach was overly generous to Mr Curzons and manifestly so.

[*Headnote by the Wolters Kluwer editors*]

D Trim QC with A Ward for the appellant (instructed by Finlaysons).

S Walsh QC with A Baker for the respondent (instructed by Mahony's Lawyers).

Before: Gray, Sulan and David JJ.

[¶81-986] Queen Elizabeth Hospital v Curtis

(2008) Aust Torts Reports ¶81-986;
Medium neutral citation: [2008] SASC 344
Supreme Court of South Australia (Full Court)
9 December 2008

Torts — Negligence — Essentials of action for negligence — Damage — Causation — Generally — Civil Liability Act 1936 (SA), s 55.

Damages — Measure and remoteness of damages — Personal injuries — Loss of earnings and earning capacity.

In December 1999, Ms Curtis (the respondent) started suffering symptoms of dizziness, nausea and headache. She attended a general practitioner who diagnosed a migraine and treated her. He advised her to attend at the appellant if her condition did not improve. The respondent attended at the emergency department of the appellant later that day when her condition had not improved. She was diagnosed as suffering from a migraine and was treated and discharged. She returned to the emergency department later that night and was again examined. At this time a presumptive diagnosis of meningitis was made and various tests were ordered. The tests confirmed that she was suffering from meningitis and treatment was commenced. The treatment commenced over 10 hours after her initial attendance at the emergency department. She recovered but during her stay in hospital her mother noticed that the respondent was unable to hear on the right side. Almost two months later the respondent underwent a hearing test which confirmed that she had a profound hearing loss on her right side. She sued the appellant in negligence for its failure to treat her appropriately when she first attended.

The trial judge found in favour of the respondent on the basis of the appellant's breach of its duty of care in failing to make a timely differential diagnosis of meningitis which caused a delay in treatment by more than 10 hours. The breach of duty was a material cause of the loss of hearing suffered by the respondent. The respondent was awarded $222,546.65 in damages.

The appellant appealed the decision on the basis that the trial judge was in error in relation to her finding of causation. In the alternative the appellant argued that even if causation had been made out, the damages should have been reduced because there was a real possibility that the respondent would have suffered hearing loss in any event. It also argued that the damages awarded were manifestly excessive. The respondent cross-appealed with respect to damages and costs.

Held: **appeal dismissed. Cross-appeal allowed.**

Per Gray J (David J agreeing)

1. The scope of the duty of care was to meet the standard of care observed by a competent medical practitioner in the area of emergency medicine, to make a differential diagnosis of meningitis, and to provide treatment to avoid or minimise the risk of mortality or permanent disability.

2. Proof of causation is to be assessed in a practicable and robust manner. The inherent difficulty in establishing scientific causation where, for example, the aetiology of a disease is

uncertain, does not preclude the court from reaching a decision as to causation on the balance of probabilities.

3. There was direct, relevant, cogent and probative evidence from well-qualified experts that the respondents' right-sided deafness was materially caused by the breach of duty of care owed by the appellant.

4. Evidence that a particular act or omission increased the risk of loss being suffered, and proof that loss was suffered, may, depending on any other evidence in the case, justify an inference that the act or omission materially caused the loss.

5. The appellant was under a legal duty to take precautions to protect the respondent from the risks associated with the illness of meningitis, and by omitting proper treatment, the appellant substantially increased the risk of the respondents' loss of hearing. In these circumstances, when the loss of hearing has in fact occurred, the law treats that increasing risk as a sufficient basis, in the absence of evidence showing how the meningitis occurred, for an inference that the omissions of proper treatment materially contributed to the respondent's loss of hearing.

Per Gray J (David J and Kourakis agreeing)

6. The fact that the respondent had a permanent total loss of hearing in one ear for the balance of her life from the age of 16 called for a substantial award in damages. The damages awarded were not excessive.

7. The correct approach when calculating loss of earning capacity is to use an interest rate of five per cent, and prospective mortality rates.

8. Rule 6A.05 of the Supreme Court Civil Rules 1987 (SA) provides a discretion in the court to deprive a plaintiff who does not comply with Rule 6A of the whole or part of the costs of the action. The discretion is enlivened by non-compliance with the rule. Once enlivened the discretion is unfettered. The rule by its terms does not cast an onus on either party. However, the party seeking the exercise of the discretion in its favour would in the ordinary case be expected to show reason why an order should be made. In the present case the discretion should not be exercised to deprive the respondent of any portion of her costs. The question of causation both as to liability and damages was factually and medically complex.

Per Kourakis J

9. An injury can only be a foreseeable result of a breach of duty if it is accepted that the breach is capable of causing such an injury. In short, the capacity of the breach to cause the injury suffered by the plaintiff supports an inference that the breach did in fact cause the injury with which it is "coupled".

10. A plaintiff cannot prove that a breach of duty has caused the injury for which damages are sought without proving that he or she did not suffer that injury before the occurrence of the acts or omissions by which the duty was breached.

[*Headnote by the Wolters Kluwer editors*]

A Harris QC with J White for the appellant/cross-respondent (instructed by Fountain & Bonig).

WJN Wells QC with B Doyle for the respondent/cross-appellant (instructed by Turner Freeman Lawyers).

Before: Gray, David and Kourakis JJ.

[¶81-820] Neindorf v Junkovic
(2005) Aust Torts Reports ¶81-820
Medium neutral citation: [2005] HCA 75
High Court of Australia
8 December 2005

Negligence — Duty of care — Standard of care — Occupier's liability — Domestic Premises — Obviousness of risk — Economic relationship between parties — Respondent was injured when she tripped on the driveway of a house owned by the appellant — Appellant had been on respondent's property as an invitee attending a garage sale — Whether risk posed by the uneven surface of the driveway was obvious and relatively minor — Whether appellant should have taken preventative measures to obviate the risk — Whether such considerations justified the conclusion that there was no breach of duty of care — Whether economic relationship between the parties affected the standard of care — Whether respondent had contributed by her negligence — Civil Liability Act 1936 (SA)s 20 — Wrongs Act 1936 (SA)s 17C.

The appellant was the owner and occupier of a house located in the suburbs of Adelaide. Adjacent to the house was a carport and a concrete driveway which extended from the carport to the road. The driveway was of a type that was no different from many concrete driveways on residential properties throughout South Australia. However, an expansion joint ran from the road along the length of the driveway. On the left side of the joint, the driveway was approximately 10 to 12 millimetres higher than on the right side. There was consequently a height differential of that magnitude within the driveway across the expansion joint. That difference in height was clearly visible and obvious to those walking on the driveway. A height differential created by the expansion joint in a driveway was also not to be regarded as uncommon, or unexpected of a suburban residence in South Australia. In fact, there were even greater irregularities in the surface of the footpath in front of the appellant's residence.

In February of 2000, the appellant advertised, and then held, a garage sale at her house. She had conducted four such garage sales at her home in the preceding two years without incident. The respondent, a woman then aged 53, decided to attend the garage sale which the appellant held in February of 2000. She accordingly went to the appellant's house, where she walked up the driveway towards a table under the carport. As the respondent did so, she tripped over the height differential caused by the expansion joint. More specifically, her right foot rolled on the elevation of one concrete slab as it adjoined the adjacent slab. The respondent fell towards the ground but regained her footing before she fell over completely. However, in the course of this motion, she felt a crack in her right foot. That motion was subsequently diagnosed as having caused a fracture. At the time this injury occurred, the respondent had been looking at, or towards, the goods on offer and had not been paying attention to the driveway. The weather had been fine, and the surface upon which the driveway had been constructed was generally flat and open.

The respondent commenced the proceedings against the appellant in the Magistrates Court of South Australia seeking damages for negligence. The Magistrate concluded that the appellant, having invited visitors such as the respondent, owed a duty of care to prevent injury from reasonably foreseeable hazards. In addition, the Magistrate held that simple and inexpensive steps could and should have been taken to diminish, or eliminate, the particular hazard presented to the respondent. The Magistrate also rejected a defence of contributory negligence before entering judgment in favour of the respondent for $24,464. The appellant then appealed to the Supreme Court of South Australia. In that court, Besanko J reversed the finding of the magistrate. The basis of that conclusion was that the duty of care of the occupier of a domestic property did not extend to include risks which were obvious and which it was well known were likely to be encountered. Nevertheless, Besanko J's decision was reversed by the Full Court. By majority, it held that because simple steps could have been

taken to guard against the danger presented by the driveway, judgment for the respondent was to be restored. The appellant then appealed that finding to the High Court.

Held: Appeal allowed.

Per Gleeson CJ

1. The appellant, as occupier of the premises, owed the respondent a duty of care. The issue presented by the case consequently concerned the standard of care owed by the appellant to the respondent, and whether there was, in the circumstances of the case, a breach of duty.

2. If doing nothing about a hazard were of itself sufficient to constitute negligence, every occupier of land in South Australia would potentially have been liable. Furthermore, the type of hazard presented by the case was likely to have existed in most suburban houses in South Australia.

3. The conduct of the appellant did not constitute a failure to take reasonable care for the safety of the respondent. In addition, the unevenness of the surface upon which the respondent tripped was so ordinary, and so visible, that reasonableness did not require any action on the part of the occupier.

Per Kirby J (dissenting)

1. A relevant duty of care existed in this case. It had firmly been established that an occupier owed a duty of care to entrants in respect of risks of physical injury arising out of the condition of the occupier's premises. There was no need for the scope of that duty to be defined with any greater precision for the purposes of the case.

2. Defining the standard of care owed by the appellant depended on a full understanding of the relationship between the parties. That relationship was one established by the appellant's invitation to the public to do business with her from which she stood to make a modest economic gain.

3. In such circumstances, there was a higher standard of care than was to be expected in relation to total strangers, unexpected visitors or uninvited charity collectors. Those who invited for economic gain were to be expected, at the very least, to turn their attention to dangers that were be faced by those who accepted their invitation.

4. The appellant had the knowledge, the power and the economic interest to protect the public at large whom she had invited onto her property. In terms of fault, for failure to act in the circumstances, the responsibility fell mainly on the appellant for not taking preventative measures.

5. It was not unreasonable to expect considerations of visitor safety (and in many cases insurance) to attract the appellant's attention. Had that been done in the present case, the precautions that should have been taken were obvious, inexpensive and comparatively trivial.

Per Hayne J

1. It was readily apparent that the issues presented by the case raised no point of principle. That was because the decision turned only on an assessment of what would have been reasonable and practicable for the occupier to do in the circumstances of the case.

2. This inquiry about what would have been reasonable and practicable was not to be undertaken in hindsight. Nor was it to be confined to what could have been done to eliminate, reduce or warn against the danger. Asking what could have been done revealed what was practicable.

3. In the present case, the relevant danger was presented by the uneven surface of the appellant's driveway. Neither the fact that the driveway paving was uneven nor its degree of unevenness could be regarded as uncommon in the driveways of suburban housing.

Per Callinan and Heydon JJ

1. The appeal raised no question of principle. It simply presented a question whether an occupier of residential premises owed entrants a duty of care to prevent a minor and obvious risk of injury which an entrant, exercising reasonable care for his or her own safety, could reasonably have been expected to notice and avoid.

2. The appellant's premises were modest residential premises in the Adelaide suburbs. In entering those premises, the dangers that the respondent encountered were minor, obvious, and of a type that were encountered unexceptionally on suburban footpaths.

3. It was to be acknowledged that the circumstances of the injury did include the selling of goods, and an invitation to the respondent to come onto the appellant's premises to buy them. But such an occasion was far removed from the selling of goods on a daily basis by a commercial retailer.

4. It was an overstatement to describe the slightly raised concrete on one side of the driveway as a danger of which the appellant was, or should have been aware. It was therefore not unreasonable for the appellant not to have taken measures to guard against that slight risk.

[*Headnote by the Wolters Kluwer editors*]

R J Whitington QC with K G Nicholson (instructed by Thompson Playford) for the appellant.

S Walsh QC with A Rossi (instructed by Moody Rossi & Co) for the respondent.

Before: Gleeson CJ, Kirby, Hayne, Callinan and Heydon JJ.

Tasmania

[¶82-756] Port Sorell Bowls Club Inc v Dann

(2022) Aust Torts Reports ¶82-756

Medium neutral citation: [2022] TASFC 2

Supreme Court of Tasmania, Full Court

2 February 2022

Contributory negligence — Volunteer cooking sausages at bowling club barbeque — Fat caught fire due to negligence of club — Volunteer burned hand removing cup of burning fat from below barbeque plate — Findings of contributory negligence and 15% reduction of damages — Assessment of damages — Income and loss of earning capacity — Wrongs Act 1954 (Tas), s 4 — Civil Liability Act 2002 (Tas), ss 11, 17, 23.

On 17 November 2015, Mr Kraig Dann (Mr Dann) was working as a volunteer at the Port Sorell Bowls Club Inc (the Club), during a "barefoot bowlers" evening. Mr Dann had previously worked voluntarily at the Club by cooking sausages and he was asked to do the same job again. The Club's gas barbeque was an unsophisticated 4-burner barbeque. A makeshift method to collect the fat from the barbeque involved a ceramic mug positioned out of sight underneath the barbeque plate. Soon after Mr Dann began cooking the sausages, the mug overflowed and caught fire. He turned off the gas, but the contents of the mug remained alight. Mr Dann then tried to move the mug which was sitting on a bracket. As he moved it, the cup caught on the upturned corners of the bracket and the fat spilt, causing partial thickness burns to Mr Dunn's right hand.

Mr Dann commenced proceedings in the Supreme Court of Tasmania against the Club, in negligence and claimed damages. He claimed that the Club failed to provide him with safe barbeque equipment with an adequate fat run-off collection system and also failed to provide him with protective equipment such as a heat-proof mitt and fire safety equipment. Also, Mr Dann alleged that the Club failed to provide adequate instruction as to the use of the equipment he was required to use and failed to provide adequate instruction in fire prevention and fire extinguishing.

The Club denied liability. It relied on the fact that there were fire extinguishers and a fire blanket at the Club, as well as at least 2 fire extinguishers within sight of the barbecue. The Club argued that it was not foreseeable that Mr Dann would have acted in such an unsafe manner in removing the cup of fat. It also contended that, even if it was found to have breached its duty to him in that respect, Mr Dann was contributorily negligent.

The primary judge found that the method that the Club used to catch the fat in the mug was completely flawed and that the sequence of events that occurred had been reasonably foreseeable. If the Club had simply taken the step of ensuring that the cup did not already contain fat when Mr Dann started to use the barbeque, then the accident would not have occurred. As to the voluntary assumption of risk defence, the primary judge found that the evidence established that Mr Dann had felt compelled to act to avoid a risk of harm to others resulting from the mug exploding. In a real and practical sense, his choice to act or not to act was constrained. He did not voluntarily agree to the risk that eventuated and so the defence of voluntary assumption of risk could not be maintained.

As to contributory negligence, Mr Dann failed to make observations which could have been made and he did not note the turned-up corners of the tray. Damages were assessed at $1,074,880, taking into account a 15% reduction for contributory negligence: *Dann* v *Port Sorell Bowls Club Inc* (2020) Aust Torts Reports ¶82-574; [2020] TASSC 47.

The Club appealed the primary judge's findings on apportionment and argued that the reduction of 15% for contributory negligence was grossly inadequate. Mr Dann cross appealed the finding of contributory negligence and argued that the primary judge erred by any contributory negligence.

Held: appeal dismissed.

Per Blow CJ and Pearce J:

1. As to the cross appeal, the primary judge was correct to find that Mr Dann unreasonably and imprudently exposed himself to a high risk of foreseeable injury, and that there was contributory negligence. Mr Dann decided to reach under the barbeque, when flames were still extending from the front vents and through the hole in the hot plate, with an effectively unprotected hand to grab a cup which he knew to be not sitting squarely, which he knew to be full and overflowing with boiling and burning fat, and when he did not know whether he could remove the cup without resistance or obstruction. There was a significant probability of serious harm. Although there were reasons for his decision to attempt to remove the mug, a reasonable person in the same circumstances would not have regarded the exigencies of the situation as so overwhelming or urgent as to sufficiently explain the respondent's decision to expose himself to such risk of injury. The primary judge was correct to find that Mr Dann should have taken greater stock than he did before exposing himself to such risk. His actions in attempting to remove the mug went beyond misjudgment and amounted to a failure to take reasonable care for his own safety, and contributed to his injury. [36]–[38]

2. As to the grounds of appeal, contributory negligence was to be measured against the same objective standard of reasonable conduct as is applicable to negligence: Civil Liability Act, s 23. The Wrongs Act, s 4, permits reduction in damages for up to 100% for contributory negligence. [67]

3. The essential aspect of the Club's argument was that it was the actions of Mr Dann which were the immediate cause of the harm he suffered, and that those actions were entirely under his control. It argued that Mr Dann had time to assess the situation, but then proceeded to do something which was "just plain stupid". The task of cooking the sausages was delegated to Mr Dann, and that it thereafter became, at least, a joint responsibility. The Club's argument that Mr Dann should have emptied the mug of fat before using the barbeque, and that he was on an equal footing to the Club in terms of decision-making, was rejected. [68], [69]

4. The reduction of 15% for contributory negligence was not unreasonable. [71]

Per Marshall AJ:

1. The primary judge did not err in determining that the just and equitable apportionment for Mr Dann's negligence was 15%. That figure was not manifestly inadequate or attended with any error. [145]

2. As to Mr Dann's cross-appeal, that no finding of contributory negligence should have been made, that the primary judge examined the actions of Mr Dann from the viewpoint of the manner in which he assessed and conducted the task of removing the mug, was not an impermissible approach, having regard to all the evidence before her. The primary judge, on the evidence, was entitled to take the view that Mr Dann's failure to observe the difficulty he would have in extracting the mug from the tray due to the turned-up corners of the tray, was negligence on his part. However, having considered that because of the exigencies of the situation Mr Dann found himself in, that negligence was insignificant compared to the

negligence of the Club. Even if a person has a decision forced upon him or her in the "agony of the moment", it does not mean that the person may not have contributed in some way to the injury caused. [150]–[153]

[*Headnote by the Wolters Kluwer editors*]

KE Read SC and TD Cox (Barry Nilsson Lawyers) for the appellant.

BR McTaggart SC and P Griffits (Griffits and Griffits) for the respondent.

Before: Blow CJ, Pearce J, Marshall AJ.

[¶82-725] Girmay v Green

(2021) Aust Torts Reports ¶82-725
Medium neutral citation: [2021] TASSC 52
Supreme Court of Tasmania
4 November 2021

Motor accidents — Pedestrian — Child running across road into side of moving car — Driver travelling slowly but unable to avoid collision — Civil Liability Act 2002 (Tas), s 11.

At about 2.10 pm on 9 September 2005 the plaintiff, Brehane Girmay, who was 12 years old at the time, was hit by a car driven by 36-year-old Jason Green. He fell backwards onto the roadway, hit his head, and suffered permanent brain damage.

By agreement, the action has proceeded to trial only in relation to the issues relating to liability. The quantum of the plaintiff's claim has been agreed, subject to Court approval, the plaintiff being under a disability.

The motor accident occurred on a long straight section of road. Mr Green had a clear view of the road ahead after travelling over a slight rise.

Mr Girmay commenced negloigence proceedings against Mr Green in the Supreme Court of Tasmania. He alleged that Mr Green was negligent in that he failed to keep a proper lookout, drove at an excessive speed, failed to observe Mr Girmay in time to avoid a collision, and failed to brake, stop, slow down or manoeuvre his vehicle sufficiently or at all so as to avoid a collision.

Mr Green denied liability. He claimed that he was keeping a proper lookout and driving at a reasonable speed, and braked and swerved to the left on seeing Mr Girmay but that a collision was unavoidable because Mr Girmay suddenly ran across the road.

The matter proceeded to hearing as to liability only.

Held: judgment for the defendant.

1. The evidence established that Mr Girmay ran out from behind the car in which he had been travelling. If he had been moving slowly as he crossed the road, and not running, it was highly likely that the accident would not have occurred. [23]

2. A person who drives a motor vehicle on a road always owes a duty of care to persons on or near that road, including pedestrians. Provisions in the *Civil Liability Act 2002* (Tas) apply to breaches of that duty of care. Provisions as to the standard of care are to be found in s 11 of that Act. [27]

3. This accident occurred during school hours. There was no reason to expect children to be in the vicinity of the takeaway shop. There was no reason for special vigilance on the part of Mr Green. His duty of care required him to keep a proper lookout as to what was in front of him and behind him, to keep a lookout for vehicles approaching from his right or left, and to be aware of his vehicle's speed. It does not follow that Mr Green was not exercising reasonable care. Mr Green could not have avoided a collision unless he had been travelling significantly more slowly than the assumed speed of 45 kilometres per hour. The risk of a

pedestrian suddenly running across the road on a collision course with an approaching car was not so significant that a reasonable motorist in Mr Green's position would have travelled so slowly that a collision could have been avoided. Mr Green did not breach his duty of care. [31], [32]

[*Headnote by the Wolters Kluwer editors*]

PGJ Zeeman (Murdoch Clarke) for the plaintiff.

KE Read SC, DW Symes (Dobson Mitchell Allport) for the defendant.

Before: Blow CJ.

[¶82-468] Keller v Phillips

(2019) Aust Torts Reports ¶82-468
Medium neutral citation: [2019] TASSC 35
Supreme Court of Tasmania
21 August 2019

Torts — Negligence — Duty of care — Breach of duty — Liability — Contributory negligence — Motor vehicles — Expert evidence — Damages — Pre-existing injury — Quantification — Motorcycle being ridden by plaintiff collided with car being driven by defendant while he was turning right at a traffic light — Contested evidence as to how fast each party had been travelling — Plaintiff suffered injuries as a result of collision and commenced proceedings seeking damages — Collision occurred entirely due to defendant's negligence in not remaining stationary when traffic light was orange — Plaintiff had not been contributorily negligent — Plaintiff's back pain symptoms were not pre-existing and had not been exaggerated — Defendant required to pay plaintiff general damages as well as damages for past and future economic loss.

On 12 February 2014, Jess Klaas Keller, who was 17 at the time, was riding a motorcycle along William Street in Devonport in Tasmania. Mr Jiah Johnson Phillips was driving his car along the same street in the opposite direction. As they both approached a traffic light, Mr Phillips made a right hand turn ahead of the oncoming traffic, which included Mr Keller on his motorcycle. At the time that Mr Phillips turned, the traffic lights were orange. The exact details of what then happened and the speed each party was travelling were contentious, however the circumstances resulted in a collision occurring between Mr Keller's motorcycle and Mr Phillips' car. As a result of that collision, Mr Keller sustained injuries including a fractured third metacarpal, and an aggravation of a pre-existing mid to low back strain.

Mr Keller commenced proceedings in the Supreme Court of Tasmania against Mr Phillips, in negligence and claimed damages. As well as seeking damages for pain and suffering and loss of amenities of life, he claimed that he had lost earning capacity as a result of the back injury.

Mr Phillips alleged that both he and Mr Keller had been negligent, in that they both fell short of their required duties in driving their vehicle on the road. Mr Phillips alleged that Mr Keller had not been keeping a proper lookout, had been driving too fast and had increased his speed as he approached the intersection when it was not safe to do so. He also claimed that Mr Keller failed to stop at the orange light or to slow down or manoeuvre so as to avoid Mr Phillip's vehicle. In relation to damages, Mr Phillips argued that Mr Keller's back injury was entirely pre-existing.

Held: judgement for the plaintiff.

Per Estcourt J:

1. The evidence established that both Mr Keller and Mr Phillips had been travelling within the speed limit just prior to the collision and that neither accelerated immediately

before the impact. Neither party had been doing anything out of the ordinary. There was no speed or squealing of tyres. [33]–[40]

2. Although Mr Phillips claimed that Mr Keller accelerated just prior to the accident as the traffic lights changed, there was no evidence to support that claim. Mr Phillips' evidence that he heard the gears of the motorcycle change to allow Mr Keller to accelerate was not convincing. [41]–[54]

3. Mr Phillips' negligence in moving off from a wholly stationary position to turn right in front of Mr Keller's oncoming motorcycle was the sole cause of the collision. Mr Keller's evidence that it was unsafe for him to suddenly stop at the traffic light because it was orange was to be accepted and he was not contributorily negligent. [55]–[58]

4. Mr Keller's uncontradicted evidence was that he did not have disabling back pain prior to the accident, but that he had ever since he commenced to explore employment opportunities upon leaving school shortly afterwards in about March 2014. There was nothing to suggest that any other incident afterwards could account for the pain. [59]–[74]

5. The evidence was inconsistent with Mr Phillips' contention that Mr Keller had been fabricating his back pain symptoms. That notion was entirely at odds with his continued and determined efforts to find and maintain employment. It was also inconsistent with the clear evidence given by his family of Mr Keller's symptoms. [86]–[106]

6. Damages are awarded in the total sum of $430,472.87, made up of past lost earning capacity, assessed at $52,850 plus lost superannuation, future lost earning capacity and superannuation assessed at $282,622.87, and general damages assessed at $90,000.

[*Headnote by the Wolters Kluwer editors*]

Ken Read SC and Andrew Gaggin (Murdoch Clarke Lawyers) for the plaintiff.

Sandra Taglieri SC and John Pedder (Pedder Schuh Lawyers) for the defendant.

Before: Estcourt J.

[¶82-290] Raper v Bowden

(2016) Aust Torts Reports ¶82-290
Medium neutral citation: [2016] TASSC 35
Supreme Court of Tasmania
Judgment delivered 15 July 2016

Torts — Negligence — Employer and employee — Causation — Quad bike accident — Inference drawn as to defendants' negligence — Inadequate training — Safety helmet not worn — Inoperative rear brakes — Kuhl v *Zurich Financial Services Australia Ltd [2011] HCA 11; 243 CLR 361, applied — Aust Dig Torts [36].*

Torts — Negligence — Particular cases — Other cases — Whether excessive speed — Safety helmet not worn — Whether employee in breach of rule or system — Defendants' overarching negligence — Davies v *Adelaide Chemical & Fertiliser Company Limited (1946) 74 CLR 541, considered — Aust Dig Torts [66].*

Torts — Statutes, regulations, etc — Applicability and effect in actions for negligence — Whether Civil Liability Act applies — Mercer v *Allianz Insurance Ltd (No 2) [2013] TASSC 35, considered — Aust Dig Torts [87] — Civil Liability Act 2002 (Tas), s 3B(2), (3) — Workers Rehabilitation and Compensation Act 1988 (Tas), s 97(3), Pt X, Div 2 — Motor Accidents (Liabilities and Compensation) Act 1973 (Tas), s 97, Pt III.*

Damages — Measure and remoteness of damages in actions for tort — Measure of damages — Personal injuries — Method of assessment — Other matters — Whether Todorovic v Waller applies to overseas plaintiff — Todorovic v *Waller [1981] HCA 72; 150 CLR 402, applied — Aust Dig Damages [37].*

Damages — Measure and remoteness of damages in actions for tort — Measure of damages — Personal injuries — Method of assessment — Medical and hospital expenses — Whether catastrophically injured plaintiff residing in United Kingdom obliged to rely on NHS benefits — Whether "double dipping" or failure to mitigate damage — Griffiths v *Kerkemeyer [1977] HCA 45; 139 CLR 161; Diamond* v *Simpson (No 1) [2003] NSWCA 67, applied — Aust Dig Damages [38].*

Damages — Measure and remoteness of damages in actions for tort — Measure of damages — Personal injuries — Other matters — Award for pain and suffering — Catastrophically injured plaintiff in minimally conscious state — Whether insight into condition — Skeleton v *Collins (1966) 115 CLR 94; Victorian Workcover Authority* v *Asixa Pty Ltd [2010] VSC 467, considered — Aust Dig Damages [38].*

Damages — Measure and remoteness of damages in actions for tort — Measure of damages — Personal injuries — Other pecuniary damage — Brain injury — Future lost earning capacity — Life expectancy — Lost years — Fitch v *Hyde-Cates [1980] 2 NSWLR 757, considered — Aust Dig Damages [47].*

Damages — Measure and remoteness of damages in actions for tort — Measure of damages — Personal injuries — Other pecuniary damage — Cost of adapted housing and transport — Offset by costs which plaintiff would have incurred had injury not occurred — Aust Dig Damages [47].

On 30 December 2011, Holly Raper, a 24-year-old British backpacker, was employed working on a dairy farm on King Island, which was owned and operated by David and Jocelyn Bowden. On the morning of 30 December 2011, Ms Raper was asked by the dairy manager, Jason Haines to move a herd involving six bulls down a lane at the farm. Ms Raper used a 2007 Honda all terrain vehicle, known as a quad bike. She walked over to the quad bike, reversed it and turned it around and began to slowly follow the bulls down the lane. She was then required to go to paddock 8 to collect the herd in that paddock and escort the herd to paddock 24.

A short time after she had left, Mr Haines noticed that the cows in paddock 8 had not moved. He saw the quad bike Ms Raper had been riding sitting in the middle of the paddock. When he went to investigate, he saw her lying beside the quad, unconscious. The motor was still running, and the quad bike was upright.

Ms Raper was not wearing a safety helmet.

An emergency call was raised and the police and ambulance attended shortly thereafter. Ms Raper was flown to the Royal Hobart Hospital where she was diagnosed with multiple and catastrophic injuries, including a traumatic brain injury. She was later flown to the Royal Preston Hospital in England, where she remained until she was discharged in April 2013, nearly 18 months after the accident.

Since her accident, Ms Raper has been in a vegetative state (classified as an absence of self-awareness and the environment). She can move her head but does not have any movement in her limbs. She is unable to communicate, has a permanent tracheostomy in place and is fed through a tube directly in her stomach. She is confined to her bed or a wheelchair and requires 24 hours a day attendant care.

Ms Raper commenced proceedings in the Supreme Court of Tasmania against Mr and Mrs Bowden, in negligence and claimed damages. She claimed that Mr and Mrs Bowden, as her employers, breached their duty of care in negligence on the basis that the rear brakes of the quad bike were inoperative, that the rear tyre was only partially inflated, that Ms Raper had not been provided with adequate training and instruction to allow her to ride the quad bike safely, and that she was allowed to ride without being required to wear a safety helmet.

She also alleged a breach of statutory duty.

Mr and Mrs Bowden denied liability. They argued that it could not be shown how Ms Raper came to be separated from the quad bike, and that it cannot be proved how the

accident happened, therefore it follows that Ms Raper is not able to prove that any alleged breach of duty of care was causative of the accident. They also argued that Ms Raper had not proven on the balance of probabilities that her failure to wear a helmet would have prevented the injuries she suffered.

Held: **judgment for the plaintiff in the total sum of £6,970,426.**

Per Estcourt J:

1. The provisions of s 138AA of the *Workers Rehabilitation and Compensation Act 1988* (Tas) apply to the claim brought on behalf of Ms Raper. Further, the argument by Mr and Mrs Bowden, that the claim brought on behalf of Ms Raper is in respect of civil liability relating to an injury to which the *Motor Accidents (Liabilities and Compensation) Act 1973* (Tas) applied with the consequence that the *Civil Liability Act 2002* (Tas) applied, is not correct.

2. Accordingly, the provisions of the Civil Liability Act have no application to Ms Raper's claim. In deciding whether there has been a breach of duty of care, the common law applies and regard is to be had to the well-known passage in *Wyong Shire Council* v *Shirt* [1980] HCA 12; 146 CLR 40 at 47.

3. Mr and Mrs Bowden owed a common law duty of care to Ms Raper as her employer.

4. The evidence established that the rear brakes were inoperative, that the right tyre was only partially inflated, and that Ms Raper was allowed to ride without being required to wear a helmet. Further, the basic instruction provided to her did not amount to proper training on how to ride the quad bike. Mr and Mrs Bowden were in breach of their duty of care to Ms Raper in each of the four identified respects.

5. Ms Raper lost control of the quad bike after encountering a drain in the paddock, and she suffered injuries as a result of impacting the bike and/or ground, or both. On the balance of probabilities, Ms Raper's injuries were caused by Mr and Mrs Bowden's breaches of duty. Whatever the actual dynamics of the accident, the absence of operative rear brakes, a lack of appropriate training, were causes of the accident. Ms Raper's failure to wear a safety helmet caused or materially contributed to the injury to the brain. Further, had Ms Raper been properly instructed and trained in the use of the quad bike, she would not have lost control. The accident would on the balance of probabilities have been prevented had Ms Raper been properly trained.

6. As Ms Raper is a British citizen and residing in Britain, she is subject to the *Health and Social Care (Community Health and Standards) Act 2003* (UK) and the *Social Security (Recovery of Benefits) Act 1997* (UK).

7. Total damages are assessed at £6,970,426 including funds management.

[*Headnote by the Wolters Kluwer editors*]

K Read SC and T Cox (instructed by Slater + Gordon Lawyers) for the plaintiff.

C Bridge SC and A G Melick SC (instructed by Hicksons Lawyers) for the defendant.

Before: Estcourt J.

[¶82-259] Chu v Russell

(2016) Aust Torts Reports ¶82-259
Medium neutral citation: [2016] TASFC 1
Supreme Court of Tasmania, Full Court
Judgment delivered 12 February 2016

Torts — Negligence — Contributory negligence — Particular cases — Road accident cases — Collision between car and bicycle — Cyclist diverged from left edge of lane into path of vehicle behind him — Motorist inattentive and travelling too fast — Civil Liability Act 2002 (NSW), ss 11, 12, 13, 23 — Wrongs Act 1954 (Tas), s 4.

Daniel Russell was on a cycling holiday in Tasmania in December 2008. He was travelling with a friend, Robert Dunn. At approximately 10 am on 16 December 2008, the pair were riding north on Colebrook Road and intended to turn right at the junction with Fingerpost Road on their way to Orford, Tasmania. They were riding single file on the left hand side of the road. Honfei Chu was the driver of a motor vehicle and was also travelling north on Colebrook Road. He drove around a bend and saw the two cyclists in front of him on a straight stretch of road before the junction with Fingerpost Road. As Mr Russell moved toward the centre of the road and commenced his turn into Fingerpost Road, Mr Chu collided with Mr Russell, who sustained serious injuries as a result of the accident including breaking his back in three places.

Mr Russell commenced proceedings against Mr Chu in the Supreme Court of Tasmania, in negligence and claimed damages. Mr Russell claimed that immediately before the collision, he put his hand up to signify a right-hand turn and continued to ride along the dotted line while giving that signal. Mr Chu denied any liability and claimed that the cyclists were on the left side of the roadway and then suddenly they turned right. He went right to avoid hitting Mr Russell and braked suddenly, but could not avoid the collision. Mr Chu claimed that at no stage did Mr Russell give any signal before he made the sudden turn and that Mr Russell moved into his path in a sudden and unheralded fashion.

Her Honour Wood J found that Mr Russell did not turn and look before diverging towards the centre line, did not signal an intention to turn right and did not signal before diverging from the broken line. Wood J also found that Mr Chu's speed at the point of collision was within a range of 95–100 km/h and within the speed limit. However, Wood J also found Mr Chu only made partial observations of Mr Russell's manoeuvre; if he had been paying attention, he would have seen Mr Russell gradually diverging from the broken line. Although Mr Chu was travelling within the speed limit, it was still necessary for Mr Chu to reduce his speed, given the inherent dangers when a cyclist and motorist share a road. Mr Chu's speed, and his failure to keep a proper lookout, amounted to a breach of duty to other road users including the cyclists.

Wood J also found that Mr Russell did not look behind him immediately before diverging from the edge of the road and did not signal an intention to move towards the centre line. He failed to keep a proper lookout and had his damages reduced by 30% on account of contributory negligence.

Mr Chu appealed the trial judge's decision. He argued that he should not have been found liable and alternatively, that the reduction of 30% for contributory negligence was manifestly inadequate.

Held: appeal allowed.

Per Blow CJ (with whom Porter J agreed):

1. The evidence established that Mr Chu failed to keep a proper lookout, evidenced by the fact that he suddenly applied the brakes so hard that all four wheels locked up and the vehicle skidded. But for Mr Chu's failure to keep a proper lookout and his speed, the collision would not have occurred.

2. However, Mr Russell rode into the path of Mr Chu's vehicle without looking, and unnecessarily created a dangerous situation where none had existed. Mr Russell's conduct involved a gross departure from the standard of care required of a reasonable cyclist.

3. It is appropriate to take into account the inequalities of size, weight, speed and manoeuvrability between Mr Chu's vehicle and Mr Russell's bicycle, and the consequent vulnerability of Mr Russell. While Mr Russell alone created a dangerous situation, that factor was more or less cancelled out by the inequality between the car and the bicycle in relation to size, weight, speed and Mr Russell's vulnerability as a cyclist.

4. The extent of Mr Russell's departure from the standard of care of a reasonable cyclist was equal to the extent of Mr Chu's departure from the standard of care of a reasonable driver.

5. The trial judge's finding against Mr Chu is to be upheld, however Mr Russell's contributory negligence is to be increased to 50%.

Per Estcourt J (dissenting):

1. The evidence established that Mr Chu was not exceeding the speed limit and there was no evidence that he breached his duty of care to Mr Russell by not slowing down to any particular speed.

2. The evidence was equally consistent with Mr Russell moving, without warning, into the path of Mr Chu's vehicle as it was with any breach of duty on the part of Mr Chu by failing to keep a proper lookout.

3. No evidence established any causal connection between the speed of Mr Chu's vehicle and the fact of the collision occurring. On the other hand, it is clear that in moving into the path of Mr Chu's vehicle and failing to signal his intention to do so, Mr Russell was in breach of his duty to take reasonable care for himself and for other road users. But for those breaches on the part of Mr Rusell, it is more probable than not the collision would never have occurred.

4. Mr Chu did not breach his duty of care to Mr Russell, and if he did, any possible breach was not causative of his injuries.

5. Mr Russell's own negligence was the sole cause of his injuries.

[*Headnote by the Wolters Kluwer editors*]

P Jacskon SC with A Denehey (instructed by Murdoch Clarke) for the appellant.

K Read SC with R Phillips (instructed by Phillips Taglieri) for the respondent.

Before: Blow CJ, Porter, Estcourt JJ.

Victoria

[¶82-785] Kozarov v Victoria

(2022) Aust Torts Reports ¶82-785
Medium neutral citation: [2022] HCA 12
High Court of Australia
13 April 2022

Torts — Negligence — Workplace safety — Occupational health and safety — Personal injuries — Psychological injuries — Exposure to stressors — Duty of care — Notice of harm — Breach of duty — Causation — Appellant worked as a solicitor in Office of Public Prosecutions for which respondent was responsible — Work performed by appellant required her to deal with challenging material including evidence relating to child sex offences — Respondent becomes aware that such work could have repercussions for mental health of its employees — Appellant begins to experience psychological symptoms and is diagnosed with post-traumatic stress disorder and depression — Appellant commences proceedings claiming employer breached its duties to her — Primary judge held that respondent had been put on notice of risk to appellant and that she would have accepted an offer of rotation to a different department had it been offered — Damages of $435,000 are awarded to appellant — Respondent appeals to Court of Appeal, which agreed that respondent had been put on notice but did not agree that appellant would have accepted rotation — Appellant is granted leave to appeal to High Court and respondent files notice of contention — Whether evidence established that employer had been put on notice of risk of injury to appellant — Whether error in application of decision of High Court in Koehler v *Cerebos (Australia) Ltd (2005) 222 CLR 44 — Whether evidence demonstrated that appellant would have accepted an offer of rotation.*

Appeal from: *State of Victoria* v *Kozarov* (2020) Aust Torts Reports ¶82-587; [2020] VSCA 301.

The appellant, Ms Zagi Kozarov (Ms Kozarov), was a solicitor who worked for the Victorian Office of Public Prosecutions (the OPP). From June 2009, Ms Kozarov worked in the OPP's Specialist Sexual Offences Unit (the SSOU). In the course of that work, she was routinely exposed to crimes involving sexual violence, including towards children. This meant that Ms Kozarov frequently had to assess graphic and disturbing evidence of such violence, including child pornography. Her position also required her to regularly meet with the victims of these crimes and their families. The work entailed long hours and frequently Ms Kozarov worked late into the night.

In 2009, the OPP become aware that the challenging nature of this work was leading to high level of staff turnover within the SSOU. For that reason, the OPP introduced support strategies, including an Employee Assistance Programme (EAP) that offered staff free counselling. Ms Kozarov twice booked into the EAP but was unable to attend because of work commitments and instead started seeing a psychologist privately. Despite that, Ms Kozarov experienced growing levels of stress due to the work she was doing within the SSOU. She found it difficult to sleep and had problems in her personal relationships.

In 2011, she was one of a number of members of the SSOU's staff who signed a memorandum addressed to the SSOU's management (the 2011 staff memo). In it, the staff expressed a number of concerns about the volume and nature of the work that they were being required to undertake. By way of response, the SSOU's management undertook to make the workload more manageable. More particularly, it advised employees that it would take steps to increase its levels of staffing and to better organise the system for allocation of case files. It also undertook to augment the EAP that it had put in place in 2009.

Ms Kozarov's condition nevertheless deteriorated, and she began to experience symptoms like insomnia, weight loss and more problems with her personal relationships. She also felt paranoid and anxious about her own children and did not want to leave them with other people. In August 2011, she went on sick leave for 2 weeks due to these symptoms. Over the following 8 months, she made several attempts to return to work, but her symptoms returned on each occasion. In February 2012, Ms Kozarov was diagnosed with post-traumatic stress disorder (PTSD). She stopped working for the OPP in April 2012.

Ms Kozarov commenced proceedings against the defendant, the State of Victoria (Victoria), as the entity responsible for the OPP. She claimed that the OPP's negligence had caused her to develop the PTSD as well as a major depressive disorder (MDD). In making that claim, Ms Kozarov pleaded that the OPP had been put on notice that she could suffer psychological harm due to the nature and intensity of the work. She claimed that the 2011 staff memo raised the alarm about that possibility, but the OPP had not taken adequate steps to address the concerns raised. Ms Kozarov also pleaded that the OPP failed to protect her once she began to exhibit signs of impaired mental health.

At first instance, the primary judge held that the OPP had been placed on notice of a risk to Ms Kozarov's mental health by the end of August 2011 (the notice finding). This meant that the OPP had been required to take steps by way of reasonable response which included offering her rotation out of the SSOU to work in another section of the OPP. Her Honour also found that, at the end of August 2011, Ms Kozarov would have accepted an offer of rotation out of the SSOU to work in another section of the OPP (the rotation finding), thereby avoiding the exacerbation of her PTSD that occurred between August 2011 and February 2012. Damages of $435,000 were awarded.

Victoria then appealed to the Court of Appeal. That Court unanimously upheld the notice finding but rejected the rotation finding. In that context, the Court rejected Ms Kozarov's claim that she would have accepted an offer to rotate out of the SSOU. As such, the Court found that the OPP's breach of duty had not caused the exacerbation of Ms Kozarov's psychiatric injury between August 2011 and her departure from the SSOU in February 2012. On that basis, the award of damages was set aside. Ms Kozarov was then granted special leave to appeal to the High Court to challenge the Court of Appeal's rejection of the rotation finding.

The OPP filed a notice of contention seeking to also have the notice finding rejected. That notice of contention raised the proper application of the decision of the High Court in *Koehler* v *Cerebos (Australia) Ltd* (2005) 222 CLR 44 (*Koehler*). In that respect, Victoria emphasised the statement of the High Court that an employer was "entitled to assume, in the absence of evident signs warning of the possibility of psychiatric injury, that the employee considers that he or she is able to do the job". Victoria contended that Ms Kozarov had not established "evident signs" of the type contemplated by the High Court in Koehler.

Held: appeal allowed; cross-appeal dismissed.

Per Kiefel CJ and Keane J (who otherwise agreed with Gageler and Gleeson JJ):

1. The circumstances of a particular type of employment could be such that the work to be performed by the employee was inherently and obviously dangerous to the psychiatric health of the employee. The decision in Koehler was therefore not to be understood as requiring proof of "evident signs" in such cases. [4]–[6]

2. Given the policies that the OPP had in place from the beginning of Ms Kozarov's employment, it was clear that it had a "lively appreciation" of the serious risk to Ms Kozarov's mental health posed by her work within the SSOU. No further warning signs were necessary to oblige the OPP to take further protective steps. [7]

3. The OPP failed to properly implement those policies and did not take those further protective steps. Ms Kozarov had therefore not needed to show that there were additional

"evident signs" after the commencement of her employment, although it could be doubted that they would have independently put the OPP on notice. [8]–[19]

Per Gageler and Gleeson JJ:

1. The evident signs which manifested in Ms Kozarov's conduct from August 2011 provided a sufficient basis for the OPP to have been put on notice that she was at risk of the psychological injuries which she suffered. Those evident signs signified more than merely the inevitable and universal experience of vicarious trauma in the workplace of the SSOU. [50]–[54]

2. In setting aside the rotation finding, the Court of Appeal had not placed sufficient weight on the evidence that Ms Kozarov had consulted with medical professionals who had advised her about the risks of her employment to her psychological state. It was likely that she would have heeded their advice had she been given the chance. [58], [59]

3. While there was evidence that suggested that Ms Kozarov would have elected to stay in the SSOU even if she had been offered a rotation, the preferable view was that she would have acted in the interests of her mental health and accepted the alternative work. The primary judge's conclusion in that regard was to be restored. [60]–[62]

Per Gordon and Steward JJ:

1. Based on the evident signs that had then manifested in her conduct, Victoria had been put on notice about the risk of a psychological injury to Ms Kozarov no later than in August 2011. The conclusions of both the Court of Appeal and the primary judge in that respect were to be upheld. [67]–[80]

2. Contrary to what the Court of Appeal held with respect to the rotation finding, Ms Kozarov would have co-operated and her exposure to trauma would have been reduced had she been offered rotation to a different department. It was especially likely that she would have taken that option had she been fully advised of the relative risks to her health. [81]–[97]

Per Edelman J:

1. When Ms Kozarov commenced work in the SSOU in June 2009, the nature of the work undertaken in the SSOU required immediate precautions in relation to every employee in that unit. In Ms Kozarov's case, the necessity for those precautions increased and had been made clear by August 2011 as the "evident signs" emerged. [108]–[111]

2. Had the OPP offered Ms Kozarov appropriate psychological counselling about the risks which staying in the SSOU posed to her health, then it was probable that she would have accepted any offer to be rotated out of the SSOU. Had that happened, her injuries would not have been exacerbated. [112]–[113]

[*Headnote by the Wolters Kluwer editors*]

JT Rush QC and AM Dinelli with JB Richards QC and GD Taylor (Bowman & Knox) for the appellant.

BW Walker SC with GA Worth and NA Wootton (Russell Kennedy Lawyers) for the respondent.

Before: Kiefel CJ and Gageler, Keane, Gordon, Edelman, Steward and Gleeson JJ.

[¶82-782] Singh v Ward

(2022) Aust Torts Reports ¶82-782
Medium neutral citation: [2022] VSC 155
Supreme Court of Victoria
29 March 2022

Motor accidents — Pedestrian struck on highway — Pedestrian out of vehicle to change drivers — Driver did not see collision — Whether plaintiff contributorily negligent — Whether collision occurred in emergency lane or northbound left lane — Whether plaintiff parked car in safe position — Contributory negligence — Wrongs Act 1958 (Vic), s 26(1)(b).

On 31 December 2014, the plaintiff, Mr Gurtej Singh, was driving his family and a friend between Queenscliff and Melbourne. In the course of the journey, Mr Singh's 2-year-old daughter became upset and started to cry. After this had gone on for some time, Mr Singh decided to stop the car and swap seats with his friend in the front seat so that he could assist in the comforting of his daughter. He pulled over into the emergency lane and stopped at a point in the road where it swept gently to the right. After getting out, he closed the door and walked towards the front of the car with the intention of getting into the front driver's side seat.

The plaintiff, Mr Grant Ward, had been driving behind Mr Singh. As Mr Singh was walking towards the front of his car, part of Mr Ward's car (the left side-view mirror) struck him. At the time, Mr Ward had been travelling at approximately 100km/h. He claimed that he did not realise that his car struck Mr Singh and carried on driving (although he subsequently returned to the scene). The collision was witnessed by the passengers in the car behind Mr Ward's car, Mr Benjamin Ades and Ms Nicole Ades. After being struck by the car, Mr Singh's was knocked forward and his leg was broken. An ambulance attended and took him to hospital.

Mr Singh commenced negligence proceedings against Mr Ward. He claimed that he had remained entirely in the emergency lane when walking to the front of his car and that Mr Ward had negligently veered into the emergency lane from the northbound lane. Mr Singh relied upon the evidence given by Mr and Ms Ades, both of whom were very familiar with the area and travelled on the road around 5 times a week. Mr and Ms Ades both maintained that Mr Singh remained in the emergency lane, that Mr Ward veered to the left and that this movement caused the collision. They also attested that Mr Ward had not applied his brakes or slowed down before or after hitting Mr Singh. They both formed the view that Mr Ward had engaged in a "hit and run". They followed Mr Ward, flashing their lights and honking their horn. They pulled up next to Mr Ward and told him that they had seen him hit Mr Singh.

Mr Ward nevertheless denied that he drove negligently. He argued that Mr Singh had walked into the northbound lane. He relied on the contemporaneous police report that recorded that Mr Singh had been hit by a passing car after he walked onto the northbound lane. He also argued that Mr Singh had been contributorily negligent in that he had stopped his car very close to the northbound lane upon which traffic was rapidly passing.

Held: judgment for plaintiff.

1. The photograph upon which Mr Singh relied showed his car parked facing north with the right half of the car in the emergency lane and the left half his car on the open grassed area to the left of the emergency lane. There was therefore a gap to walk in the emergency lane. The notion that the car had been moved prior to the photograph was unfeasible. [4]–[6]

2. None of the people who gave evidence about the incident made a sworn statement at the time. It followed that each was giving evidence in March 2022 as to what had happened in

December 2014, unassisted by any contemporaneous record of events. There were marked divergences in the evidence given. [8], [9]

3. At the time that the police report was written, Mr Singh had been badly hurt and was being attended to by his family and his friend. It was also to be noted that English was not their first language. As such, it was likely that the version of events that the police officer recorded was the version that he was told by Mr Ward. [11]–[15]

4. Mr Ward's claims that he made efforts to return to the scene as soon as he realised what happened were not supported by the evidence. His claim that he tried to call the police before Mr Ades and Ms Ades reached him was not supported by the telephone transcript. It was also not supported by the evidence that Mr And Ms Ades had given. [21], [22]

5. Both Mr Ades and Ms Ades were impressive witnesses who had no reason not to give honest and consistent accounts of what happened. Their evidence about exactly where the collision took place was nevertheless affected to some degree by their age and by the passage of time. [33]–[51]

6. On balance, the evidence supported an inference that Mr Ward had lost concentration and veered into the emergency lane. Mr Singh had nevertheless been contributorily negligent by stopping so close to the northbound lane. Liability for the incident was to be apportioned at 90% to Mr Ward and 10% to Mr Singh. Damages were agreed between the parties. [52]–[72]

[*Headnote by the Wolters Kluwer editors*]

M Pilipasidis and T Nathanielsz (Slater & Gordon Ltd) for the plaintiff.

WR Middleton QC and AW Middleton (Transport Accident Commission) for the defendant.

Before: Gorton J.

[¶82-748] DP (a pseudonym) v Bird

(2021) Aust Torts Reports ¶82-748
Medium neutral citation: [2021] VSC 850
Supreme Court of Victoria
22 December 2021

Historic child sexual abuse — Institutional liability — Vicarious liability — Reasonable care — Psychological injuries — Post-traumatic stress disorder — Identification of causes — Expert medical evidence — Pain and suffering — Future economic loss — Wrongs Act 1958 (Vic), Pt X, s 48 — Legal Identity of Defendants (Organisational Child Abuse) Act 2018 (Vic), s 7(2)(b).

The plaintiff, DP, was born in Port Fairy in Victoria in 1966. His family were strict Catholics and DP regularly attended the local Catholic church (St Patrick's). From 1971, DP was also a pupil at the local Catholic school of the same name and continued there until 1976. Both the school and the church fell within the Diocese of Ballarat (the Diocese). In 1969, Mr Bryan Coffey (Mr Coffey) was ordained as a Catholic priest and in 1966 he was appointed by the Diocese as assistant priest at St Patrick's. He also worked as a teacher at the school. DP regularly saw Mr Coffey both at the school and his home, where he was a regular visitor and well known to his parents.

DP asserted that on 2 occasions in 1971 he was sexually abused by Mr Coffey. Both instances were alleged to have occurred in DP's home. The first incident occurred during his grandmother's wake. Mr Coffey was alleged to have carried DP to his bedroom on the pretext of putting him to bed. DP then claimed to have woken up to find Mr Coffey touching his genitals. The second incident took place on Boxing Day. DP had been given a tent as a Christmas present and Mr Coffey entered the tent with him. At that point, Mr Coffey started tickling DP's abdomen and then moved his hands down towards his genitals.

DP experienced a number of problems over the subsequent years. His father was said to be physically abusive and he also claimed to have been physically abused by another teacher at the school. He had difficulties in education and finished high school in Year 11. In 1985, when he was 19, DP's parents were both involved in a fatal motor accident and he formed the view (which was rejected by the Coroner) that his father had deliberately caused the accident to kill his mother. Following this, DP had difficulties with substance abuse. He also had problems finding work and maintaining relationships. Business ventures that he tried ended in failure and he was bankrupted in 2006.

In February 1999, Mr Coffey was convicted in the County Court of multiple accounts of indecent assault against children and ordered to serve a suspended sentence. Up to 2019, DP nevertheless had not disclosed his allegations to any other person. In particular, he did not disclose them in the course of multiple consultations that he had with psychologists or in the context of a complaint he made against the school in relation to the other teacher's physical abuse. DP first disclosed the allegations to the solicitors who placed an advertisement about civil proceedings for the benefit of Mr Coffey's victims in Port Fairy's local newspaper.

In March 2020, by which time Mr Coffey had died, DP commenced negligence proceedings in the Supreme Court of Victoria against the Diocese through the defendant, Mr Paul Bird, who was the Diocese's presiding Bishop. DP claimed that the assaults by Mr Coffey had caused him long-term psychological damage (including post-traumatic stress disorder) which had caused major pain and suffering and destroyed his earning capacity. DP maintained that the Diocese was vicariously liable for the actions of Mr Coffey. Additionally, he claimed that it was liable in negligence by reason of the Diocese's (and the relevant Bishop's) failure to exercise reasonable care in its supervision and control of Mr Coffey's conduct.

The Diocese did not admit that Mr Coffey assaulted DP and denied that it was vicariously liable for his actions. The Diocese did accept that it owed a duty of care to DP, but asserted it was not breached. If the Diocese was to be held liable, it claimed that the primary sources of DP's mental health issues were unrelated to the sexual abuse perpetrated by Mr Coffey. More particularly, the Diocese contended that the problems DP experienced in his later life were caused by factors other than Mr Coffey's assaults and so there was no cogent evidence to sustain an award of damages for economic loss.

Held: judgment for plaintiff in part.

DP's credibility and claims

1. There were multiple reasons for not accepting that the sexual assaults had affected DP in the way that he claimed. In particular, the fact that he had not disclosed them until 2019, despite multiple consultations with mental health professionals in the decade before, told against the claim that they had profoundly affected his life. [54]–[60]

2. The notion that DP had been too embarrassed or too ashamed to disclose the assaults prior to then, or that he had supressed them in some way, was also to be rejected. He had given detailed accounts of other intimate aspects of his life to mental health professionals and then had been prepared to disclose the assaults to solicitors over the phone in 2019. [61]–[77]

3. It could nevertheless be accepted that the sexual assaults, as pleaded by DP, had in fact happened. Key evidence in that respect was the testimony of 9 other people who had been sexually assaulted by Mr Coffey. DP's claims were consistent with the tendencies which that evidence established, including Mr Coffey's modus operandi. [78]–[115]

Vicarious liability of Diocese

4. An analysis of the authorities demonstrated that the principles of vicarious liability had been adapted for the purposes of child sexual abuse cases. Vicarious liability was to be imposed where the employer significantly increased the risk of harm by putting the employee in his or her position and requiring him [or her] to perform the assigned tasks. [116]–[162]

5. The authorities nevertheless did not support the Diocese's contention that vicarious liability only attached to situations where the relevant act took place in the context of the employment relationship. That proposition could not be reconciled with the decision of the High Court in *Prince Alfred College Incorporated* v *ADC* (2016) 258 CLR 134. [163]–[210]

6. DP's claim of vicarious liability did not fail because Mr Coffey could not be regarded as the Diocese' employee. It was instead necessary to undertake a holistic assessment of the facts to determine whether vicarious liability was to be imposed upon the Diocese for Mr Coffey's conduct. [211]–[224]

7. That assessment of the facts supported the imposition of vicarious liability. Mr Coffey had been the "essence" of the Diocese in Port Fairy and had been acting in that capacity when he took the opportunity to exploit children, including DP. Notwithstanding that he had acted unlawfully, the Diocese was to be held vicariously liable for Mr Coffey's conduct. [225]–[282]

Direct liability of Diocese

8. There was no evidence that the Diocese had any evidence to the affect that Mr Coffey had preyed on children prior to sexually assaulting DP. There was evidence that it had information to that effect about other clergy, but there was nothing to suggest that it was aware of specific allegations against Mr Coffey. [283]–[303]

9. It was impossible to conclude that allegations against other clergy should have led the Diocese on a path to reasonably suspect other priests, and more particularly Mr Coffey, as being potentially responsible for similar conduct towards young boys. The Diocese had therefore not breached its direct duty to DP. [304]–[308]

Assessment of damages

10. Consistently with the findings on DP's credibility, it was not to be accepted that Mr Coffey's conduct towards him had profoundly affected his later life. To the extent that the medical expert evidence that he called purported to support such a claim, that evidence was to be rejected. [309]–[383]

11. DP's claim of lifelong symptoms on account of Mr Coffey's assaults was squarely contradicted by several out-of-court statements made by DP and histories to treating professionals. Not only did he not refer to the assaults, but he described a normal childhood up until the school abuse. [384]–[423]

12. DP was therefore not to be awarded damages for any long-term psychological injuries, including PTSD. He was, however, to be awarded damages for pain and suffering (both past and ongoing) and medical expenses. Aggravated damages were also to be awarded given the nature of the assaults. Damages were award in the total sum of $230,000, including aggravated damages of $20,000. [424]–[484]

[*Headnote by the Wolters Kluwer editors*]

G Boas with E Kelly (Ken Cush & Associates) for the plaintiff.

R Annesley QC with T Skvortsova and A Dinelli (Colin, Biggers & Paisley Lawyers) for the defendant.

Before: Forrest J.

[¶82-722] PCB v The Geelong College

(2021) Aust Torts Reports ¶82-722
Medium neutral citation: [2021] VSC 633
Supreme Court of Victoria
1 October 2021

Historic child sexual abuse — Institutional abuse — Liability of school — Vicarious liability — Duty of care — Breach of duty — Damages — Psychological and psychiatric injuries — Post Traumatic Stress Disorder (PTSD) — Pain and suffering — Past and future economic losses — Plaintiff attended school conducted by defendant from 1987 to 1992 — Activity centre associated with school offered students range of afterschool activities — Between 1988 to 1990 plaintiff suffered sexual abuse by an honorary member of that activity centre who was not formally employed by the school — Vicarious liability — Wrongs Act 1958 (Vic), Pt VB.

In 1987, the plaintiff, who was born in 1975, commenced Year 7 at The Geelong College (the school). At that time, the school was divided into a junior and a senior campus and the plaintiff spent most of his time on the junior campus. However, in 1988, the plaintiff began to regularly attend the "House of Guilds" on the senior campus after school. The House of Guilds was an activity centre in which students of the school could pursue woodwork, ceramics and other crafts. Students from other schools and members of the public could also pursue activities in the House of Guilds upon payment of a fee. The plaintiff regularly attended the woodwork room in the House of Guilds.

Mr Bert Palframan, who was in his seventies at the time, also regularly attended the woodwork room as an honorary member of the House of Guilds. Mr Palframan was not trained as a teacher and had no formal affiliation with the school. Between 1988 and 1990, Mr Palfram sexually abused the plaintiff. The sexual abuse typically commenced in the woodwork room and then continued in Mr Palfram's car and then in his apartment. The sexual abuse stopped in mid-1990. Mr Palfram died in around 1999.

The plaintiff did not tell anyone about the sexual abuse at the time. He completed his higher education in 1992 but then was initially unable to complete a tertiary qualification, although he subsequently completed a bachelor's degree in commerce in 2000. However, over the following 19 years, he experienced ongoing difficulties in maintaining employment. The plaintiff met his wife in 2004 and they married in 2007. However, in that same year he had a mental breakdown and was unable to work until 2011. He then worked intermittently until 2019. From late 2019, the plaintiff began regularly seeing a psychologist and in 2021 he was diagnosed as having suffered post-traumatic stress disorder (PTSD) and generalised anxiety disorder (GAD) as a consequent of the sexual abuse he suffered. These diagnoses were subsequently confirmed by a psychiatrist.

The plaintiff commenced proceedings in the Supreme Court of Victoria against the school, in negligence and claimed damages. He claimed that the school was either directly liable for breaching its duty to him or vicariously liable for the sexual abuse perpetrated by Mr Palfram. As to damages, the plaintiff claimed that the "trajectory" of his life had been affected by the abuse and so he sought damages for past and future losses.

The school did not dispute that Mr Palfram had committed the sexual abuse in the manner, and over the time period, that the plaintiff claimed. It was also not in contention that the plaintiff had suffered PTSD and GAD as a consequence of that abuse. However, the school did argue that it had not breached the non-delegable duty it owed to the plaintiff because it had instituted a system of supervision in the House of Guilds. The school also denied that it was vicariously liable for Mr Palfram's conduct. As to damages, the school argued that the trajectory of the plaintiff's life had not been affected to the extent pleaded and that he would soon be able to return to work.

Held: judgment for plaintiff.

1. The plaintiff gave consistent evidence about the sexual abuse he had suffered. He also gave convincing evidence on the effect that it had on both his professional and personal life. While he was understandably emotional in giving that evidence, his testimony was credible and was largely to be accepted. [29]–[98]

2. The evidence given by the plaintiff's wife was also consistent and credible. She gave evidence about the ongoing difficulties that he had and the manner in which she had been required to support him at various periods of their marriage because he was unable to work. Her evidence was also to be accepted. [99]–[119]

3. The plaintiff's treating psychiatrist gave evidence that the sexual abuse had "dramatically shifted" his educational and professional career. Evidence was also given to the effect that the plaintiff was "struggling gigantically" and would be unable to return to work in the foreseeable future. That evidence withstood cross-examination. [120]–[140]

4. It was not to be accepted that the school held Mr Palframan out as a teacher of the school to those attending the House of Guilds. The more likely scenario was that, for his own purposes, Mr Palframan endeavoured to infiltrate the operations of the House of Guilds by misrepresenting his affiliation with the school. [295]–[298]

5. The decisions in which vicarious liability was imposed on a school for the acts of a third party in an institutional context were generally premised on the existence of an employment relationship. Those cases were therefore to be distinguished in this case. There was no other basis upon which to impose vicarious liability on the school. [299]–[312]

Whether the school breached its duty of care to the plaintiff

6. The school was aware of the possibility that its students could be victims of sexual abuse. That was particularly because, at the relevant times, the school's headmaster had been informed that at least one other teacher and housemaster had allegedly sexually interfered with students in the junior school. [321]–[324]

7. There was also evidence that at least one other student had made a complaint to the school about the conduct of Mr Palframan in the House of Guilds. At the very least, the school was in a position to further investigate matters which would likely have led to a specific understanding of the risked posed by Mr Palframan. [325]–[343]

8. In response to this information, the school did nothing. It took no steps to further investigate the allegations and took no steps to ensure that additional systems were put in place at the House of Guilds to prevent such abuse occurring. The school considered that the existence of a fulltime warden at the House of Guilds was sufficient. [344]–[345]

9. However, the general system relied upon by the school was not a reasonable response to the specific risk presented by the complaints made about Mr Palframan. To the contrary, Mr Palframan should have been either excluded from the House of Guilds or should have been "watched like a hawk". [346]–[384]

10. The duty of care owed to the plaintiff by the school was breached in respect of the extensive abuse suffered by him at the hands of Mr Palframan on the premises of the defendant and, on the evidence, that abuse was a cause of the psychiatric injury that he had suffered. No question of "apportionment" arose in that context. [385]–[429]

11. The expert evidence established that the sexual abuse had a "crippling" effect on the plaintiff's life. While he had sometimes affected a confident manner, it could be accepted that this was a façade for the humiliation he felt as a consequence of the abuse. He was entitled to general damages for pain and suffering in the amount of $300,000. [430]–[473]

12. The sexual abuse had affected the "trajectory" of the plaintiff's life. In particular, if it had not occurred then he would have achieved the level that he achieved in 2019 some 4

years earlier. He also would have been able to keep working. He was therefore entitled to additional damages for past and future economic losses to give a total of $2,632,319.25. [474]–[553]

[Headnote by the Wolters Kluwer editors]

FM McLeod SC with T Hammond (Rightside Legal) for the plaintiff.

JT Rush RFD QC with RL Kaye (HWL Ebsworth) for the defendant.

Before: O'Meara J.

[¶82-648] Simmonds-Thatcher v Kamari

(2021) Aust Torts Reports ¶82-648
Medium neutral citation: [2021] VSCA 133
Supreme Court of Victoria, Court of Appeal
14 May 2021

Motor accidents — Respondent struck by applicant's vehicle when crossing road after alighting from taxi — Contributory negligence — Whether trial judge erred in finding applicant negligent by reason of not slowing down, having seen respondent alight from taxi onto nature strip — Whether open to find that applicant not keeping proper lookout — Whether causal relationship established.

On 14 November 2015, Ms Sudabh Kamari attended a lunchtime social gathering with her 2 children and a group of friends. At the conclusion of the gathering Ms Kamari and 3 of her friends engaged a maxi taxi to take them, together with their children, back to their respective homes.

The first drop-off was at one of Ms Kamari's friends. The taxi pulled up at the kerb and the front wheels of the taxi were positioned on a speed hump. Ms Kamari opened the sliding door on the passenger's side of the taxi and stepped out into the gutter and onto the nature strip. She took a blanket in a plastic bag from her friend in order to help her friend disembark from the taxi and cross the road, because her friend needed to place an infant in a pram before crossing the road. Ms Kamari walked around the rear of the taxi before crossing the road. She looked to her right but did not look to her left and stepped out from behind the taxi. Shortly after stepping out into the roadway, Ms Kamari was struck by a motor vehicle driven by Mr Brandon Simmonds-Thatcher and fell to the ground, suffering injury as a result.

Mr Simmonds-Thatcher stated that as he approached the taxi, he saw Ms Kamari alight from it, but she then went out of view behind the taxi as his car moved forward. As he drove over the speed hump Ms Kamari suddenly ran out from behind the taxi and collided with the passenger side of the vehicle.

Ms Kamari commenced proceedings against Mr Simmonds-Thatcher in the County Court of Victoria, in negligence and claimed damages. The primary judge found in favour of Ms Kamari and found that she had suffered injury as the result both of her own negligence as a pedestrian and the negligence of Mr Simmonds-Thatcher in that, having observed Ms Kamari get out of the taxi, he was negligent in that either he failed to keep a proper lookout and/or was travelling too fast. Damages were assessed in the total sum of $515,000 but with a reduction of 75% on account of contributory negligence: *Kamari* v *Simmonds-Thatcher* [2020] VCC 961.

Mr Simmonds-Thatcher sought leave to appeal the primary judge's liability finding that he was 25% liable for the accident. He argued that the primary judge erred in imposing a duty of care which was beyond a duty to take reasonable care and by holding that the duty was breached, and erred in finding that causation had been established, that at a walking pace for Ms Kamari, Mr Simmons-Thatcher if travelling at an appropriate speed would have had ample time to avoid the collision.

Held: leave to appeal granted; appeal allowed.

1. The only circumstance relied upon to put Mr Simmons-Thatcher on notice of any kind of risk as he was driving along Hartington Street was the sight of Ms Kamari alighting from the taxi onto the adjacent nature strip and then disappearing from view. Ms Kamari was an adult woman who, it should be assumed, would behave rationally and not put herself at risk by entering onto the roadway without looking. [48]

2. It was not open to the primary judge to find that Ms Kamari alighting from the taxi onto the nature strip was a factor that should cause a motorist, acting reasonably, to reduce his or her speed below the applicable speed limit. It was not open to hold that it was incumbent on Mr Simmonds-Thatcher "to travel at a speed where he could stop", especially as it was entirely unclear where that point would be. The primary judge's analysis suffered from the flaw identified in *Mobbs* v *Kain* (2009) Aust Torts Reports ¶82-037; [2009] NSWCA 301: it was self-fulfilling as to breach of duty — because there was an accident, the speed was too great. It was the product of impermissible hindsight reasoning. [49]

3. If drivers were required to anticipate in any and all circumstances that a pedestrian might suddenly stray onto the road, traffic would come to a standstill. In the present case there was no line of stationary cars from which a pedestrian might unexpectedly emerge. The primary judge erred in finding that it was incumbent on Mr Simmonds-Thatcher to travel at a speed at which he could stop so as to avoid a collision of the type which occurred. [51], [52]

4. Mr Simmonds-Thatcher was not required to slow down just because he saw Ms Kamari alight from the taxi from further up the street. The primary judge's finding on causation was infected by the error identified concerning the extent of Mr Simmonds-Thatcher's duty of care. [55]

5. The finding with respect to error in the primary judge's approach to duty of care and breach of that duty was not dispositive of the appeal in itself. The facts may permit an inference that Mr Simmonds-Thatcher breached his duty of care to Ms Kamari by failing to keep a proper lookout and that that breach was a cause of the injury to Ms Kamari. [56]

6. It was open to find on the evidence that Mr Simmonds-Thatcher breached his duty of care to Ms Kamari by failing to keep a proper lookout at the point when Ms Kamari emerged onto the roadway from behind the taxi and proceeded to cross a substantial part of the roadway in front of him. Whilst the primary judge erred in relation to both duty and causation, the court would be prepared to infer that Mr Simmonds-Thatcher was not keeping a proper lookout when Ms Kamari emerged from behind the taxi. However, the evidence does not permit the court to be satisfied that had Mr Simmonds-Thatcher been keeping a proper lookout, he could have stopped his car so as to avoid hitting Ms Kamari. [61]–[70]

7. On any view, Mr Simmonds-Thatcher's opportunity to react to the presence of Ms Kamari on the roadway was very brief. The extent and adequacy of Mr Simmonds-Thatcher's opportunity to react to the presence of Ms Kamari on the roadway was attended by material uncertainty. Whilst it may be inferred that it was possible the collision may have been avoided if Mr Simmonds-Thatcher had kept a better lookout, it could not be inferred that it was more probable than not that the collision would have been avoided or that Ms Kamari would not have fallen into the road and been injured if Mr Simmonds-Thatcher had kept a better lookout. [71]

[*Headnote by the Wolters Kluwer editors*]

J Ruskin QC with G Cooper (Transport Accident Commission) for the applicant.

ADB Ingram QC with M Pilipasidis (Kenyon Legal) for the respondent.

Before: Kyrou, Emerton and Osborn JJA.

[¶82-604] Marks v Skydive Holdings Pty Ltd

(2021) Aust Torts Reports ¶82-604
Medium neutral citation: [2021] VSC 21
Supreme Court of Victoria
1 February 2021

Skydiving — Inherent risks — Waivers — Exclusions — Dangerous recreational activities — Plaintiff entered into contract with defendant skydive operator to undertake a recreational skydive — Plaintiff was injured in course of heavy landing after undertaking tandem skydive with her instructor — Proceedings commenced by plaintiff against defendant seeking damages in respect of her injuries — Plaintiff claimed that her instructor had been negligent in way that he had landed parachute — Defendant invoked waiver in denying liability — Alternatively defendant claimed that plaintiff's injuries had been caused by inherent risks of skydiving — Injuries suffered by plaintiff were an inherent risk of skydiving materialised — Wrongs Act 1958 (Vic), s 55.

The plaintiff, Ms Hayley Marks (Ms Marks), undertook a recreational tandem skydive with her partner, Mr Dane Cummins (Mr Cummins), on 18 August 2018. Ms Marks had earlier booked the 2 tandem skydives with the defendant, Skydive Holding Pty Ltd (Skydive Holdings). The booking process was completed online. It prompted Ms Marks to join the Australian Parachute Federation (APF), membership of which was included in the price. She accordingly electronically completed the APF membership form which included a section headed "Waivers". In that section, VPF (meaning Victorian Parachute Federation) was written with a start date of 15 August 2018.

This process automatically created a waiver form in Ms Marks' electronic membership record. That form essentially purported to exclude the liability of APF or any of its operators from common law or statutory liability in respect of death or injuries occurring to Ms Marks as a consequence of the skydive. In addition, the waiver form contained a risk warning which stated that the recreational activities supplied by APF and its providers were inherently dangerous and involved some degree of risk. That risk warning further stated that accidents could and often did happen and that they could result in personal injury, death or property damage where they did occur.

On the day of the skydive, Ms Marks and Mr Cummins went to the Lilydale airfield in the Yarra Valley, where they checked in for their jump. They met Mr Cummins' tandem instructor, put on their harnesses, and watched an instructional video. Ms Marks met her tandem instructor, Mr Sam Dale (Mr Dale), just before they went up in the plane. Ms Marks and Mr Cummins were clipped on to the front of their tandem instructors before each pair jumped out of the plane at an altitude of about 13,000 feet. Mr Cummins completed his jump without incident. However, a short time later, Ms Marks and Mr Dale landed very heavily. As a consequence, Ms Marks fractured her lumbar spine and required surgery. She was subsequently able to return to full-time work, but she claimed to be living in constant pain and to have ongoing disabilities. She also claimed to have become anxious and depressed.

Ms Marks commenced proceedings in the Supreme Court of Victoria against Skydive Holdings in negligence, for breach of contract, and for breaches of guarantees in the Australian Consumer Law. She alleged that her injuries were caused by a lack of care and skill on the part of Mr Dale, for whom Skydive Holdings was vicariously liable. Skydive Holdings relied on the waiver form and, in the alternative, argued that Ms Marks' injury occurred due to the manifestation of the inherent risks of skydiving within the meaning of s 55 of the *Wrongs Act 1958* (Vic).

Held: proceedings dismissed.

Whether the waiver formed part of the contract

1. The waiver was not part of the contract that Ms Marks entered into with Skydive Holdings on 1 August 2018 when she booked and paid for 2 tandem jumps. The waiver was

part of the APF membership, which was an "added extra" for the purchase price. But the booking process had not required Ms Marks to complete the membership form before the skydive. [23], [24]

2. Membership of the APF was not a prerequisite to undertaking a skydive with Skydive Holdings. Such a contention was inconsistent with the non-mandatory wording of the membership form. There was also no evidence that Skydive Holdings took steps to ensure that the form was completed prior to the skydive. [25]–[27]

3. It was not clear that Ms Marks would, or should, have understood the waiver form to be waiving her rights to make any claim against Skydive Holdings. The waiver form contained no specific reference to Skydive Holdings and its relationship with APF was not specified. [28]–[30]

Whether Skydive Holdings had been negligent

4. The heavy landing and Ms Marks' injuries were not the result of any failure by Mr Dale to exercise reasonable care for Ms Marks' safety. He performed the landing with due care and skill, aligning the parachute into the wind on his final approach and braking early to slow the parachute's unusually fast descent. [4], [79], [80]

5. The evidence established that, in the final few moments before landing, Ms Marks and Mr Dale encountered a downdraft. It was this downdraft, which was an inherent risk of skydiving, that led to Ms Marks' injuries. As such, Ms Marks was not able to establish that Skydive Holdings had breached any common law or statutory duty that it owed her. [86]–[91]

[*Headnote by the Wolters Kluwer editors*]

S McCredie with PG Hamilton (Zaparas Lawyers) for the plaintiff.

R Annesley QC with A Baker (Lander & Rogers) for the defendant.

Before: Richards J.

[¶82-512] Yeung v Santosa Realty Co Pty Ltd

(2020) Aust Torts Reports ¶82-512
Medium neutral citation: [2020] VSCA 7
Supreme Court of Victoria, Court of Appeal
6 February 2020

Torts — Negligence — Delegated duty of care — Owner liability — Delegation to real estate agent — Inspection of premises — Tenant injuries — Apportionment of liability — Equitable apportionment — Appeals — Tenant of premises owned by appellant slipped and fractured her right ankle — Proceedings brought by tenant against appellant and first respondent real estate agent — Primary judge awarded damages to tenant and apportioned two-thirds of responsibility to appellant and one-third to first respondent — Appellant appealed against apportionment — Held: appeal allowed — Appellant had delegated his duty of care to first respondent — Second respondent's failure to carry out that duty led to tenant's injuries — First respondent required to fully indemnify appellant in respect of his liability to tenant.

Ms Potter was a tenant of residential premises owned by Mr William Yeung and managed by Santosa Realty Co Pty Ltd (Santosa). On 19 May 2014, Ms Potter slipped at night on the back stairs of the premises that she was renting. Those stairs were worn, slippery, unlit and had no handrail. As a consequence of slipping, Ms Potter fractured her right ankle.

Ms Potter commenced proceedings in the County Court of Victoria against Mr Yeung and Santosa, in negligence and claimed damages. At first instance, the primary judge found that Mr Yeung and Santosa had each breached their duty of care to Ms Potter and were

liable to pay damages totalling $433,899.80. The primary judge apportioned two-thirds of that liability to Mr Yeung and one-third to Santosa.

Mr Yeung sought leave to appeal from the primary judge's apportionment. He claimed on appeal that Santosa had failed, through Ms Hunter who was a licensed real estate agent employed by Santosa, to inspect the back stairs and detect their defects, especially their slipperiness, and report those defects back to Mr Yeung for repair. Mr Yeung also claimed that he had relevantly delegated the performance of his duty of care as landlord and occupier to Santosa. The failure of Santosa to discharge that duty was why the injury to Ms Potter occurred. Alternatively, Mr Yeung claimed that the court should make a just and equitable apportionment having regard to the extent of each party's actual responsibility for the injury to Ms Potter.

Held: leave to appeal granted, appeal allowed.

1. Under Pt IIA of the *Wrongs Act 1958* (Vic), Mr Yeung was defined as the "occupier" of the premises because he was the landlord of the premises let under a tenancy who was under an obligation to the tenant to maintain or repair the premises. The issue was whether he had delegated that obligation to Santosa. [68]–[78]

2. It had been well established that the duty of a landlord and deemed occupier of premises to take reasonable care to avoid foreseeable risk of injury to tenants could be discharged by the exercise of reasonable skill and care in engaging an apparently competent contractor, such as Santosa in the present case. [79]–[80]

3. Santosa had been engaged to conduct routine inspections of the premises and, in its inspection reports, indicate what repairs were needed. It was also not in contest that Santosa had failed to carry out an inspection of the back stairs at the relevant time, as it was bound to do. [81]–[82]

4. The factual findings of the primary judge supported the conclusion that, had Santosa done what Mr Yeung required of it under the management agreement, Ms Potter would not have fallen and suffered injury. Those findings revealed that Mr Yeung in fact delegated the performance of his relevant duty of care to Santosa. [83]–[92]

5. The primary judge erred in finding that Mr Yeung failed to take any real steps to ensure the premises were in good repair. There was no basis for rejecting the proposition that it was reasonable for Mr Yeung to appoint Santosa as a management agent for the purposes of conducting inspections that required no specialist expertise. [93]–[99]

6. The duty to inspect, detect and report on obvious hazards was a duty that had been delegated by Mr Yeung to Santosa. Santosa had not discharged that duty and accordingly, it was liable to indemnify Mr Yeung fully for the injuries suffered by Ms Potter. [100]–[114]

7. Paragraphs 4 and 5 of the orders of the primary judge dated 5 February 2019 ought be set aside and, in their place, it be ordered that Santosa indemnify Yeung with respect to all Yeung's liability under paras 1 and 2 of those orders whereby the judge ordered that there be judgment for the plaintiff in the sum of $433,899.80 plus interest in the sum of $40,960 and that the defendants pay the plaintiff's costs (including reserved costs) on an indemnity basis. [114]

[*Headnote by the Wolters Kluwer editors*]

J Ruskin QC with S Gladman (Mills Oakley) for the appellant.

J Gorton QC with C Madder (Moray Agnew) for the first respondent.

No appearance for the second respondent.

Before: Tate, Kaye and Niall JJA.

[¶82-506] State of Victoria v Thompson

(2019) Aust Torts Reports ¶82-506
Medium neutral citation: [2019] VSCA 237
Supreme Court of Victoria, Court of Appeal
25 October 2019

Torts — Negligence — Breach of statutory duty — Intentional injuries — Claim for non-economic loss — Statutory limitations on claims — Statutory interpretation — Appeals — Respondent was injured when another prison inmate stabbed him — Proceedings commenced by respondent against appellant State seeking damages for his injuries — Respondent's claims sought damages for non-economic loss — Statutory scheme imposed general rule that non-economic loss could only be awarded for a "significant injury" — Exception to rule could be invoked where claim "related to" an intentional act — Primary judge held that exception applied — State appealed — Plain meaning of exception and legislative intent supported its application in circumstances — Wrongs Act 1958 (Vic), s 28LC and 28LE.

On 13 June 2014, the respondent, Mr Allan Thompson, who was then an inmate at Dhurringile Prison at Murchison, was injured when he was stabbed by another prisoner. He subsequently commenced proceedings against the appellant, the State of Victoria (the State), claiming damages in respect of his injuries.

In his statement of claim, Mr Thompson pleaded that his injuries were caused by the negligence and/or breach of statutory duty of the State and that those injuries had caused him non-economic loss. Section 28LE of the *Wrongs Act 1958* (Vic) (the Wrongs Act) provided that a person was "not entitled to recover damages for non-economic loss in any proceeding in a court in respect of an injury to a person caused by the fault of another person unless the person injured had suffered significant injury". For that purpose, Pt VBA of the Wrongs Act set out the requirements for proving the existence of a "significant injury" to satisfy s 28LE.

Although Mr Thompson initially began the process of attempting to prove that he had suffered a significant injury under Pt VBA, he subsequently relied upon s 28LC(2) of the Wrongs Act. That provision relevantly stated that Pt VBA did not apply to claims for the recovery of damages for non-economic loss where the fault concerned "is, or relates to, an intentional act that was done with intent to cause death or injury or that was sexual assault or other sexual misconduct". In that respect, Mr Thompson contended that, because he had been the victim of an intentional stabbing, s 28LC(2) had the effect of excluding s 28LE from applying to his case.

The State nevertheless maintained that, because Mr Thompson was actually pleading negligence and breach of statutory duty as his causes of action, s 28LC(2) could not apply. At first instance, the primary judge held that the words "or relates to" in s 28LC(2) meant that the provision could apply.

The State appealed the primary judge's findings.

Held: appeal dismissed.

1. The historical context in which Pt VBA was enacted was relevant. That context was that Pt VBA was part of the State Government's legislative response to an alleged crisis "in the affordability and availability of several key insurance products". As such, the Part dealt with limitations on the assessment of personal injury damages. [27]–[35]

2. Although that was the broad purpose of Pt VBA, the words "or relates to" in s 28LC(2) represented the State Government's attempt to "balance the rights of people to sue for personal injuries and the need for access to affordable insurance". Those words broadened the exception to the limitations where a plaintiff had been intentionally injured. [36], [37]

3. It followed that there was no basis for giving the words "or relates to" in s 28LC(2) some different or narrower meaning than they bore on their face. In particular, there was no justification for reading the provision so that the relevant intentional act had to be done by a defendant. [38], [39]

4. As such, the primary judge was correct to conclude that there was a sufficient nexus between the intentional stabbing of Mr Thompson (done with intent to cause death or injury) and his claim for s 28LC(2)(a) to be applicable. That nexus obviated the need for Mr Thompson to comply with Pt VBA of the Wrongs Act. [40], [41]

[*Headnote by the Wolters Kluwer editors*]

SA O'Meara QC with R Kaye (Victorian Government Solicitor) for the appellant.

JP Brett QC with YC Chen (LY Tonge & Co) for the respondent.

Before: Beech and Osborn JJA, and Kennedy AJA.

[¶82-354] Sim Development Pty Ltd v Greenvale Property Group Pty Ltd

(2017) Aust Torts Reports ¶82-354
Medium neutral citation: [2017] VSC 335
Supreme Court of Victoria
Judgment delivered 16 June 2017

Contract — Construction — Consultancy and management agreement — Agreement terminated prior to completion of property development project — Whether consultant entitled to 20% of net profit arising on sale of property — Entitlement to 20% net profit contingent on completion of project — Entitlement of consultant to be paid at agreed hourly rate for Services performed up to the date of termination — Contractual definition of Services — Whether evidence supports hourly amount claimed.

Tort — Negligence — Concurrent duties in contract and tort — Whether failure to advise of electricity substation constituted breach of duty — Whether failure to advise caused loss and damage — Wrongs Act 1958 (Vic), s 51 — Civil Liability Act 2002 (NSW), s 5D(1).

Real property — Caveats — Application for removal of caveat — Whether amounts owing pursuant to consultancy and management agreement were secured by a charge over property — Whether the charge constituted a caveatable interest — Whether caveat lodged without reasonable cause — Transfer of Land Act 1958 (Vic), ss 89(1), 90(3), 118.

On February 2013, Cai, a property developer and the sole director of Sim Development Pty Ltd (Sim Development), discussed the development potential of a property with an associate, Jonathan Wang ("Wang"). Two property inspections were conducted to a group of potential investors.

On 22 May 2013, Greenvale Property Group Pty Ltd (Greenvale) entered into a contract of sale with Sim Development for the purchase of the Property for the sum of $4.1m. Greenvale also contracted with Sim Development to provide consulting and management services in relation to the proposed development. In return, Greenvale agreed to pay 20% of the net profit resulting from the project to Sim Development.

The Sim Consultancy and Management Agreement (the Agreement) was executed and backdated to 29 May 2013. Sim Development undertook a substantial amount of work in relation to the Project.

In September 2014, Greenvale decided to sell the Property and that it would no longer pursue the development and ceased making payments to Sim Development. Sim Development continued to undertake work in relation the Property. On 10 July 2015, Greenvale sent an

email notifying Sim Development of its intention to terminate the Agreement with effect from 28 August 2015.

On 15 July 2015, Sim Development lodged the Caveat over the Property to secure the moneys alleged to be owed by Greenvale and rendered an invoice to Greenvale for the sum of $380,280 in respect of fees and services provided to Greenvale.

On 17 August 2015, Wyndham Developments offered to purchase the Property for $6.8m, however, it later decided not to pursue the purchase due to uncertainty in relation to the cost of dealing with a substation.

Sim Development commenced proceedings in the Supreme Court of Victoria against Greenvale, making a claim for declarations that it is entitled to 20% of the net profit to be realised on the sale of the Property by Greenvale. Greenvale made a counterclaim against Sim Development and Cai in relation to the substation and claimed to have suffered loss and damage as a consequence of Sim Development's alleged breach of duty, including by having to incur wasted fees and expenditure. It alleged that it suffered loss and damage to the extent of the cost of remedying the defect which led to a diminution in the value of the Property, and alleged that prospective purchasers of the Property were discouraged by the cost and uncertainty associated with moving the substation.

Held: **Sim Development is entitled to payment of $153,260. Its claim will otherwise be dismissed. Greenvale is entitled to payment of the sum of $20,000 on its counterclaim. Its claims will otherwise be dismissed. There should be a set off in relation to claims in (a) and (b). The Caveat Proceeding will be dismissed.**

Per Sifris J:

1. It is clear from the evidence that substantial work was performed by Sim Development. Sim Development was entitled to "full payment for all work performed" up to the date of termination pursuant to clause 16(b) of the Agreement. Greenvale knew and intended the work to continue and cannot escape liability for payment of consultancy fees. The basis for the calculation of such fees is the agreed rate.

2. Sim Development's failure to mention the Substation was a minor breach of duty and of little consequence. Greenvale bears the burden of proving, on the balance of probabilities, any fact relevant to the issue of causation and in accordance with s 51 of the *Wrongs Act 1958* (Vic), and also considering s 5D(1)(a) of the *Civil Liability Act 2002* (NSW) (which is identical to s 51 of the *Wrongs Act 1958* (Vic) save for two respects).

3. Greenvale failed to demonstrate, on the balance of probabilities, that Sim Development's failure to warn of the presence of the Substation caused the particular harm identified and failed to demonstrate factual causation, namely that Sim Development's negligence was a necessary condition of the occurrence of the harm. There was no basis in the evidence to suggest that all of the work done was wasted and that Greenvale would have to start again. The wasted work is estimated to be in the amount of about $20,000.

[*Headnote by the Wolters Kluwer editors*]

Mr S V Palmer with Mr P J Rule (instructed by Moray & Agnew) for the plaintiff.

Mr A Kirby (instructed by Brand Partners) for the defendant.

Before: Sifris J.

[¶82-287] **Scott v Wanklyn**

(2016) Aust Torts Reports ¶82-287

Medium neutral citation: [2016] VSC 382

Supreme Court of Victoria

Judgment delivered 8 July 2016

Negligence — Personal injury — Occupier's liability pursuant to the Wrongs Act 1958 (Vic) s 14B(3) — Plaintiff stepped into a trench dug on the defendant's property and fell — Defendant ran business part-time from premises — Defendant in breach of duty to take care to avoid injury to plaintiff by reason of the state of the premises — Roads and Traffic Authority of NSW v *Dederer (2007) 234 CLR 330; Erickson* v *Bagley [2015] VSCA 220 cited — Wrongs Act 1958 (Vic), ss 14B(3), (4), 48.*

In December 2014, Mr Scott attended a property owned and occupied by Mr Wanklyn. Mr Scott had been driven to Mr Wanklyn's property by his daughter, Carol Tompkins, to collect a wooden chair which Mr Wanklyn was repairing for him. After alighting from Mrs Tompkins' car, Mr Scott walked across a gravel driveway area intending to step into a shed where he understood the chair to be. As he stepped forward, he placed his left foot on the driveway close to the concrete floor of the shed. Mr Scott alleged that his foot went into a trench which was about eight or nine inches wide and about six inches deep, as a consequence of which he lost his balance, fell backwards and fell onto his left hip. As a result of the fall, Mr Scott suffered a subcapital fracture of the left femur.

Mr Scott commenced proceedings in the Supreme Court of Victoria, in negligence and claimed damages. He alleged that there was negligence, or a breach of the duty owed by Mr Wanklyn for the purposes of s 14B(3) of the *Wrongs Act 1958* (Vic) (the Wrongs Act), which was a cause of his injuries.

There was no dispute between the parties as to the trench's existence. However, there was a critical dispute about its size and nature. Mr Wanklyn denied all liability. He claimed that he had dug the trench that morning, and that it was about 75 millimetres by 75 millimetres in dimension. He alleged there were a number of circumstances, including the nature of the premises, the frequency of visitors, the size of the trench and the fact that its existence should have been obvious to a person walking across the driveway, to argue that there was no breach of the duty owed by him to take any precautions to protect Mr Scott from falling and suffering injury. Mr Wanklyn also alleged that Mr Scott had been contributorily negligent.

In addition to liability, there was also a dispute between the parties as to the assessment of damages for non-economic loss and for gratuitous attendant care services provided to Mr Scott as a consequence of his injuries.

***Held:* judgment for the plaintiff.**

Per Keogh J:

1. Mr Scott was consistent and clear as to the manner in which he fell, and as to the cause of that fall. The inconsistencies in his evidence did not impugn Mr Scott's credit. Mr Scott's evidence as to the manner of his fall, that is stepping forward with his left foot close to the concrete floor of the shed, intending to step up onto the floor when his left foot went into the trench, causing him to lose balance and fall backwards is to be accepted.

2. Mr Wanklyn gave inconsistent evidence in relation to the filling in of the trench, what was seen in the photographs, what he previously said had occurred on the day and the frequency of attendance of customers and potential customers at his premises. On that basis, reliance could not be placed upon his evidence.

3. The risk of harm for the purposes of the Wrongs Act was properly identified as the risk that an entrant onto the property would step into, or lose their footing in a trench located across the doorway of the shed immediately next to the slab which was the floor of the shed, fall and suffer injury.

4. The nature of the danger posed by the trench weighed in favour of Mr Scott. Every visitor to the premises entering the shed would be exposed to that danger. The trench was not in the nature of an imperfection or irregularity that might be expected on such a premises.

5. It was easily foreseeable that a visitor attempting to enter the shed without warning of the existence of the trench might step into it and suffer injury. While the frequency of visitors could be expected to be relatively low, the risk of any one visitor not warned of the existence of the trench coming to grief, was high.

6. Mr Wanklyn breached his duty of care owed to Mr Scott in leaving the trench unguarded and without warning as to its existence, which was a cause of Mr Scott stepping into the trench, falling and suffering injury. Total damages were assessed at $230,000.

[*Headnote by the Wolters Kluwer editors*]

T Monti, QC with M Seelig (instructed by Garden & Green) for the plaintiff.

D McWilliams (instructed by DLA Piper) for the defendant.

Before: Keogh J.

[¶82-192] Powney v Kerang and District Health

(2015) Aust Torts Reports 82-192

Medium neutral citation: [2014] VSCA 221

Victorian Court of Appeal

Judgment delivered 11 September 2014

Negligence — Causation — Allegedly negligent medical treatment causing personal injury — Jury trial — Factual causation — Necessary condition of the occurrence of harm — Scope of liability — Whether negligence cannot be established as a necessary condition of the occurrence of harm — Whether appropriate for jury to determine issue pursuant to s 51(2) of the Wrongs Act 1958 — Whether defendant negligent — Whether negligence caused injury — Whether evidentiary gap bridged — Why responsibility for harm should be imposed where factual causation cannot be established — Whether an appropriate case — Whether in accordance with established principles — Importance of pleadings — Wrongs Act 1958, Pt X, s 51, 51(2), 52.

On 20 August 2008, the appellant, Mr Wayne Powney, was admitted to Kerang Hospital (the Hospital), which was managed by the respondent, Kerang and District Health, for the purpose of undergoing nasal surgery. The surgery was performed between 10.15 am and 10.45 am. Mr Powney experienced post-operative pain in his nose and at 4.00 pm he was given an injection of pethidine. Mr Powney was discharged from the hospital at approximately midday the following day.

Over the next few days, Mr Powney developed a severe infection in his left upper arm, which progressed to septicemia with a significant abscess in the arm. On 24 August, Mr Powney was admitted to Bendigo Base Hospital with a high fever. On 2 September, the abscess was surgically drained.

Mr Powney commenced proceedings in the County Court against the Hospital relating to his treatment, claiming negligence. Mr Powney claimed that an intramuscular injection of pethidine was injected into his left arm by a nurse in a negligent manner, and that it was an uncapped and unsterile needle, which caused the infection in his left arm. He claimed that the hospital staff failed to respond to his complaints of pain in his arm, caused by the infection. He alleged that the infection led him to suffer a significant permanent injury to his left arm with an associated psychiatric condition.

Mr Powney had no direct recollection of his time as an inpatient at the Hospital. He relied on the evidence of his wife, his young daughter and his niece that the needle was uncovered and did not have a cap on it. He also relied on the evidence of an infectious diseases expert, Dr Hudson, that the risk of infection would have been reduced if appropriate steps had been taken. The Hospital relied on the evidence of the nurse who administered the injection. She had no specific recollection of the injection but said that it was her usual practice to administer injections of that kind into the buttock. If not, it would be administered into the arm. It was her invariable practice to keep the cap or wrapper on the needle until it was administered. No complaint of pain or other relevant symptoms were recorded in the hospital notes. The Hospital argued that no such complaint was ever made by Mr Powney; if it had been made, it would have been in the notes.

The Hospital accepted that an intramuscular injection given to Mr Powney on 20 August 2008 was the source of the infection. However, it denied Mr Powney's claim and argued that the injection was not given negligently. The Hospital relied on the evidence of an infectious diseases expert, Dr Eisen, that even if the nurse used a needle which had been uncapped for a period of minutes and placed in a kidney dish without a cap, the risk of infection would not be significantly increased. He also stated that it would take a period of months to years for an uncapped needle to become overly contaminated. Both Dr Hudson and Dr Eisen accepted that there was a small risk of contracting an infection from an intramuscular injection such as the one given to Mr Powney, even if all due care had been taken when giving the injection.

The issue to be determined was whether the conduct of the Hospital did materially increase the risk of infection. A further issue was whether there was likely to have been complaints of pain prior to Mr Powney's discharge, and whether there would have been any clinical signs or symptoms at the time of discharge (1.15 pm on 21 August), less than 12 hours after the injection (given at 4.00 pm the previous day).

On the last day of the trial at the conclusion of the evidence, counsel for Mr Powney made an oral submission as to the application of s 51(2) of the *Wrongs Act 1958* (the Act) and argued that s 51(2) of the Act only came into play if the jury was not satisfied of the "but for" test, and that only then would the jury look to s 51(2) as to whether this was an appropriate case to deal with in that way. Mr Powney argued that if he could, in the alternative, rely on s 51(2) he wanted the jury to be in a position to, if they thought it was an appropriate case, to have regard to those principles; s 51(2) should be left open, the jury should do the best they could and decide whether it was an appropriate case or not. The Hospital argued that Mr Powney had not proven what he needed to prove in respect of causation because he had not proven that what the Hospital was alleged to have done wrong in relation to the injection materially increased the risk of infection.

The trial judge ruled that the jury was confined to determining factual causation under s 51(1) of the Act and not to considering the matters in s 51(2) of the Act. The requirements of s 51(2) were not considered to be an issue for the jury. The jury ultimately found in favour of the Hospital.

Mr Powney appealed and raised issue with how s 51(2) of the Act was to be applied in negligence cases, and whether a jury had a role to play in determining questions of causation. Mr Powney argued on appeal that all parts of s 51(2) should have been determined by the jury and the trial judge was wrong to not permit the jury to consider the matters contained in that subsection. He also argued that the trial judge had erred by failing and refusing to give a direction to the jury in accordance with s 51(2) of the Act, that if negligence in the Hospital was not established to be a necessary condition of the occurrence of harm to Mr Powney, negligence on the part of the Hospital that could not be established as a necessary condition of such harm could be taken to establish factual causation. Mr Powney also argued that the trial judge erred by failing and refusing to give a direction to the jury as to whether this case was an appropriate case in which negligence should be taken to establish factual causation.

Held: **appeal dismissed.**

Per Osborn JA, Beach JA and J Forrest AJA:

1. The common law and state legislation as well as the 2001 Ipp Report were considered at length as to causation. Section 51(2) of the Act enabled a court to find causation was made out in certain cases where the plaintiff cannot satisfy the first test, that of factual causation. Section 51(2) was a recognition by the legislature that in certain circumstances the "but for" test may produce unjust results and a court may, in appropriate cases, bridge the evidentiary gap. It was not intended as a fall back provision in a conventional case for a plaintiff who is unable to establish factual causation. Rather, it was designed to accommodate cases quiet out of the ordinary.

2. The trial judge was correct in rejecting Mr Powney's submission that the jury determines the issue raised by s 51(2). It was the trial judge's function to determine what was, or was not, an appropriate case to impose liability, not that of a jury. Section 51(2) required a normative judgment to be made by the trial judge, not the jury.

3. Mr Powney failed to prove what was a very weak case. He was unable to prove his case beyond demonstrating a somewhat increased risk of injury arising out of a contentious single event, the injection. Section 51(2) was not directed to Mr Powney's claim; where there is one alleged tortious act, it is not the sort of case that would be regarded as appropriate for the operation of s 51(2).

4. The jury finding in favour of the Hospital may not have been any different even if the jury had been directed to consider s 51(2). It was far from certain that the jury ever reached the question of factual causation. Mr Powney's case relied on the evidence of his daughter and niece (one a child and the other a teenager) being accepted over that of the trained nurse and her standard practice. The jury may not have been persuaded that there was any breach of duty on the Hospital's part.

5. The trial judge was correct in refusing to permit the jury to consider the requirements of s 51(2). It was appropriate for the trial judge to direct the jury to determine only the issue of factual causation.

[*Headnote by the Wolters Kluwer editors*]

Mr CP Locke with Mr G Boas (instructed by Arnold Dallas McPherson) for the appellant.

Mr AN Murdoch QC with Ms PR Riddell (instructed by Minter Ellison) for the respondent.

Before: Osborn JA, Beach JA and J Forrest AJA.

[¶82-181] Victorian YMCA Community Programming Pty Ltd v Nillumbik Shire Council & Anor

(2014) Aust Torts Reports ¶82-181
Medium neutral citation: [2014] VSCA 197
Supreme Court of Victoria, Court of Appeal
Judgment delivered 1 September 2014

Torts — Workplace injury — Contribution between tortfeasors — Occupier's liability — Accident compensation — Recovery proceedings against third party — Two occupiers of premises were owner and operator of premises — Damages claimed by employee of operator against owner and operator — Judgment for employee against both defendants — Operator breached contractual duty to owner to have public liability insurance in name of itself and owner — Owner sought to be indemnified by operator in respect of judgment amount against it — Whether operator's breach of contract causative of loss to owner — Whether inference favourable to owner could be drawn as to terms of approved form of policy when policy not in evidence — Whether owner's duty of care to injured employee relevantly delegable — Whether trial judge's ruling that duty non-delegable affected decision with respect to contribution — Effect of successful appeal in respect of contribution proceeding between defendants on recovery proceedings — Accident Compensation Act 1985 (Vic), s 138 — Wrongs Act 1958 (Vic), Pt IIA.

In April 2005 Ms Balassone sustained injury when she fell from the edge of a pool deck at the Eltham Leisure Centre (the Centre) owned by Nillumbik Council (the Council). When she sustained her injury Ms Balassone was engaged in her employment by Victorian YMCA Programming Pty Ltd (YMCA) as a swimming teacher. YMCA was the manager and operator of the Centre pursuant to a contract with the Council dated 24 September 2001 (the Contract). Under the Contract YMCA was obliged to hold a current public liability (PL) insurance policy in the name of YMCA, its subcontractors and the Council. When Ms Balassone suffered injury YMCA held no such policy.

Ms Balassone brought a claim for damages against YMCA and the Council alleging that YMCA owed her duties both as employer and occupier of the premises, which duties it had breached. She further alleged that the Council owed her duties both at common law and as occupier, which duties it had also breached. At trial, Ms Balassone confined her claim against YMCA to alleged breach of duty of care as her employer; and she confined her claim against the Council to breach of its duty as occupier under Pt IIA of the *Wrongs Act 1958* (Vic). YMCA and the Council both denied liability.

The Council argued that, by operation of the Contract, YMCA had been placed into a position akin to that of an independent contractor which had been assigned the performance of certain tasks by an occupier. In respect of those tasks, the Council had delegated the discharge of its duty to Ms Balassone to YMCA. What had been delegated, the Council argued, was the performance of so much of its duty of care to Ms Balassone as was confided, by the Contract, to YMCA. The Council also alleged that, if it was found liable to Ms Balassone, it was entitled to full indemnity from YMCA (the contribution proceedings) because the latter had breached the term of the Contract requiring YMCA to hold a current PL policy in the approved form which had caused the Council loss and damage. It was alleged that proof that such an insurance policy was not in force when Ms Balassone was injured established breach.

Ms Balassone's proceedings went to trial in October 2013. There was also a second proceeding concerning accident compensation that she had been paid. Victorian WorkCover Authority (VWA) made a claim (the recovery proceedings) on the Council pursuant to s 138 of the *Accident Compensation Act 1985* (Vic). The Council joined YMCA as a third party. It claimed indemnification from YMCA in the event that it was held liable to VWA, again relying upon the alleged contractual breach.

Ms Balassone's proceedings against YMCA and the Council was tried by jury. The recovery proceedings was deferred for determination until the resolution of Ms Balassone's proceedings. The jury's verdict was that Ms Balassone had suffered injury by reason of breach of duty whether viewed from the standpoint of an employer or an occupier and it awarded damages in favour of Ms Balassone against both YMCA and the Council in an amount of $250,000. The trial judge entered judgment in her favour: see *Balassone v Victorian YMCA Community Programming Pty Ltd and Anor* and *VWA* v *Nillumbik Shire Council and Anor* (Unreported, County Court of Victoria, 30 October 2013).

The trial judge then considered the Council's claim that it should be indemnified by YMCA because of the latter's alleged contractual breach, the issue of contribution between tortfeasors which would arise in the event that the claim for indemnification failed, and the outcome of the recovery proceedings. YMCA argued that there was no evidence of any policy that would have in fact indemnified the Council for Ms Balassone's claim. Thus while a breach might have occurred, on the evidence, the Council had not suffered any loss. The trial judge held that on the evidence including inferences to be drawn from that evidence, and from the failure of the YMCA to produce any relevant PL policy that would exclude the risk, it was accepted that a PL policy that the parties contemplated under the Contract would have responded to the claim by Ms Balassone alleging liability by the Council under the *Wrongs Act 1958* (Vic) (Wrongs Act). Therefore the Council's claim for indemnification succeeded both with respect to the judgment in favour of Ms Balassone and the recovery proceedings. The trial judge determined further that, if it was not for indemnification, each of YMCA and the Council should contribute equally to the judgment entered in favour of Ms Balassone.

The appeal

There was no appeal from judgment in favour of Ms Balassone. But YMCA appealed against the trial judge's order that, in consequence of its breach of the Contract which his Honour found was established, it must indemnify the Council against the latter's liability to Ms Balassone. YMCA also challenged the order that it indemnify the Council against judgment in the recovery proceedings.

YMCA submitted that an exclusion in its PL policy in respect of injuries which would have been covered by its accident compensation insurance policy had the potential to somewhat reduce the cost of that insurance, this supporting an inference that the policy which the trial judge had inferred had been approved by the Council contained such an exclusion.

YMCA also contended that the question whether the approved PL policy would have responded so as to protect the Council against Ms Balassone's claim was not to be answered by what an "objective bystander" would have regarded as YMCA's obligation to hold a policy pursuant to the Contract. The question was what inference was to be drawn by the finder of fact on consideration of all the circumstances. Having regard to all the circumstances, YMCA submitted, the approved policy would have excluded cover in respect of a claim for damages made by an injured employee of YMCA.

The cross-appeal

The Council cross-appealed in respect of a ruling by the trial judge that as a matter of law and as a matter of fact the jury could not have found that the Council had delegated its duty. The Council further contended that the trial judge's finding of equal contribution between defendants could not have been sustained because the trial judge's erroneous rejection of the delegation of duty submission meant that his Honour did not fully address relevant circumstances. In addition the trial judge's disposition of the contribution claim focused upon an attempt by his Honour to interpret the jury's verdict as to the circumstances of the accident, rather than being his Honour's independent consideration of the evidence, and then his reaching conclusions which were consistent with the jury's verdict in favour of Ms Balassone.

Held: appeal allowed. Cross-appeal allowed.

Per Ashley JA (with whom Nettle and Hansen JJA agreed):

Indemnification

1. The trial judge's conclusion that YMCA breached the Contract, such breach being causative of loss and damage to the Council, was erroneous. Therefore the Council was unable to maintain a claim to be indemnified against its liability to Ms Balassone and to VWA.

2. There was no direct evidence that a PL policy was produced to the Council for approval, or approved, before or after the commencement of the Contract. However, on the balance of probabilities, it should have been inferred that a PL policy in which the Council was named as an insured was produced to the Council and was approved. The issue which then arose was what inference should have been drawn as to the terms of the policy, including any exclusions. The Council's submission that proof that a policy in the approved form was not in force when Ms Balassone was injured established breach did not establish that a policy in the approved form would have responded to that incident. Contrary to the trial judge's conclusion, the Council carried the evidentiary, as well as the ultimate, burden of proof that the policy would have responded.

3. Although the trial judge decided that the inference was "available" and was "a reasonable one" that an approved policy would have responded to Ms Balassone's claim, the question was whether the Council had established, more probably than not, as a matter of inference, that the policy would have responded. In all the circumstances that inference on the balance of probabilities could not have been drawn. At best for the Council the inference was neither more nor less likely than the competing inference advanced for YMCA that the approved policy would have excluded cover in respect of a claim for damages made by an injured employee of YMCA.

Delegation of duty of care

4. The trial judge erred in ruling, as a matter of law, that discharge of the duty of care which the Council owed to Ms Balassone as occupier under Pt IIA of the *Wrongs Act 1958* (Vic) was non-delegable. A duty of care was non-delegable when its discharge was not permitted to be confided to some other person, usually by the engagement of a competent independent contractor. A non-delegable duty was a more stringent duty than the duty to take reasonable care. It was a duty to ensure that reasonable care was taken by the other person for the persons to whom the duty was owed. This special duty arose only in confined areas such as the relationship between master and servant, school authority to student, and hospital to patient. It would have been wrong to recognise, or create, such a new category in the absence of very clear indications leading to that conclusion.

5. There was no reason in principle why an occupier's duty of care should have been accounted non-delegable. There was no indication in Pt IIA of the Wrongs Act which led to the recognition of a new category of non-delegable duty. The question therefore was whether an occupier's duty under Pt IIA of the Wrongs Act was or was not non-delegable in fact. If the trial judge found there was no evidence which could have supported a finding of delegation in fact, that conclusion was not available.

The contribution proceeding

6. There was no challenge to the judgment entered in favour of Ms Balassone even though the Council was prevented from putting to the jury its contention that the Council had delegated to YMCA the discharge of particular aspects of the duty of care which it owed to Ms Balassone. In consequence of his Honour's conclusion that delegation by the Council of performance of its duty of care to Ms Balassone was not open in law or in fact, his consideration of the contribution issue between defendants was incomplete. For that reason, and also because the trial judge appeared to have been concerned to interpret the jury's

verdict, rather than find relevant facts consistent with that verdict for himself, his Honour's determination of the contribution proceeding could not stand.

The recovery proceedings

7. Both because the trial judge erred in concluding that YMCA was in breach of the Contract, such breach being causative of loss and damage to the Council, and because his Honour's resolution of the contribution proceeding was flawed, consequences ensued for the order made in the recovery proceedings. The application by YMCA for leave to appeal against that order out of time, not opposed by the Council or by VWA, should have been granted.

8. It was inappropriate for this court to consider and determine the interrelated questions of delegation and contribution between defendants, and the implications of the eventual resolution of the contribution proceeding for the recovery proceedings. The contribution proceeding and the recovery proceedings should be remitted for hearing and determination by a different judge of the County Court upon the evidence adduced at the trial held in October 2013.

[*Headnote by the Wolters Kluwer editors*]

R P Gorton QC with R Kumar (instructed by Hall & Wilcox) for the appellant.

C J Blanden QC with J Frederico (instructed by Minter Ellison) for the first respondent.

J P Gordon QC with M Norton (instructed by Russell Kennedy) for the second respondent.

Before: Nettle, Ashley and Hansen JJA.

[¶82-155] **Odisho v Bonazzi**

(2014) Aust Torts Reports ¶82-155
Medium neutral citation: [2014] VSCA 11
Supreme Court of Victoria, Court of Appeal
Judgment delivered 18 February 2014

Negligence — Medical practitioners — Duty to warn — Duty to warn of rare risks — Extent of duty — Breach of duty — Causation — Factual causation — Scope of liability — Whether warning would have made any difference — Whether medical causation established — Wrongs Act 1958, s 48, 50–52, 58 and 60.

On 17 April 2006, the plaintiff (and appellant on appeal) Grazilda Odisho presented to the Royal Melbourne Hospital with symptoms that were eventually diagnosed as multiple pulmonary emboli. Over the course of the next few days she was admitted to the Royal Women's Hospital where she received treatment for her pulmonary emboli. Subsequently, she commenced proceedings for damages against specialist gynaecologist Marcia Bonazzi (defendant at first instance and respondent on appeal) whom she had consulted for abnormally heavy bleeding initially in February 2006. The plaintiff alleged that her pulmonary emboli were caused by the negligence of the specialist in failing to provide her with an appropriate warning concerning the side effects of a drug, tranexamic acid, which was prescribed to treat the bleeding condition. Specifically, the plaintiff alleged that the specialist was negligent for failing to warn her in respect of a risk that consumption of the drug may cause her to suffer a thromboembolic event.

The specialist contended that at the time she prescribed the drug in 2006, she had never heard that the oral dose in gynaecological use could cause thromboembolism. Her position at the time she prescribed the drug was informed by, among other things, her access to the full version of the product information provided by the manufacturer of the drug through her subscription to the MIMS Annual. In the MIMS entry for tranexamic acid it was recorded that "Although clinical evidence shows no significant increase in thrombosis, possible risks of thrombotic complication cannot be ruled out". In that same entry, adverse reactions were

dealt with as "Rare side effects (< 1/1,000) Thromboembolic events, impaired colour vision. Exceptional cases of giddiness have been reported".

At first instance, Succardo J dismissed the plaintiff's proceedings concluding that:

(a) the exercise of reasonable care on the part of the specialist did not require her to warn the plaintiff that taking the drug carried with it the rare risk of thromboembolic events

(b) the plaintiff had failed to establish that the tablets she took were a cause of her pulmonary emboli, and

(c) even if the plaintiff had been given a warning that the drug carried with it a small risk of suffering a thromboembolic event, the plaintiff would not have been dissuaded from taking the drug to treat her condition. She had not presented to the specialist as someone with "special needs or concerns" who would be likely to attach particular significance to a warning about the risks of thromboembolism.

The plaintiff appealed on the following grounds:

(a) The judge erred in failing to find that a reasonable person in the plaintiff's position would, if warned of the risk, have been likely to attach significance to a warning about the risks of thromboembolism.

(b) The judge erred in failing to find that in all the circumstances the plaintiff as "the particular patient" would, if warned of the risk, have been likely to attach significance to it.

(c) The judge erred in failing to find that a cause of the plaintiff's injuries was the breach of duty by the specialist in failing to warn her of the remote risk that the drug might cause pulmonary emboli.

Held: appeal dismissed.

Per Beach JA and McMillan AJA:

1. There was a real issue, on the evidence, as to whether a warning in the terms of the MIMS publication should have been given on the basis that a reasonable person in the appellant's position would be likely to attach significance to it. Although the risk of thromboembolism was described in MIMS as being rare and less than one in a thousand, the evidence did disclose that the risk of thromboembolism was a serious matter and potentially life threatening.

2. Notwithstanding the evidence that suggested it might not have been normal practice for gynaecologists who prescribe tranexamic acid to give warnings to their patients of the rare risk of thromboembolism, there were reasonable grounds for contending that reasonable care required a warning.

3. When the expert evidence was considered and the evidence summarised by the trial judge, the court was left with the conclusion that the trial judge was correct when he held that the appellant had not established that the tranexamic acid she consumed was a cause of her pulmonary emboli. Consequently, the appellant had failed to establish factual causation as required by s 51(1) of the *Wrongs Act 1958*.

4. Evidence of what a person would have done if warned of a risk that materialised, which is given with the benefit of hindsight of what actually occurred, has been described as "so hypothetical, self-serving and speculative as to deserve little (if any) weight". The exaggerated nature of the appellant's answers to the questions put to her on the issue of what she would have done had she received a warning well justified the trial judge's rejection of the evidence.

5. It is highly unlikely that an appropriate warning of the risk of pulmonary emboli would have made any material change to the events that occurred.

Per Nettle JA (in agreeing the appeal should be dismissed):

1. As the appellant presented to the respondent as a particularly anxious patient, she was therefore more likely, if warned of that risk, to attach significance to it. Consequently, it was at least fairly arguable that the respondent was under a duty to warn the appellant of the risk.

2. Allowing that her anxiousness may have led to her attaching significance to the risk, it was inherently improbable that even the most anxious patient in her position, or thus she, would have declined the treatment offered.

3. The trial judge was undoubtedly right to conclude that the appellant failed to prove on the balance of probabilities that her ingestion of tranexamic acid was a physical cause of her pulmonary emboli. On the evidence, it was no more than possible that it played some part.

[*Headnote by the Wolters Kluwer editors*]

Dr I R L Freckelton SC with Mr Rolf Sorenson (instructed by Mendis & Gibson Lawyers) for the appellant.

Mr Jeremy Ruskin QC with Ms S L Keeling (instructed by Holman Webb Lawyers) for the respondent.

Before: Nettle, Beach JJA and McMillan AJA.

[¶82-034] Gosling & Ors v Lorne Foreshore Committee of Management Inc and Surf Coast Shire

(2009) Aust Torts Reports ¶82-034;
Medium neutral citation: [2009] VSCA 228
Supreme Court of Victoria, Court of Appeal
Judgment delivered 8 October 2009

Torts — Negligence — Duty of care — Nervous shock resulting from daughter's death — Whether Committee breached duty of care to appellants — Characterisation of risk — "Obviousness" of risk.

The appellants sued the first respondent (the Committee) for damages in negligence for the nervous shock they suffered as a result of the death of their daughter, Samantha Gosling. The deceased suffered fatal injuries as a result of falling down a steep embankment and striking her head on a concrete drain at the bottom. The Committee was responsible for the management of some 15 km of foreshore area along the Lorne coast, an area that included the embankment where the death occurred.

The evidence showed that the embankment was regularly used as the most direct route to walk from the Lorne Hotel to the Lifesaving Club and the beach. Several "goat tracks" on the embankment attested to its frequent use by pedestrians. There was no lighting at night, nor was there any fencing along the perimeter. At the place where the accident occurred, directly opposite the hotel, the embankment was more than 13 m in height with a very steep slope. Near its base the slope became almost vertical, flattening out slightly just before reaching the drain cover at the bottom.

At trial, it was not disputed that the Committee owed a duty of care to the deceased, and by extension to the appellants. The sole issue for determination was whether the Committee was in breach of its duty by failing to take any steps to guard against the risk posed by the embankment. The trial judge concluded that there had been no breach. The relevant risk arose as a result of the steepness of the embankment, which ought to have been sufficiently obvious to anyone attempting to traverse it. Installing a light or warning sign would only have drawn attention to something that was already apparent. Given that it was impractical to fence off all areas under the Committee's control, there was nothing about the particular area in question to suggest the necessity of fencing it off.

On appeal it was submitted that the trial judge had wrongly assessed the risk posed by the embankment. The real risk arose as a result of the hidden drop-off located near the bottom of the slope. By failing to attach sufficient weight to this hidden danger, the trial judge had erroneously concluded that the risk was so obvious that the Committee's lack of action was a reasonable response in the circumstances.

Held: **appeal allowed.**

1. The trial judge's conclusion that the Committee's inaction was a reasonable response to the foreseeable risk of injury posed by the embankment was based on an erroneous identification of the true risk in issue.

2. The risk was constituted by the hidden danger of the drop-off in combination with the concrete drain cover at the bottom. Once the risk is properly characterised, it becomes clear that neither the likelihood nor the magnitude of the danger would have been obvious to a person in the position of the deceased.

3. The "obviousness" of a risk is only one fact among many in determining whether the response of a person with a duty of care is reasonable in the circumstances. The trial judge had attached considerable weight to this factor, without correctly identifying the real nature of the risk posed.

4. Similarly, the frequency with which a particular risk is taken by persons to whom a duty of care is owed is clearly a factor in determining what discharge of that duty requires. However, the fact that the embankment had been used for many years without incident does not necessarily mean that the Committee's inaction was reasonable — a response may be called for, even where the risk of serious injury or death might be objectively low. What is required in all such cases is an assessment of the risk along with the cost and practicality of possible responses.

5. In the present circumstances, the Committee's failure to take any steps at all in relation to the risk was unreasonable and constituted a breach of duty. The erection of a fence would have been an easy and cost-effective way to ameliorate the risk, as would the installation of lighting and/or a warning sign.

[*Headnote by the Wolters Kluwer editors*]

JH Mighell SC with BF Quinn and A Pillay for the appellants (instructed by Slater & Gordon).

CJ Blanden SC with DA Siemensma for the first respondent (instructed by Herbert Geer).

Before: Ashley JA, Redlich JA and Kyrou AJA.

[¶81-936] Kirkland-Veenstra v Stuart & Ors

(2008) Aust Torts Reports ¶81-936;
Medium neutral citation: [2008] VSCA 32
Victorian Court of Appeal
Judgment delivered 29 February 2008

Torts — Duty of care — Psychiatric injury suffered by wife of deceased who committed suicide — Whether police owed duty of care to wife — Power to detain mentally ill — Whether failure to exercise statutory power — Mental Health Act 1986 (Vic) s 10

The appellant suffered psychiatric injury following the suicide of her husband, Mr Veenstra. She brought proceedings against two police officers (the respondents) and the State of Victoria, claiming that the respondents had breached the duty of care which they owed to her deceased husband, both at common law and under the statutory provisions of the Mental Health Act 1986 (the Act). Mr Veenstra had worked as a finance manager until 1998, when his employer's belief that he had been involved in fraud forced him to resign. He was subsequently made aware that he would be served with a brief containing criminal charges on 22 August 1999.

At around 5.40 am on the morning of 22 August, the respondents came across Mr Veenstra's parked car while on a routine patrol. The car was the only vehicle in the carpark, and had a tube running from the exhaust of the car through to the rear window (the engine was not running, however). The respondents approached Mr Veenstra, who was sitting in the driver's seat, and spoke to him for 10–15 minutes. Mr Veenstra admitted that he had been contemplating doing "something stupid", but had changed his mind. The respondents conducted a search of the vehicle and carried out a number of checks to verify the identity of Mr Veenstra. Although concerned for the welfare of Mr Veenstra, noting in their patrol log that he was depressed and referring to suicide, they did not exercise their statutory power to apprehend Mr Veenstra as a person who appeared to have a mental illness and to have attempted (or to be likely to attempt) suicide.

Mr Veenstra, who returned home and briefly spoke to the appellant that morning, committed suicide later that day by asphyxiating himself with exhaust fumes. The appellant, returning home to find her husband lying on the ground, tried to revive him orally. She was unsuccessful, however, and immediately went into shock. At trial, the appellant submitted that the respondents owed a duty of care to her husband to take reasonable steps to protect him from committing suicide, and that they owed her a duty to take reasonable steps to protect her from the reasonable foreseeable consequences of her husband's suicide, namely the kind of psychiatric injury which she suffered. However, the trial judge dismissed the proceeding on the ground that the duties of care alleged to be owed to Mr Veenstra and the appellant did not exist at law.

Held: Appeal allowed (retrial ordered).

Per Warren CJ (Maxwell P agreeing)

1. The respondents owed a duty of care to Mr Veenstra.

2. The issue of the existence of a duty of care to Mr Veenstra must be considered in the context of the legislation and whether there is a duty to exercise reasonably the statutory power of detention for the purpose of protecting those whom the Act seeks to protect. However, the respondents' duty of care to the deceased was a common law duty arising independently of the Act.

3. The court should apply a multi-factorial or "salient features" approach in determining duty of care, bearing in mind that the former importance accorded to the idea of "reliance" has been replaced by the concept of "vulnerability" or the duty to protect from a "great harm": *Pyrenees Shire Council* v *Day* (1998) Aust Torts Report ¶81-456.

4. In the present case, Mr Veenstra was vulnerable in the sense that he could not reasonably be expected to adequately safeguard himself from harm. Further, the respondents ought reasonably to have foreseen, once they had "entered the field" of unfolding events, that a failure to exercise police powers of apprehension may result in Mr Veenstra committing suicide.

5. The respondents owed a duty of care to the appellant. It was reasonably foreseeable that a failure to exercise reasonable care to protect Mr Veenstra from suicide would create a real risk of psychiatric injury of the kind suffered by his spouse. It was also reasonable to expect the respondents to have contemplated the appellant as a person "closely and directly affected" by their acts or omissions in relation to her husband: *Tame* v *State of New South Wales* (2002) Aust Torts Reports ¶81-672; [2002] HCA 35 and *Annetts* v *Australian Stations Pty Ltd* (2002) Aust Torts Reports ¶81-672; [2002] HCA 35.

6. The respondents had almost complete control over the circumstances giving rise to the risk of psychiatric injury to the appellant, whereas the appellant had no way of protecting herself against that risk.

Per Chernov JA (dissenting)

7. Imposing a duty of care of the kind claimed by the appellant would be incompatible with the framework of the Act. It would create a "distorting" influence on the discretionary power to apprehend conferred by s 10(1), the exercise of which required police officers to balance the aim of providing mentally ill people with the best possible care against the principle of keeping any restrictions upon their rights and their dignity to the minimum necessary in the circumstances.

8. Given the deceased's conduct in deceiving the police and the appellant, it is not clear that exercising the power of apprehension could have removed the risk to the deceased. Nor was there relevant "vulnerability" or "dependence" by the deceased on the police officers.

[*Headnote by the Wolters Kluwer editors*]

JHL Forrest QC with P Halley for the appellant (instructed by Slater & Gordon).

J Ruskin QC with R Orr for the first and second respondent (instructed by Victorian Government Solicitor).

BM Dennis for the third respondent (instructed by Deacons).

Before: Warren CJ, Maxwell P and Chernov JA.

Western Australia

[¶82-790] Greenslade v Hiew

(2022) Aust Torts Reports ¶82-790
Medium neutral citation: [2022] WASCA 47
Supreme Court of Western Australia, Court of Appeal
4 May 2022

Occupiers liability — Ceiling collapse — Water ingress — Extreme weather events — Scope of duty of care — Causation — Appeals — Adequacy of reasons — Expert evidence — Primary judge dismissed claim on ground that damage to ceiling had been caused by extreme weather events and appellant had fault had not been observable prior to collapse — Appellant appealed on ground that primary judge had given inadequate reasons for rejecting report of expert upon which he had relied — Civil Liability Act 2002 (WA), s 10 — Occupiers Liability Act 1985 (WA), s 9.

In 1995, the respondent, Ms Lee Hiew, purchased residential premises (the premises) that were built in 1994. She bought the premises as an investment property and carried out some initial improvements and painting. Between 1995 and 1999, Ms Hiew let the premises to her sister-in-law. Commencing in 1999, the premises were let to a series of tenants. None of those tenants raised any issue about the state of the premises' ceiling. A property condition report dated 19 October 1999 noted that the premises had some minor non-structural cleaning and maintenance issues, but all the ceilings were "ticked" as being undamaged.

The premises were also periodically inspected during the time that they were rented to those tenants. Those inspections made references to some minor non-structural and maintenance issues, but no reference was made to the state of the ceilings. On 22 June 2013, the appellant, Mr Philip Greenslade, entered into a tenancy agreement over the premises. Ms Hiew did not do a thorough inspection of the premises prior to letting them to Mr Greenslade, but she did look through them from room to room. At that time, she saw no sagging of the ceiling and she did not have the roof space inspected. Mr Greenslade also did not report any issues with the ceiling at that time.

Between October and December 2014, there were a series of extreme wet weather events including heavy hail which caused ingress of water into the roof space. However, Mr Greenslade did not notice any defect in the ceiling and made no report of any concerns to Ms Hiew. On 11 January 2015, the ceiling of the premises' family room collapsed suddenly and caused injury to Mr Greenslade and members of his family.

Mr Greenslade commenced negligence proceedings against Ms Hiew. Mrs Hiew denied liability and alleged that Mr Greenslade was contributorily negligent because he had failed to identify and report to Mrs Hiew that the ceiling required repairs and had failed to inspect and report to her of any damage to the ceiling. Mrs Hiew submitted that if she had been informed of any cracking or sagging she would have had the ceiling inspected. She denied that her husband had carried out any ceiling repairs at the premises. The primary judge noted that the duty of care of a landlord was no more than a duty to take reasonable care. Liability was not strict and depended on all the circumstances of the case. The primary judge found that the ceiling collapsed without having exhibited any observable sign of damage or defect. It collapsed due to water damage likely to have been initiated or exacerbated by weather events in October and December 2014 and there were no special circumstances that would have created an affirmative duty to inspect the ceiling at the inception of the tenancy, or any time prior to the ceiling collapse: *Greenslade* v *Hiew* (2020) Aust Torts Reports ¶82-564; [2020] WADC 120.

Mr Greenslade appealed the primary judge's findings. He argued that the primary judge erred in failing to find that a linear crack was observable on the ceiling prior to its collapse.

Further, that the primary judge erred in failing to accept the evidence of his construction expert, that the crack should have prompted a layperson to have the ceiling inspected by a professional who would then have observed and rectified long-term water ingress.

Held: appeal dismissed.

1. There had been no evidence before the primary judge of any significant mark or crack on the ceiling prior to the collapse. That was despite the fact that there had been numerous property inspections carried out in relation to the premises after Ms Hiew started to rent it out after 1999. [60]–[63]

2. The primary judge's reasons clearly set out the reasons for not imposing liability upon Ms Hiew. Foremost of those, was that, even if it was assumed that the water ingress had begun earlier than the severe weather events, there had been nothing to put Ms Hiew on notice that such water ingress was taking place. [64]–[67]

3. In relation to the linear crack photograph, the primary judge held that the linear crack was not observable before the ceiling collapse. That finding was open upon the evidence given that no one, including the Mr Greenslade or anyone in his family, had made raised any issue about the linear crack until after the incident. [68]–[76]

4. Because the finding that the linear crack had not been observable had been upheld, it was not strictly necessary to determine whether a layperson would have been prompted to engage a professional inspection of the roof. In turn, it was not necessary to determine whether such an inspection would have prevented the collapse. [94], [95]

5. However, if those issues of causation had arisen for determination, there had been no error or deficiency in the primary judge's reasons for preferring the evidence of Mr Jones over Mr Greenslade's expert. Mr Jones' report fitted more conformably with the objective facts, including the absence of any signs of water ingress prior to the collapse. [96]–[111]

[*Headnote by the Wolters Kluwer editors*]

BL Nugawela & R Hinchliffe (Soul Legal) for the appellant.

CC Rimmer (Sparke Helmore Lawyers) for the respondent.

Before: Murphy JA, Beech JA and Vaughan JA.

Wolters Kluwer Note: The full text of the judgment is accessible through the District Court of Western Australia database on the AustLII website.

[¶82-694] Garnett v Qantas Airways Ltd

(2021) Aust Torts Reports ¶82-694
Medium neutral citation: [2021] WASCA 110
Supreme Court of Western Australia, Court of Appeal
30 June 2021

Negligence — Airline carriers — Personal injuries to passengers — Occupiers liability — Contractor liability — Carrier liability — Limitation of actions — Agents — Scope of agency — Watson-type implied terms — Safe access implied terms — Apportionment of liability — Passenger tripped over a concrete plinth when walking between aircraft and airport terminal — Passenger awarded damages against aircraft carrier by consent up to statutory limit of carrier's liability — Carrier recouped half of its damages from contractor by consent — Primary Judge held that contractor not liable to passenger because of statutory time limitation — Occupier held to be liable to both passenger and carrier — Appeals bought by passenger and occupier — Appeal — Civil Aviation (Carriers' Liability) Act 1959 (Cth), s 33 — Civil Liability Act 2002 (WA), s 5B — Occupiers' Liability Act 1985 (WA), s 5.

Qantas Airways Ltd (Qantas), operated air carrier services between Perth and Karratha airports. For that purpose, Qantas was a designated carrier within the meaning of the *Civil Aviation (Carriers' Liability) Act 1959* (Cth) (CACL Act) as incorporated into Western

Australian law by the *Civil Aviation (Carriers' Liability) Act 1961* (WA). The City of Karratha (Karratha), had exclusive responsibility for the design and construction of Karratha airport, including the structures on and around the tarmac. Skystar Airport Service Pty Ltd (Skystar), contracted with Qantas to provide ground handling services at Karratha Airport. It was responsible for marking the path along which passengers walked in between the plane and the terminal.

On 4 November 2012, Mr Rodney Garnett was a passenger on a Qantas flight that traveled from Perth to Karratha. At around 6:30 pm, the flight arrived at Karratha and Mr Garnett disembarked via its rear stairs. He then proceeded to follow a path across the tarmac to the terminal. The path was marked on the left side by bunting with flags strung between wheelie bins. At the intersection of the tarmac and a footpath leading to the terminal, the bunting was tied between a wheelie bin and around a lighting tower designed to light the adjoining area of the tarmac. As Mr Garnett approached the lighting tower, his left foot struck the corner of a raised concrete plinth at its base and he fell over and suffered injuries.

Mr Garnett commenced proceedings in the Supreme Court of Western Australia against Qantas, Karratha and Skystar, in negligence and claimed damages. Judgment was subsequently entered by consent for Mr Garnett against Qantas in the amount of $500,000, which was the limit of Qantas' strict liability under the CACL Act. Qantas pursued a third-party claim against Skystar in which it sought to recoup the damages that it had agreed to pay Mr Garnett. On that claim, judgment was entered by consent for Qantas with Skystar being ordered to pay 50% of Qantas' liability to Mr Garnett. That then left 4 claims for determination, namely claims by Mr Garnett against Karratha and Skystar, a claim by Karratha against Skystar, and a claim by Qantas against Karratha.

At first instance, the primary judge firstly held that Karratha, as the occupier of the premises on which the injuries occurred, was liable to Mr Garnett pursuant to s 5 of the *Occupiers' Liability Act 1985* (WA) (the OL Act) when read in conjunction with s 5B of the *Civil Liability Act 2002* (WA) (the CL Act). That was because the plinth had posed a risk of injury that could have been avoided and Mr Garnett had not been contributorily negligent. Secondly, the primary judge held that Skystar was not liable to Mr Garnett because it had been the agent of Qantas and s 33 of the CACL Act imposed a 2-year limitation period (which had expired) on claims brought against agents of airline carriers. Thirdly, the primary judge rejected Karratha's claim that it could seek contribution from Skystar on the basis that the lease between the 2 parties (the lease) compelled Skystar to obtain public indemnity insurance. In that context, it was held that Karratha could not expect to recover under the lease agreement in respect of damages which it had caused or had contributed to. Fourthly, the primary judge held that Qantas could seek damages from Karratha for breaching its obligation to provide passengers with a safe path (the safe access implied term). That term was found to exist in the contract under which Qantas was allowed to use the Karratha Airport (the Karratha Airport Agreement).

Mr Garnett appealed the primary judge's finding that he could not maintain his claim against Skystar. In that respect he argued that the primary judge erred in the construction and application of s 33 of the CACL Act by finding that Skystar had been an "agent" of Qantas. Karratha lodged a separate appeal in which it contended that the primary judge had mistakenly found that it had breached its duty to Mr Garnett pursuant to s 5(1) of the OL Act read with s 5B of the CL Act. It also argued that Skystar had not been entitled to the benefit of the limitation in s 33 of the CACL Act because it had not been Qantas' agent.

Karratha additionally reiterated its claim that Skystar had breached clause 6.2 of the lease between Skystar and Karratha by failing to take out public liability cover of not less than $10 million. With regard to its liability to Qantas, Karratha claimed that the primary judge erred in finding that the safe access implied term was implied in the Karratha Airport Agreement and that Karratha had breached that term. Qantas responded with a notice of

contention claiming that the Karratha Airport Agreement had contained a warranty of the type recognised by the High Court in *Watson* v *George* (1953) HCA 41 (the Watson-type implied term) and that Karratha had breached that warranty.

Held: both appeals dismissed.

Construction of the Karratha Airport Agreement

1. The Karratha Airport Agreement contained a Watson-type implied term because Karratha impliedly warranted to Qantas (the warranty being implied by law) that the land was and would remain, during the currency of the Karratha Airport Agreement, as safe as reasonably possible for the purpose of its use as an airport. [110]–[121]

2. Where such a Watson-type implied term was implied as a matter of law, there was no scope to imply the safe access implied term found by the primary Judge as a matter of fact. Such an implied term could not be regarded as necessary for the reasonable or efficient operation of contract. [121], [122]

3. It followed that the primary judge erred in holding that the Karratha Airport Agreement contained the safe access implied term which Karratha was found to have breached. But the Karratha Airport Agreement did contain the Watson-type implied term which Karratha had breached and so Qantas' notice of contention was to be allowed. [123]

Liability of Karratha to Mr Garnett

4. It was reasonably foreseeable that disembarking passengers might trip and fall over the plinth unless it were cordoned off or otherwise made distinguishable. Karratha knew it was not always cordoned off and it knew (as was the case) that it had left the plinth in a state indistinguishable from the pathway since maintenance works in June 2012. [131]–[134]

5. It had not been contended, at first instance or appeal, that the risk posed by the plinth was "not insignificant" for the purposes of s 5B(1)(b) of the CL Act. It followed that the primary Judge was correct to find that the risk was reasonably foreseeable in that Karratha knew, or ought to have known, of it, within the meaning of s 5B(1)(a) of the CL Act. [135]–[137]

Whether Skystar was entitled to invoke limitation under s 33 of the CL Act

6. The purpose of s 33 of the CL Act was to be considered in the context of the Conventions regarding carriage by aviation (relevantly, the Warsaw Convention and the Hague Protocol) to which Australia was a party, not the common law generally or the general law of Australia in particular. [244]–[245]

7. The essential purpose of s 33 was to prevent a plaintiff from circumventing the protection afforded to the carrier under Pt IV of the CL Act. It did so by providing to other defendants, who may have claimed or procured indemnity against the carrier, the benefit of the same limitations as were available to that carrier. [246]–[252]

8. The phrase "servant or agent" in s 33 of the CL Act included an independent contractor engaged by Qantas (in this case, Skystar) to marshal passengers from the aircraft to the terminal in the performance of a function required of Qantas under the contract of carriage. That conclusion was sufficient to dispose of the submissions of Mr Garnett and Karratha. [253], [254]

Liability of Skystar to Karratha under lease

9. It was sufficient to observe that Karratha had no right or interest pursuant to the lease concerning its position as occupier of the airport generally and, in particular, the tarmac and the area between bay 1 and the terminal. The lease was a demise to use the premises only, with Skystar's other obligations governed by its agreement with Qantas. [272], [273]

10. None of the clauses of the lease to which Karratha referred had any bearing on its interests in its capacity as an occupier of the airport land, including the area in which the lighting tower and plinth were located. The lease therefore did not provide a basis for

inferring a requirement that Skystar should have indemnified Karratha for its liability to Mr Garnett. [274]–[276]

[*Headnote by the Wolters Kluwer editors*]

T Lampropoulos SC & B Bradley (Bradley Bayly Legal) for Mr Garnett.

A Casselden SC & CV Wren (HWL Ebsworth Lawyers) for Qantas.

JRB Ley SC & RJS French (McCabe Curwood) for Skystar.

D Lloyd SC & GJ Pynt (GSG Legal) for Karratha.

Before: Murphy, Mitchell and Vaughan JJA.

Wolters Kluwer Note: The full text of the judgment is accessible through the District Court of Western Australia database on the AustLII website.

[¶82-681] Herridge Parties v Electricity Networks Corporation T/AS Western Power

(2021) Aust Torts Reports ¶82-681
Medium neutral citation: [2021] WASCA 111
Supreme Court of Western Australia, Court of Appeal
2 July 2021

Torts — Negligence — Liability for bushfires — Multiple plaintiffs — Appeal from test case — Electrical fires — Liability of electricity distributor — Liability of contractor — Liability of landowner — Contribution between defendants — Private nuisance — Damages — Physical inconvenience — Bushfire that started when an electrical pole collapsed caused damage to multiple properties — Plaintiffs all claimed to be owners of real and personal property damaged by bushfire — 4 sets of proceedings commenced against owner of electrical pole, owner of electricity distribution network and contractor that had been engaged to service electrical pole — Primary Judge held that owner of electrical pole and contractor were liable to plaintiffs in negligence and private nuisance but that network owner was not — Damages awarded to test case plaintiffs but primary Judge refused to include damages for physical inconvenience — 12 appeals and cross-appeals brought against primary Judge's decisions — Civil Liability Act 2002 (WA), s 5AI — Electricity Act 1945 (WA), s 25.

In this decision, the only successful contention on appeal or cross-appeal was that the owner of an electricity distribution network should have been held liable in negligence to plaintiffs for failing to regularly inspect relevant electricity poles. The primary Judge's decisions on all remaining aspects were upheld. Liability was reapportioned as 50% to the owner of distribution network, 35% to the contractor and 15% to the owner of the relevant electricity pole.

Ms Noreen Campbell (Ms Campbell) was the owner of real property in Parkerville in Western Australia. She was also the owner of a jarrah electricity pole standing on that property. That electricity pole was known in the trade as a point-of-attachment pole (the PA pole) because it attached the external electricity distribution system to the property's electricity supply. The external electricity distribution system was owned and operated by Electricity Networks Corporation trading as Western Power (Western Power). As part of its operations, Western Power contracted third parties, including Ventia Utility Services Pty Ltd (formally known as Thiess Services Pty Ltd) (Thiess), to maintain and service its electricity distribution network.

In July 2013, Western Power contracted Thiess to undertake work near Ms Campbell's property. The work included replacing a termination electrical pole outside the property and inspecting the PA pole for "serviceability". On 19 July 2013, a crew engaged by Thiess accordingly replaced the termination pole and connected it to the PA pole. There was some

dispute about whether the then crew undertook an inspection of the PA pole, however it was accepted that, even if they did conduct an inspection, that inspection did not involve an adequate "hammer test". The hammer test involved digging around the base of the pole to create enough space to allow the pole to be hit with a hammer. The purpose of the test was to determine whether a pole was compromised by fungal decay or termite damage.

On 12 January 2014, the PA pole fell towards the ground due to fungal decay and damage by termites. As the PA pole fell, the sub-mains cable was pulled through the cable hole at the base of the main switchboard enclosure, which then exposed the conductor's single insulation to the sharp metallic edges of the hole. That damaged the insulation which caused a short circuit fault resulting in electrical arcing. Hot molten metal globules from the conductors and the metal enclosure then dropped to the ground and ignited the dry vegetation around the base of the PA pole. The fire soon spread around Ms Campbell's property and into nearby bushland. The bushfire that ensued damaged many surrounding properties.

More than 500 plaintiffs who owned those properties subsequently commenced 4 separate proceedings against Ms Campbell, Western Power and Thiess. Those plaintiffs were allocated to 3 groups depending upon which set of proceedings they had joined, namely, the Herridge Parties, the IAG/Allianz Parties and the RAC Parties. Preliminary issues in all of the actions were tried together before the primary Judge with the main issue at trial being the liability of Ms Campbell, Western Power and Thiess for the failure and collapse of the PA pole and the subsequent fire and damage. The trial also concerned the assessment of damages of the nominated test case plaintiffs in the Herridge Parties' action, Mr and Ms Elwood.

At first instance, the primary Judge found Ms Campbell and Thiess liable to the plaintiffs in negligence and nuisance. All claims against Western Power were dismissed. Liability as between Thiess and Ms Campbell in both negligence and nuisance was apportioned as follows: Thiess 70% and Ms Campbell 30%. In assessing damages in favour of Mr and Mrs Elwood, the primary Judge rejected a claim for compensation for the physical inconvenience resulting from the fire. All of the parties, other than Western Power, then appealed in the 4 sets of proceedings. Each of those parties then also cross-appealed, resulting in 12 appeals and 12 cross-appeals which gave rise to the following issues for the Court of Appeal's determination:

- **Whether Western Power was liable in negligence on the basis that it had breached a common law duty of care owed to the plaintiffs by failing to implement a system for the periodic inspection of the PA pole. In this context, Ms Campbell argued that the primary Judge erred in concluding that Western Power did not have a duty to periodically inspect the PA pole because s 25 of the *Electricity Act 1945* (WA), which set out the duties of suppliers of electricity, did not prescribe such a duty.**
- **Whether Western Power owed the plaintiffs a non-delegable duty to ensure that Thiess took reasonable care in carrying out the July 2013 works. The notion that Western Power did owe such a duty was based on a contention that the duty was particularly hazardous and failure to properly discharge it could have significant consequences.**
- **Whether Western Power failed to take reasonable care in engaging and instructing Thiess to carry out the July 2013 works. This was based on an argument that Western Power had breached its duty to the plaintiffs in its choice of Thiess and by not properly auditing its work.**
- **Whether Ms Campbell should have been held liable in negligence and nuisance. Ms Campbell claimed in this respect that, although she owned the PA pole and the land to which it was affixed, for all practical purposes it remained under the control of Western Power. She therefore did not have a duty of care to the plaintiffs with respect to its regular inspection and her use of it had not been unreasonable for the purposes of the action in private nuisance.**

- Whether the plaintiffs' claims against Ms Campbell and Thiess in nuisance were "apportionable claims" as defined in s 5AI of the *Civil Liability Act 2002* (WA) (the CL Act). The plaintiffs contended that the primary Judge had erred in concluding that they were so apportionable.
- Whether Mr and Mrs Elwood proved their claims for physical inconvenience and whether those claims were compensable at law.
- If Western Power was liable to the plaintiffs, how were damages to be apportioned between it, Ms Campbell and Thiess.

Held: Western Power was liable in negligence; all other contentions rejected; liability reapportioned.

Liability of Western Power in negligence

1. Western Power owed a duty to persons in the vicinity of its network to take reasonable care to avoid or minimise the risk of injury to those persons, and loss or damage to their property, from the ignition and spread of fire in connection with the delivery of electricity through its electricity distribution system. [151]–[161]

2. That duty required it to undertake periodic inspections of wooden poles more than 15 years old, especially in rural areas where there was an elevated risk of bushfires. The risk of harm from a falling pole was foreseeable and known and the probability that harm would occur if PA poles were not inspected was high, approaching certainty over time. [162]–[167]

3. The cost of a scheme for inspection of all PA poles, including those on private property, would have been significant. However, particularly given the degree of risk and the magnitude of ensuing damage, that cost was not unreasonable. Such a duty was also consistent with the terms of s 25 of the Electricity Act. Western Power therefore breached its duty to the plaintiffs. [168]–[180]

4. If Western Power had implemented a system for periodically inspecting wooden PA poles, the PA pole would probably have been inspected and its deterioration identified prior to its collapse. As such, causation had also been established with respect to the cause of action in negligence against Western Power. [181]–[185], [203], [204]

Whether Western Power owed a non-delegable duty

5. Because Western Power had been found negligent in failing to implement a system for regularly inspecting to PA poles, it was strictly unnecessary to determine whether the primary Judge erred in rejecting the contention that it owed a non-delegable duty to ensure that Thiess took reasonable care in carrying out the July 2013 works. [205]–[207]

6. However, if it had been necessary to decide the matter, there was no basis for interfering with the primary Judge's finding that such a non-delegable duty had not been owed. Contrary to the submissions of the plaintiffs, the duty owed by Western Power did not fall within any of the established categories of non-delegable duties. [225]–[235]

Whether Western Power failed to take reasonable care in engaging and instructing Thiess

7. It was again strictly unnecessary for the Court to determine whether Western Power had breached this narrower duty. But as the primary Judge concluded, there was no basis for finding that the selection of Thiess had been inappropriate or inadequately researched. Western Power had also audited its performance from time to time. [254]–[263]

Whether Ms Campbell had been liable in negligence and private nuisance

8. A reasonable person in Ms Campbell's position would have appreciated that, at least by the time that the PA pole had been *in situ* for 25 years, there was a risk that its integrity might be compromised. Given the high magnitude of the risk if the pole failed, a reasonable person in Mrs Campbell's position would have arranged for the pole to be inspected. [296]–[299]

9. It had not been incumbent upon the primary Judge to formulate how regularly Ms Campbell should have had the PA pole inspected. The evidence was that she had never had

the PA pole inspected and so the primary Judge had been entitled to find that she had breached her duty to the plaintiffs and that she had committed the tort of nuisance. [300]–[302], [308]

Whether the claims in nuisance were apportionable

10. The claims in nuisance advanced by the plaintiffs and found to be established in the present case did arise from a failure to take reasonable care within the meaning of the definition of "apportionable claim" in s 5AI of the CL Act. It followed that those claims were apportionable under that provision. [321]–[333]

Whether claims for physical inconvenience had been established and were compensable

11. The evidence given by Mr and Mrs Elwood fell short of establishing that they suffered such a nature or degree of physical inconvenience that an award under a separate head of compensation was necessary. There was therefore no need to quantify that head of damage. [346]

Re-apportionment of damages

12. Given the finding that Western Power had been liable to the plaintiffs for failing to conduct regular inspections of PA poles, it was necessary to re-apportion damages. Liability between Western Power, Thiess and Ms Campbell was to be re-apportioned at 50%, 35% and 15% respectively. The primary Judge's orders were otherwise to be upheld. [349]–[360]

[*Headnote by the Wolters Kluwer editors*]

PJ Dunning QC and T Smyth (Slater & Gordon) for the Herridge Parties.

CM Harris QC and P Mendelow (Hall & Wilcox) for the IAG/Allianz Parties.

RJ Price for (Civic Legal) the RAC parties.

B Dharmananda SC and MJ Sims (DLA Piper) for Western Power.

JC Giles SC and TN Owen (Minter Ellison) for Ms Campbell.

GM Watson SC and SCM Wong (Wotton + Kearney Lawyers) for Thiess.

Before: Buss P, Murphy and Mitchell JJA.

Wolters Kluwer note: The full text of the judgment is accessible through the Supreme Court of Western Australia, Court of Appeal database on the AustLII website.

[¶82-615] Wreford v Lyle [No 3]

(2021) Aust Torts Reports ¶82-615
Medium neutral citation: [2021] WASCA 20
Supreme Court of Western Australia, Court of Appeal
11 February 2021

Motor vehicle accident — Motor vehicle collided with cyclist — Duty of care owed to road users — Contributory negligence — Departure from the standard of care of a reasonable cyclist — Whether trial judge erred in assessing contributory negligence — Whether trial judge erred in assessing damages — Civil Liability Act 2002 (WA), s 5K.

At approximately 4:00 pm on 12 June 2013, the appellant, Ms Wreford was travelling eastbound on her bicycle toward the intersection of Mill Point Road and Tate Street in South Perth when she was struck by a Toyota Land Cruiser driven by the respondent, Mr Lyle, and suffered significant injuries as a result. As Mr Lyle was exiting a car park, his vehicle crossed the footpath. Ms Wreford's progress along the path was obstructed by the vehicle. Mr Lyle stopped before entering the road in order to make a right turn. Ms Wreford was approaching from his left-hand side. Mr Lyle did not see her. Ms Wreford decided to proceed around the front of the vehicle. Mr Lyle still did not see her. He proceeded to make his turn, resulting in Ms Wreford being hit by the vehicle and run over.

Ms Wreford commenced proceedings in the District Court of Western Australia against Mr Lyle, in negligence and claimed damages. Mr Lyle admitted liability. Damages were

assessed in the total sum of $808,644 with a reduction of 30% for contributory negligence on account of Ms Wreford's conduct in riding her bicycle in front of Mr Lyle's car: *Wreford* v *Lyle* [2018] WADC 173.

Ms Wreford appealed the primary judge's findings as to the assessment of damages and the findings as to contributory negligence. Ms Wreford was unrepresented in the appeal.

Held: appeal dismissed.

1. The general principles concerning liability for harm caused by the fault of road users, and in particular in relation to contributory negligence, are to be found in the *Law Reform (Contributory Negligence and Tortfeasors' Contribution) Act 1947* (WA) and *Civil Liability Act 2002* (WA) (Civil Liability Act). The *Law Reform (Contributory Negligence and Tortfeasors' Contribution) Act 1947* provides that where a court is satisfied that a plaintiff is guilty of contributory negligence it shall reduce the damages recoverable "to such extent as the court thinks just in accordance with the degree of negligence attributable to the plaintiff". Section 5K of the Civil Liability Act prescribes how contributory negligence is to be determined in such a case. [18]–[20]

2. The standard of care for contributory negligence is the same as it is for negligence itself. In that context, contributory negligence of a plaintiff was to be assessed against the risk of harm to himself or herself rather than the risk of harm to others. [22]

3. There was no dispute, at trial or on appeal, that Ms Wreford rode her bicycle in front of Mr Lyle's car. Accordingly, whether Ms Wreford was guilty of contributory negligence depended upon whether she had unreasonably exposed herself to a foreseeable and not insignificant risk of harm by riding in front of the car. [26]

4. The primary judge's finding that Ms Wreford had failed to take reasonable care for her own safety, and that that failure directly contributed to the accident, was based upon (a) the fact that Ms Wreford deliberately rode her bicycle in front of Mr Lyle's car, when (b) she knew that Mr Lyle had not seen her. Neither of those essential facts was in dispute. Those facts alone provided a sufficient basis for finding that Ms Wreford's negligence contributed to the accident that caused the harm that she suffered. [106]

5. The primary judge had not been shown to be in error in relation to her findings as to the circumstances of the accident. [134]

6. As to contributory negligence, the primary judge recognised that Mr Lyle bore the greater responsibility for the accident, particularly having regard to the greater capacity for damage from his car and the significant obligation to keep a proper lookout. Nevertheless, Ms Wreford's actions were a significant departure from the standard of care of a reasonable cyclist. It was a deliberate decision by Ms Wreford to move to the front of Mr Lyle's car, she knew Mr Lyle was intending to pull out, and on the primary judge's findings, there was nothing to prevent Mr Lyle from doing so. Ms Wreford took a deliberate risk that was "tantamount to reckless". That characterisation of Ms Wreford's conduct was correct. In all of the circumstances, it cannot be concluded that a reduction of damages by 30% was outside the range of reasonable judgment. [138]–[140]

[*Headnote by the Wolters Kluwer editors*]

Appellant appeared in person.

DR Clyne (Moray & Agnew Lawyers) for the respondent.

Before: Quinlan CJ, Murphy and Pritchard JJA.

Wolters Kluwer Note: The full text of the judgment is accessible through the Supreme Court of Western Australia, Court of Appeal database on the AustLII website.

[¶82-613] Gregory Spencer Ward trading as Ward's Stock Transport v Watson

(2021) Aust Torts Reports ¶82-613
Medium neutral citation: [2021] WASCA 44
Supreme Court of Western Australia, Court of Appeal
12 March 2021

Torts — Negligence — Workplace injury — Appeal — Duty of care — Employer duties — Safe systems of work — Obvious risks — Training and induction — Relevance of employee experience — Breach of duty — Contributory negligence — Quantification — Appellant employed respondent as driver of trucks transporting cattle — Respondent seriously injured by bull when he entered pen of truck — Respondent commenced proceedings claiming that appellant had been negligent by failing to provide training against entering pen of truck — Appellant claimed obviousness of risk meant not necessary to train experienced drivers of that risk — Primary Judge held that appellant had breached its duty but that respondent also 20% liable for contributory negligence — Civil Liability Act 2002 (WA), s 5O — Law Reform (Contributory Negligence and Tortfeasors' Contribution) Act 1947 (WA), s 4.

Appeal from: *Gregory Spencer Ward trading as Ward's Stock Transport v Watson* (District Court of Western Australia, CIV 2758 of 2017).

The respondent employee, Mr Kerry Watson (the employee), commenced employment with the appellant employer, Mr Gregory Ward (the employer) on 31 March 2014. The employer was the sole proprietor of Ward's Stock Transport and carried on a business of general livestock transport. As part of his employment, the employee drove road trains, mainly transporting cattle. The employee did not receive any formal training or induction before commencing the position and the employer did not contest that it generally did not provide its employees with such training. However, the employer did claim to have a policy of not employing a driver who did not have at least 3 years' experience.

On 18 February 2015, the employee and 3 co-workers, including Mr Gary Page (Mr Page), were directed to transport cattle from the Cullalla feedlot in Gingin to Fremantle. Each of the employees had a separate road train. As the trailers of Mr Page's road train were being loaded with cattle, one of the bulls baulked before entering the front pen of the trailer and remained in the rear pen. The employee then entered the rear pen to encourage the bull to move forward into the front pen. At that point, the bull turned on the employee and forced him up against part of the loading dock, causing him serious injuries.

The employee sued the employer for damages on the basis that the employer was in breach of his duty of care as his employer. The employee's essential contention was that the employer had breached his duty of care to his employees by failing to provide them with adequate training about what to do in these situations. More particularly, the employee contended that the employer should have instructed his employees never to enter a pen with a baulked animal. The employee contended that there was a safe method of dealing with a baulked animal, which the employees should have been instructed to use.

At first instance, O'Neal DCJ in the District Court of Western Australia found that the employer's failure to instruct his employees never to enter a pen with a baulking animal was in breach of his duty of care and that the breach caused the employee's injuries. However, the primary judge also concluded that the employee was guilty of contributory negligence and so reduced his damages by 20% pursuant to the *Law Reform (Contributory Negligence and Tortfeasors' Contribution) Act 1947* (WA) (the CNTC Act). On 12 December 2019, judgment was entered for the employee against the employer in the sum of $1,232,429.02 plus costs.

On appeal, the employer submitted that the primary judge had erred in 2 respects. Firstly, it was submitted that the primary judge had erred in finding that the employer was in breach of his duty of care to the employee and that his breach caused the employee's loss.

More particularly, the employer argued that the obvious danger of getting into a pen with a bull meant that the employer had not been obliged to train its employees not to do so. That was particularly the case given the employer's policy of only employing drivers who had at least 3 years' experience. Secondly, the employer contended that the assessment of contributory negligence at 20% was manifestly inadequate.

Held: appeal allowed in part.

Breach of duty and causation

1. The duty owed by the employer was a duty to use reasonable care to ensure that the loading and unloading of cattle was carried out in a safe manner. The content of that duty was informed by the relevant risk, which was the risk to employees of injury when undertaking the task of loading cattle into the road train trailer. [108]–[115]

2. It followed that the relevant risk was not, as the employer had submitted, the risk that an experienced cattle operator would enter a trailer in order to coax a bull that had stalled in one of the pens. That risk that was to inform the content of the employer's duty in the circumstances. [116], [117]

3. In determining whether the employer had taken adequate steps to discharge its duty, the obviousness of the risk that eventuated was one factor that was to be taken into account. However, the fact that a risk was obvious did not foreclose consideration of whether an employer such as the appellant should have taken steps to prevent that risk occurring. [127]–[140]

4. The experience of an employee such as the respondent was also a consideration that was relevant to assessing an employer's response to a risk. However, it also had to be recalled that a safe system of work was one that was safe for an "average" worker within an employer's enterprise. [141]–[148]

5. As such, the primary judge had been correct to conclude that the putative instruction never to enter a trailer with a baulking animal was part and parcel of the only safe system of dealing with a baulking animal. Baulking was quite common in the industry and the risks to employees who were not properly trained was significant. [149]–[170]

6. The employer had therefore been obliged to instruct the employee never to enter a trailer with a baulked animal at all. It was not established at first instance that the employee would have ignored this instruction. As such, both breach of duty and causation were established. [171]–[185]

7. The employee's unreasonable belief that it was appropriate to enter the trailer was not relevant to whether the employer should, in the exercise of reasonable care, have instructed the employee never to do so. That meant that the primary judge had not needed to resolve factual disputes about the exact circumstances of the accident. [186]–[199]

Contributory negligence

8. The employee's conduct went beyond mere inadvertence; it fell below the standard of a driver acting reasonably for his safety. For those reasons, the primary judge was correct to conclude that it was necessary to apportion responsibility having regard to the comparison of the culpability of each party. [200]–[207]

9. However, the primary judge failed to give sufficient weight to the employee's own appreciation of the nature and magnitude of the risk in the present case and the degree to which, objectively, he departed from the standard of conduct expected of someone in his position. [208]–[211]

10. Even allowing for the imperative of appellate restraint, it was therefore necessary to re-exercise the discretion. On that assessment, the relative state of the knowledge of the parties and their comparable experience demonstrated that their culpability was similar. The employee was therefore to be held 40% contributorily negligent. [212]–[214]

[*Headnote by the Wolters Kluwer editors*]

T Lampropoulos SC (Greenland Legal Pty Ltd) for the appellant.

TJ Hammond (Perth City Legal) for the respondent.

Before: Quinlan CJ, Murphy and Vaughan JJA.

Wolters Kluwer Note: The full text of the judgment is accessible through the AustLII database for Western Australian cases.

[¶82-583] Nikolich v Webb

(2020) Aust Torts Reports ¶82-583
Medium neutral citation: [2020] WASCA 169
Supreme Court of Western Australia, Court of Appeal
21 October 2020

Negligence — Occupiers' liability — Whether operation of s 5O limited to defence of volenti non fit injuria — Duty to warn — Whether obvious risk — Short stay rental property — Slip in bathroom — Liability of owner — Civil Liability Act 2002 (WA), s 5O.

On 14 February 2014, Mr and Mrs Nikolich occupied a short stay accommodation rental property owned by Matthew and Karen Webb (the Webbs). Mrs Nikolich suffered injury to her right arm after she slipped on a wet bathroom floor at the property.

Mrs Nikolich commenced proceedings in the District Court of Western Australia against the Webbs, in negligence and claimed damages. She claimed that the Webbs owed her a duty of care and that they breached their duty and caused her injury. The Webbs admitted that they owed Mrs Nikolich a duty of care but denied breaching their duty. The primary judge found that the risk of slipping on a wet bathroom floor and suffering injury was an obvious risk within the meaning of s 5O of the *Civil Liability Act 2002* (WA) (the Act) and dismissed Mrs Nikolich's claim.

Mrs Nikolich appealed the primary judge's findings. She argued on appeal that the primary judge erred in misconstruing s 5O of the Act by finding that it had the effect that the Webbs did not owe a duty of care to warn of an obvious risk and in finding that the relevant risk was an "obvious risk" for the purpose of s 5O of the Act.

Held: appeal dismissed.

1. The primary judge identified the relevant risk of injury as being the risk of a person slipping and falling on the wet bathroom floor. There was no evidence or finding that the bathroom floor was "unusually slippery". The relevant factual finding was that there was a high or very high risk of slipping in the case of a barefooted person walking on the wet bathroom floor; however, when dry, the risk was no more than very low to moderate. [60]–[62]

2. The primary judge referred to the risk of slipping on the bathroom floor when it was wet in the context of considering whether there was a foreseeable risk and in assessing breach. There was no error in so doing. [70]

3. There was no finding or evidence that the bathroom floor was unusually, innately or uniquely slippery. The slipperiness of the bathroom floor — and the risk of injury in slipping and falling — was a function of the water on the floor rather than the floor being unusually, innately or uniquely slippery. There was no evidence and no finding that the bathroom floor when wet was more (or less) slippery than other bathroom floors when wet. The primary

judge's unchallenged finding was that, when dry, a person walking on the bathroom floor in bare feet would have a very low to moderate risk of slipping. The obviousness of a risk was a question of fact. It turned on the evidence of what occurred and why the risk was one that was obvious. The finding that there was an obvious risk for the purpose of s 5O of the Act should be upheld. [89], [90], [109]

[*Headnote by the Wolters Kluwer editors*]

GMG McIntyre SC with JR Brooksby (Percy Kakulas Gleeson) for the appellant.

JRB Ley SC (Greenland Legal Pty Ltd) for the first and second respondents.

Before: Murphy, Beech and Vaughan JJA.

Wolters Kluwer Note: The full text of the judgment is accessible through the Supreme Court of Western Australia, Court of Appeal database on the AustLII website.

[¶82-575] Gors by his Plenary Administrator Gors v Tomlinson

(2020) Aust Torts Reports ¶82-575
Medium neutral citation: [2020] WASCA 164
Supreme Court of Western Australia Court of Appeal
30 September 2020

Torts — Negligence — Occupier liability — Duty of care — Breach of duty — Causation — Warnings — Failure to warn — Obvious risks — Respondents were occupiers of house that had a patio roof made of laserlite polycarbonate panels — Appellant fell through those panels and suffered significant injury in course of removing a hot water system from main roof — Primary judge held that occupier's duty to warn only extended to risks that were not obvious and that risks of placing weight on patio roof were obvious — Appellant appealed — Civil Liability Act 2002 (WA), s 5O.

The respondents, Mr Tomlinson and Mrs Tomlinson, were the occupiers of a house in Yathroo in Western Australia. Their property comprised a large farmhouse with a patio on the north side. The main roof of the house, including the veranda, was tiled and was angled at approximately 20 degrees. A patio extended the width of the house. Over the patio there was a roof constructed of a laserlite polycarbonate material which was approximately 2.1 to 2.2 metres above the brick paved area of the patio. The patio roof was angled at approximately 2 degrees and the laserlite panels were corrugated. There was a gutter at one edge of the tiled roof where it met the patio roof. On the main roof of the house, there was a Solhart hot water unit (the unit) attached to the tiling. The weight of that unit was approximately 80 kgs.

On 19 August 2014, by arrangement with the respondents, Mr Kevin Gors (Mr Gors) and his brother attended the respondents' property for the purposes of removing the unit from the roof of the respondents' house. Having ascended to the roof on a ladder, Mr Gors and his brother managed to detach the unit and then proceeded to move it to where the ladder was resting. However, because of the weight of the unit, they paused briefly and put the unit down. At that point, Mr Gors took two steps backwards without looking behind him and stepped from the main roof onto the laserlite panels which comprised the patio roof. Those panels were unable to support his weight and Mr Gors fell through them onto the ground below and suffered significant injuries as a result.

Mr Gors commenced proceedings in the District Court of Western Australia against the respondents, in negligence and claimed damages. Mr Gors conceded that if he placed his weight on the laserlite panels, it had been reasonably foreseeable that the panels would fracture and he would fall through them. Mr Gors' case was pleaded on the basis that the respondents had breached their occupier's duty owed to him under s 5O of the *Civil Liability Act 2002* (WA) (the CLA) by failing to warn him of the risk that the patio roof was constructed of laserlite panels and/or that it was not safe to walk on.

The primary judge noted that Mr Gors had visited the respondents' house on a number of occasions and had seen the laserlite roof and that he had a laserlite roof over the pool of his own house and found that it would have been obvious to Mr Gors that the laserlite patio roof would not support his weight if he walked upon it. As such, the respondents' duty under s 5O of the CLA did not extend to warning Mr Gors of the risks of walking upon that roof. The primary judge also held that, even if the risk had not been obvious, it was reasonable of the respondents to assume that Mr Gors would take precautions for his own safety: *Keven Gors by his Plenary Administrator of Janet Christine Gors* v *Tomlinson* (2019) Aust Torts Reports ¶82-474; [2019] WADC 88.

Mr Gors appealed the primary judge's findings. He argued that if the risk was obvious, the primary judge was bound to hold that the respondents had a duty of care to Mr Gors in relation to that risk and that the respondents could not escape liability on the ground that they reasonably expected Mr Gors to take care of his own safety. Mr Gors also argued that the primary judge erred in finding that the patio roof was translucent and that it was constructed of material similar to his own pool roof and that such findings could not sustain a finding that he was aware of the dangers of the respondents' patio roof. Mr Gors also argued that the defence in s 5O of the CLA could not apply because the respondents had not pleaded voluntary assumption of risk.

Held: appeal dismissed.

1. Mr Gors did not identify any basis for concluding that key findings of fact were drawn in error. [42]–[52]

2. The authorities established that, in some circumstances, a foreseeable risk was so obvious and the remoteness of its occurrence so small that reasonableness might require no response to the risk at all. That is evidently what the primary judge concluded in the present case and there was a basis for that conclusion. [53]–[65]

3. There was a firm foundation for the primary judge's finding that Mr Gors, a regular visitor to the property, would have seen the patio roof for himself. There was also evidence to substantiate the finding that he had a roof made of laserlite and that he understood the dangers of walking upon it. [66]–[80]

4. The text of s 5O of the CLA was clear and unambiguous. It provided, in terms, that in circumstances in which a risk to the plaintiff was an obvious risk, a defendant had no duty to warn the plaintiff of that risk. The defence was not only engaged where a defendant pleaded voluntary assumption of risk. [81]–[106]

5. Section 5O did not have the effect that a defendant would probably have no duty to do anything in relation to an obvious risk. It was only concerned with the duty to warn and left a defendant's duty to take reasonable care otherwise unaffected. However, Mr Gors in this case did not identify any other step that the respondents should have taken to avoid the harm. [107]–[134]

6. The primary judge found that Mr Gors stepped back onto the patio roof without looking behind him even though he was aware that it would not support his weight. As such, the conclusion that causation would not have been established in any event was also irresistible. [135]–[144]

[*Headnote by the Wolters Kluwer editors*]

G McIntyre SC and JR Brooksby (Donna Percy & Co) for the appellant.

GR Hancy (Greenland Legal Pty Ltd) for the respondents.

Before: Quinlan CJ, Murphy JA and Vaughan JA.

Wolters Kluwer note: The full text of the judgment is accessible through the Supreme Court of Western Australia Court of Appeal database on the AustLII website.

[¶82-517] Lawrence v Province Leader of the Oceania Province of the Congregation of the Christian Brothers

(2020) Aust Torts Reports ¶82-517
Medium neutral citation: [2020] WADC 27
District Court of Western Australia
11 March 2020

Damages — Psychiatric injury — Historical institutional child sexual abuse cause of action —Definition of "child sexual abuse" — Loss of past earning capacity — Malec v JC Hutton Pty Ltd — Pre-judgment interest —Exemplary damages — Aggravated damages — Limitation Act 2005 (WA), s 6A — Civil Liability Act 2002 (WA), s 15A — Supreme Court Act 1935 (WA), s 32.

In 1952, when John Lawrence was eight years of age, he was transported by ship from England to Western Australia as a child migrant. Upon his arrival at Fremantle, he was taken to St Vincent's Orphanage Clontarf (St Vincent's) operated by the Christian Brothers. When he was nine years old, Mr Lawrence lived at another orphanage operated by the Christian Brothers, the Castledare Junior Orphanage (Castledare), for a year. He then returned to St Vincent's where he remained until he was 16 years old, at which time he was told to leave St Vincent's.

During Mr Laurence's time at both St Vincent's and Castledare he was repeatedly subjected to sexual abuse and assault by the Brothers and by others, including a teacher working at St Vincent's. He was also subjected to physical abuse, cruelty, intimidation, humiliation, degradation and neglect.

Mr Lawrence commenced proceedings in the District Court of Western Australia against the Christian Brothers, in negligence and claimed damages, including exemplary and aggravated damages. Mr Lawrence was able to make a claim against the Christian Brothers because of recent amendments to the *Limitation Act 2005* (WA) making special provision for child sexual abuse actions by removing the limitation period and it was brought pursuant to Pt 2A of the *Civil Liability Act 2002* (WA) (the CLA).

Mr Lawrence alleged that by reason of the abuse he suffered psychiatric injury which impacted upon all aspects of his life, including his ability to work and earn an income. Mr Lawrence claimed damages for the psychiatric injury caused by the sexual abuse as a child. [2]

On the first day of the trial the Christian Brothers admitted liability for the claim for damages but disputed the quantum of damages. By way of amended defence, the Christian Brothers also admitted that as of January 1957, they had, over a period of approximately 38 years, received reports from time to time relating to allegations of sexual abuse directed against Brothers who were members of the Christian Brothers at both St Vincent's and Castledare and also at other institutions in Australia operated by the Christian Brothers. They further admitted that the relevant office holder of the Christian Brothers ought to have known that at the time Mr Lawrence was a resident at St Vincent's and Castledare there was a reasonably foreseeable risk of sexual abuse being committed against boys who were resident at St Vincent's and Castledare. [27]

The Christian Brothers admitted that, besides sexually abusing Mr Lawrence, they also physically and verbally abused him, and physically abused other boys in his presence, which they pleaded is unrelated to the sexual abuse and for which he is not entitled to claim damages. The Christian Brothers pleaded that, because Mr Lawrence suffered injury and damage caused by their other maltreatment of him, the damages he is entitled to receive for any injury or loss caused by the sexual abuse must be reduced, relying on the amending legislation which only allows damages to be awarded for child sexual abuse, not for any other type of abuse such as physical or emotional abuse. The Christian Brothers took issue with whether other forms of abuse, particularly physical abuse to which Mr Lawrence was

subjected, came within the meaning of the terms "child sexual abuse" or "sexual abuse", for the purposes of those terms in s 15A of the CLA and s 6A of the Limitation Act. [31]–[33]

The matter ultimately proceeded to hearing as to an assessment of damages only.

***Held:* judgment in favour of the plaintiff in the total sum of $1,329,500.**

1. The evidence demonstrated that the sexual abuse of Mr Lawrence was bound up with physical and emotional abuse in the context of a pervasive atmosphere created by the Christian Brothers of violence, fear and terror. If any harm had been caused to Mr Lawrence because of how he was maltreated while in the care of the Christian Brothers, that maltreatment and any consequent harm are so entwined with the child sexual abuse and the harm which was caused by that abuse that the causes and the harm cannot be disentangled. The inability to disentangle the competing causes and effects impacts upon the assessment of damages. [96]

2. If in the context of an institution, or indeed any relationship where an adult has power over a child, any conduct which heightens the child's vulnerability and allows him or her to be exploited for purposes of sexual gratification may be considered to be sexual abuse. If, in an institutional setting, a child is regularly physically beaten and threatened which causes a child to be fearful, frightened and defenceless, or unable to turn to anyone for help, thereby heightening or increasing the child's vulnerability to do what the child is directed or forced to do, that conduct may fall within the meaning of the expression "sexual abuse". If the child's resistance to sexual abuse, or sexual overtures, is lowered or reduced because of feelings of fear, helplessness and defencelessness, the conduct, the physical abuse, may come within the meaning of the term "sexual abuse". That is so even if the person administering the physical abuse is not the sexual abuser, providing the physical abuse aides or assists, whether intentionally or otherwise, the sexual abuse to occur. If a child is physically beaten because of reporting sexual abuse, that conduct makes the child more vulnerable to being sexually abused by adding to the child's feelings of fear, helplessness and defencelessness. It is likely to reduce a child's resistance against being sexually abused. Even if the child is not physically abused for reporting sexual abuse, if the child is aware of others being physically punished for reporting sexual abuse, that knowledge increases the child's feelings of helplessness and fear and increases his or her vulnerability to being sexually abused. [101]

3. Therefore, if an atmosphere or environment has been allowed to develop by which children feel they cannot report sexual abuse because of the threat or fear of being physically abused, the physical abuse may fall within the meaning of the term sexual abuse. That term must be given an expansive meaning to cover any other forms of abuse which surround and allow the sexual abuse to occur. However, for this other conduct, specifically physical abuse, to fall within the meaning of the term sexual abuse, there must be some connection to or association with the conduct which is sexual, that is, for the purposes of sexual gratification of the abuser. If the physical abuse is not connected to or associated with conduct for sexual gratification, the physical abuse does not fall within the meaning of the term sexual abuse. [102]

4. The physical and other abuse, including emotional deprivation, perpetrated against Mr Lawrence when he was young boy while he was living at St Vincent's and Castledare is so inextricably intertwined and associated with the child sexual abuse that it cannot be separated from the sexual abuse. The physical and emotional abuse, and other forms of maltreatment, to which Mr Lawrence, and the other boys, were subjected while at Castledare and St Vincent's, aided the occurrence of the child sexual abuse. The violence, cruelty and threats to which Mr Lawrence was subjected by, among others, Brothers Murphy and Doyle created an atmosphere of fear, intimidation and subjugation which provided the basis for and which allowed the sexual abuse to occur and flourish. [258]

5. The other forms of abuse to which Mr Lawrence was subjected by the Christian Brothers exacerbated the harmful impact of the child sexual abuse because it increased his

sense of hopelessness and fear and his inability to do anything about it, while he was being sexually abused. The physical abuse perpetrated by Brother Doyle, and Mr Lawrence's knowledge of other boys being physically abused when they reported allegations of sexual abuse, caused Mr Lawrence to believe he would be beaten if he reported the sexual abuse, adding to his sense of helplessness and exacerbating the harmful impact of the child sexual abuse. The physical abuse caused the child sexual abuse to have a greater harmful impact on Mr Lawrence. [260]

6. As to damages, while it is accepted that Mr Lawrence's psychiatric illness has had some impact upon his poor physical health, the evidence does not establish that the primary medical conditions, the heart disease, the peripheral vascular disease, the back condition, the knee condition and the diabetes are caused by Mr Lawrence's poor mental health. [550]

7. Mr Lawrence's psychiatric illness, the predominant cause of which is the child sexual abuse, significantly interfered with Mr Lawrence's capacity for work. Mr Lawrence's inability to obtain permanent full-time employment, and instead lead an itinerant working life in labouring and semi-skilled positions, was directly caused by his psychiatric illnesses which in turn were caused by the sexual abuse. [713]

8. As a negligent defendant the Christian Brothers must take an injured plaintiff, Mr Lawrence, as they find him. To the extent Mr Lawrence was already vulnerable to psychiatric injury because of his early childhood experiences before he was sexually abused by the Christian Brothers, and because of that vulnerability the trauma of the sexual abuse had a greater impact upon him, the Christian Brothers are liable for the full consequences of that injury. [749]

9. As to economic loss, the opportunity to work in other areas or industries, that chance was denied Mr Lawrence because of the child sexual abuse. The sexual abuse perpetrated upon Mr Lawrence made it almost inevitable he would suffer psychiatric injury and as a consequence face significant challenges in being able to hold down stable, full-time, permanent employment. [790]

10. The various factors identified from Mr Lawrence's life which may have impacted upon the trajectory of his working life require a greater than the normal discount of 3% to 6% but do not justify a discount beyond 10%. [812]

11. The amendments to the *Civil Liability Act 2002* (WA) provide that any liability that a former office holder would have had in relation to the "cause of action" is taken to be held by the current office holder. Therefore, if there was a cause of action in tort in 1960 against the then office holder, there is a legal basis for a plaintiff to now bring an action in relation to that tortious cause of action against the current office holder. The remedy for a cause of action in tort is damages. Damages are assessed at the time of trial. Mr Lawrence's damages are to be assessed in accordance with the law as it currently stands. It follows that there is an entitlement to pre-judgment interest on past loss pursuant to s 32(1) of the *Supreme Court Act 1935* (WA) (SCA) which applies to all proceedings commenced in this court. The court has power pursuant to s 32(1) of the SCA to award pre-judgment interest to Mr Lawrence on his past economic loss, essentially his past loss of earnings. [889]–[895]

12. It is appropriate to adopt an interest rate of 6% over the entire period in which the loss was suffered. [914]

13. As to exemplary damages, while the evidence does establish the Christian Brothers, through the Superior, at some point in time became aware of allegations Brother Murphy, and Brothers Marques and Angus, were abusing boys, there is no evidence which establishes they were aware of the nature and extent of the abuse. When allegations of sexual abuse were put to both Brothers Angus and Marques, they each denied the allegations and accused the boys of lying. It seems the Christian Brothers felt that in those circumstances there was little they could do. However, it does indicate that, rather than keep the allegations hidden, they did at least raise the allegations with the alleged abusers. [1012]

14. Neither does the evidence establish that the Christian Brothers deliberately established an environment in which boys were regularly threatened and physically beaten when allegations of sexual abuse were reported for the purpose of allowing the sexual abuse to continue. The evidence did not establish that a deliberate course of action was taken by the Christian Brothers' hierarchy for the purpose of allowing the sexual abuse to occur. Had the court been satisfied the Christian Brothers had acted in such a way, then that may have provided a sufficient basis upon which exemplary damages could be awarded. [1013]

15. Because of the historical nature of the allegations and the time which has long since passed, and all of the steps the Christian Brothers have taken in recent times to acknowledge their appalling behaviour, and also having regard to the fact that the Christian Brothers no longer exist as an institution having the care of children, the court is not of the view that this is one of those rare cases which justify an award of exemplary damages. [1050]

16. The award of general damages to Mr Lawrence for pain and suffering and loss of amenities takes into account the insult and humiliation and the degrading nature of the abuse suffered by Mr Lawrence, particularly when he was sexually abused by Brother Murphy. The purpose of aggravated damages is satisfactorily addressed in the award of general damages and it is not appropriate to make any specific award for aggravated damages. [1053]

[*Headnote by the Wolters Kluwer editors*]

TJ Hammond (M Howard SC appeared on pre-judgment interest on 5 February 2020) (Rightside Legal) for the plaintiff.

BA Mangan and A Liscia (SK Dharmananda SC appeared on pre-judgment interest on 5 February 2020) (Irdi Legal) for the defendant.

No appearance for first third party (Australian Government Solicitor) (relied on written submissions)

CJ Thatcher SC (appeared on pre-judgment interest on 5 February 2020) (State Solicitor's Office) for the second third party

Before: Herron DCJ.

Wolters Kluwer note: The full text of the judgment is accessible through the District Court of Western Australia database on the AustLII website.

[¶82-504] J-Corp Pty Ltd v Thompson

(2019) Aust Torts Reports ¶82-504
Medium neutral citation: [2019] WASCA 173
Supreme Court of Western Australia, Court of Appeal
7 November 2019

Torts — Negligence — Liability — Occupier's duty — Duty of care — Breach of duty — Standard of care — Negligent construction — Building contractors — Subcontracting of construction — Inspection of works — Appellant was head contractor in construction of a house — Brickwork was subcontracted out — Subcontract provided for appellant to inspect works — Respondent was injured when brickwork collapsed while he was in process of constructing roof — Primary judge held appellant liable for failure to properly carry out inspection obligations — Appellant appealed against finding of liability — Primary judge erred by using hindsight to inform requisite duty of care — Correct test of standard of care would nevertheless have led to same result — Civil Liability Act 2002 (WA), s 5B — Occupiers' Liability Act 1985 (WA), s 5.

The respondent, Mr Alex Thompson, was working as a roof carpenter on a house being built by the appellant, J-Corp Pty Ltd. Mr Thompson was not employed by J-Corp, but instead contracted his services to TJO Roofing, a contract roof carpentry business that had been contracted to build the house's roof. The house's design was such that it included a porch area at the front of the house and an isolated brick column referred to as a ''pier''. A

wooden beam traversed the span from the pier to the brickwork of the master bedroom. A second wooden beam traversed the span from the pier to the brickwork of the garage, so that it ran at a right angle to the other wooden beam. Those beams were nailed together at the top of the pier. The brickwork and the pier had been constructed by a subcontractor engaged by J-Corp. That subcontract enabled J-Corp to inspect the subcontractor's work and obliged the subcontractor to execute the works in accordance with any directions of J-Corp's supervisors.

Construction of the roof began on 12 August 2014. On that day, Mr Thompson was walking along the wall plates on the top of the brick walls and was marking the wall plates to show where the roof rafters would be fixed. In so doing, Mr Thompson walked across the beam which traversed the span from the master bedroom to the pier. As he stepped onto the beam, the pier collapsed and he suffered significant injuries as a result.

Mr Thompson commenced proceedings in the Supreme Court of Western Australia against J Corp, in negligence, and claimed damages. The trial judge found negligence to be established and awarded damages on the basis that J-Corp had not taken steps to ensure that the pier was properly constructed.

J-Corp appealed against the primary judge's findings. It argued that such a finding was not substantiated by the evidence. Mr Thompson also filed a notice of contention asserting that, even if that claim was upheld, a correct application of the applicable principles would yield the same result.

Held: appeal dismissed.

1. It was axiomatic that, in determining whether a duty of care had been breached, the court was to look forward to identify what a reasonable person in the defendant's position would have done, not backwards to identify what would have avoided the risk to the plaintiff in the circumstances. [33]–[38]

2. Contrary to this, the primary judge focussed too narrowly on the particular circumstances in which Mr Thompson came to be injured. As such, the primary judge failed to address the question of what a reasonable builder and occupier in J-Corp's position would have done from the proper perspective. [39], [40]

3. The primary judge also found that J-Corp ought to have known that the unfilled pier was too weak to support loads such as those applied by the feet of roof carpenters. However, J-Corp was not a structural engineer and there was no other evidence upon which to base this conclusion. [41]–[48]

4. A reasonable builder and occupier would nevertheless have been aware that a fall due to the failure of elevated brickwork on which a roof carpenter was stepping in carrying out his/her work was likely to result in serious injury to the roof carpenter. That was so even if the builder and occupier did not have the expertise of a structural engineer. [49]–[56]

5. In those circumstances, a reasonable builder and occupier in J-Corp's position would have inspected the brickwork to check that structural elements had been constructed in accordance with structural engineering specifications. By not doing so, J-Corp breached its duty to Mr Thompson and so his notice of contention was to be upheld. [57]–[66]

[*Headnote by the Wolters Kluwer editors*]

GR Hancy (Greenland Legal Pty Ltd) for the appellant.

T Lampropoulos SC and DM Bruns (Stephen Browne Lawyers) for the respondent.

Before: Murphy, Mitchell and Vaughan JJA.

Wolters Kluwer Note: The full text of the judgment is accessible through the Supreme Court of Western Australia Court of Appeal database on the AustLII website at www.austlii.edu.au.

[¶82-430] East Metropolitan Health Service v Jane Elizabeth Popovic as executrix of the will of Emil Popovic

(2019) Aust Torts Reports ¶82-430

Medium neutral citation: [2019] WASCA 18

Supreme Court of Western Australia Court of Appeal

31 January 2019

Tort — Negligence — Medical negligence — Patient suffered severe brain injury due to meningitis and due to delay in administering antibiotics — Whether medical practitioner breached duty of care to patient — Whether inference should be drawn that practitioner failed to give appropriate advice to client — Whether causation was proved — Whether if patient had attended hospital earlier antibiotics would have been administered earlier.

In December 2005, Mr Peter Panagoulias was diagnosed as having a benign tumour near the pituitary stalk in his brain. On 23 January 2006, Mr Popovic performed a left supra orbital (above the eye socket) craniotomy and a subtotal resection of the tumour, removing about 90% of the tumour mass. Later, on 14 September 2007, Mr Panagoulias had further brain surgery to remove the remaining 10% of the mass. The second surgery was abandoned due to bleeding after Mr Popovic nicked Mr Panagoulias' carotid artery. The lacerated artery was treated and he was transferred to Royal Perth Hospital intensive care unit. Mr Panagoulias was discharged from hospital on 20 September 2007.

On 5 October 2007, Mr Panagoulias sneezed and lump of fatty tissue was expelled from his nose. He called Mr Popovic. In the early hours of the following morning, Mr Panagoulias woke with a bad headache, worse than usual. After speaking again with Mr Popovic, by 9:53 am he presented to the emergency department at RPH. Later that afternoon, a diagnosis was made of bacterial meningitis and intravenous medication was first administered. However later that same evening, Mr Panagoulias was found unresponsive in his bed. He had lost consciousness and was unresponsive. He was intubated. He had developed bacterial meningitis which had caused Mr Panagoulias severe and irreversible brain damage. As a result, he has sustained permanent disabilities that will require 24-hour monitoring and supervision for the rest of his life.

Mr Panagoulias commenced proceedings in the District Court of Western Australia against East Metropolitan Health Service, in negligence and claimed damages. East Metropolitan is legally responsible for the liabilities of Royal Perth Hospital (RPH) where Mr Panagoulias was admitted on 6 October 2007. He also sued his neurosurgeon, Mr Popovic.

Mr Panagoulias alleged that Mr Popovic's failure to provide the required warning or advice resulted in a delay in Mr Panagoulias' arrival and treatment at RPH. That, in turn, caused delay in the appropriate antibiotic treatment of Mr Panagoulias' bacterial meningitis, to the point that severe and irreversible brain damage was caused. Further, that the staff at RPH failed to act in a timely way to diagnose and treat his bacterial meningitis. In particular, he alleged that RPH staff failed to conduct appropriate tests to diagnose or exclude bacterial meningitis, thereby allowing the meningitis to reach the stage where it caused severe and irreversible brain damage. As against both East Metropolitan and Mr Popovic, Mr Panagoulias alleged that but for their neglect, causing treatment to be delayed, he would have recovered without long-term harm.

It was agreed at trial, by all parties and by the experts, that Mr Panagoulias contracted bacterial meningitis and that he did so by virtue of a cerebrospinal fluid (CSF) leak, as a result of a puncture of the dura mater during the second surgery. [16]

There was very limited first-hand evidence; Mr Panagoulias' severe brain injury meant that he could not give evidence, Mr Popovic had died in March 2011, and only one member of RPH staff was called to give evidence. As against East Metropolitan, the primary judge found in favour of Mr Panagoulias, that RPH staff breached the duty owed to Mr Panagoulias by failing to act in a timely way to diagnose and treat the bacterial meningitis, and that the failure by RPH staff to treat Mr Panagoulias in a timely way was a necessary condition of the severe brain injury he acquired. However, the claim against the surgeon, Mr Popovic, was dismissed on the basis that neither breach nor causation had been established. Damages were awarded in the total sum of $11,634,527.

East Metropolitan appealed the primary judge's findings as against Mr Popovic. It does not challenge the finding that it is liable in negligence. Rather the appeal challenges the judge's dismissal of Mr Panagoulias' claim against Mr Popovic.

Held: appeal dismissed.

Per Murphy, Beech JJA and Allanson J:

1. East Metropolitan's case on breach was and is founded on a telephone conversation between Mr Panagoulias and Mr Popovic. It was and is common ground that Mr Popovic's duty of care required him to give certain advice to Mr Panagoulias during that conversation. There was no direct evidence of the content of the telephone conversation from either of the parties to it. The issue as to breach was and is whether an inference could be drawn that Mr Popovic failed to give the required advice. [5]

2. The primary judge's finding that Mr Panagoulias did not tell his wife that he had received the appropriate advice from Mr Popovic does not sustain an inference that Mr Popovic failed to give such advice in his telephone conversation with Mr Panagoulias on 5 October 2007. The circumstances relied on by East Metropolitan do not, individually or in combination, sustain an inference that Mr Popovic failed to give the appropriate advice. [116] – [117]

3. Mr Panagoulias acted consistently with what the primary judge found to be the appropriate advice in that at about 8.30 am, but not earlier, Mr Panagoulias experienced a headache of a severity or kind that was out of the ordinary, and then contacted Mr Popovic. [202]

4. Assuming Mrs Panagoulias' evidence is admissible, East Metropolitan failed to prove that Mr Popovic did not provide the appropriate advice to Mr Panagoulias in the course of the telephone conversation. Consequently, East Metropolitan failed to prove a breach by Mr Popovic. [202]

5. Further, East Metropolitan failed to prove that any breach by Mr Popovic caused the harm suffered by Mr Panagoulias. [202]

[*Headnote by the Wolters Kluwer editors*]

G R Donaldson SC (State Solicitor's Office) for the Appellant.

R Weinstein SC & G P Bourhill (Avant Law) for the First Respondent.

No appearance for the Second Respondent.

Before: Murphy, Beech JJA and Allanson J.

[¶82-418] Lightfoot v Rockingham Wild Encounters Pty Ltd

(2018) Aust Torts Reports ¶82-418

Medium neutral citation: [2018] WASCA 205

Supreme Court of New South Wales, Court of Appeal

23 November 2018

Torts — Negligence — Plaintiff injured while on dolphin watching tour — Whether navigation through passage in reef rather than via a deeper channel was negligent — Whether there was a foreseeable and not insignificant risk of injury to passengers if boat travelled through reef passage — Civil Liability Act 2002 (WA), ss 5B, 5I, 5J.

On 23 September 2012, Ms Lightfoot went on a dolphin watching tour run by Rockingham Wild Encounter Pty Ltd (RWE), signing a waiver of liability in relation to it. As part of the tour, the passengers were transferred from the mainland to Penguin Island by a small ferry. Once at Penguin Island, they boarded another boat.

On the boat's return voyage, the skipper navigated the boat through the Reef Passage, rather than through a deeper and wider marked channel, known as South Channel. While navigating through the Reef Passage, the boat encountered a large wave which caused Ms Lightfoot to rise out of her seat and come down hard on it, striking her back against the seat's edge. Ms Lightfoot sustained a serious spinal injury and underwent spinal surgery two days later.

Ms Lightfoot commenced proceedings in the District Court of Western Australia against RWE, in negligence and claimed damages. She alleged that RWE was negligent in navigating into and through the Reef Passage rather than proceeding via South Channel.

In denying liability, RWE relied on s 5I and 5J of the *Civil Liability Act 2002* (WA). The main issues at trial were whether RWE breached its duty of care; whether a risk warning was given, so that s 5I of the CLA operated to mean there was no duty of care; and whether any liability was effectively waived pursuant to s 5J of the CLA. Damages were also in issue.

The primary judge found that RWE did not breach its duty of care; the risk of a sudden steep wave arising in those waters was remote, and without the benefit of hindsight it was not unreasonable for the skipper to navigate through the channel.

Ms Lightfoot appealed the primary judge's findings. She argued that the primary judge erred in finding no breach of duty of care.

***Held:* appeal dismissed.**

Per Buss P, Murphy JA, Beech JA:

1. Ms Lightfoot pleaded that what was foreseeable was the risk of large swell or waves endangering the safety of passengers. There was no suggestion of any relevant risk of injury to passengers arising from anything other than the effect of large swell or waves on the boat. [48]

2. The relevant risk was of a passenger suffering an injury as a result of the boat encountering a large swell or wave during its navigation of the Reef Passage. It was, and is, necessary for Ms Lightfoot to establish that this risk (1) was foreseeable, (2) not insignificant and (3) that, in the circumstances, a reasonable person in the skipper's position would have taken the precaution of navigating the boat through South Channel and avoided the Reef Passage. [50] – [51]

3. The primary judge's findings of fact do not sustain a conclusion that, at the time the skipper decided to navigate through the Reef Passage, there was, to a reasonable person in the position of the skipper, a foreseeable and not insignificant risk that, if the boat were navigated through the Reef Passage, a passenger may have suffered an injury as a result of the boat encountering a large swell or wave. [70]

4. Ms Lightfoot had not established that there was a foreseeable and not insignificant risk that, if the boat was navigated through the Reef Passage, the boat might encounter a large swell or wave which could cause injury to a passenger. [79]

[*Headnote by the Wolters Kluwer editors*]

Dr A S Morrison QC & Mr N F Morrissey (CLP Legal Pty Ltd) for the appellant.

Mr D R Clyne (SRB Legal) for the respondent.

Before: Buss P, Murphy and Beech JJA.

***Wolters Kluwer note**: The full text of the judgment is accessible through the Supreme Court of Western Australia Court of Appeal database on the AustLII website at www.austlii.edu.au.*

[¶82-118] Town of Port Hedland v Reece William Hodder by next friend Elaine Georgina Hodder [No 2]

(2012) Aust Torts Reports ¶82-118
Medium neutral citation: [2012] WASCA 212
Supreme Court of Western Australia, Court of Appeal
Judgment delivered 26 October 2012

Torts — Negligence — Liability — Duty of care — Breach of duty — Standard of care — Damage — Causation — Contributory negligence — Subjective test — Disabilities — Plaintiff suffered from intellectual disabilities and cerebral palsy — Defendants were Town and community organisation that had responsibility for a pool that plaintiff attended — Plaintiff climbed onto diving blocks adjacent to shallow end of pool and dived in — Shallowness of water meant that plaintiff struck his head on pool floor and he was rendered quadriplegic as a result — Proceedings commenced by plaintiff against both defendants claiming negligence in relation to the position of the diving blocks and the lack of warning — Defendants claimed that plaintiff was also liable for contributory negligence — Primary judge held that Town was liable for plaintiff's injuries because risk was foreseeable and easily avoided — Plaintiff was also found to be liable for contributory negligence and so his damages were decreased by 10% — Appeals brought by Town against finding of liability and by plaintiff against finding of contributory negligence — Whether Town had been in breach of its duty of care — Whether Town had delegated its responsibility to community organisation — Whether Town was contractually indemnified in respect of its liability — Whether plaintiff was liable for contributory negligence — Whether contributory negligence was to be assessed by an objective or a subjective standard — Civil Liability Act 2002 (WA), s 5K.

Mr Reece Hodder (Mr Hodder) was born in 1983 with cerebral palsy and an intellectual disability. Soon after birth, he was found to be profoundly deaf, practically blind and virtually unable to speak. Mr Hodder also suffered from epileptic fits which had left him in a long term coma on at least one occasion. His cerebral palsy also caused weakness in the cartilage in his throat and that caused his windpipe to collapse. That meant that, until his windpipe was repaired in 2005, Mr Hodder had to have a tracheotomy in order to breathe. Despite those difficulties, Mr Hodder attended school where he learnt sign language to communicate. He also learnt to read and write and was able to take part in basic activities like swimming and running. Mr Hodder also learnt to follow television programs and to play computer games. During the performance of those activities, however, Mr Hodder constantly required close supervision. In particular, his tracheotomy meant that any physical activity that Mr Hodder performed had to be closely monitored. The person who took most responsibility in that respect was his mother, Mrs Elaine Hodder (Mrs Hodder).

In 2006, when Mr Hodder was 23, he attended the Aquatic Centre in South Hedland in Western Australia. At that time, the swimming pool was owned by the Town of Port Hedland (the Town), and managed by the Young Men's Christian Association of Perth (the YMCA)

pursuant to a contract between the Town and the YMCA. The pool itself was 50 m long and was used for both competitive and recreational swimming. At the pool's shallow end, the pool had a depth of 1.1 m. The pool then became progressively deeper so that it was 3.5 m deep at the opposite end. Diving boards had been constructed at that end and diving was frequently performed into the deeper water. However, at the shallow end, eight diving blocks had been constructed to allow swimmers to dive in during competitive swimming. Those blocks, which were 0.97 m above the water level, were not removed when recreational swimming took place. The existence of the diving blocks therefore contravened Fédération Internationale De Natation (FINA) regulations which stated that blocks could be a maximum of 0.75 m above water of that depth.

Mr Hodder attended the pool in the company of family members but his mother was not present (she had been given some rest from his ongoing care). By that time, his tracheotomy had been removed and he was able to completely submerge himself in water. He was therefore left unattended for a short time while his relatives were either swimming or preparing to swim. It was during that brief period that Mr Hodder mounted one of the diving blocks at the shallow end of the swimming pool. One of the lifeguards who was on duty at the pool (Ms Cooper) saw Mr Hodder climbing onto the diving block. However, Ms Cooper's duty post was not on the pool deck itself. She therefore could not stop Mr Hodder diving head first into the pool. As soon as he dived in, Ms Cooper knew that Mr Hodder was likely to be injured. She consequently shouted "spinal" and dived into the pool to pull him out (together with another lifeguard). At that time, Mr Hodder's head was bleeding profusely from a cut that occurred when he struck his head on the bottom of the pool. Subsequent investigations established that that same impact caused a fracture of his cervical spine. Mr Hodder was rendered quadriplegic as a result.

Proceedings were subsequently commenced on Mr Hodder's behalf against each of the Town and the YMCA, claiming damages for personal injury allegedly caused by their negligence. The Town claimed contribution and indemnity from the YMCA in respect of any damages it was ordered to pay Mr Hodder. At first instance, the primary judge found that the Town had breached its duty to Mr Hodder by failing to remove the diving blocks from the shallow end of the pool. His Honour also found that the Town's breach of duty caused the injuries suffered by Mr Hodder as he would not have dived into the pool but for the presence of the diving blocks. The primary judge additionally held that the YMCA had breached the duty it owed to Mr Hodder in two respects: by failing to have a lifeguard supervising on the deck by the main pool; and in failing to provide adequate signs, indicating to recreational users of the facility, the dangers arising from use of the diving blocks situated at the shallow end of the pool.

The primary judge nevertheless also concluded that neither of the YMCA's breaches of duty made any material contribution to Mr Hodder's injuries. In other words, the primary judge held that the injuries would have occurred even if the YMCA had not been in breach of its duties. For that reason, his Honour dismissed Mr Hodder's claim against the YMCA, and the Town's claim for contribution and indemnity. The primary judge then held that it was necessary to assess whether Mr Hodder was liable for contributory negligence by failing to take adequate care for his own safety. His Honour ultimately determined that issue of contributory negligence on an entirely objective basis — that is, without regard to Mr Hodder's various disabilities. According to the primary judge, such an approach was necessitated by the terms of s 5K of the *Civil Liability Act 2002* (WA) (the CL Act). Following that assessment, the primary judge held that responsibility for Mr Hodder's injuries was to be apportioned 90% to the Town and 10% to Mr Hodder. It was also agreed between the parties that the damages to which Mr Hodder would have been entitled, but for the finding of contributory negligence, were $6.5m.

The Town then appealed to the Court of Appeal. In that respect, the Town argued that the primary judge had been wrong to find that it was liable to Mr Hodder in negligence. It also contended that his Honour was wrong to conclude that the YMCA was not liable to Mr Hodder. The Town argued that the primary judge should instead have found the YMCA liable to contribute to the damages it was ordered to pay Mr Hodder, or alternatively to indemnify the Town in respect of those damages. In that respect, the Town relied upon a provision in the contract between the Town and the YMCA by which the latter managed the pool. The Town also asserted that the primary judge should have apportioned a greater liability for the accident to Mr Hodder. For his part, Mr Hodder brought a separate appeal against the primary judge's decision to dismiss his claim against the YMCA. Mr Hodder also contended that his Honour had been wrong to assess his contributory negligence without regard to his various disabilities. On that point, Mr Hodder argued that, when allowance was made for those disabilities, he should not have been found to have failed to take adequate care for his own safety.

Held: Town's appeal dismissed. Mr Hodder's appeal allowed in part.

Per Martin CJ

The Town's liability

1. The evidence established that the risk of someone suffering injury by striking their head on the bottom of the pool was relatively low, given that there was only one such incident in 27 years of operation of the pool. But at the same time, the risk, which was potentially catastrophic, was known and had been recognised.

2. The risk which the presence of the diving blocks posed to inexperienced, disabled or immature users of the pool could be, and eventually was, cheaply and effectively removed entirely by the removal of the blocks from the shallow end of the pool.

3. Assessment of the relevant facts and considerations therefore compelled the conclusion that the primary judge was correct to conclude that for the Town to discharge its duty of care it needed to remove the diving blocks, and that the Town was in breach of duty by failing to remove the blocks prior to Mr Hodder's accident.

4. The Town had delegated duties with respect to supervision of swimmers and the placement of signage to the YMCA. However, the Town was not found liable for breach of those duties and their breach had not caused Mr Hodder's accident. The Town had therefore not delegated its responsibility to the YMCA.

The YMCA's liability

5. There was no evidence, and nor did the primary judge find that any employee of the YMCA knew, or had any reason to know, that Mr Hodder was completely deaf, practically blind and intellectually disabled. The YMCA was therefore not put on notice of the accident's potentiality.

6. The proposition that the primary judge should have found that the YMCA had a duty to supervise Mr Hodder of a kind which, if discharged, would have averted his accident therefore had to be rejected. The duty that would otherwise have been imposed upon the YMCA was impractical.

7. There was only one way of ensuring that recreational swimmers would not suffer injury diving off the blocks at the shallow end of the pool and the means of achieving that was solely in the Town's hands. It followed that the Town could not avoid its liability by relying upon its contract with the YMCA.

Mr Hodder's liability

8. An objective approach to the assessment of contributory negligence required an unrealistic approach which required the Court to consider some parallel universe in which the blind could see, the deaf could hear, the lame could walk or even run, and the cognitively impaired were somehow restored to full functionality.

9. There was no basis for such an approach in the decided authorities on the point. To the contrary, those cases suggested that a plaintiff's physical or mental disability was properly taken into account when deciding whether there had been contributory negligence.

10. Taking into account the legislative background to s 5K of the CL Act, the provision required that the court determine whether a plaintiff had failed to take reasonable care for his or her own safety by reference to the conduct that was to be expected of a reasonable person in the position of the plaintiff.

11. However, that reasonable person was also to be assessed as having any physical defects or incapacities suffered by the plaintiff. The objective nature of the test to be imposed only required the court to exclude from consideration idiosyncrasies of temperament, behaviour or personality.

12. The primary judge was therefore wrong to assess contributory negligence without regard to Mr Hodder's disabilities. The proper approach to the question was to ask what conduct might have been expected from a reasonable person in Mr Hodder's situation having regard to his relevant physical disabilities.

13. However, in the present circumstances, it was not necessary to have regard to any disability suffered by Mr Hodder other than his visual impairment in order to conclude that he did not fail to take reasonable care for his own safety. The finding of contributory negligence was therefore to be set aside.

Per McLure J

14. There was no intermediate appellate court decision on equivalent legislation in other states suggesting or holding that the standard of care in contributory negligence was subjective or that there was an attenuated standard of care for any class other than children.

15. However, the Town had not discharged its onus of establishing that a reasonable person would have understood that he should not dive from the blocks without first making an independent safety assessment. The nature of the Town's breach of its duty therefore exculpated Mr Hodder from any contributory negligence.

16. It followed that a finding of contributory negligence was not open on the evidence. The onus of establishing contributory negligence was on the Town but it had not discharged that onus. As such, the primary judge's finding of contributory negligence against Mr Hodder was to be set aside.

Per Murphy JA (dissenting on the question of contributory negligence only)

17. A review of the relevant case law indicated that, until the High Court indicated otherwise, the standard of care was, in general principle, objective and applied equally in the case of negligence and contributory negligence, to activities voluntarily and autonomously undertaken.

18. The applicable objective standard precluded exculpation on the basis that the person failed, through intellectual impairment or otherwise, subjectively to comprehend the risk which they were posing to themselves or others in undertaking the activity in question.

19. It followed that Mr Hodder's conduct in diving into the pool when he could not see the depth of the water below him was to be judged according to the objective standard. The fact that he did not subjectively appreciate the risk of the activity he was undertaking did not lead to an attenuated standard of care in this case.

20. In addition, the words "a reasonable person in the position of that person" in s 5K(2) of the CL Act were to be read as a whole. The words "in the position of that person" were not to be read as separately conveying that a subjective standard was to be applied in determining questions of contributory negligence.

21. The primary judge was therefore correct to conclude that Mr Hodder was liable for contributory negligence because he ought to have known that he could not do so safely,

having regard to the height of the block, the ascertainable depth of the water and his own inexperience and lack of skill.

[*Headnote by the Wolters Kluwer editors*]

S Walsh QC and J Campbell (instructed by DLA Piper) for the Town.

Dr AS Morrison QC and G Droppert (instructed by Donna Percy & Co) for Mr Hodder.

Before: Martin CJ, McLure P and Murphy JA.

[¶82-047] Department of Housing and Works v Smith

(2010) Aust Torts Reports ¶82-047
Medium neutral citation: [2010] WASCA 25
Supreme Court of Western Australia, Court of Appeal
Judgment delivered 19 February 2010

Torts — Negligence — Duty of care — Breach of duty — Landlord liability — Maintenance of surrounds — Hazards — Obligation to take remedial action — Respondent lived in a unit owned by appellant — Appellant organised for an independent contractor to tend and mow lawn and garden at rear of units — Indentation on lawn caused by a bird bath left by another tenant — Respondent allegedly tripped and fell on indentation — Proceedings commenced by respondent claiming appellant breached its duty to adequately maintain lawn — District Court at first instance held that appellant had breached its duty — Appellant appealed to Court of Appeal — Whether appellant owed duty of care to respondent — Whether content of that duty required appellant to fill in indentation — Whether actual cause of accident had been respondent's failure to take care — Civil Liability Act 2002 (WA), s 3, 3A, 5A, 5B, 5C, 5D, 5E, 5F, 5M, 5N, 5O, 5W — Occupiers' Liability Act 1985 (WA), s 4, 5, 6, 7, 9.

The respondent, Ms Irene Smith (Ms Smith) resided in a rented unit in Balga in Western Australia. That unit was one of a block of 16 residential units, all of which were owned by the appellant, the Department of Housing and Works (the Department). Ms Smith thus leased the unit directly from the Department which accordingly took on the role of landlord. In that capacity, the Department (among other things) engaged an independent contractor to mow the lawn and tend the garden at the rear of the block of units. That independent contractor came reasonably regularly to perform those tasks. However, the lawn was patchy in some areas. There was also an indentation in the lawn which was caused by a bird bath left on it by one of the other tenants. When that bird bath was subsequently removed, the indentation remained but was quite difficult to see. The indentation had a depth of approximately one inch. Its diameter was between one and two feet.

In September 2006, Ms Smith, who was then aged 72 years, fell on an area of lawn proximate to that indentation. She had been hurrying at the time and had not seen the indentation. Ms Smith was subsequently found on the lawn by her son. She suffered personal injuries as a consequence of the fall. Ms Smith soon after commenced proceedings in the District Court against the Department. In that context, Ms Smith alleged that her injury was caused by the Department's breach of a duty of care owed to her as her landlord. The action was tried before Keen DCJ.

In determining the content of the Department's duty of care, his Honour noted that the units were all rented by elderly persons. Such persons were likely to be less stable on their feet and also likely to suffer significant consequences from any fall. In those circumstances, his Honour found that the "reasonable response" to the risk would have been to take some action to alleviate the risk of an elderly person stepping into the indentation left by the bird bath. On that basis, his Honour found that the Department was liable to Ms Smith and awarded her damages in the sum of $38,000.

The Department then appealed to the Court of Appeal against the finding of liability. In that context, it claimed that Keen DCJ had made three errors. The first was in finding that the depression in the lawn created a foreseeable risk of injury which was not an insignificant risk for the purposes of s 5B(1)(a) of the *Civil Liability Act 2002* (WA). Keen DCJ was secondly said to have erred in finding that the depression constituted a danger for the purposes of s 5(1) of the *Occupier's Liability Act 1985* (WA). The third error that his Honour was said to have made was in finding that a reasonable person in the Department's position would have taken a precaution of the type contemplated by s 5B(1)(c) of the Civil Liability Act, namely, to fill the indentation with sand.

***Held:* appeal allowed.**

Per Pullin JA (with whom Newnes JA agreed)

1. A reasonable person in the position of the Department would have done nothing by way of remedial work to deal with the risk of injury which might have been caused by the slight depression in the lawn, the existence of which was obvious to a person choosing to look where they were going.

2. The cause of Ms Smith's fall was that she was hurrying, in her words "almost running". She thus did not take sufficient care to observe where she was going and did not proceed with appropriate care for her own safety. There was no poor original design in the lawn and there was no history of previous accidents.

3. It followed that the trial judge erred in concluding that the Department was under a duty to fill the depression with sand "to alleviate the risk of an elderly person stepping into the depression and falling in some way or other". Such a duty went beyond what a reasonable person would have done.

Per Buss JA

4. The appeal raised questions about the interaction between the Occupiers' Liability Act and the Civil Liability Act and their relationship to the common law. Those questions could not be simply ignored as they had been in the submissions of the parties.

5. When those interactions were taken into account, it became evident that the landlord's duty required the Department to exercise reasonable care to avoid risks of physical injury to Ms Smith by reason of any dangers due to the state of the premises or to anything done or omitted to be done on them.

6. In considering the application of that duty, it had to be appreciated that a lawn in an ordinary suburban block of home units was not perfectly level. It was to be expected that the surface would have some unevenness. This may have occurred by the action of human beings or by natural means.

7. It was therefore clear that Keen DCJ was in error in deciding that the applicable standard of care (that is, the measure of the discharge of the Department's duty of care to the respondent) required the appellant to fill in the depression with sand.

8. It was also clear that his Honour wrongly held that the Department had breached its duty. That was because the indentation was not a trap. It was not a hazard of a kind requiring some warning. Indeed, it was not a hazard at all for most people over the age of 55 years taking reasonable care for their own safety.

[*Headnote by the Wolters Kluwer editors*]

S Sirett for the appellant (instructed by Downings Legal).

K Pratt for the respondent (instructed by Trewin Norman & Co).

Before: Pullin JA, Buss JA and Newnes JA.

[¶82-012] Shire of Gingin v Coombe

(2009) Aust Torts Reports ¶82-012
Medium neutral citation: [2009] WASCA 92
Supreme Court of Western Australia, Court of Appeal
Judgment delivered 25 May 2009

Torts — Negligence — Duty of care — Breach of duty — Public authority — Off-road motorbike riding — Whether warning sign adequate — Obviousness of risk — Causation — Class to whom duty is owed — Effect of encouragement by public authority to use area.

The respondent, Mr Coombe, was injured while riding his motorbike on sand dunes that had been gazetted for use by off-road-vehicles under the Control of Vehicles (Off-Road Areas) Act 1978 (WA). The area of land, known as the Lancelin Off Road Vehicle Area (ORVA), was under the control and management of the Shire (the appellant). Situated on the access road leading to the main carpark was a large sign (approximately 2 m x 2 m), which depicted a map of the ORVA in a blue rectangular area overlaid with the words "THE OFF ROAD AREA IS A HAZARDOUS ENVIRONMENT MANY SERIOUS INJURIES OCCUR EACH YEAR". Underneath this text was the warning "BEWARE" in large red lettering, followed by the text "Sudden steep descent, collisions with vehicles/pedestrians". Below this was set out the regulations governing the use of the ORVA.

The respondent was injured as a result of falling down the steep side of a large dune, the slope of which was almost vertical. The circumstances of the accident indicate that he had been travelling at such a speed along the gentle incline at the back of the dune that he was unable to stop in time to avoid the steep descent at the crest.

The respondent sued the Shire in negligence, alleging that it had failed to discharge its duty of care as the occupier of the ORVA. The trial judge, having dismissed the contentions that the Shire should have either implemented a system of inspection to identify and restrict access to the most dangerous areas or excluded the public from the area altogether, accepted the respondent's submission that the Shire had breached its duty to warn him of the particular dangers he faced. It was held that the large sign erected by the Shire was inadequate for two principal reasons: (i) as it was designed primarily to designate the off road area in pictorial fashion and direct people to the regulations governing its use, the warning sign itself was "perfunctory and easily lost within the scheme of the sign"; (ii) the placement of the sign on an access track rather than in the main carpark, in circumstances where there was no requirement to stop and read the warnings, was a breach of the Shire's duty. The trial judge concluded that the plaintiff's injuries would have been averted if he had been presented with an adequate warning sign, because he would have been prompted to carry out an initial inspection of the terrain over which he was to planning to ride.

***Held:* appeal allowed.**

Per Martin CJ (Miller JA agreeing; McLure JA dissenting)

1. The trial judge had erred in concluding that the Shire, by failing to warn the respondent of the particular dangers involved in the activity in which he engaged, had breached its duty of care.

2. The content of the duty of care owed by a public authority having control of a large area of land to which the public have access is to be assessed by looking at the entire area under the control of the authority (rather than the particular site where the injury occurred), and by reference to the class of entrants to that area generally (rather than the plaintiff as an individual).

3. In the present case, the class of persons to whom the Shire owed its duty of care voluntarily undertook obviously hazardous recreational activities — a factor which tended to constrain the extent of the Shire's duty.

4. The trial judge assessed the reasonableness of the care taken by the Shire by reference to the hazards posed by the particular dune upon which the respondent suffered his injuries, rather than by reference to the range of risks to which all entrants to the ORVA were exposed as a class.

5. In order to avoid the distortions of "hindsight bias", the assessment of the existence and content of a duty of care is to be undertaken looking forward from a time before the occurrence of the injury giving rise to a claim, rather than backward from the time of the claim.

6. The trial judge's description of the warning as "perfunctory and easily lost within the scheme of the sign" is not an accurate description of the warning. The word "beware", coloured red against a blue background, was obvious and designed to attract attention. Nor is it clear how the words "sudden steep descent" were inadequate to warn entrants of the kind of terrain which led to the respondent's accident.

7. As far as the placement of the sign, the issue was not whether it would have been better to place the sign in the carpark; the question was whether, by placing the sign on the access road, the Shire had departed from a standard of reasonable care. On the evidence, it was entirely reasonable to situate the sign on the access road, where the prominence of the area map was likely to encourage first time visitors to stop and read the contents of the sign.

8. The obviousness of the risk may be of such significance and importance as to be conclusive in some cases. Although the risk of encountering dunes with a steep drop-off would not, in the absence of a sign, have been obvious to persons unfamiliar with the ORVA, it must be obvious to any driver of an off road vehicle that they risk significant injury if they travel at such a speed that they cannot stop within the area of land surface visible to them.

[*Headnote by the Wolters Kluwer editors*]

MH Zilko SC & Mr J Eller for the appellant (instructed by John Eller).

TH Offer for the respondent (instructed by Friedman Lurie Singh & D'Angelo).

Before: Martin CJ, McLure JA and Miller JA.

[¶81-785] Koehler v Cerebos (Australia) Ltd

(2005) Aust Torts Reports ¶81-785
Medium neutral citation: [2004] HCA 15
High Court of Australia
6 April 2005

Torts — Negligence — Duty of care — Employment relationship — Obligation to provide safe system of work — Appellant accepted part time employment as a merchandising representative with respondent — Complaints were made by appellant to respondent about the amount of work that was expected of her — Respondent took no action to decrease amount work — Appellant developed psychiatric injuries as a result of her work — Proceedings were commenced by appellant against respondent seeking damages for injuries suffered — Whether respondent could have reasonably foreseen psychiatric injuries suffered by appellant — Occupational Safety and Health Act 1984 (WA).

The appellant had been employed by the respondent as a full-time sales representative between 1994 and 1996. In May of 1996, the respondent retrenched the appellant but offered to re-engage her as a part-time merchandising representative. The appellant accepted that offer and it was thus agreed that she would work three days a week. However, the appellant immediately complained to the respondent about the size of the territory that she was obliged to cover in that period. In response, her supervisor told her to try it for one month to see if she could manage it. For a period of some six months, the appellant did cover the entirety of the area that she was expected to, but she simultaneously made a number of oral and written complaints about it to the respondent. By those complaints, the appellant sought to have the area that she was required to cover reduced or the number of days that she worked

increased. Nevertheless, the respondent took neither of those steps. In October of 1996, the appellant felt that she could no longer cope with the workload and consulted her doctor. She was diagnosed with a recognised psychiatric illness of which her work was found to be a cause.

On that basis, the appellant commenced proceedings in the District Court of Western Australia claiming that the respondent's failure to reduce her work area or increase her hours breached an employer's common law duty to provide a safe system of work. It was also alleged that the respondent had breached an implied term of the employment contract that the employer would provide a safe system of work in addition to breaching the statutory duty owed under the *Occupational Safety and Health Act 1984* (WA). At first instance, Commissioner Greaves found that the appellant's workload had been excessive and that the respondent had consequently failed in its duty to ensure that a safe system of work had been provided. On appeal, however, a Full Court of the Supreme Court of Western Australia held that the respondent could not reasonably have foreseen that the appellant was exposed to a risk of psychiatric injury as a consequence of her duties at work. The Full Court accordingly allowed the respondent's appeal. An appeal was then brought by the appellant to the High Court.

Held: appeal dismissed:

Per McHugh, Gummow, Hayne and Heydon JJ

1. To begin the relevant inquiry by simply focusing on questions of breach of duty invited error. It invited error because the assumption that was made about the content of the duty of care failed to take fundamental aspects of the relationship between the parties into account. That was so even though in the present case the question of reasonable foreseeability was determinative.

2. Because the appellant did not prove that the respondent ought reasonably to have foreseen that she was at risk of suffering psychiatric injury as a result of performing her duties at work, her claim in negligence should have failed at trial.

3. There were two reasons for not inferring negligence on the part of the respondent. Firstly, the appellant agreed to perform the duties which were a cause of her injury. Secondly, the respondent had no reason to suspect that the appellant was at risk of psychiatric injury. The appellant's agreement to undertake the work ran contrary to the contention that the employer ought reasonably to have appreciated that the performance of those tasks posed a risk to her psychiatric health.

4. It was generally acknowledged that some recognisable psychiatric illnesses could be triggered by stress. It could not be said, however, that all employers were under an obligation to recognise that all employees were at risk of psychiatric injury from stress at work.

5. The evidence of the complaints that the appellant made to the respondent did not establish any basis for imposing an obligation on it to foresee her psychiatric injury. That is, the complaints provided no reason for the respondent to believe that the appellant was jeopardizing her health by fulfilling her assigned tasks.

Per Callinan J

6. It was "far-fetched" to think that the appellant — a "competent, seemingly well woman" — would suffer disabling psychiatric injuries within six months of taking up her position. Although a psychiatrist might have been able to foresee her injuries in the circumstances of the case, it was not reasonable to expect an employer to have done so.

[*Headnote by the Wolters Kluwer editors*]

AG Braddock with NJ Mullany (instructed by Marks & Sands) for the appellant.

BW Walker SC with DR Clyne (instructed by Dibbs Barker Gosling) for the respondent.

Before: McHugh, Gummow, Hayne, Callinan and Heydon JJ.

Appendix
Other noteworthy cases

In addition to the top 100 cases featured in this book, we would like to acknowledge the following cases which are also prominent across the jurisdictions. These cases have been grouped according to their jurisdiction and noting the area of claim:

Australian Capital Territory

Medical negligence

- *Old* v *Miniter* (2021) Aust Torts Reports ¶82-657; [2021] NSWCA 92
- *Kempster* v *Healthscope Operations Pty Ltd* (2019) Aust Torts Reports ¶82-483; [2019] ACTSC 248
- *Spence* v *Neilson* (2018) Aust Torts Reports ¶82-416; [2018] ACTSC 273
- *Robinson* v *Ng* (2015) Aust Torts Reports ¶82-193; [2014] ACTSC 227

Motor accident

- *Carvalho* v *Town* (2020) Aust Torts Reports ¶82-519; [2020] ACTSC 1
- *Lee* v *McGrath* (2019) Aust Torts Reports ¶82-436; [2019] ACTCA 6
- *Dow* v *Elbarbary* (2018) Aust Torts Reports ¶82-370; [2017] ACTSC 418
- *Casey* v *Alcock* (2009) Aust Torts Reports ¶81-991; [2009] ACTCA 1

Occupiers' liability

- *SMA* v *John XXIII College (No 2)* (2020) Aust Torts Reports ¶82-552; [2020] ACTSC 211
- *Meyers* v *Commissioner for Social Housing* (2018) Aust Torts Reports ¶82-406; [2018] ACTSC 193

Public authority

- *Hartigan* v *Commissioner for Social Housing in the ACT* (2017) Aust Torts Reports ¶82-341; [2017] ACTSC 100

Workers' compensation

- *Roberson* v *Icon Distribution Investments Ltd and Jemena Networks (ACT) Pty Ltd trading as ActewAGL Distribution* (2020) Aust Torts Reports ¶82-593; [2020] ACTSC 320

New South Wales

Aviation

- *Parkes Shire Council* v *South West Helicopters Pty Ltd* (2019) Aust Torts Reports ¶82-439; [2019] HCA 14
- *Pel-Air Aviation Pty Ltd* v *Casey* (2017) Aust Torts Reports ¶82-327; [2017] NSWCA 32

Intentional tort

- *NSW* v *Ibbett* (2005) Aust Torts Reports ¶81-825-1; [2006] HCA 57

Motor accident

- *Yebdoo* v *Holmewood* (2021) Aust Torts Reports ¶82-663; [2021] NSWCA 119
- *Connors* v *Nominal Defendant (No 4)* (2020) Aust Torts Reports ¶82-554; [2020] NSWDC 438
- *Serrao (by his tutor Serrao)* v *Cornelius (No 2)* (2016) Aust Torts Reports ¶82-305; [2016] NSWCA 231
- *Solomons* v *Pallier* (2015) Aust Torts Reports ¶82-244; [2015] NSWCA 266
- *Roads and Traffic Authority of NSW* v *Dederer & Anor* (2007) Aust Torts Reports ¶81-905; [2007] HCA 42

Public authority

- *Port Macquarie Hastings Council* v *Mooney* (2014) Aust Torts Reports ¶82-172; [2014] NSWCA 156

Recreational activity

- *Carter* v *Hastings River Greyhound Racing Club* (2020) Aust Torts Reports ¶82-559; [2020] NSWCA 185
- *Castle* v *Perisher Blue Pty Ltd* (2020) Aust Torts Reports ¶82-596; [2020] NSWSC 1652
- *Menz* v *Wagga Wagga Show Society Inc* (2020) Aust Torts Reports ¶82-542; [2020] NSWCA 65
- *Singh bhnf Ambu Kanwar* v *Lynch* (2020) Aust Torts Reports ¶82-543; [2020] NSWCA 152
- *Goode* v *Angland* (2017) Aust Torts Reports ¶82-369-3; [2017] NSWCA 311
- *Perisher Blue Pty Ltd* v *Nair-Smith* (2015) Aust Torts Reports ¶82-219; [2015] NSWCA 90
- *Stewart & Ors* v *Ackland* (2015) Aust Torts Reports ¶82-210; [2015] ACTCA 1
- *Campbell* v *Hay* (2014) Aust Torts Reports ¶82-169; [2014] NSWCA 129
- *Fallas* v *Mourlas* (2006) Aust Torts Reports ¶81-835; [2006] NSWCA 32
- *Falvo* v *Australian Oztag Sports Association & Anor* (2006) Aust Torts Reports ¶81-831; [2006] NSWCA 17

School authority

- *Oyston* v *St Patrick's College (No 2)* (2013) Aust Torts Reports ¶82-148; [2013] NSWCA 310

Workers' compensation

- *Optus Administration Pty Ltd* v *Glenn Wright by his tutor James Stuart Wright* (2017) Aust Torts Reports ¶82-326; [2017] NSWCA 21
- *Caltex Refineries (Qld) Pty Ltd* v *Stavar* (2009) Aust Torts Reports ¶82-045-1; [2009] NSWCA 258
- *CSR Ltd* v *Eddy* (2005) Aust Torts Reports ¶81-808; [2005] HCA 64

Northern Territory

Aviation

- *Cook & Ors* v *Modern Mustering Pty Ltd & Ors* (2017) Aust Torts Reports ¶82-369-4; [2017] NTCA 1

Intentional tort

- *Johnson* v *Northern Territory of Australia* (2016) Aust Torts Reports ¶82-322-1; [2016] NTSC 49

Recreational activity

- *Kent* v *City of Darwin* (2018) Aust Torts Reports ¶82-424-1; [2018] NTSC 3

Workers' compensation

- *Kampourakis* v *DCT (NT) Pty Ltd* (2013) Aust Torts Reports ¶82-154-1; [2013] NTSC 76

Queensland

Motor accident

- *Allen* v *O'Donnell & Anor* (2021) Aust Torts Reports ¶82-627; [2021] QSC 63
- *Brown* v *Holzberger & AAI Ltd* (2017) Aust Torts Reports ¶82-335; [2017] QSC 54
- *Smith* v *Randall & Anor* (2016) Aust Torts Reports ¶82-301; [2016] QSC 191
- *McQuitty* v *Midgley & Anor* (2016) Aust Torts Reports ¶82-260; [2016] QSC 36
- *Perfect* v *MacDonald & Anor* (2012) Aust Torts Reports ¶82-123-2; [2012] QSC 11
- *Allwood* v *Wilson* (2011) Aust Torts Reports ¶82-098-1; [2011] QSC 180
- *Hawira* v *Connolly & Anor*; *Connolly* v *Hawira & Anor* (2008) Aust Torts Reports ¶81-989-1; [2008] QSC 4
- *Clement* v *Backo & Suncorp Metway Insurance Ltd* (2007) Aust Torts Reports ¶81-877; [2007] QCA 81

Occupiers' liability

- *Wright* v *KB Nut Holdings Pty Ltd* (2013) Aust Torts Reports ¶82-128; [2013] QCA 66
- *Ellis* v *Uniting Church in Australia Property Trust (Q)* (2008) Aust Torts Reports ¶81-983; [2008] QCA 388
- *Green* v *Hanson Construction Materials Pty Ltd* (2007) Aust Torts Reports ¶81-907; [2007] QCA 260

Workers' compensation

- *Schokman* v *CCIG Investments Pty Ltd* (2022) Aust Torts Reports ¶82-775; [2022] QCA 38
- *Giles* v *State of Queensland* (2021) Aust Torts Reports ¶82-689; [2021] QCA 206
- *Caffrey* v *AAI Ltd* (2019) Aust Torts Reports ¶82-433; [2019] QSC 7
- *Eastment* v *State of Queensland* (2018) Aust Torts Reports ¶82-412; [2018] QCA 253
- *Kerle* v *BM Alliance Coal Operations Pty Ltd & Ors* (2016) Aust Torts Reports ¶82-320; [2016] QSC 304
- *Downes* v *Affinity Health Pty Ltd* (2016) Aust Torts Reports ¶82-269; [2016] QCA 129

- *Boon* v *Summs of Qld Pty Ltd* (2016) Aust Torts Reports ¶82-261; [2016] QCA 38
- *Heywood* v *Commercial Electrical Pty Ltd* (2013) Aust Torts Reports ¶82-145; [2013] QCA 270

South Australia

Motor accident

- *Elliott* v *Cottrell* (2021) Aust Torts Reports ¶82-704; [2021] SADC 103
- *Eicas* v *Dawson* (2016) Aust Torts Reports ¶82-316; [2016] SASCFC 124

Occupiers' liability

- *Battunga Country Lions Club* v *Paues* (2021) Aust Torts Reports ¶82-750-3; [2021] SASCA 72
- *Clutterbuck* v *Pollifrone* (2021) Aust Torts Reports ¶82-750-4; [2021] SADC 15
- *Stringer & Or* v *Westfield Shopping Centre Management Co (SA) Pty Ltd* (2017) Aust Torts Reports ¶82-369-5; [2017] SASCFC 138

Tasmania

Intentional tort

- *ZAB* v *ZWM* (2021) Aust Torts Reports ¶82-750; [2021] TASSC 64

Motor accident

- *Scattergood* v *Commonwealth* (2022) Aust Torts Reports ¶82-780; [2022] TASSC 21

Property tort

- *Prestage* v *Barrett* (2021) Aust Torts Reports ¶82-680; [2021] TASSC 27

Workers' compensation

- *Allianz Australia Insurance Ltd* v *Mercer* (2016) Aust Torts Reports ¶82-258; [2016] TASFC 2

Victoria

Abuse law

- *Lonergan* v *Trustees of The Sisters of Saint Joseph & Anor* (2021) Aust Torts Reports ¶82-732; [2021] VSC 651
- *Perez* v *Reynolds & Anor* (2020) Aust Torts Reports ¶82-582; [2020] VSC 537

Medical negligence

- *Phelan* v *Melbourne Health* (2019) Aust Torts Reports ¶82-487; [2019] VSCA 205

Mental harm

- *Puleio* v *Olam Orchards Australia Pty Ltd* (2018) Aust Torts Reports ¶82-374; [2018] VSC 109
- *Homsi* v *Homsi* (2016) Aust Torts Reports ¶82-285; [2016] VSC 354

Motor accident

- *Walker* v *Smith* (2022) Aust Torts Reports ¶82-779; [2022] VSC 188
- *Biggs* v *O'Connor* (2021) Aust Torts Reports ¶82-743; [2021] VSC 826

Occupiers' liability

- *Tanah Merah Vic Pty Ltd* v *Owners' Corporation* (2021) Aust Torts Reports ¶82-642; [2021] VSCA 72
- *Bucic* v *Arnej Pty Ltd* (2019) Aust Torts Reports ¶82-446; [2019] VSC 330
- *A Woodley Osteopathic Services Pty Ltd* v *TAC & Brendan Woodley; Brendan Woodley* v *TAC & A Woodley Osteopathic Services Pty Ltd* (2013) Aust Torts Reports ¶82-154; [2013] VSCA 350
- *Duffy* v *Salvation Army (Victoria) Property Trust* (2013) Aust Torts Reports ¶82-149; [2013] VSCA 253
- *Campaspe Shire Council* v *De Young* (2008) Aust Torts Reports ¶81-960; [2008] VSCA 129
- *Raciti* v *Wadren Pty Ltd* (2006) Aust Torts Reports ¶81-848; [2006] VSCA 132

Professional negligence

- *Swansson* v *Harrison & Ors* (2014) Aust Torts Reports ¶82-162; [2014] VSC 118

Property tort

- *GG & PM Burrell Pty Ltd* v *Butler Market Gardens Pty Ltd* (2020) Aust Torts Reports ¶82-520; [2020] VSCA 31

Public authority

- *Greater Shepparton City Council* v *Clarke* (2017) Aust Torts Reports ¶82-340; [2017] VSCA 107
- *Central Goldfields Shire* v *Haley* (2009) Aust Torts Reports ¶82-018; [2009] VSCA 101

Pure economic loss

- *Roo Roofing Pty Ltd & Anor* v *Commonwealth of Australia* (2019) Aust Torts Reports ¶82-460; [2019] VSC 331

Recreational activity

- *Archer* v *Garcia* (2022) Aust Torts Reports ¶82-759; [2022] VSC 57
- *West* v *Rosenlis* (2021) Aust Torts Reports ¶82-614; [2021] VSC 41

Scienter liability

- *Jolly* v *Kondos* (2021) Aust Torts Reports ¶82-730; [2021] VCC 1397

Workers' compensation

- *Shearer* v *iSelect Services Pty Ltd* (2021) Aust Torts Reports ¶82-736; [2021] VSCA 328
- *Shahid* v *Alpha Trading Engineering Pty Ltd* (2021) Aust Torts Reports ¶82-708; [2021] VSC 551
- *The Age Company Ltd* v *YZ (a pseudonym)* (2020) Aust Torts Reports ¶82-507; [2019] VSCA 313

Western Australia

Medical negligence

- *O'Loughlin* v *McCallum* (2021) Aust Torts Reports ¶82-733; [2021] WADC 77
- *Lazarevski* v *North Metropolitan Health Service* (2019) Aust Torts Reports ¶82-463; [2019] WADC 84

Motor accident

- *O'Connor* v *Insurance Commission of Western Australia* (2016) Aust Torts Reports ¶82-280; [2016] WASCA 95
- *Miller* v *Miller* (2009) Aust Torts Reports ¶82-040; [2009] WASCA 199

Occupiers' liability

- *Gentle* v *Wright* (2021) Aust Torts Reports ¶82-691; [2021] WADC 63
- *Apostolic Church Australia Ltd* v *Dixon* (2018) Aust Torts Reports ¶82-411; [2018] WASCA 146

School authority

- *Sidhoum* v *Minister for Education* (2022) Aust Torts Reports ¶82-791; [2022] WADC 35

Workers' compensation

- *Smith* v *High Energy Service Pty Ltd* (2021) Aust Torts Reports ¶82-710; [2021] WADC 101
- *MR & RC Smith Pty Ltd t/as Ultra Tune (Osbourn Park)* v *Wyatt (No 2)* (2012) Aust Torts Reports ¶82-108; [2012] WASCA 110

Case Table

Paragraph

L

M

N

O

P

Made in the USA
Monee, IL
07 May 2026

49713176R00138